*ĐẠI VIỆT AND CHAMPA:
OCCUPATION AND LIBERATION
THE DYNASTIES OF HỒ AND
HẬU (LATER) LÊ*

Volume 3C of "*A Traveller's Story of Vietnam's Past*"
From the 13th to the 16th centuries CE
by Tan Pham

© 2025 Tan Pham

All rights reserved. No part of this book may be reproduced or modified in any form, including photocopying, recording, or by any information storage and retrieval system, without permission in writing from the publisher, 315Kio Publishing.

First edition 2025
For any inquiries, please email: nxb315kio@gmail.com

Cover designed by Son La Pham
Published by 315Kio Publishing, Auckland, New Zealand

ĐẠI VIỆT AND CHAMPA: OCCUPATION AND LIBERATION THE DYNASTIES OF HỒ AND HẬU (LATER) LÊ

Volume 3C of "*A Traveller's Story of Vietnam's Past*"
FROM THE 13TH TO THE 16TH CENTURIES CE

TAN PHAM

Contents

Foreword	11
Preface	15
Eight periods of history	16
Convention and references	17
Abbreviation	22
Acknowledgements	23
Chapter 1: A summary of this book	25
Chapter 2: The Trần dynasty's historical exit	31
2.1 - Three sisters, four brothers and the end of a dynasty	31
2.2 - Famines, earthquakes, solar eclipses and operas	38
2.3 - A Trần princess and a Cham king	39
2.4 - Kingdoms in the west	47
2.5 - Inscriptions on a rock – Bia Ma Nhai	51
2.6 - Chế Bồng Nga – Cham hero and Đại Việt villain	53
Chapter 3: The Hồ Dynasty (1400–1407)	67
3.1 - Lê Quý Ly (1336–1407) – The father	67
3.2 - Relationship with Champa	72
3.3 - The Ming is coming	75
3.4 - Relationship between Đại Việt, Champa and the Ming dynasty in the late 14th and early 15th centuries according to Ming shilu	80
3.5 - The Ming invasion of Đại Việt	83
Chapter 4: Under the Ming's rule – Đại Việt fights back	95
4.1 - A six-year resistance, 1407–1413	95
4.2 - The Ming occupation, 1414–1417	107
Chapter 5: Lê Lợi, a national hero and the liberation of Đại Việt	113
A timeline	113
5.1 - Lê Lợi (1385–1433), a national hero	114
5.2 - Nguyễn Trãi (1380–1442), a scholar, a poet and a state counsellor	120
5.3 - *Lam Sơn Thực Lục* [Veritable Records of Mount Lam]'s account of the liberation campaign (1414–1428)	121

5.4 - *Bình Ngô Đại Cáo* (Great Proclamation upon the Pacification of the Wu)	157
5.5 - The aftermath	160

Chapter 6: The Early Lê (Lê Sơ) Dynasty (1428–1527) — 167

6.1 - Lê Lợi (King Lê Thái Tổ, r.1428–1433)	167
6.2 - A reflection on Lê Lợi – An analysis of success	172
6.3 - Three kings over 30 years	183
6.4 - One king over nearly 40 years – Lê Tư Thành (King Lê Thánh Tông, r.1460–1497)	190
6.5 - Đại Việt invasions and the breakup of Champa	201
6.6 - The Cham records of the 1471 event	211
6.7 - The court of Ming and Champa	212
6.8 - Wars in the west with Laos	213
6.9 - Six kings over 30 years of chaos and decay	221
6.10 - The final resting place – Lam Kinh	228

Chapter 7: Conclusion — 233

A turbulent time	233
A risky royal succession	234
A challenge of unity	234
The scholar-officials	235
The innovators	236
A militaristic regime	236
An era of economic hardship?	238
A travel plan	238

Appendix 1: Prefectures, Subprefectures and Counties under the Ming occupation — 239

Appendix 2: Ming shilu's records — 243

The war against Lê Lợi (1418–1428)	243
Ming - Champa - Đại Việt relations in the mid to late 15th century	257

Bibliography — 261

Endnotes — 267

Tables

Table 2-1: Kings of the Trần dynasty (1126-1400).	36
Table 2-2: The kings and lords of Champa from the 11th to the 15th centuries.	65
Table 5-1: The timeline of Lê Lợi's liberation campaign.	114
Table 6-1: Kings of the Early Lê (Lê Sơ) dynasty (1428-1527).	228
Table A1-1: Household records from some prefectures under the Ming occupation.	241
Table A1-2: Household records from some subprefectures under the Ming occupation.	241
Table A1-3: A summary and comparison of households between regions under the Ming occupation.	242

Figures

Figure 0-1: A timeline illustrating the eight periods of Vietnamese history, with each text box proportionally scaled to reflect the duration of its respective period. — 18

Figure 2-1: The Trần and Hồ family tree, 14th century. — 37

Figure 2-2: A Vietnamese opera (*hát bội*) character prepares for her act. — 38

Figure 2-3: A statue of Princess Huyền Trân at her temple, Huế, 21st century, bronze, H. 2.37 m. — 41

Figure 2-4: A view of the back of the Princess Huyền Trân's temple. — 41

Figure 2-5: Map of Đại Việt and northern Laos. — 50

Figure 2-6: Bia Ma Nhai (rock inscriptions). — 52

Figure 2-7: Bronze tubiform gun — 63

Figure 3-1: The Hồ Citadel, south gate (main entrance). — 70

Figure 3-2: The Hồ Citadel, north gate. — 70

Figure 3-3: A panoramic view of the Hồ Citadel, viewed from the top of the main gate looking toward the north gate. — 71

Figure 3-4: Map of the Ming's invasion of Đại Ngu, 1406–1407. — 85

Figure 5-1: Map of historic Lam Kinh and other locations related to Lê Lợi's early years of the uprising. — 117

Figure 5-2: Vĩnh Lăng stele, Lam Kinh, Thanh Hóa, 1433, stone, H. 2.79 m, W. 1.94 m, D. 0.27 m. — 119

Figure 5-3: The turtle base of the Vĩnh Lăng stele. — 119

Figure 5-4: Details of the dragons around the perimeter of the Vĩnh Lăng stele. — 119

Figure 5-5: The junction of the Hiếu and Cả Rivers. — 132

Figure 5-6: View of the Cà River, looking west from Cây Chanh Bridge. — 132

Figure 5-7: Map of Lê Lợi's southern campaign (1424–1425). — 135

Figure 5-8: The Old Fort of Lam Thành (15th century). — 136

Figure 5-9: Map of Lê Lợi northern campaign (1425–1426). — 140

Figure 5-10: Map of the battle of Tốt Động – Chúc Động. — 143

Figure 5-11: Quán Bến, the temple for the battle of Tốt Động, viewed looking east.	144
Figure 5-12: The Đáy River by Quán Bến Temple, viewed looking north.	144
Figure 5-13: The communal house of Tốt Động village.	144
Figure 5-14: A shrine near the burial ground of the Ming soldiers.	144
Figure 5-15: View of the Đáy River from Mai Lĩnh Bridge, viewed looking south.	145
Figure 5-16: Xương Giang historic site.	145
Figure 5-17: Chi Lăng Pass, viewed looking south.	153
Figure 5-18: A painting of the beheading of Liu Sheng in the Chi Lăng Museum.	153
Figure 5-19: Map of Ming reinforcements at the end of 1427.	156
Figure 6-1: The statue of 'National Hero Lê Lợi' at Thanh Hóa City.	169
Figure 6-2: National examinations under the Later Lê dynasty.	193
Figure 6-3: Đoan Môn Gate, viewed from the outside; viewed looking north-east.	195
Figure 6-4: Đoan Môn Gate, inside view from above; viewed looking south-west.	195
Figure 6-5: The dragons at the Kính Thiên Palace (southern steps), Hanoi, 15th century, stone.	196
Figure 6-6: Head of the Kính Thiên dragon (southern steps).	196
Figure 6-7: The dragons at the Kính Thiên Palace (northern steps), Hanoi, 15th century, stone.	197
Figure 6-8: Detail of the side of the Kính Thiên dragon (northern steps).	197
Figure 6-9: Map of An Nam reproduced from *Hồng Đức Bản Đồ* (Atlas of Hồng Đức).	199
Figure 6-10: Map of the 1471 invasion of Champa.	209
Figure 6-11: Seal, History Museum of Ho Chi Minh City, 1471, bronze.	212
Figure 6-12: Map of the western campaign against Bồn Man and Lão Qua.	216
Figure 6-13: The Early Lê family tree, 14th–16th century.	227
Figure 6-14: Main entrance to Lam Kinh with the Main Hall building located behind.	229
Figure 6-15: The well before the main entrance, Lê Lợi's actual tomb?	229
Figure 6-16: *Nghê*, a mythical animal, 19th century? painted wood.	229

Figure 6-17: *Nghê*, 17th-19th century? stone.   229

Figure 6-18: Dragon at the steps to the Main Hall.   230

Figure 6-19: Head of the dragon at the Main Hall.   230

Figure 6-20: The tomb of King Lê Thánh Tông (Lê Tư Thành).   230

Figure 6-21: The tomb of Ngô Thị Ngọc Dao, mother of King Lê Thánh Tông.   230

Figure 6-22: A rare statue of a female attendant at the tomb of Ngô Thị Ngọc Dao, Lam Kinh, stone, 17th-19th century?.   231

Figure 6-23: Small figures of an elephant, a rhinoceros and a horse, 15th century, stone.   231

FOREWORD

The present volume is a very welcome addition to the author's exploration of the making of Viet Nam. It is a name that only came into being in the early nineteenth century through negotiations between the newly installed Nguyen dynasty and the Qing court. Even then, the name was not used domestically as the Nguyen preferred to refer to their empire as Dai Nam, the Great South. During the period covered in this volume, from the mid-1300s to the mid-1500s, the country was called Dai Viet and briefly Dai Ngu, though Ming China insisted on referring to it as An Nan (Pacified South) as during the Tang dynasty or even Jiaozhi (Vietnamese Giao Chi) as during the Han era.

Before the mid-1300s, Dai Viet extended only to the area just south of modern Hue (and this thanks to the marriage of a Tran princess to a Cham king in 1306). By the end of the 1400s, Dai Viet had vanquished Champa, and had expanded its territory southward to present-day Binh Thuan and Ninh Thuan (Panduranga). So the history of Viet Nam is the story of a country-as-project that unfolded over centuries through a drawn-out process of nation-building and cycles of expansion, division and unification.

This is the story that Tan Pham has undertaken to tell in his travelers' guides to the past as if it were a museum, using visual aids such as photographs, diagrams, maps, genealogical trees to accompany his narrative. It combines information culled from Chinese and Vietnamese historical sources, archaeological data, stele inscriptions and poetry as well as modern scholarship. The abundant footnotes, some stretching over pages, testify to his meticulous research. The sources contain valuable information about military confrontations between Dai Viet, Ming, Champa and Ai Lao as well as among feuding members of royal clans and rebellious commoners. They allow the author to identify sites of ancient battles and the associated forts, ramparts and encampments that over time became rice-fields. The author painstakingly excavates their submerged histories together with information about the sizes of the armies, military resources (including war elephants), food supplies and routes taken. But there are also sites unconnected to warfare. The pagodas, stupas and monasteries that dot the northern landscape were built not only as manifestations of the Buddhist piety of the Ly and Tran rulers (1010-1400); besides being places of worship and pilgrimage destinations, the temples also served as resting places for weary travelers and markers of the reach of imperial power. In the country's center, towering monuments, heavily damaged by time and war, attest to the presence of Hindu-Buddhism in Champa and to the wealth generated by long distance maritime trade between the Cham principalities and South and Southeast Asia. In the period covered in the present volume, Dai Viet and Champa fought fiercely for supremacy in the Indochinese peninsula. On several occasions, Cham armies went all the way to the Dai Viet capital, Thang Long (present-day Ha Noi).

The Ming Occupation (1407-1427) brought enormous changes in the society and culture of Dai Viet. Buddhist temples were replaced by communal houses as centers of village life and of (male) power. Confucian morality was enforced through education and the law. The reforms enacted during the Ming Occupation were continued by the Le emperors, enabling Dai Viet to mount a decisive attack against Champa in 1471. The capital Vijaya that had once served as a hub for maritime trade was sacked. Champa never recovered, Dai Viet's territory now extend south to Panduranga in present-day Binh Thuan and Ninh Thuan where Cham communities endured until the nineteenth century. Dai Viet's campaign against Ai Lao was far less successful, the long mountain range forming a natural barrier between Laos and northern Vietnam. That episode seldom features in standard histories of Vietnam and its inclusion in the present volume is highly welcome.

Not all wars took place on battlefields. Some happened on paper. Tan Pham has mined the copious correspondence between Dai Viet and Ming China, some threatening, some conciliatory, over issues of dynastic legitimacy, tribute missions, precious commodities and disputed territory. Other conflicts took place within royal palaces and harems. Included in the volume are portraits of emperors, both good and bad, as well as of some significant historical figures. Alas, the lives and personal names of women, including royal ones, seldom made it into the pages of dynastic histories.

Tan Pham's multi-volume history of Viet Nam is a labor of love. Readers will be able to follow in the footsteps of emperors, officials, soldiers and rebels; to visualize monuments, temples and shrines and to conceive of the landscape as the repository of the past.

Hue-Tam Ho Tai
KENNETH T. YOUNG PROFESSOR OF SINO-VIETNAMESE HISTORY EMERITA
HARVARD UNIVERSITY

PREFACE

This Volume 3C, the third instalment of the third volume in my series on Vietnamese history, covers the period from the 13th to the early 16th centuries. It focuses on the Hồ and Hậu (Later) Lê dynasties of Đại Việt, a kingdom located in present-day north and north-central Vietnam, north of the Hải Vân Pass.

As a methodology, I have selected and approached the stories from a traveller's perspective, which explains the series title, *A Traveller's Story of Vietnam's Past*. However, my books are not travel guides; readers will not find information on accommodations or other travel-related details, though I occasionally include notes from my visits to the historical sites discussed.

My primary goal is to examine the meaning and significance of these stories, and to trace the connections between historical events and the locations where they occurred. While such knowledge exists, it is often scattered across various sources in different languages and levels of complexity. This series seeks to bring these threads together in one place, using geography as the unifying structure.

In preparation for this volume, I visited most of the historical sites related to the period covered in the book between late 2019 and early 2025. Unless specified otherwise, I took most of the photographs shown in this volume. Some images have been edited to add clarity and presentation.

Eight periods of history

As mentioned in the previous volumes, I have divided Vietnam's history into eight periods based on the major events that marked the key turning points that altered the course of its history. The selection of these eight periods is mine and not necessarily based on the historical timeline I was taught at school.

In broad terms, **Period I** covers the ancient times to 111 BCE (BCE=Before Common Era, same as BC=Before Christ), a time when the people of present-day Vietnam governed themselves. Volume One, entitled *The Bronze Drums and The Earrings*, deals with this period.[1] In the following millennium, **Period II**, the land of northern and north-central Vietnam was under the control of various Chinese dynasties, barring a few years of Vietnamese autonomy. The country gained independence in 938 at the beginning of the second millennium in the 10th century CE (CE=Common Era, same as AD=Anno Domini, the year of our Lord); hence the title of Volume Two, *One Thousand Years - The Stories of Giao Châu, the Kingdoms of Linyi, Funan and Zhenla*. The names refer to different political entities that existed in present-day Vietnam over that time.

From 938 CE onward, Vietnam regained its autonomy—despite several episodes of foreign occupation, internal divisions, and prolonged conflict—and expanded significantly, more than doubling its territory compared to the previous millennium. I have divided this second millennium into Periods III to VIII.

Period III spans roughly 600 years, from the 10th to 16th centuries, when there were three polities in Vietnam: Đại Việt (formerly Giao Châu) in the north, Champa (formerly Linyi) in the central and parts of the Khmer empire in the south.[2] This southern region was called Zhenla and, earlier, Funan. Volumes 3A, *Đại Việt and Champa: The Early Centuries - The Dynasties of Đinh, Tiền (Former) Lê, Lý, and Trần*; Volume 3B, *Đại Việt and Champa: Panduranga, Kauthara, and Indrapura*; this current Volume 3C, and the forthcoming Volume 3D, cover this period.[3]

Period IV follows, marking a time when Champa lost most of its land to Đại Việt. Đại Việt itself became fragmented, ruled by competing northern and southern lords for nearly 200 years, from the early 17th century until the end of the 18th century.

Following a thirty-year civil war at the end of the 18th century, Đại Việt was united, expanded its territory south and west, and absorbed Champa and southern Vietnam to become what is today Vietnam. This is **Period V**, a brief time of around 60 years in the first half of the 19th century.

The expansion ended with the arrival of the French arrived in the middle of the 19th century and their expulsion nearly a century later. This stretch of history is **Period VI**. In **Period VII**, Vietnam was once again divided and at war for another 21 years until its unification in 1975. Finally, **Period VIII** covers the era from 1975 to the present.

The eight periods are summarised in Figure 0-1.

My upcoming volumes will cover periods IV, V, and VI, until 1954, when the French finally departed from the country after first bombarding and landing in Touraine (Đà Nẵng) in 1858. I have chosen to end my contribution at 1954, as Period VII has already been well documented by existing historical works, and Period VIII remains too recent for a historical traveller.

To avoid repeating the full introduction from Volume One, I have provided a simplified overview of the eight historical periods, but the contents of Volume 3C are unique to this book.

Convention and references

As in the previous volumes, I have generally used local spellings for the names of people and places in their respective countries. Vietnamese names and locations are written with full diacritical marks. For Chinese names, I use Pinyin romanization rather than the older Wade-Giles system. However, for the benefit of readers more familiar with Vietnamese transliterations of Chinese names—such as Mu Sheng (*Mộc Thạnh*)—I have included the Vietnamese equivalents in parentheses, and vice versa.

Vietnamese kings traditionally held several names. Before ascending the throne, they were known by their personal names—for example, *Lê Tư Thành*. Upon accession, they received a Reign Name (*Tôn Hiệu* or *Đế Hiệu*) from the royal court. After their death, they were given a Temple Name (*Miếu Hiệu*), such as *Lê Thánh Tông*.

PERIOD I — AUTONOMY (~500 YEARS: 630-111 BCE) ANCIENT TIMES TO PRE-HÙNG KINGS, HÙNG KINGS TO NAN-YUE	PERIOD II — NORTHERN RULE [NOTE] (~1000 YEARS: 111 BCE-938 CE)

Figure 0-1: A timeline illustrating the eight periods of Vietnamese history, with each text box proportionally scaled to reflect the duration of its respective period.

Note: The thousand-year period mainly addresses the land north of the Ngang Pass. Immediately south, the territory became autonomous from around the 3rd century. The southern border marks the extent of Northern Rule, which kept changing from Ngang to Hải Vân Passes; from the 5th century, it settled at Ngang Pass.[4] The kingdoms to the south of this pass, Linyi/Champa and Funan/Zhenla, maintained their independence.[5]

PERIOD VII — DIVISION AND WAR
(21 YEARS: 1954-1975 CE)

PERIOD IV — DIVISION
(~200 YEARS: 1558-1802 CE)

| PERIOD III — INDEPENDENCE (~600 YEARS: 938-1558 CE) | IV | V | VI | VIII |

PERIOD V — ONE COUNTRY
(~60 YEARS: 1802-1858 CE)

PERIOD VI — FRENCH RULE
(~100 YEARS)

PERIOD VIII — UNITED VIETNAM
(50 YEARS: 1975–PRESENT)

The Reign Names are often very long and complex, and the Temple Names often share a common root. For example, Lý Thái Tổ (1009-1028) and Lê Thái Tổ (1428-1433) are the founders (*Thái Tổ* or founding ancestor) of two different dynasties. Since the king's personal name is unique to him, in this book I have used these names to avoid confusion if I were to use their temple names.[6] I want to emphasize that this choice is made for clarity and is not intended as a sign of disrespect, even though using a monarch's personal name is a taboo and traditionally frowned upon in Vietnamese culture.

It is also worth noting that Vietnamese names are structured with the family name first, followed by a middle name and given name. For example, *Lê Bang Cơ* and *Lê Tư Thành* are brothers in the Lê family; *Cơ* and *Thành* are their given names.

In contrast, most Vietnamese women had their family name followed by the word *Thị*, a term that originally indicated lineage but later came to denote a female. Later records often added *Thị* and *Ngọc* to the names of royal women in this period—for example, *Ngô Thị Ngọc Dao*—even when earlier texts referred to them more simply, in this case as *Ngô Dao*. The equivalent term for Vietnamese men was *Văn*.

Lastly, the dates found in Chinese and early Vietnamese sources are based on the lunar calendar, which generally lags behind the Gregorian calendar by about one month. Where appropriate, I have converted these dates into the Gregorian calendar for consistency and clarity.

Vietnamese and Chinese records use different names for the same location at different times. Although it may be simpler to use one a single name throughout the book, I have retained the names as indicated in the original sources. To avoid confusion, these names are: Thăng Long (under Lý, Trần dynasties) = Đông Quan (under the Ming dynasty) = Đông Đô (under the Hồ dynasty) = Đông Kinh (under the Later Lê dynasty) = Hanoi (present-day) and Đại Việt = Đại Ngu (under the Hồ dynasty) = An Nam = Annam = Jiao-zhi = Giao Chỉ = north and north-central, approximately the land north of Hải Vân Pass of present-day Vietnam.

Similarly, the capital of Champa from the 11th to the 15th centuries was Vijaya, located at the site of present-day Hoàng Đế Citadel in Bình Định province.[7] However, Đại Việt chronicles refer to it as Đồ Bàn and Chà Bàn, while the Chinese sources record it as Dazhou or Xinzhou (Tân Châu).[8] For the sake of consistency, I use the name Vijaya throughout this book, even though SKTT does not.

Vietnamese history includes two Lê dynasties. The *Tiền* Lê (Former Lê) dynasty ruled from 980 to 1009. The *Hậu* Lê (Later Lê) dynasty had two distinct phases: the Early Lê or Initial (*Lê Sơ*) dynasty, which lasted from 1428 to 1527, and the Restored or Revival Lê (*Lê Trung Hưng*) period, which continued from 1533 to 1789. Volume 3A covers the Former Lê dynasty; this volume focuses on the Early Lê dynasty, while the Restored Lê period will be explored in the following volume.

I have made every effort to cite the primary reference sources used in this volume. These have included major Vietnamese historical chronicles such as:

Đại Việt Sử Ký Toàn Thư (Complete Book of the Historical Records of Great Viet, 15th-17th century),

Đại Việt Thông Sử (Complete History of Đại Việt, 18th century), and

Khâm Định Việt Sử Thông Giám Cương Mục (The Imperially Ordered Annotated Text Completely Reflecting the History of Viet, 19th century).[9]

From Chinese sources, I have drawn extensively on:

Ming shilu (明實錄, *Minh Thực Lục*) (also known as the Veritable Records of the Ming Dynasty), a collective name for the successive reign annals of the emperors of Ming China (1368-1644),

Ming shi (明史, History of Ming, *Minh Sử*, 17th century), and

Annan Zhiyuan (*An Nam Chí Nguyên*, 17th century).

For the Ming shilu, I have relied on the English translation by historian Geoff Wade.

The Appendices and End Notes provide many details and reference sources that I have used to construct the stories. While this level of detail may not appeal to every reader, it is intended to assist those interested in deeper study or further research.

Finally, this book was written before Vietnam's provincial reorganisation on 12 June 2025, which reduced the number of provinces from 63 to 34. For example, at the time of writing, Bình Định was still a separate province; from 12 June 2025, it was merged with Gia Lai to form the new Gia Lai province.

Abbreviation

ANCN	*An Nam Chí Nguyên* (Annan Zhiyuan, 安南志原, Original Record of Annam or Annam Chronicles).[10]
BNĐC	*Bình Ngô Đại Cáo* (平吳大誥, Great Proclamation upon the Pacification of the Wu).[11]
CM	*Khâm Định Việt Sử Thông Giám Cương Mục* (欽定越史通鑑綱目, The Imperially Ordered Annotated Text Completely Reflecting the History of Viet).[12]
ĐVTS	*Đại Việt Thông Sử* (大越通史, Complete History of Đại Việt).[13]
LSTL	*Lam Sơn Thực Lục* (藍山實錄, Veritable Records of Mount Lam).[14]
QTTMT	*Quân Trung Từ Mệnh Tập* (軍中詞命集, Compilation of Writings and Commands from the Military Camp).[15]
SA MSL	Southeast Asia in the Ming Shi-lu, https://epress.nus.edu.sg/msl/.[16]
SKTT	*Đại Việt Sử Ký Toàn Thư* (大越史記全書, Complete Book of the Historical Records of Great Viet).[17]

Acknowledgements

I wish to thank my wife, Mỹ Thành, my son, Sonla Pham, and my daughter Mai-Linh Pham, who have given me much encouragement and support for this book. I am deeply grateful to Professor Hue-Tam Ho Tai and Associate Professor Dr Nguyễn Thị Mỹ Hạnh, who have both taken time out of their busy lives to read my manuscript and provide very valuable comments and suggestions.

Special thanks go to Lê Quỳnh Trang and Ngô Viết Hùng for their assistance with photography and translations from Chinese used in this volume. I wish to thank Nguyễn Trọng Doãn and his wife, Lê Thị Phương, for their warm hospitality during my stay in Thanh Hóa. I also want to express my gratitude to Minh Bui Jones, Trần Mỹ Hạnh, and Nguyễn Hải Yến, who accompanied me on a memorable journey along Highway QL7A retracing the route of Lê Lợi's southern campaign.

My gratitude goes to Nguyễn Ngọc Tân, who dedicated many hours to drawing the maps. Finally, my thanks go to Minh Bui Jones for his meticulous proofreading of the manuscript. Any remaining errors or omissions are, of course, entirely my own responsibility.

Lastly, I would like to thank Google Maps for granting permission to use their mapping content.

CHAPTER 1

A SUMMARY OF THIS BOOK

This book recounts the history of Đại Việt and Champa over the two centuries following the Trần dynasty's victory over the Mongol-led Yuan invasions in the late 13th century, as detailed in Volume 3A, up to the early 16th century. Beginning in the mid-14th century, the Trần dynasty gradually fell into decline, weakened by internal strife and increasing external pressure from Champa. The weakening of Đại Việt encouraged Champa to invade, culminating in the multiple sackings of Thăng Long (present-day Hanoi) by Chế Bồng Nga, the formidable king of Champa in the late 14th century.

Champa's northern offensives came to an end after Chế Bồng Nga was killed by a stray cannonball during a fierce river battle between the two kingdoms. These events are explored in detail in **Chapter 2**.

The wars with Champa paved the way for the rise of Lê Quý Ly from Thanh Hóa province, who ultimately forced the last Trần king to abdicate. He, then, changed his surname to Hồ and established the Hồ dynasty, with his two sons and relations from the same province. They built a massive citadel and established it as their capital in Tây Đô, located about 45 kilometres north-east of Thanh Hóa City. Having spent years fighting against the Chams, Hồ (Lê) Quý Ly was intimately familiar with the southern frontier. Once on the throne, he and his sons launched an aggressive campaign against Champa, seeing their dynasty's future in the expansion of the south. They quickly gained territory and initiated an ambitious resettlement program, moving people from Thanh Hóa and Nghệ An to areas now known as Huế, Quảng Nam, and Quảng Ngãi.

Their expansion was achieved through force, seizing Cham lands and pushing Đại Việt's southern border as far as the Vệ River in Quảng Ngãi province. Unfortunately for the Hồ family, their rise to power coincided with the dawn of the vastly more powerful Ming dynasty in China. The third Ming emperor demanded full submissions from neighbouring states, and the Hồ family's overthrow of the Trần dynasty provided him a convenient pretext for invasion. Early policies implemented by the Hồ court, including the introduction of paper currency and ruthless purge of the Trần descendants, were unpopular and fuelled public resentment.

The Ming army crossed into Đại Việt on 19 November 1406. Although the Hồ court mounted a determined resistance, they were unable to halt the Ming advance. Tây Đô fell within two months, and by mid-June 1407, Hồ Quý Ly and his two sons were captured and taken to Nanjing. His youngest son later served the Ming court, but all three eventually died in exile in China. Meanwhile, Champa seized the opportunity to reclaim the territories lost to the Hồ dynasty and forced the recent settlers to flee.

The Hồ Citadel at Tây Đô, along with their domestic policies, southern expansion into Champa and the Ming invasion of Đại Việt are examined in **Chapter 3.**

Chapter 4 opens with a 1407 order from the Ming emperor to his commanders in Đại Việt, declaring the kingdom's pacification and instructing them to establish a civil-military administration, while preparing to withdraw the army to China. The Ming administration was soon established, reorganising Đại Việt into a system of prefectures and subprefectures, while also constructing military forts and barracks to consolidate control. They recruited learned and skilled individuals to be sent to China and set up mining operations and tax offices to exploit local resources.

However, much to the emperor's frustration, Đại Việt was far from subdued. A Trần descendant soon proclaimed himself king, rallied a large following, and posed a serious threat to Ming control. His forces managed to reclaim much of the territory taken by the Ming army—until he executed his top general, causing the resistance to collapse. The struggle reignited when another Trần descendant emerged and united the remaining resistance forces under the banners of two Trần kings. Together, they fought the Ming occupiers for nearly six years. Ultimately, with reinforcements from China, the Ming army crushed the resistance in 1414. Both Trần kings and their commanders were either captured, killed, or taken to China and executed. The Ming commanders were finally able to depart Đại Việt, reaching Beijing in October 1415.

With the resistance suppressed, the Ming colonial administration then intensified its colonisation efforts, implementing a range of policies, including the establishment of local Confucian schools, the expansion of resource exploitation—particularly gold and silver mining—and the monopolisation of salt production. They also confiscated books written by the Vietnamese and built shrines to various deities. In addition, they reasserted control over the territories that Champa had reclaimed from the Hồ dynasty.

The Ming occupation of Đại Việt might have continued for years were it not for the uprising led by a man from the foothills west of Thanh Hóa—Lê Lợi—who ultimately drove them out. **Chapter 5** tells the story of this remarkable figure, a national hero deeply revered by the Vietnamese people.

In 1416, at the age of 31, Lê Lợi, then a local chief, gathered 18 like-minded men and held a blood oath ceremony at Lũng Nhai, near his home in Lam Sơn, Thanh Hóa. Together, they pledged to defend their homeland against Ming rule. Among them was Nguyễn Trãi, a 36-year-old scholar from Thăng Long, who would become a key figure in the rebellion. He composed all of Lê Lợi's official correspondence with the Ming commanders, and later wrote a detailed account of the events that led to the end of the occupation.[1]

In the early years, Lê Lợi and his men struggled against the Ming forces which, together with the help of local collaborators, were determined to destroy him. They desecrated his ancestors' graves, took his young daughter, scattered his family, and forced him to seek refuge in the nearby mountains and the rugged terrain of northern Laos, where they barely survived. However, from 1424 onward, the tide began to turn when Lê Lợi achieved a series of victories as he moved east and south, away from Lam Sơn. The victories enabled him to recruit and train more men while also capturing many weapons from the Ming army, including small cannons.

By 1425, Lê Lợi had reclaimed the territories south of Thanh Hóa, including former Cham lands, from Ming control. That year and in early 1426, they launched a northern campaign aimed at retaking Đông Đô. Alarmed by these developments, the Ming emperor dispatched reinforcements to Đông Đô in late 1426. Although the Ming forces initially scored some victories, they suffered a major defeat at the battle of Tốt Động, east of the capital, and retreated to Đông Đô, where they were besieged for several months before the Ming court attempted a relief effort.

Around October 1426, two Minh relief columns crossed into Đại Việt— one from the north-east and the other from the north-west. Confident of an easy victory, the commander of the northeastern column was lured into an ambush and quickly killed. Lê Lợi then sent the seal of the dead commander to the head of the northwestern column, who decided to take a safe course and retreat. With no possibility of getting reinforcements, the Ming garrison in Đông Đô surrendered. On 3 January 1428, they departed the capital on foot, horses and aboard ships provided by Lê Lợi. The Ming occupation of Đại Việt was over.

Chapter 6 opens with Lê Lợi relocating his wartime headquarters across the Red River to Đông Đô, where he established the Later Lê dynasty around May 1428. Lacking close family members to fill senior positions, he instead appointed trusted comrades who had fought alongside him, including Nguyễn Trãi, who assumed the highest civil post. Nevertheless, real power remained with the military leaders, while Lê Lợi retained ultimate authority. A strict disciplinarian, he maintained a strong and well-organised army throughout his brief reign.

Lê Lợi ruled for just under five years before his death. His young son ascended the throne and, in an attempt to assert his authority, initiated a purge of some of his father's former allies. Nguyễn Trãi and his family were executed after the king died after a night spent with Nguyễn Trãi's young wife, who was accused of causing the king's death. In the decades that followed, political intrigue and continued purges of former wartime commanders slowed the kingdom's progress.

In 1460, Lê Lợi's grandson, Lê Tư Thành, became king, ushering in a period of progress across multiple domains, including education, civil and military examinations, legal reform, and cartography. He also rehabilitated Nguyễn Trãi and several of Lê Lợi's former allies. Relations with Champa deteriorated during his reign, however, eventually leading Lê Tư Thành to launch a major military campaign in 1471. He led a large army into Champa, captured its capital in what is now Bình Định province, and took the Cham king prisoner. The king died on the way to Đông Kinh. After the conquest, Lê Tư Thành dismantled the Champa kingdom, creating two smaller states and reducing its territory to the modern-day provinces of Ninh Thuận and Bình Thuận.

Eight years later, in 1479, Lê Tư Thành launched a major campaign into what is now northern Laos, dispatching five armies that, according to Vietnamese sources, advanced as far as present-day Luang Prabang and southern Myanmar. They returned in triumph. However, Laotian historical records tell a different story, claiming that the Đại Việt forces were eventually forced to retreat. Although Lê Tư Thành personally led a contingent of troops, he ultimately turned back and never crossed into Laotian territory.

Despite Lê Tư Thành's accomplishments, the Later Lê dynasty began to unravel just seven years after his death with the rise, in 1504, of a ruler who would later be remembered as the Demon King. Over the following two decades, intense political infighting and factional struggles brought an end to the early phase of the Later Lê dynasty, paving the way for the emergence of the Mạc dynasty. The Later Lê would eventually reclaim the throne—a story that will be explored in my next volume.

CHAPTER 2

THE TRẦN DYNASTY'S HISTORICAL EXIT

2.1 - Three sisters, four brothers and the end of a dynasty

The Trần dynasty, which began in 1226, is chronicled in Volume 3A, up to the reign of its fourth king, Trần Thuyên (King Trần Anh Tông, 1276–1320). His son, Trần Mạnh (King Trần Minh Tông, 1300–1357), succeeded him and was noted for introducing reforms that overhauled the nation's political system. According to *Đại Việt Sử Ký Toàn Thư* (Complete Book of the Historical Records of Great Viet, abbreviated as SKTT), he upheld loyalty, honoured his ancestors, demonstrated foresight, preserved domestic harmony and order, and earned respect from foreign nations.[1] His achievements are reflected in the inscription of *Bia Ma Nhai*. However, after his reign, the Trần dynasty entered a period of decline, ultimately ending in 1400. While external factors such as the Ming dynasty's rise in 1368 and increased aggression from Champa contributed to its downfall, internal factors involving three key sisters also played a significant role.

Like other Đại Việt kings, Trần Mạnh had several queens and concubines. Among his consorts were two sisters, known in history as *Lê thị* or the Lê women, who became the mothers of three Trần kings: Trần Vượng, Trần Phủ, and Trần Kính. Their personal names are unknown, and they are referred to by their titles, Minh Từ *Hoàng thái phi* and Đôn Từ *Hoàng thái phi*, with *Hoàng thái phi* being a term for a royal consort who is also a king's mother. Based on the known birthdays of their sons, if they bore them at around the age of 18, Minh Từ was likely born around 1298, making Đôn Từ, born around 1315, her younger sister.

Trần Mạnh also married his cousin, Hiến Từ, who, according to SKTT, was the sisters' sibling, explaining how the Lê sisters came to be his consorts.[2] During their time at court, they introduced their nephew, Lê Quý Ly, who would later play a pivotal role in the dynasty's collapse and the establishment of the Hồ dynasty, a subject discussed in the next chapter. Hiến Từ herself gave birth to one king, Trần Hạo, and was instrumental in enthroning another king, Nhật Lễ.

Before Hiến Từ gave birth to a son, Minh Từ became embroiled in a court intrigue that resulted in her son, Trần Vượng, ascending the throne in 1329 as King Trần Hiến Tông (1319–1341). His reign lasted 12 years, ending prematurely at the age of 23. During this period, Trần Mạnh, who held the title of senior king (*Thái Thượng Hoàng*, also translated as Emperor Emeritus or Father of the King), had the final say in most significant decisions.

Trần Vượng was tutored by a scholar, Chu Văn An (1292–1370), who is considered as the Founding Father of Vietnamese Confucianism. Around this time, Lý Tế Xuyên (?–?) wrote *Việt Điện U Linh Tập* (Compilation of the Departed Spirits in the Realm of Viet), a compilation of legends about Vietnamese deities and spirits from ancient times, that has survived to the present time.[3]

In 1336, five years before Trần Vượng's death, Hiến Từ gave birth to Trần Hạo, who succeeded the throne after Trần Vượng's passing. The transition of power was peaceful under the watchful eyes of the senior king. However, in 1357, Trần Mạnh (the senior king) passed away, leaving no successor to fulfil the stabilizing role he had provided. Following his death, Trần Hạo, his mother, Hiến Từ, and likely the two Lê sisters—Minh Từ and Đôn Từ—along with their nephew, Lê Quý Ly, began to dominate the Trần court.

Trần Hạo (King Trần Dụ Tông, 1336–1369) ruled for 28 years but died young at 34. According to SKTT, the Trần dynasty began to decline during his reign as Trần Hạo became increasingly indulgent and debauched. A few years before his death, a significant event unfolded involving his brother, Nguyên

Dục. While watching an epic play about *The Queen Mother Offers the Peaches of Longevity*, Nguyên Dục fell in love with a pregnant actress from the production.[4] He married her and adopted her child, naming him Dương Nhật Lễ. After Trần Hạo's death in 1369, his mother, Hiến Từ, insisted that Nhật Lễ should inherit the throne. She justified her decision by arguing that Nguyên Dục, her eldest son and the rightful heir, had died five years earlier, in 1364.

Later historians were highly critical of Hiến Từ's decision to enthrone Dương Nhật Lễ, arguing that she should have selected a candidate from the Trần bloodline, particularly as there were more capable and suitable options available.[5] Their criticism proved justified; Nhật Lễ was a deeply unfit ruler. According to SKTT, he indulged excessively in drinking, singing, dancing, and sex, showing little interest in governance.[6]

Within just six months of ascending the throne, in the last lunar month of 1369, Nhật Lễ poisoned Hiến Từ—the elderly queen who had secured his place as king. By that time, Hiến Từ had come to regret her decision to install him, but it was too late to reverse the damage caused by her choice.[7]

Why Hiến Từ made the fateful decision to enthrone Nhật Lễ—a choice that ultimately led to her death—remains a mystery. Nhật Lễ held no power over her at the time, and she was free to choose any other Trần nephew as king. However, later events suggest that even selecting a blood relative might not have guaranteed her safety. In the declining years of the Trần dynasty, family loyalty was a fragile concept, often broken by personal ambition and political intrigue.

Hiến Từ's death became the catalyst for her family to rally and seek vengeance against Nhật Lễ. Their first attempt at retaliation failed, but in 1370, Hiến Từ's daughter, Princess Thiên Ninh, and her half-brothers, Trần Phủ and Trần Kính, raised an army in Thanh Hóa and sailed to Thăng Long. As they advanced along the Red River, court officials defected to their side, welcoming them as liberators.

When Nhật Lễ realized the inevitability of their victory, he came out to surrender as they approached the landing. He was immediately seized and imprisoned near today's Hàng Buồm Street in Hanoi. While in captivity, Nhật Lễ strangled a servant and Trần Phủ had him beaten to death.[8]

After Nhật Lễ's death, his mother, the actress, fled to Champa and sought revenge for her son by urging the Cham court to invade Đại Việt. Champa readily agreed, and in 1371, Cham forces reached Thăng Long, where they burned and pillaged the capital, though the Trần court managed to escape.[9]

Meanwhile, the accession of Trần Phủ (King Trần Nghệ Tông, 1321–1394) proved advantageous for Lê Quý Ly. Trần Phủ's mother, Minh Từ, was Lê Quý Ly's aunt, creating a familial connection that elevated his status at court. In 1372, just a year after ascending the throne, the king married his daughter to Lê Quý Ly and appointed him as a representative of the Secret Council (*Khu Mật Viện Đại Sứ*), a prestigious position. At the age of 34, this marked Lê Quý Ly's first recorded appearance in SKTT, setting the stage for his eventual rise to power.[10]

Trần Phủ had never aspired to be king, and in 1372, just two years into his reign, he abdicated to become the senior king. He passed the throne to his half-brother, Trần Kính, who succeeded him as King Trần Duệ Tông (1337–1377). Unlike Trần Phủ, Trần Kính was known for his more combative nature. When Champa attacked and burned Thăng Long in 1371, it was Trần Kính who preserved the army and weapons during the retreat.

By this time, Champa had grown into Đại Việt's most formidable existential threat. Determined to eliminate this danger once and for all, Trần Kính embarked on extensive preparations for a military campaign. At the end of 1376, he launched an expedition into Champa. However, the Chams lured Trần Kính and his forces into a planned ambush. In early 1377, the Chams decisively defeated the Đại Việt army, and Trần Kính was killed in battle.[11] Trần Kính's mother, Đôn Từ, was the youngest of the three Lê sisters.

Later historians characterised Trần Phủ as an indecisive figure. Under his long reign of 22 years as a senior king until he died in 1394, Đại Việt suffered, *externally*, [when] *the enemy invaded the capital and internally*, [when] *traitors threatened the throne. The country declined and then perished.*[12] A contemporary account, *Nam Ông Mộng Lục* (Dream Memoir of a Southern Man), by his grandson, Hồ Nguyên Trừng, described him more sympathetically as *gentle, filial, respectful, frugal, wise and decisive. He studied history and did not like pomposity.*[13]

Before embarking on his ill-fated campaign to Champa, Trần Kính married his daughter to Prince Húc, the son of his half-brother, then the senior king.[14] After his death, his son, Trần Hiện, succeeded him as King Trần Phế Đế (1361–1388). According to SKTT, Trần Hiện was both foolish and weak.[15] He made an enemy out of the senior king, his uncle Trần Phủ, by having Húc, his brother-in-law who had surrendered and joined the Chams in 1377, lured into a trap and killed. This act enraged Trần Phủ, who sought retribution for the death of his son.

However, Trần Hiện was astute enough to recognize the growing influence of Lê Quý Ly, who had become a trusted ally of Trần Phủ. Sensing the threat posed by Lê Quý Ly's unchecked power, Trần Hiện sought to remove him before he became too difficult to control. However, Lê Quý Ly learned of the king's plans and acted pre-emptively, persuading the senior king to depose Trần Hiện. Trần Phủ, already seeking vengeance for Prince Húc's death, needed little convincing.

In late 1388, Trần Phủ invited Trần Hiện to a meeting under the pretence of discussing state affairs. Upon his arrival, Trần Hiện was seized, imprisoned, and subsequently hanged. His loyal generals initially planned a rescue mission, but Trần Hiện ordered them to stand down. This decision proved fatal, as Lê Quý Ly later had most of them executed.

After deposing Trần Hiện, Trần Phủ placed his youngest son, Trần Ngung, on the throne as King Trần Thuận Tông (1378–1399). At just 11 years old, the new king was too young to wield power, leaving the court firmly under the control of Lê Quý Ly. To consolidate his influence further, Lê Quý Ly arranged for his daughter to marry Trần Ngung once the king reached adulthood.

In 1394, Trần Phủ, the senior king, passed away. Before his death, Lê Quý Ly had sworn to protect the Trần dynasty, but this promise was soon broken. In 1398, Lê Quý Ly compelled the young king to abdicate in favour of his infant son, Trần An (King Trần Thiếu Đế, (1396-?)). However, that was not enough for a man like Lê Quý Ly, and a year later, he had Trần Ngung killed by hanging after first attempting poisoning and starvation.[16] Trần Ngung was 21 years old at the time of his death.

Strangely, before he died at 73, Trần Phủ told Lê Quý Ly to assist Trần Ngung if he could, but if the latter *proved to be weak and stupid, then you* [Lê Quý Ly] *could take the throne for himself.*[17] Despite the implicit permission from the last senior Trần king, Lê Quý Ly, a political survivor in his early 60s, took no chances. In 1399, when a plot to assassinate him from members of the Trần allies failed, Lê Quý Ly ordered them all killed, including Trần Khát Chân – the hero who stopped Cham King Chế Bồng Nga in 1390 – and 370 other family members and relatives. The destruction of the Trần clan was complete and relentless in the following few years; *their property was confiscated, their daughters were forced into servants, and their sons from one year old and older were buried alive or drowned. Hunting and arresting* [the plotter's] *associates persisted unabated for several years. People who knew each other only signalled the acquaintance by looking at each other, not daring to talk. People's houses were not allowed to accommodate travellers. Whenever they had overnight guests, the homeowners had to report the guests to their neighbours. Together, they would examine the guests' documents, belongings, and reasons for travelling as proof of guarantee* [that the guests were unrelated to the plotters]. *Every commune had checkpoints that were controlled by guards day and night.*[18]

After a brief two-year reign, Lê Quý Ly forced Trần An to abdicate and declared himself king, marking the end of the Trần dynasty and the beginning of the Hồ dynasty in 1400. The list of the Trần kings is shown in Table 2-1, and the complex relationship between their family members is shown in Figure 2-1.

KINGS OF THE TRẦN DYNASTY

	NAMES (BIRTH-DEATH)	TEMPLE NAMES (MIẾU HIỆU) (R=REIGN)
1	Trần Cảnh (1218–1277)	Trần Thái Tông (r.1226–1258)[19]
2	Trần Hoảng (1240–1290)	Trần Thánh Tông (r.1258–1278)
3	Trần Khâm (1258–1308)	Trần Nhân Tông (r.1278–1293)
4	Trần Thuyên (1276–1320)	Trần Anh Tông (r.1293–1314)
5	Trần Mạnh (1300–1357)	Trần Minh Tông (r.1314–1329)
6	Trần Vượng (1319–1341)	Trần Hiến Tông (r.1329–1341)
7	Trần Hạo (1336–1369)	Trần Dụ Tông (r.1341–1369)[20]
8	Trần Phủ (1321–1394)	Trần Nghệ Tông (r.1370–1372)
9	Trần Kính (1337–1377)	Trần Duệ Tông (r.1372–1377)
10	Trần Hiện (also Nghiễn) (1361–1388)	see note below
11	Trần Ngung (1378–1399)	Trần Thuận Tông (r.1388–1398)
12	Trần An (1396–?)	Trần Thiếu Đế (r.1398–1400)

Table 2-1: Kings of the Trần dynasty (1126-1400).

Note: SKTT refers to Trần Hiện as Trần Phế Đế (r.1377–1388), with Phế Đế meaning 'deposed emperor'. He was not given a temple name.

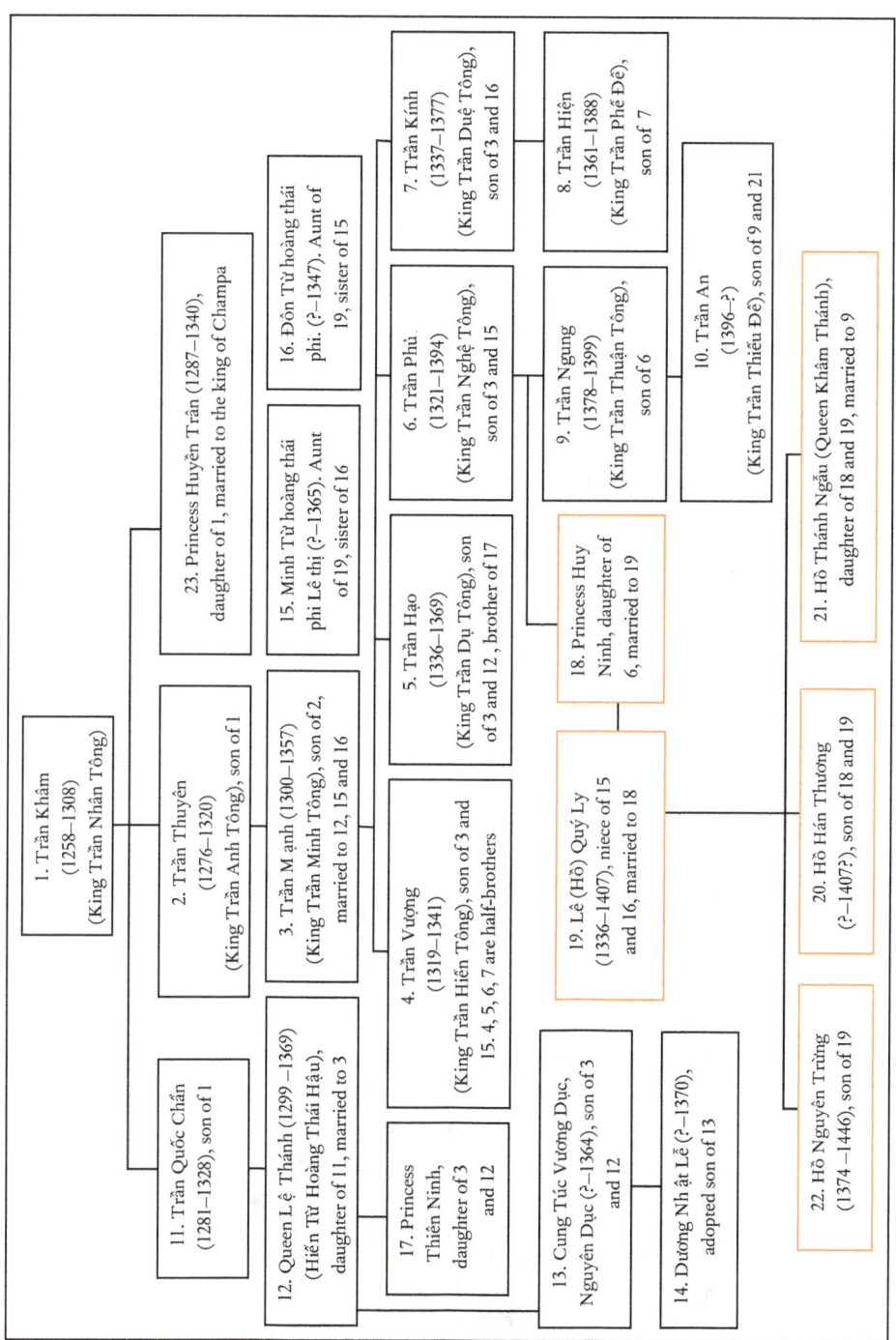

Figure 2-1: The Trần and Hồ family tree, 14th century.[21]

Note: Minh Từ Hoàng thái phi is also known as Anh Tư Phu nhân or Anh Tư Nguyên phi.

2.2 - *Famines, earthquakes, solar eclipses and operas*

In addition to chronicling historical events, the compilers of SKTT also document natural and man-made disasters. Famine was a recurring hardship in Đại Việt, as the country suffered from regular floods, crop-destroying insects, and occasional droughts. It is interesting to note that Thăng Long was also struck by earthquakes in 1355 and 1393.[22] SKTT mention solar eclipses on 10 December 1349, 26 May 1351 and 25 March 1354.[23] These dates align with NASA's (National Aeronautics and Space Administration) catalogue of solar eclipses between 1301 and 1400, with the latter two events precisely matching NASA's documented occurrences.[24]

In 1362, Trần Hạo, often described as a 'debauched' king, required members of the royal family to submit various forms of stage entertainment for his amusement and rewarded those he favoured. Among these submissions was an opera form that eventually became known as '*tuồng* (傳)' or '*hát bội*', Vietnamese opera, which continues to be performed in Vietnam today. The characters in the opera dress in elaborate costumes and paint their faces with vibrant colours. Figure 2-2 illustrates one such character.[25]

The origins of *tuồng* trace back to the Mongol-Yuan invasions at the end of the 13th century, when a captured prisoner-of-war, Li Yuanjishan (*Lý Nguyên Cát*), introduced the art form to Đại Việt. Notably, as mentioned earlier, Nhật Lễ's mother was an actress in such an opera.[26]

Figure 2-2: A Vietnamese opera (*hát bội*) character prepares for her act.

2.3 - *A Trần princess and a Cham king*

PRINCESS HUYỀN TRÂN (HUYỀN TRÂN CÔNG CHÚA)

Volume 3A tells the stories of the Mongol-Yuan invasions of Đại Việt in 1257–1258, 1284–1285, 1287–1288 and Champa in 1283–1284. Both kingdoms survived these onslaughts and successfully expelled the invaders. These terrible times brought the two kingdoms closer together. In the third lunar month of 1301, the senior king of Đại Việt, Trần Khâm (King Trần Nhân Tông, 1258–1308), visited Champa and returned to Thăng Long (Hanoi), in the 11th lunar month of the same year. The capital of Champa at the time was in today's Bình Định province, so it is likely that he spent most of his time there during his visit.[27]

While in Champa, he promised to marry his daughter to the lord (*chúa*) of Champa. Four years later, in the spring of 1305, a delegation from Champa arrived in Thăng Long to formalise the marriage proposal. Chế Bồ Đài led the delegation of more than 100 people and brought gifts of gold, silver, precious agarwood and other foreign objects. Most people at the Trần court objected to the proposal, but *Hành Khiển* (Chief Administrator), Trần Khắc Chung supported the marriage alliance. Such political marriage was not unprecedented; for instance, in 1154, the king of Champa, Chế Bì La Bút, offered his daughter to Lý Thiên Tộ (King Lý Anh Tông, 1135–1175) of the Lý dynasty (1009–1226).[28]

A year later, in the sixth lunar month of 1306, Princess Huyền Trân married Chế Mân, the lord of Champa. The story would have ended there as a minor footnote in Vietnamese history but for the subsequent events which transformed Princess Huyền Trân into a Vietnamese legend that most Vietnamese still remember to this day.

What happened?

Between 1306 and 1307, Chế Mân presented the two provinces of Ô and Lý to Đại Việt as a wedding present, or a 'marriage exchange', following his union with Princess Huyền Trân. In the first lunar month of 1307, Đại Việt renamed these provinces Thuận Châu and Hóa Châu. However, resistance arose among the inhabitants of three hamlets – La Thủy, Tác Hồng, and Đà Bồng – who refused to accept the new administration.[29]

To address the dissent, Đại Việt dispatched the court official Đoàn Nhữ Hài, who negotiated with the locals by awarding titles to some individuals, granted land, and offered tax exemptions to secure their cooperation.[30] These territories, encompassing parts of present-day southern Quảng Trị and Huế provinces, stretched between the Hiếu/Thạch Hãn Rivers and the Thu Bồn River, marking a significant territorial expansion for Đại Việt. The administrative centres of these prefectures were located at two citadels, which are detailed in Volume 3B.³¹

A few months after the names change, in the summer of 1307, during the fifth lunar month (or about June), Chế Mân died. In the intervening year, it appears that Princess Huyền Trân had a son with Chế Mân and named him Đa Da. According to SKTT, Princess Huyền Trân had to be cremated with her husband after his death in accordance with Champa customs. Worrying about this possibility, five months later, her brother and Đại Việt king, Trần Thuyên, sent Trần Khắc Chung to Champa under the pretext of attending Chế Mân's funeral to save her and her son.

The king told Trần Khắc Chung to suggest to the Chams that no one would be available to perform the required rituals properly if the princess were cremated. Instead, he recommended a ceremony at the beach where they could summon spirits from heaven before returning to the funeral pyre. The Chams concurred. When the funeral procession reached the shore, Trần Khắc Chung used a small boat to rescue the princess secretly. According to SKTT, during their extended journey at sea, as they spent a long time travelling in circles to delay their return, Trần Khắc Chung and Princess Huyền Trân had a sexual liaison.³² However, this account is difficult to accept, as Trần Khắc Chung was already sixty years old and a contemporary of the princess's father. The delay in their return to Thăng Long is more plausibly explained by a storm that forced them ashore.

There are gaps in the stories, such as how the Chams managed to preserve Chế Mân's body for at least six months after his passing and before his cremation. Similarly, why Trần Khắc Chung did not leave immediately after hearing of Chế Mân's death, which could have been in July, but waited until November before departure? If he were, he would have been at the funeral in August. The two-month duration is due to the distance between the capitals of the two kingdoms. It would have taken about a month for the news of Chế Mân's death to reach Thăng Long and a month for Trần Khắc Chung to travel from Thăng Long to Bình Định to attend the funeral to rescue the princess.

Perhaps the Chams decided to delay the cremation until December 1307, as it would be an auspicious date, and would also allow time for travel by other foreign leaders.

Regardless, the story of Princess Huyền Trân has captivated the imagination of the Vietnamese for centuries. She is honoured with temples and streets bearing her name. In 2006, to celebrate the 700th anniversary of the founding of Thuận Hóa, the People's Committee of the Thừa Thiên-Huế province began the construction of a temple in her honour. It is situated on a hill covered in beautiful pine trees, approximately 10 kilometres south-west of Huế Imperial City.[33] A giant bronze statue of her at the temple is shown in Figure 2-3.[34] Thuận Hóa prefecture is the combination of Thuận Châu and Hóa Châu in today's southern Quảng Trị and Huế respectively.

Figure 2-3: A statue of Princess Huyền Trân at her temple, Huế, 21st century, bronze, H. 2.37 m.

Figure 2-4: A view of the back of the Princess Huyền Trân's temple.

The statue of Princess Huyền Trân as the Buddhist nun Hương Tràng is in the gazebo.

According to the inscription on the temple stele, Princess Huyền Trân was born in 1287. In 1306, she was 19 when she embarked on a trip south to wed the Cham lord Chế Mân. One can only imagine how terrified she must have been to leave the familiar comforts of home in Thăng Long. However, such marriages were not uncommon in Đại Việt. Đại Việt kings, including the Trần and the Lý before them, used their princesses as diplomatic tools, marrying them to tribal chiefs in order to secure their loyalty and strengthen the realm's alliances.[35]

The temple inscription also notes that she returned to Thăng Long around August or September 1308, nearly nine months after she was rescued. A year later, she became a Buddhist nun. She died in 1340 at the age of 53 at the Hổ Sơn pagoda, in Nam Định province.[36] As for her son, Prince Đa Da, we have no information on what happened to him. Since he was a Cham prince and SKTT does not mention him again, he likely remained in Champa. Given that he was barely a year old at the time of the rescue, it is reasonable to assume he did not accompany his mother on the perilous sea journey. The dangers of the escape would have made it unlikely for him to travel with her.

The Vietnamese are grateful to Princess Huyền Trân for her sacrifices for the land that Champa gifted to Đại Việt in return. To understand the significance, the combined area of present-day Quảng Trị and Thừa Thiên-Huế provinces is 9,825 square kilometres or roughly 65 per cent of the total area of the Red River Delta, where most people of Đại Việt lived at the time.[37] Although Thuận Hóa (harmonious and civilised, formerly Champa's Ô and Lý) is smaller than Quảng Trị and Thừa Thiên-Huế provinces, the comparison highlights the magnitude of the territorial gain. Through a single act of marriage, the total land area of Đại Việt expanded considerably, and all of this was achieved without any bloodshed. Incidentally, contemporary 'Huế' is a distortion of 'Hóa'.[38]

CHẾ MÂN AND PRINCE HARIJIT

So who was Chế Mân? Since the discovery of the Cham inscriptions in the 19th century, most historians have identified Chế Mân (as mentioned in Vietnamese SKTT) with Prince Harijit (from Cham inscriptions) and Prince Bu Di (as recorded in Chinese Yuan shi).[39] However, I have some reservations about this connection, which I will explain below.

In the early 20th century, a stele was found on a mound somewhere in the village of Čaklin (or Chakling, present-day Mỹ Nghiệp in Ninh Thuận province). The stele, coded C. 22, contains 31 lines of inscription in Cham and includes five dates: 1274, 1298, 1300, 1301, and 1306.[40] Étienne Aymonier (1844–1929), a French linguist and explorer, translates the inscription which recounts the story of Prince Harijittāmaja (Hari-jitt-āmaja, the victorious son of Hari (Vishnu or Khrisna) or winning with Vishnu's blessing), the eldest son of Jayasiṃhavarman (Jaya-siṃha-varman, the victorious lion-protector), a rājādhirāja, or 'king of kings'. According to the inscription, Prince Harijittāmaja was born in 1196 śaka (1274 CE). The inscription also mentions three queens: the chief queen, Queen Parameśvarī (Param-Īśvarī, the supreme goddess), Queen Tapasī (a female sage), and another chief queen Bhāskara] devī [of Latumvek].[41]

According to Aymonier, Queen Parameśvarī is identified as Princess Huyền Trân, based on a term in the inscription, 'King Devādideva', which refers to a king of divinities, a title commonly used by the Cambodians to describe a Đại Việt king.[42] However, another French archaeologist Louis Finot (1864–1935), disagrees, suggesting that this term should read 'Javādhideva', meaning the supreme king of Java and thus unrelated to Đại Việt.[43] Finot also argues that Prince Harijit and Prince Harijittāmaja are distinct individuals. Prince Harijit, as mentioned in inscription C. 11 found at the Po Klong Garai tower in Ninh Thuận, is another name for Jayasiṃhavarman, while in C. 22, he is described as the father of Prince Harijittāmaja. The three queens listed in C. 22 are likely Prince Harijit's wives, and the third queen probably a Cham.

According to sinologist Georges Maspero (1872–1942), Prince Harijit ascended the throne in 1287. If he was 20 years old at the time, he would have been born in 1247. By 1306, he would have been 59 years old, making it unlikely that he would marry Princess Huyền Trân as his chief queen at such an advanced age.

During the Mongol-Yuan invasion in 1283, Yuan shi mentions a young prince named Bu Di (*Bố Đích*) and an elderly Cham king named Bột Do. As discussed in Volume 3A, Marco Polo also recorded the account of an older Cham king in his travel diaries.[44] Prince Harijit's father was King Indravarman, who ruled for a very long time – between 20 and 30 years, according to inscription C. 11. This duration would fit the age profile described by both Marco Polo and Yuan shi.[45]

On this basis, there is a plausible argument that Chế Mân could be identified as Prince Harijit. However, one might question why Chế Mân would give away so much land, especially since Prince Harijit, a 'king of kings', had fought a long and hard campaign against the Mongols to preserve Cham's sovereignty over his domain. While we may never know the answer, it is possible to speculate that Chế Mân either believed that Champa would not lose the land because Đại Việt people would not settle there, or he may have considered the land to be of little value after the Mongols devastated it in early 1284. He might have been right in that the territory he offered to Đại Việt as a marriage exchange remained a contested frontier between the two kingdoms throughout much of the 14th century.

For now, in the absence of additional information, I would accept Chế Mân is Prince Harijit since they existed the same time, but not for the reasons outlined by Aymonier.

TRẦN KHẮC CHUNG – A BRAVE ROGUE

Trần Khắc Chung, the man who rescued Princess Huyền Trân, is a fascinating figure in this period of Vietnamese history. Born with the surname Đỗ, he later adopted the name Trần as he advanced through the ranks of the imperial bureaucracy. Serving three consecutive Trần kings – Trần Khâm, Trần Thuyên and Trần Mạnh – he rose to become the highest-ranking official at court during his time.[46]

A fearless negotiator

Twenty-one years earlier, the Mongol-led armies of the Yuan dynasty had invaded Đại Việt, and around August of 1285, they were outside Thăng Long. Đại Việt king, Trần Khâm, was looking for a messenger to go to the camp of the Yuan commander to request a ceasefire. He could not find anyone until a minor official named Đỗ Khắc Chung volunteered. Đỗ Khắc Chung made his way to the Mongol camp. He met with the commander, Omar Baghatur, who inquired why the king had not surrendered and come to pay respects when the mighty Yuan army arrived, remarking, *what to become of a mantis that* [tries to] *stop the wheel?*. Đỗ Khắc Chung retorted that the Yuan army should have sent the offer of capitulation at the border. Now that two sides were engaged in battle, he said, *animals would have fought and birds would have pecked, let alone humans*.[47]

Omar Baghatur reiterated the Yuan threat, stating that the great army only sought to borrow the roads through Đại Việt to attack Champa. He told Đỗ Khắc Chung that if King Trần Khâm agreed to negotiate, the kingdom would remain unharmed. However, if not, *mountains and rivers would be flattened, and the king and his subjects would turn into grass* in a short time.[48]

Omar Baghatur initially allowed Đỗ Khắc Chung to leave but then changed his mind. But it was too late. He remarked to his subordinates that conquering Đại Việt would not be easy, as the kingdom still had talented individuals like Đỗ Khắc Chung. In the early hours of 18 February 1285, Đỗ Khắc Chung returned, and the Yuan forces followed him, launching an attack on the Đại Việt camp. Volume 3A tells the stories of the Mongol-Yuan invasions.

Court intrigue

Princess Huyền Trân had an older brother, Trần Quốc Chẩn. His daughter married his nephew, Trần Mạnh, and became Queen Lệ Thánh (also known as Hiến Từ). However, after 15 years of marriage, she could not produce an heir. Meanwhile, others at the court began to conspire over the succession, favouring another prince, Trần Vượng, the nine-year-old son of a different queen, to become the next king. Unsurprisingly, Trần Quốc Chẩn vehemently opposed this idea, insisting that the court should wait for Queen Lệ Thánh's yet-to-be-born child.

In 1328, the conspirators bribed Trần Phẩu, a servant of Trần Quốc Chẩn, to falsely accuse him of treason. The king believed the accusation, arrested Trần Quốc Chẩn and sought Trần Khắc Chung's counsel. Trần Khắc Chung responded with a cautionary proverb: *catching a tiger is easy,* [but] *releasing a tiger is difficult*. Understanding the implications, Trần Mạnh locked Trần

Quốc Chẩn away, denying him food and water. Queen Hiến Từ visited her father in prison and soaked her gown in water to offer him a drink, but he died soon after. More than 100 people connected to Trần Quốc Chẩn were also arrested.[49]

The conspirators, along with Trần Khắc Chung, hailed from the same district, and Trần Khắc Chung had once been a teacher to Trần Vượng. This connection meant that he stood to gain significantly if Trần Vượng were to become the next king. As a highly esteemed figure in court, Trần Khắc Chung's opinions carried considerable weight. In this instance, however, his part in the scheme led to tragic consequences, resulting in the loss of lives and the downfall of Trần Quốc Chẩn and his supporters.

A few years later, one of Trần Phẩu's wives revealed the bribery to the king. Trần Phẩu was apprehended and sentenced to death. However, before the execution could take place, a servant of Trần Quốc Chẩn's son killed Trần Phẩu by eating him alive.

While one of the plotters was banished, the others were unaffected. Two years later, in 1330, Trần Vượng ascended the throne as the next king. Trần Khắc Chung died in the same year, but shortly after his burial, a servant of Trần Quốc Chẩn's son exhumed his body and mutilated it, cutting it into pieces.[50]

Trần Khắc Chung was a gambler who would wager all night for two or three days at a time.[51] He was a risk taker with a sharp wit, an opportunist, a rogue and craved the good things in life. For his behaviour, not surprisingly, he has received harsh criticism from historians.[52] I have included his story in this volume to contrast the stereotyped scholars of the day.

As fate would have it, Hiến Từ gave birth to a son, Trần Hạo, in 1336; Trần Vượng died young at 22 in 1341, and Trần Hạo succeeded him. In 1344, Trần Hạo honoured his grandfather, Trần Quốc Chẩn, restoring him to full status. Still, he chose not to punish Trần Vượng's mother, one of the conspirators involved in the plot against his grandfather 16 years earlier. Hiến Từ died in 1369 at 70, as mentioned previously.[53]

ĐOÀN NHỮ HÀI — A YOUNG DIPLOMAT

Within the temple complex of Princess Huyền Trân, there is an altar dedicated to Đoàn Nhữ Hài (1280–1335), the man who was tasked with persuading the Cham villagers to come over to Đại Việt as cited earlier. A contemporary of Trần Khắc Chung, but Đoàn Nhữ Hài was at least 20 years younger. When Trần Khắc Chung went to the Mongol camp in 1285, Đoàn Nhữ Hài was only a boy of five. While studying in Thăng Long, he did a favour for Trần Thuyên and became the latter's confidant. When Trần Thuyên became king, he appointed Đoàn Nhữ Hài to an official position at the young age of 19 although Đoàn Nhữ Hài had not passed the national examination with distinction.[54]

1303

Four years later, in 1303, the king sent Đoàn Nhữ Hài to Champa as Đại Việt envoy. Upon arriving, he presented Trần Thuyên's official letter to the lord of Champa. According to custom, the envoy was supposed to bow to the Cham lord before opening the letter. However, Đoàn Nhữ Hài defied this tradition. He bowed to the letter first, explaining that reading it was akin to looking into his king's face. For that reason, he had to bow to the letter before anything else. The Cham lord, unable to oppose this bold gesture, accepted it. From then on, Đại Việt envoys no longer bowed to the Cham lord.[55]

While at the court of Champa, Đoàn Nhữ Hài put up a sign at the port of Tỳ Ni (also known as Thi Lị Bì Nại, Thi Nại (Sri Vijaya)) in modern Quy Nhơn in Bình Định province declaring that trading at the port was forbidden, but he then instructed the port manager to remove the sign after he left.[56] At the time, Đoàn Nhữ Hài was just 23; on his return, Trần Thuyên praised him for his actions. I have included these episodes to demonstrate Đại Việt's dismissive attitude towards Champa in the early 14th century.

Chế Mân died in 1307; his death marked the end of the peaceful coexistence between Đại Việt and Champa. Following his passing, tensions escalated between the two kingdoms. From that point until the end of the 14th century, Đại Việt and Champa engaged in 20 conflicts, with the majority of the battles occurring in the second half of the century.[57]

1311

Four years later, in 1311, Đại Việt invaded Champa because its lord, Chế Chí, they claimed, was 'treacherous'.[58] The invasion of 1311 appeared to be a major military campaign, with Đại Việt forces divided into three main columns: Trần Thuyên, the king, taking the coastal road, his brother; Trần Quốc Chẩn, the mountain route; and a naval commander veteran from the Đại Việt-Mongol/Yuan wars, Trần Khánh Dư, the sea route. Đoàn Nhữ Hài was part of the advance party, sent to negotiate with Chế Chí in the hopes of securing his surrender. Although the details of his negotiation remain unrecorded, Chế Chí was captured in Vijaya without a fight and brought back to Thăng Long. He died in captivity and was cremated according to Cham customs two years later, in 1313.[59] In the aftermath, Đại Việt replaced Chế Chí with his brother, Chế

Đà A Bà Niêm, granting him the title of *Á Hầu* (a second-rank marquis as compared with *Chính Hầu* as a full marquis). As a result, Champa effectively had no king and was controlled by Đại Việt at this time.

1318

In 1318, Trần Quốc Chẩn, alongside Phạm Ngũ Lão, a seasoned veteran of the Đại Việt-Mongol/Yuan wars, led another military expedition against Champa. This time, the Chams put up fierce resistance, and the lord of Champa, Chế Năng, fled to Trảo Oa (present-day Java) seeking external assistance. Despite this effort, Đại Việt prevailed, capturing many Cham prisoners.[60] According to sinologist Georges Maspero, Chế Năng was Chế Đà A Bà Niêm, suggesting that after being installed by Đại Việt, Chế Đà A Bà Niêm eventually resisted their control and sought help from other regions in an attempt to regain independence for Champa.[61]

1326

Đại Việt invaded Champa again in 1326 but without success.[62] In 1335, Đoàn Nhữ Hài drowned during a campaign against Ai Lao (modern northern Laos), as discussed below.[63]

In this volume, I have included Đoàn Nhữ Hài and Trần Khắc Chung to illustrate how both achieved success at the Trần court not through their aristocratic lineage or academic achievement, but rather through personal ability, strategic acumen, and the opportunities they seized.

2.4 - Kingdoms in the west

Historically, Đại Việt historians referred to the various polities of the land immediately to their west as Ai Lao (哀牢), a term used at least until the 16th century to describe what is now northern Laos. The name first appeared in Hou Han shu (Book of the Later Han), compiled in the 5th century CE, to denote the region encompassing northern Laos and southern Yunnan.[64] SKTT records numerous interactions with Ai Lao—as a tributary state, a target of military campaigns by Đại Việt, and at times an aggressor along the western frontier.

To gain a better understanding of the interactions between Đại Việt and Ai Lao, I have taken a brief detour to explain the names and geographical locations of the various polities associated with Ai Lao as follows.

HISTORICAL KINGDOMS OF ZHENLA, LAN XANG, AI LAO, LÃO QUA AND CONTEMPORARY LAOS

In the mid-sixth century, the region immediately west of what is now central Vietnam was occupied by the kingdom of Zhenla, centred around present-day Champasak in southern Laos. By the early eighth century, Zhenla had split into two polities: Water Zhenla, covering parts of modern southern Cambodia and Vietnam; and Land Zhenla, based around present-day Thakhek in central Laos, as described in Volume Two.[65]

Following the decline of these kingdoms, the region fragmented into several smaller city-states that persisted until the 14th century. The recorded history of Laos began with the reign of Fa Ngum (1354–1373), founder of the Lan Xang kingdom (meaning 'a Million Elephants'). Lan Xang's capital was Xieng Thong (also known as Muang Sua), in present-day Luang Prabang, followed by Vientiane in the 16th century. The kingdom lasted for about three centuries before splintering into three regional kingdoms, from north to south: Louang Phrabang (Luang Prabang), Vientiane, and Champasak.[66] These kingdoms eventually fell under Siamese (modern Thai) control in the 18th century, until the French consolidated them in the 19th century under the colonial Protectorate of Laos. South-east of Louang Phrabang, close to the border of Đại Việt, was a small principality centred around today's Phonsavan of Xiengkhoang Province, the site of the prehistoric Plain of Jars.

Around the time Lan Xang was founded, the compilers of SKTT used the term Lão Qua (老撾) to refer to Laos. According to a 19th-century Vietnamese work, *Khâm Định Việt Sử Thông Giám Cương Mục* (The Imperially Ordered Annotated Text Completely Reflecting the History of Viet, abbreviated as CM), Lão Qua was a kingdom centred around Louang Phrabang.[67] However, there was no kingdom there, and Louang Phrabang was the capital of Lan Xang at that time, so CM may have mistaken the capital of Lan Xang as a separate kingdom. Both CM and SKTT continued to use the term Ai Lao separately from Lão Qua, although, strictly speaking, they referred the same polity as Lan Xang from the mid-14th century to the early 18th century.

However, they distinguished Chân Lạp (Zhenla) from Ai Lao, as their records identify Chân Lạp as the kingdom located in the south and southwest of Đại Việt.

GEOGRAPHICAL RELATIONSHIP

Today, the Vietnamese provinces located along the western border with Laos, north of the Ngang Pass, are, from north to south: Điện Biên, Sơn La, Thanh Hóa, Nghệ An and Hà Tĩnh. The corresponding Laotian provinces across the border are, from north to south, Phôngsali, Louang Phrabang, Houaphan, Xiangkhoang, and Bolikkhamxai. However, in the 11th century, Điện Biên, Sơn La and Phôngsali were part of a Tai kingdom mentioned in SKTT as Ngưu Hống.[68] Similarly, the territory west of Nghệ An province was named Tôn Bồn Man (meaning the barbarians (Man) in the region with the ancient jars) or shortened as Bồn Man, which is a reference to the Plain of Jars in Xiangkhoang.[69] These locations are shown in Figure 2-5.

The Annamite Range (Trường Sơn) mountain range forms a formidable natural barrier between Laos and Vietnam, making Laos a landlocked country. To reach the east coast, Laotians had to travel through Vietnam, and in the 14th century, they mostly travelled via the rivers or mountain tracks that connected the highlands of Laos to the coastal regions of Vietnam.

One such river is the Cả (also known as the Lam River), which flows by Vinh, in Nghệ An province. The road along the upstream portion of this river is Highway 7A (QL7A), which crosses the border into northern Laos. Contemporary Luang Prabang, Phonsavan and Vinh are connected by Routes 13, 7, QL7A and QL46 which traverse the Annamite Range. Another important river is the Đà River, which runs alongside the AH13 route, linking Hanoi, Sơn La, and Điện Biên Phủ before crossing the border into Phôngsali. A branch of AH13 at Mộc Châu also extends to the Plain of Jars. These routes have been used for centuries by both Vietnamese and Laotian armies during times of conflict.

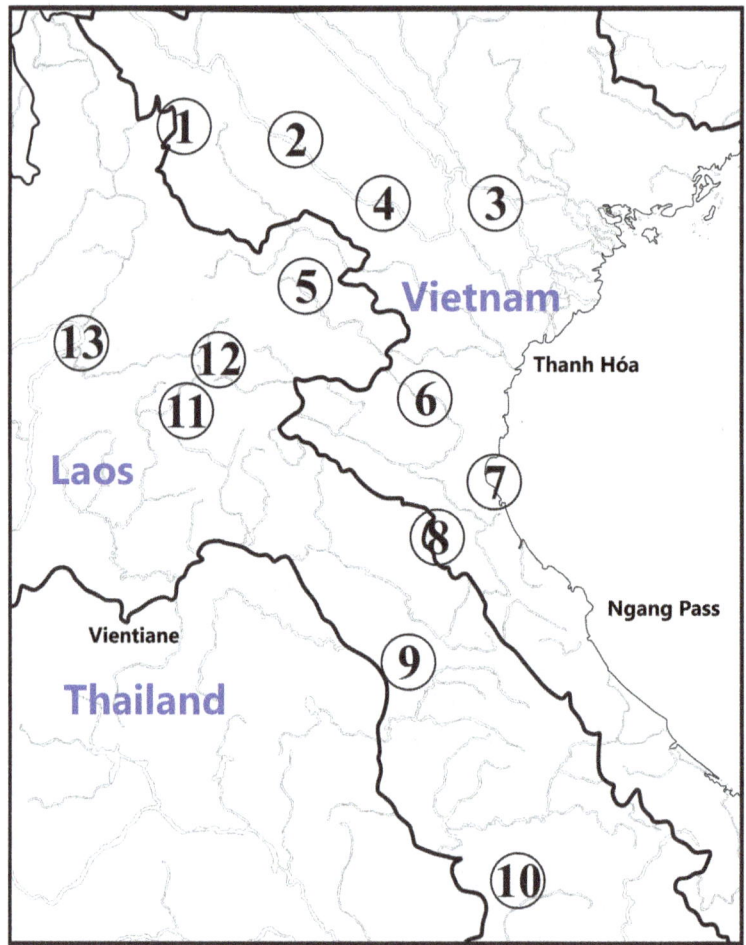

Figure 2-5: Map of Đại Việt and northern Laos.

Key: 1. Điện Biên Phủ; 2. Sơn La; 3. Hanoi; 4. Mộc Châu; 5. Sam Nuea; 6. Bia Ma Nhai; 7. Vinh; 8. Nam Phao International Checkpoint; 9. Thakhek; 10. Muang Champasak; 11. Phonavan; 12. Plain of Jars; 13. Luang Prabang.

POLITICAL RELATIONSHIP

In the early 8th century, Mai Thúc Loan—known as the Black Emperor—from Nghệ An led a major rebellion against the Tang dynasty, which then ruled northern Vietnam. He received military support from the kingdoms of Linyi, Zhenla, and Chin-lin. The revolt was ultimately crushed by Tang forces.[70] Linyi was the precursor to Champa, while Chin-lin—literally meaning 'Frontier of Gold'—was likely located on the Malay Peninsula.[71]

Nearly four centuries later, in 1150, Zhenla launched an invasion of Nghệ An but was forced to retreat after many of its soldiers succumbed to poisonous vapours near Mount Vụ Thấp, now known as Vũ Quang in Hà Tĩnh province, amid stifling heat and humidity.[72] The invading force likely followed a route that corresponds to the present-day AH15 highway, crossing Laos–Vietnam border at the Nam Phao International Checkpoint. It is possible that the Zhenla army had used this same route to join Mai Thúc Loan centuries earlier.

As the Lý dynasty became firmly established in Thăng Long in the 11th century, it considered Ai Lao and Ngưu Hống as vassal states and expected them to pay tributes. The Trần dynasty followed the same tradition and launched several military campaigns against them on multiple occasions. The final campaign in 1337 appears to have resulted in the full incorporation of Ngưu Hống into Đại Việt.[73]

2.5 - Inscriptions on a rock – Bia Ma Nhai

In 1334, Princess Huyền Trân's nephew, Trần Mạnh (then senior king), took the route along the Cả River to fight Ai Lao because the latter had moved to Đại Việt territory at Nam Nhung (present-day Tương Dương district of Nghệ An province), upstream of the Cả River.[74]

The expedition was successful as Trần Mạnh's forces reached Nam Nhung, and the Laotians fled. We know this because, on the way back to Thăng Long, Trần Mạnh instructed his top scholar, Nguyễn Trung Ngạn (1289–1370), to carve an inscription into a rock face to commemorate the victory. This inscription, known as Bia Ma Nhai (inscriptions carved in a rock at Ma Nhai), as shown in Figure 2-6, is located on the south bank of the Cả River, which one can visit by travelling around 120 kilometres north-west from Vinh City, a trip that I took in February 2025.[75] I have translated it from a Vietnamese translation of the original Chinese scripts below to illustrate how Đại Việt viewed itself in the early 14th country, as a powerful and dominant country relative to its neighbouring states.

> *The Senior King Chương Nghiêu Văn Triết was the sixth king of the Trần Dynasty, Hoàng Việt country* [Đại Việt], *under the command of heaven to unify the middle and lower worlds, everywhere on land and out at sea was obedient. That petty Ai-Lao country dares to defy his kingship. At the end of the autumn of the*

Year of the Pig [around September 1335], *the king himself led six armies to patrol the western region, the Crown Prince of Champa, Chenla, Siam and the tribal of the six barbarians, Quì, Cặm, Xa, Lạc, the recent submitted barbarian chief of Bồ and Thanh-xa tribes, all brought their products and competed to welcome the procession. Only the rebel Bổng kept hiding, afraid of his crime, and would not come to court immediately. At the end of winter, the king stationed his army in Cự field, in the Mật district, and sent his generals and barbarian troops into the country; the rebel Bổng fled with the wind. The king ordered his troops to return. At that time, it was the 12th month of the year of the Pig the 7th year of Khai-hữu,* [around January 1336], *engraved in stone.*[76]

Figure 2-6: Bia Ma Nhai (rock inscriptions).

The site in Figure 2-6 is at the foothill, some 150 metres from the southside of the Cả river. The king's camp was likely on the flat terrain below, close to the river.

However, in the following year, Ai Lao had their revenge. Despite suffering from an eye ailment, Trần Mạnh insisted on leading the expedition. Still, it was Đoàn Nhữ Hài, then the governor of Nghệ An, who commanded the two armies attacking the Laotians at Nam Nhung. He was confident of the victory, expecting to face a weak and a small Laotian force. He also planned to sail his triumphant flotilla with prisoners down the large river of Tiết La (Mekong?) to Zhenla and other neighbouring countries as a military show of force to demonstrate Đại Việt's power and encourage more royal children of these countries to pay homage to the court of Đại Việt.[77] He aimed to surpass his peers and make a grand statement of Đại Việt might.

But events went against Đoàn Nhữ Hài's plan. On the day of the battle, the clouds darkened the sky, and Ai Lao launched a surprise ambush, using horses and elephants to devastating effect. Đại Việt forces suffered heavy losses, with half of the troops drowning in the river. Đoàn Nhữ Hài was among them.[78]

2.6 - Chế Bồng Nga – Cham hero and Đại Việt villain

After the invasion of 1326, Đại Việt and Champa appeared to be at peace for the following three decades until the middle of the 14th century. In 1342, the Cham lord, Chế A Nan, died. His son-in-law, Trà Hòa Bố Đề (according to CM, a *Bố Đề* is a title equivalent to Đại Việt *tể tướng* or Prime Minister) proclaimed himself king.[79] In 1352, Chế A Nan's son, Chế Mỗ (according to CM, a *Bố Điền* is a crown (great) prince or a high-ranking noble), fled to Đại Việt and sought help to instal himself as the rightful ruler of Champa. However, other than CM interpretations, *Bố Đề* and *Bố Điền* could be a reconstruction from the Cham honorific title *Pu Lyaṅ* meaning divinity.[80]

1353 – ĐẠI VIỆT INVADES CHAMPA

SKTT does not explain why it took Chế Mỗ ten years to take this action, but in the summer of 1353, Đại Việt launched an expedition against Champa. The infantry column advanced as far as Cổ Lũy (in present-day Quảng Ngãi province) but retreated when it encountered difficulties.[81] Chế Mỗ was never able to return to Champa and died in Đại Việt. This event marked a turning point in the conflict between the two kingdoms. Later, in 1353, Champa raided Hóa Châu, and from that year, they became more aggressive as the Trần dynasty's power began to decline. Leading this resurgence was a prominent figure named Chế Bồng Nga (制蓬峩, 1340?–1390). His name remains widely recognised among the Vietnamese today.

WHO IS CHẾ BỒNG NGA?

What we know about Chế Bồng Nga comes primarily from Vietnamese and Chinese records, notably SKTT and Ming shi (History of Ming, *Minh Sử*). SKTT refers to him as Chế Bồng Nga, and the name 'Chế' appears frequently in the annals as lords, kings and members of the royal family of Champa for over 300 years, as shown in Table 2-2. It appears that Chế Bồng Nga was able to reclaim the throne following the interruption by Trà Hòa Bố Đề.[82] Ming shi mentions a Champa ruler named A-da-a-zhe (*A Đáp A Giả*, 阿荅阿者), who sent an envoy and tribute to the Ming emperor in 1369, one year after the dynasty was founded. Historian Geoff Wade suggests that A-da-a-zhe may be a contraction of the title *rājādhirāja*, meaning 'king of kings'; an interpretation which I support because *rājādhirāja* appears several times on Cham inscriptions.[83] This interpretation would explain why Ming shi does not contain a Chinese equivalent of the name 'Chế Bồng Nga'. Unfortunately, so far we have not found any inscriptions that record 'Chế Bồng Nga' in Cham or Sanskrit.

Aymonier listed a king named 'Pô Binœthuor' (reigned 1328–1373) among the legendary Cham kings, based on a chronicle given to him by a Cham man in the 19th century. In his paper, Aymonier compared this king with Chế Bồng Nga and noted that the latter died 19 years later than the date recorded in the chronicle. He also suggested that the name 'Chế Bồng Nga' might be a transcription of Chei Bangœu, which translates to 'the Flower Prince'.[84] While Aymonier was cautious in equating Chế Bồng Nga with Pô Binœthuor, later Cham writers have shown no such hesitation. Over time, Chế Bồng Nga has been widely identified with Pô Binœthuor (or its variant Po Binnasuar and Po Binthuar).[85] However, I would argue that these two names share little in common. Leaving aside the mismatched dates; one a historical figure, and the other a legendary king.

By the middle of the 14th century, the northern border between Đại Việt and Champa had shifted from the Ngang Pass nominally to the Thu Bồn River, with Đại Việt treating Champa as a vassal state, often contemptuously. However, the accession of Chế Bồng Nga to the Cham throne in Vijaya altered the power balance drastically. Over the three decades leading up to his death, Chế Bồng Nga successfully reclaimed much of the territory Champa had lost since the 11th century and even advanced further north, pushing beyond the Ngang Pass into the southern provinces of Đại Việt.

Under his command, Champa burned and looted Thăng Long at least three times in 1371, 1377, 1378 and besieged it in 1383. They lured Đại Việt troops into a trap near Vijaya, where they staged a successful ambush and killed a Đại Việt king in 1377. The Trần kings were terrified of Chế Bồng Nga, hid their treasures and relocated ancestral statues from the tombs for safekeeping. Unlike previous Cham raids, which focused on plundering and retreating, Chế Bồng Nga seemed to have a far more ambitious plan: to occupy or install a puppet ruler under Champa's control. He even incited the people of Đại Việt to follow him and counted among his entourage the brother of a Đại Việt king, who had surrendered to Champa.

However, all of these plans unravelled on 8 February 1390 when Chế Bồng Nga was betrayed by one of his subordinates and killed by shots from Đại Việt guns. Less than a decade after his death, the Trần dynasty, which had ruled Đại Việt from 1226, was no more. Shortly thereafter, the Ming dynasty (1368–1644) of China invaded Đại Việt and occupied the kingdom for 20 years. Although numerous factors led to the downfall of Đại Việt in the early 14th century, Chế Bồng Nga and Champa must be regarded as among the most significant.

The details of the Đại Việt – Champa conflict over 30 years are described below.

1361 AND 1366 – CHAMPA RAIDS ĐẠI VIỆT

Champa launched raids on Hóa Châu in 1353, 1362, 1365, and 1376, even striking Quảng Bình province, which had been Đại Việt's territory since the 11th century. In 1361, Cham forces entered the sea gate of Dĩ Lý (modern-day Lý Hòa), and in 1366, they attacked Lâm Bình (present-day Lệ Thủy district). By 1368, they escalated their demands, sending Mục Bà Ma to request the return of Hóa Châu to Champa. In response, Đại Việt assembled an expedition force that advanced to Chiêm Động (in present-day Quảng Nam province), but the Chams ambushed the troops, captured the Đại Việt commander, and forced the army to retreat.[86]

1371 – CHAMPA BURNS THĂNG LONG FOR THE FIRST TIME

But the worst was yet to come; three years later, in 1371, Cham ships arrived at the sea gate (port) of Đại An, located north of Thanh Hóa, at the Đáy River estuary. For centuries, this river entrance had been a key departure point for ships travelling south from Thăng Long, including vessels from Imperial China and Đại Việt. The last time Champa had sent ships to this sea gate was nearly four centuries earlier in 979–980. Fortunately for Đại Việt – then known as Đại Cồ Việt – was spared disaster when a storm sank most of the Cham ships, which numbered around 1000.[87]

However, in 1371, there was no storm or significant resistance from Đại Việt, and the Cham ships entered the Đáy River estuary unopposed and made their way directly to Thăng Long. Their vanguard landed at the Thái Tổ wharf, located along the west bank of the Red River close to today's Hanoi Opera House. The king of Đại Việt, Trần Phủ, fled to Đông Ngàn, located on the east bank of the Red River, at the entrance to the Đuống River.

What followed was an orgy of destruction: the Chams burned the palaces, looted books and records, and kidnapped women. This event occurred on 12 April 1371, the 27th day of the third lunar month. The Chams then withdrew seemingly unmolested.[88] The last time a foreign enemy sacked Thăng Long was a century ago, during the Mongol-Yuan invasions of 1258, 1285 and 1288.

1376/77 – ĐẠI VIỆT INVADES CHAMPA, ITS KING DIES

Two years later, Đại Việt had sufficiently recovered and began preparations for another expedition against Champa. However, the campaign did not take place until 1376. In the fifth lunar month of that year, Champa raided Hóa Châu, and a month later, Trần Kính issued an edict to prepare weapons and ships for an attack on Champa. One of his officials attempted to persuade him to send a general rather than lead the expedition, but Trần Kính did not listen. He was angry.

It transpired that Trần Kính had dispatched a senior court mandarin, Đỗ Tử Bình, to Hóa Châu to fortify the province after the Champa raid. The lord of Champa, Chế Bồng Nga, then sent ten trays of gold to Trần Kính via Đỗ Tử Bình as a gesture of goodwill, but the latter decided to keep the gold for himself and advised Thăng Long that Chế Bồng Nga was arrogant and rude, therefore suggesting that Đại Việt should invade Champa.

Trần Kính prepared his campaign thoroughly. He ordered the army and people of three southern provinces of Thanh Hoá, Nghệ An and Diễn Châu to send 50,000 *hộc* (should read picul, dan or shi 石) or roughly 3,350 to 5,000 cubic metres (or over 4,000 tonnes or milled rice) of supplies to be sent to Hóa Châu. Around November of 1376, he held a military exercise with infantry and naval contingents at Bạch Hạc, located some 75 kilometres north-west of Thăng Long.[89] Trần Kính and his father, Trần Phủ, were present at the exercise as commanding generals.[90]

In the 12th lunar month of 1376, around January 1377, Trần Kính led an army of 120,000 strong departing from Thăng Long. On the way, they encountered a funeral, which the king took as a bad omen and fined the funeral director 30 *quan*. Meanwhile, he instructed an official named Lê Quý Ly (1336–1407) to arrange for the southern provinces to transport provisions to the troops.

The Đại Việt expedition stopped at the Di Luân sea gate, which is now the estuary of the Ròn River in Quảng Bình province. Trần Kính, leading his army on horseback, camped at the Nhật Lệ river entrance for a month of further training. About two months later, on 3 March 1377, Trần Kính and his large army arrived at the port of Thi Nại, in today Quy Nhơn, where Đoàn

Nhữ Hài, over 70 years earlier, had patronisingly hung up a sign prohibiting trading.[91] The final destination of the expedition was the citadel of Vijaya, the capital of Champa, located 25 kilometres north-west of the port.

Chế Bồng Nga camped outside the citadel and sent a junior official named Mục Bà Ma to Trần Kính's camp with an offer to surrender. Mục Bà Ma explained to Trần Kính that Chế Bồng Nga had abandoned the citadel, leaving it defenceless, and urged him to move quickly to capture it.

One of Đại Việt generals, Đỗ Lễ, advised caution. He suspected it might be a trap and recommended sending an envoy to the Cham camp to verify the authenticity of the surrender offer. However, Trần Kính was having none of that. He said, *I wore hard armour, carried sharp swords, braved wind and rain, waded through rivers and climbed mountains, and went deep into enemy territory, but no one dared to confront me. That was divine assistance for me. Moreover, now that the enemy commander had heard the news, he fled and no longer had the heart to fight. The ancients once said: 'Speed is precious when using troops'. If we stop now and do not advance, it is truly a gift from heaven that we do not take. If we wait for another plan, it will be too late to regret. You are just like a woman.*

On 4 March, Trần Kính rode a horse adorned with black and white markings, while Đỗ Lễ was forced to wear a woman's dress. Đại Việt troops formed a long marching column resembling 'a string of fish', with the advance and the rear groups separated. Around the hour of the snake (*Tỵ*), between 9 and 11 am, the Chams launched a surprise attack on the column, trapping and killing Trần Kính and other officers, including Đỗ Lễ. It was a devastating defeat for the Đại Việt army. Đỗ Tử Bình, the man whose greed and deceit had started the war, was in the rear column and managed to escape. He was subsequently found guilty and demoted to a private. Lê Quý Ly, who was in charge of the supplies, survived the ambush and would go on to establish the Hồ dynasty, which is discussed in the following chapter.[92]

Trần Kính was 40 years old and had been on the Đại Việt throne for five years. He had spent the previous six months preparing for this campaign, and his overconfidence may have led to his eventual downfall. Ming shilu also records the death of Trần Kính (*Chen Tuan*).[93]

1377/1378 – CHAMPA RAIDS THĂNG LONG FOR THE SECOND AND THIRD TIMES

A little over four months later, on 16 July 1377, Cham ships reached Thăng Long, raided the capital, and withdrew the next day. However, they were caught by a storm on their return journey at the Đáy River estuary.

During the disastrous campaign in early 1377, one of the Đại Việt senior commanders, Prince Húc, Trần Phủ's son, surrendered to Champa and married a Cham princess. In 1378, the Cham sent him back to Nghệ An province, where he gathered a large number of followers. The Chams then raided Thăng Long, again, Đỗ Tử Bình had somehow regained his position and was instructed to make a stand along the Red River but failed completely.[94]

By this time, Champa had become such a threat to Đại Việt that the king ordered money be stored in the basement of a pagoda in today's Lạng Sơn, near the border with China.[95] Additionally, he instructed sacred images (idols) and statues of the Trần ancestors from various tombs in Thái Bình and Nam Định provinces be relocated to a large mausoleum in Yên Sinh, now An Sinh Temple in Đông Triều, Quảng Ninh province, some 90 kilometres east of Hanoi.[96]

The combined impact of Trần Kính's failed expedition and Champa's sack of Thăng Long had severely depleted the Đại Việt treasury. In response, in 1378, Đỗ Tử Bình suggested to Trần Hiện the imposition of a head tax on all males, drawing from a practice established during the Tang dynasty. This new levy only served to increase the already heavy tax burden on the populace.[97]

1380 – THE RISE OF LÊ QUÝ LY

The Chams were relentless. In early 1380, they incited the people of the southern provinces of Tân Bình (previously Lâm Bình) and Thuận Hóa to plunder the provinces north of Ngang Pass of Diễn Châu and Nghệ An.[98] A few months later, in the summer of 1380, they attacked Thanh Hóa. On this occasion, Lê Quý Ly led the naval contingent, and Đỗ Tử Bình commanded the infantry. Lê Quý Ly planted wooden stakes in the Ngu Giang River, located just south of the Đáy River entrance, to block the Cham advance.[99] This time, Chế Bồng Nga was defeated, forcing him to flee, thereby saving Thăng Long from another raid. Following the victory, Đỗ Tử Bình relinquished his post, claiming to be unwell, and allowed Lê Quý Ly to assume the role of the Supreme Commander of all Đại Việt forces, from Thanh Hóa to Thuận Hóa provinces. Effectively, Lê Quý Ly was in control of the north of modern Central Vietnam.[100]

Đỗ Tử Bình died a few years later, likely peacefully in bed. His name was recorded in the Temple of Literature (*Văn Miếu*), much to the dismay of later historians who did not believe he was worthy of such an honour.[101]

The battle in 1380 illustrated a tactical pattern, which was repeated several times as the river fighting between the two sides intensified in the following years. Both sides would establish defensive lines by planting stakes or wooden poles in the river, creating a barrier that also functioned as anchors for their boats. Combat typically commenced when one side broke formations, leaving the anchors to launch an attack. Meanwhile, foot soldiers, positioned along the riverbanks executed outflanking manoeuvres to support their forces.

1382 – CHAMPA LOSES AT THANH HÓA

Despite their previous defeat, the Chams returned in 1382, launching another assault on Thanh Hóa. Once again, Lê Quý Ly was dispatched to confront them. He established his camp at Mount Long Đại, while Nguyễn Đa Phương, commanding another division, fortified a defensive position behind a line of wooden stakes planted in the river bed at the sea gate of Thần Đầu.

From the high ground along the riverbank, the Chams hurled rocks and sank several Đại Việt boats as their ships advanced. However, without waiting for Lê Quý Ly's command, Nguyễn Đa Phương moved out of his defensive stakes and launched a direct attack. His assault broke the Cham's formation, resulting in heavy casualties among their forces.[102] Many Chams were killed, and their ships were set ablaze. Those who fled to the mountains faced starvation. At the same time, Đại Việt troops pursued the remnants of their army as far as Nghệ An.[103] It was a decisive victory for Đại Việt and Nguyễn Đa Phương emerged as the hero of the battle. Interestingly, three years earlier, Lê Quý Ly had promoted Nguyễn Đa Phương, who was a son of his former martial arts teacher.[104]

A year later, Lê Quý Ly led a large naval expedition to Champa but was forced to retreat when strong winds and waves damaged Đại Việt ships off the coast of what is now Quảng Bình and Hà Tĩnh provinces.

1383 – CHAMPA BESIEGES THĂNG LONG (AND RAIDS IT FOR THE FOURTH TIME)?

That summer of 1383, Chế Bồng Nga, his commander (*thủ tướng*, likely equivalent to Prime Minister), La Ngai, and their men followed the route skirting the base of the mountains from Quảng Oai, now around Ba Vì, and emerged somewhere west of Thăng Long. Their sudden appearance caused widespread panic in the capital of Đại Việt.

When Đại Việt troops confronted the Chams, they fell into an ambush and their commander was captured. Nguyễn Đa Phương constructed a defensive wall encircling the capital and commanded the troops to block the Chams from entering the city. Meanwhile, Senior King Trần Phủ crossed the Red River to Đông Ngàn and set up his court in Bảo Hoà palace at today's Phật Tích mountain in Bắc Ninh province. Once again, Thăng Long was abandoned, but it seemed the Chams could not capture the city. When winter came, Chế Bồng Nga and his forces withdrew.

The account of the 1383 event in SKTT is confusing. It is unclear how Chế Bồng Nga and the Chams reached Ba Vì on foot with war elephants.[105] It seems improbable that they travelled on foot all the way from Champa. Ba Vì is west of Thăng Long, was not along the usual approach routes as the Chams typically came up from the south via the Red River using boats. One plausible explanation is that they disembarked from their boats at an earlier point and chose an overland route to avoid the anticipated Đại Việt defensive lines along the river approaches to Thăng Long. Another possibility is that by 1383, the Chams already controlled areas south of the Ngang Pass, including Nghệ An, allowing them to use these territories as a base for their march toward Ba Vì.

The timeline also raises questions about their activities between when they arrived in the sixth and left in the twelfth lunar month. Did they lay siege to Thăng Long for this extended period? Furthermore, where were Lê Quý Ly and his men?

1390 – DEATH OF CHẾ BỒNG NGA

The next six years saw a lull in the war between Đại Việt and Champa until 1389, when the Chams returned to Thanh Hóa at the end of that year. This time, they positioned themselves upstream of a river and constructed a makeshift dam. Trần Phủ dispatched Lê Quý Ly to face the Chams. He arrived with soldiers on foot, supported by additional troops on boats—the Chams feigned retreat, luring Đại Việt troops into pursuing them. When the Đại Việt troops charged, the Chams triggered their trap: they released the dam, unleashing a surge of water downstream. This sudden flood slowed the Đại Việt boats, which struggled against the current. At the same time, Cham's war elephants ambushed Đại Việt troops on land. The coordinated attack resulted in a devastating rout of Đại Việt forces.

The date was 8 November 1389, and Đại Việt had suffered yet another catastrophic defeat; seventy officers, or generals (*tướng*), were slain, and the commander was taken prisoner. The wily Lê Quý Ly, sensing the battle was lost, delegated his command to his deputies and fled. Upon returning to Thăng Long, he requested additional warships, but Trần Phủ declined; in response, Lê

Quý Ly tendered his resignation. Back at the battlefield, Nguyễn Đa Phương, one of his deputy generals, concluded that the battle was lost. Still, to safeguard his retreat, he ordered his men to raise the flags, anchor the ships, and guard them to create the illusion of an active defence. He then boarded a small boat and made his escape.

Nguyễn Đa Phương was the hero of the 1382 rout of the Chams and the 1383 battle for Thăng Long. However, in 1389, he fled from the Chams. Soon after arriving at the capital, he openly criticised Lê Quý Ly for incompetence in handling the campaign. In response, Lê Quý Ly accused Nguyễn Đa Phương of being responsible for the failure.

Lê Quý Ly then made his next move. He reduced the number of the troops under Nguyễn Đa Phương's command. He suggested to Trần Phủ that while Nguyễn Đa Phương was a strong and brave warrior, there was a risk that he might deflect to Champa or align with the Ming dynasty. He even advised that it would be safer to eliminate him. Lê Quý Ly then forced Nguyễn Đa Phương to commit suicide.

By now, the situation was critical for Đại Việt. Their two commanding generals were fighting each other; one had resigned, and the other was coerced into taking his own life. In desperation, Trần Phủ ordered a young general, Trần Khát Chân (1370–1399), to command the army of *Long Tiệp* (translated as 'fast or winning dragon') to halt the Cham advance. Both men wept as they bid farewell, as if they feared they would never meet again. Trần Phủ was 68, had lost his son, Trần Kính, who died over a decade earlier in Champa, and now the Cham army appeared unstoppable and poised to overwhelm Đại Việt.

According to the information from the Vietnam National Museum of History, Trần Khát Chân was just 19 years old at the time, and a descendant of Trần Bình Trọng, a hero of the wars against the Mongol/Yuan invasions in the 13th century.[106] He and his men left Thăng Long sometime in December 1389, taking the river route downstream along the Lô (now the Red) River until they encountered the vanguard of the Cham army, somewhere in Hoàng Giang.[107] Assessing the terrain, Trần Khát Chân decided that the location unsuitable for battle and withdrew to the Luộc River close to present-day Hưng Yên, where he set up his defensive line to prepare for the coming clash.

Meanwhile, Chế Bồng Nga came up from Thanh Hóa, likely travelling via the Đáy and the Nam Định Rivers. It had taken him three months following the victory in early November 1389 to reach this point. He had war elephants and troops on foot, which may explain why it took that long to cover a distance of slightly over 100 kilometres. Or maybe he was waiting for reinforcements or engaging in skirmishes along the way.

The stage was set for a decisive battle between the two sides. Chế Bồng Nga had not been this close to Thăng Long in almost seven years. In early 1390, he had 100 warships with him, and his general, La Ngai, was on the riverbank with men and elephants. He also had Trần Kính's son, Trần Nguyên Diệu, with him. Nguyên Diệu had defected to Champa to revenge the death of his brother, Trần Hiện, as cited earlier. Chế Bồng Nga's adversaries who had thwarted him before – Lê Quý Ly and Nguyễn Đa Phương – were no longer in command. Instead, the man facing him was an inexperienced 19-year-old general. Victory was within his grasp, then betrayal and technology intervened.[108]

While Chế Bồng Nga was arranging his warships in formation, a minor officer in his army named Ba Lậu Khê defected. After being berated by Chế Bồng Nga, fearing execution, Ba Lậu Khê jumped ship and surrendered to Trần Khát Chân. Ba Lậu Khê identified the blue-painted ship as Chế Bồng Nga's flagship, and Trần Khát Chân ordered his men to take aim and opened fire. The bullets, or most likely cannon balls, went through the ship's wooden hull and killed Chế Bồng Nga. Chaos erupted among the Cham forces, the men on his ship cried, and in the commotion that followed, Nguyên Diệu seized the opportunity, decapitated Chế Bồng Nga and brought his head to Trần Khát Chân, presumably to claim credit for the kill.

However, Trần Khát Chân's lieutenants were not easily deceived; they promptly executed Nguyên Diệu, placed Chế Bồng Nga's head in a coffin, and carried it to Senior King Trần Phủ at Bình Than. It was about midnight on 8 February 1390 when the attendants woke the senior king, and advised him of the victory, presenting Chế Bồng Nga's head as the ultimate proof.[109] With the death of the Cham leader, the protracted war for almost 30 years between Đại Việt and Champa finally came to an end.

THE AFTERMATH

With Chế Bồng Nga's death, the Chams broke formation and retreated. La Ngai, now the de facto leader, cremated the body of Chế Bồng Nga on the riverbank before leading the remnants of the Cham army, including their elephants, back to Champa. Upon return, La Ngai proclaimed himself king of Champa. Chế Bồng Nga's sons, Chế Ma Nô Đà Nan and his younger brother, Chế Sơn Nô, fled to Thăng Long and sought the protection of Đại Việt. They were welcomed and granted the title of full and second-rank marquis, respectively. Both brothers lived out their lives and most likely died of old age in Thăng Long. La Ngai, meanwhile, ruled Champa until he died in 1400, a decade later.

SKTT records that following the passing of Chế Bồng Nga, the people of Nghệ An, who had joined the Chams, reaffirmed their support for Đại Việt, but not the people of Tân Bình and Thuận Hóa. No one was able to put an end to the fighting there. This situation was hardly surprising; Nghệ An was never part of Champa, while Tân Bình and Thuận Hóa, present-day southern Quảng Bình, Quảng Trị and Thừa-Thiên-Huế had been Cham territory for centuries, making them more resistant to Đại Việt authority.[110]

On a separate note, the use of firearms at the Luộc River was the first recorded instance of gunpowder weapons in Vietnamese annals. Firearms, in the form of rudimentary fire lances, had been in use in China as early as the Song dynasty in the 10th century. They were developed into more advanced forms like canons and matchlocks and were used extensively under the Ming dynasty (1368–1644).[111] The firearms employed by Đại Việt in 1390 to kill Chế Bồng Nga were most likely hand cannons – early portable gunpowder weapons – since matchlock firearms had not yet been introduced to the region.

An example of such a hand cannon is shown in Figure 2-7.

Figure 2-7: Bronze tubiform gun.

The caption reads: *Bronze tubiform gun (火铳) from the 11th year of Hongwu [1378] in the Ming dynasty.*[112]

The tube has a closed end (left-hand side of the photograph) and an open muzzle (right-hand side). The closed end has a small hole for ignition. The gunner operates the fire tube by packing gunpowder through the muzzle, followed by projectiles (lead balls or ceramic pellets). He then ignites the gunpowder using a slow-burning fuse through the ignition hole. When the gunpowder ignited, it rapidly expanded as hot gases. The expanding gases forced the projectile out of the open end of the tube.

THE CHAM LORDS AND KINGS KNOWN AS CHẾ

Vietnamese annals refer to the rulers of Champa by titles such as king (*vua*) and lord (*chúa*). For over 300 years, many of these rulers shared the common family name of Chế (制), indicating a royal lineage of Champa. A summary of these historical figures is shown in Table 2-2. Of these rulers, Chế Mân and Chế Bồng Nga are the most famous among present-day Chams and Vietnamese.[113]

NAMES	NAMES IN MING SHILU	YEARS FIRST APPEARED IN SKTT	RELATED EVENTS
Chế Củ		1069	Taken prisoner by Đại Việt.
Chế Ma Na		1104	Chế Ma Na retook three provinces that Chế Củ had exchanged with Đại Việt, but resubmitted them when Đại Việt attacked.
Chế Bì La Bút		1152	Killed two usurpers when Đại Việt attempted to help them.
Chế Mân		1306	Married Princess Huyền Trân.
Chế Chí		1311/1312	Captured by Đại Việt and died in Thăng Long.
Chế Đà A Bà Niêm		1312	Appointed by Đại Việt to replace Chế Chí.
Chế Năng		1326	Fled to Trảo Oa (Java) to seek help when Đại Việt invaded. There was another Chế Năng, a Champa's representative to Đại Việt, who wanted to defect in 1279 but was refused.
Chế A Nan		1342	Died in 1342 but the throne was taken by his son-in-law, Trà Hoà Bố Đề, not his son, Chế Mỗ, who fled to Đại Việt.
Trà Hoà Bố Đề		1342	Usurped the throne.
Chế Bồng Nga	A-da-a-zhe (A Đáp A Già)	1376	Offered ten trays of gold to Đại Việt.
La Ngai		1383	Led the invasion of Đại Việt with Chế Bồng Nga.

	Ge-sheng		Appeared in Ming shilu in 1391 as a minister who killed the Cham king and established himself as ruler.
Ba Đích Lại	Zhan-ba Di-lai	1400	Son of La Ngai who died in 1400, Ba Đích Lại died in 1441.
Bí Cai		1444	Raided Hóa Châu.
Ma Ha Quý Lai	Gu Lai?	1446	
Quý Do	Mo-he Gui-you	1449	Imprisoned Quý Lai, usurped the throne.
Bí Điền		1470	
Bàn La Trà Duyệt	Pan-luo Yue Pan-luo Cha-yue	1470	usurped the throne from Bí Điền.
Trà Toàn	Pan-luo Cha-quan	1470	Bàn La Trà Duyệt passed on the throne.
Bồ Trì Trì		1471	Self-claimed lord of a reduced Champa.
Trà Toại		1471	Captured by Đại Việt.
	Zhai-ya-ma-wu-an		Appeared in Ming shilu 1478, enfeoffed by the Ming emperor. Zhai-ya-ma-wu-an could be reconstructed as Jayavarman.
	Gu-Lai		Appeared in Ming shilu 1481, replaced Zhai-ya-ma-wu-an.

Table 2-2: The kings and lords of Champa from the 11th to the 15th centuries.

CHAPTER 3

THE HỒ DYNASTY (1400–1407)

3.1 - Lê Quý Ly (1336–1407) – The father

THE ROAD TO THE TOP

On 23 March 1400, Lê Quý Ly forced the very last Trần king, Trần An, to abdicate. Trần An was four years old at the time; since he was Lê Quý Ly's grandson his life was spared. However, a year earlier, his father—the former king and Lê Quý Ly's son-in-law—was strangled to death on Lê Quý Ly's order.

To legitimize his claim to the throne, Lê Quý Ly then compelled members of the Trần royal family and court mandarins to submit petitions to him suggesting he should be the next king. They had to do it three times. The first two times, Lê Quý Ly feigned modesty and declined, saying that he was near the end of his life. However, once the charade was over, he declared himself king, changed the country's name from Đại Việt to Đại Ngu (*Da Yu*, 大虞), and established his capital at Tây Đô (Western Capital) to differentiate it from Thăng Long as Đông Đô (Eastern Capital).

In 1400, Lê Quý Ly was 64 years old, and it had taken him decades to this day in March when he wore a yellow robe of a sovereign and walked under 12 yellow parasols reserved for the son of heaven. As a young man, his aunts had brought him to the court of the Trần kings sometime in the middle of the 14th century. During the years that followed, he appeared to be loyal to the Trần dynasty, serving the kings and the senior kings, particularly Trần Phủ, his father-in-law. Under Trần Phủ, who effectively became his patron, Lê Quý Ly's career advanced rapidly, culminating in his declaration on that day as *Quốc Tổ Chương Hoàng* (Country Ancestor (or founder) Chương Hoàng) and Yellow became the royal colour of his reign. However, even though he was the most powerful man in Đại Việt/Đại Ngu then, he was reluctant to address himself as 'trẫm', or the royal 'we' that a king would use, but he chose a common term of 'dư', or 'I'.[1]

Historical accounts paint a picture of a ruthless but cautious man. Lê Quý Ly was ambitious, a survivor but not a hero. He married into royalty, and when plots against him failed, he had the plotter leaders and associates killed. When his friends and allies criticised him, Lê Quý Ly had them demoted, imprisoned, and murdered. When the battles against Champa turned against him, he was one of the first to retreat, making sure that someone else got the blame for defeat. Lê Quý Ly was the ultimate 'king's whisperer' and exercised his power behind the scenes until after Trần Phủ's death.

Once he became king, he changed his family name to Hồ and claimed that his ancestor was Hồ Hưng Dật, who came from today's Zhejiang, south of Shanghai, to Đại Việt in the 10th century as a governor/prefect (*Taishou, Thái thú*) of Diễn Châu (now north of Vinh in Nghệ An province), where his family settled. According to Lê Quý Ly's narrative, his grandfather moved to Đại Lại, which is near today's Hà Ngọc commune, north of the Lèn River in Thanh Hóa province, and took on the name Lê from the adopted family.[2] After becoming king, Lê Quý Ly also researched the family genealogy of both his paternal and maternal lines (his mother was a Phạm). The aim of this genealogical research was evident. He wanted to find close relatives and appoint them to positions at court in the new capital to ensure the court's loyalty.

THE OPPOSITION

Hồ Quý Ly's accession to power was not without opposition, as he faced significant resistance from the Trần clan, which had ruled Đại Việt since the early 13th century. During that time, the Trần dynasty had been able to mobilise the whole country to repel the Mongol-Yuan invasion at the end of the century. They were 'natural' rulers then, and no one dared to challenge them. However, by the middle of the 14th century, the last of the capable Trần generals had died, and the lineage, unable to produce inspired leaders, ended.[3] Trần Kính, the younger brother of Trần Phủ, was the closest in the mould of the Trần competent kings but he died in Champa. Similarly, the long reigns of the interfering senior kings and their wives had not helped the development of future leaders.

Despite this decline, two attempted coups, if succeeded, would have removed Hồ Quý Ly. The first occurred in 1388 and was initiated by Trần Hiện, Trần Kính's son. However, it failed because the plot was quickly leaked, and Trần Hiện had placed too much trust in his uncle, Trần Phủ. The second attempt was in 1399 and was led by Trần Khát Chân. It had a better chance of success, but Trần Khát Chân stopped it at the last minute for reasons that remain unclear. Reading the details of the attempts, I am baffled by how unprepared both coups were against a man like Hồ Quý Ly. In any event, the failure of the second event provided Hồ Quý Ly with a perfect opportunity to exterminate the remaining members of the Trần royal family, as mentioned earlier.

PAPER CURRENCY

Even before formally becoming king in 1400, Hồ Quý Ly already controlled the Trần court. Following Trần Phủ's death in 1394, Hồ Quý Ly swiftly eliminated several royal family members and their associates, often using false pretences, and appointed his allies to key positions of power.[4] In 1396, he issued paper money and exchanged it for coins that were in circulation at the time. This measure was introduced with strict rules: anyone caught printing counterfeit money would be executed and their assets confiscated by the court. Using or hoarding of bronze coins was strictly prohibited and people were required to exchange their coins for paper money at the Treasury in the capital. The penalty for noncompliance would be equivalent to the penalty for printing counterfeit currency.[5]

Later historians credited Hồ Quý Ly for boldly introducing the first paper money in Vietnam, praising him for his innovative approach.[6] However, it is most likely that he used this method to collect coins from the population to enrich the royal Treasury.⁷ Besides, it was not a new idea; paper money was used in Imperial China under the Mongol-Yuan dynasty before then and by the Ming dynasty during its early years until rampant inflation forced it to suspend the practice in 1450.⁸

However, despite strict rules and an increase in treasury's holding of coins, the paper money policy ultimately failed. The population was unfamiliar with the new currency, lacked confidence in its value, and the circulation of counterfeit notes led to inflationary pressure.⁹ The Ming occupation brought an end to the Hồ dynasty's paper currency experiment, and subsequent dynasties reverted to using coins.¹⁰

THE CITADEL

Hồ Quý Ly established his capital, Tây Đô, at around 30 kilometres north-east of Hà Ngọc, the ancestral home of his grandfather's family. Tây Đô, or the Hồ Citadel (*Thành Nhà Hồ*), still stands today, with most of its walls and gates remaining intact. Today, one can spend a pleasant day exploring the site, which has an information centre/museum nearby. Figures 3-1 to 3-3 show views of the Hồ Citadel.¹¹ Figure 3-4 shows the locations of Tây Đô and other places mentioned in this chapter.

Figure 3-1: The Hồ Citadel, south gate (main entrance).

Figure 3-2: The Hồ Citadel, north gate.

The construction of the Hồ Citadel began around 1397. It was officially occupied in 1400 when Hồ (Lê) Quý Ly started his reign. The walls and gates were built from large stones, a distinguishing feature compared to other historic citadels in Vietnam, which were typically built using bricks or rammed earth. The citadel covered a nearly square area (870.5 x 883.5 metres), with gates standing 9.5 metres high. There are four gates – north, south, east, and west – though the central axis from the north to the south gates is almost 30 degrees off the true N-S axis towards the east.[12]

Located along this central axis at 3.5 kilometres to the south is the Esplanade of Sacrifice to the Heaven and Earth (*Đàn Nam Giao*) at Mount Đốn Sơn in Vĩnh Thành commune, which was built in 1402.[13] The temple dedicated to Trần Khát Chân was close by, and it was at Mount Đốn Sơn that the second coup failed and where Trần Khát Chân was executed at the age of barely 30.[14]

The citadel is surrounded by moats and further protected by the Nam Mã River on the west and the Bưởi River on the east. Information from the local museum indicates an outer wall of earthen ramparts surrounded the citadel. However, the photograph of a section of this outer wall shows a structure that appears suspiciously like a dyke.[15] Today, the palaces and other buildings inside the walls have gone, and the area is used for cultivation as shown in Figure 3-3.

Figure 3-3: A panoramic view of the Hồ Citadel, viewed from the top of the main gate looking toward the north gate.

HỒ HÁN THƯƠNG (?–1407?) – THE SON

In less than a year after ascending to the throne, Hồ Quý Ly became a senior king and allowed his son, Hồ Hán Thương, to succeed as the next king. Hồ Hán Thương followed his father's policy of strengthening the Hồ clan by identifying the Hồ people in Diễn Châu and Thanh Hóa, who shared the Hồ surname and granting them senior positions.[16] He also implemented a policy of limiting the number of servants a person could have and the size of the land that a person could own.[17] The policy was designed to reduce the power and influence of the Trần clan.

These policies, along with the relocation of the capital from Thăng Long to Tây Đô, helped ensure that the Hồ dynasty's ruling class were largely composed of individuals from Thanh Hóa and Nghệ An provinces, in contrast to the Trần elites of Nam Định and Thái Bình further north. Such a practice of regional consolidation was not entirely new, as previous dynasties like the Lý and Trần had also used similar strategies to strengthen their rule by favouring their tribes.

3.2 - Relationship with Champa

INVASIONS OF CHAMPA

Before becoming king, Hồ Quý Ly fought the Chams many times over 20 years since the ill-fated campaign of 1376/77, when he was in charge of supplies. By 1380, Hồ Quý Ly had risen to the position of Supreme Commander of all Đại Việt forces from Thanh Hóa to Thuận Hóa provinces. This role allowed him to become very familiar with the central region of Vietnam, from Ngang to Hải Vân Passes. Hồ Quý Ly's subsequent actions suggest that he intended to extend his domain southward, encroaching on Cham territory from his base in Thanh Hóa and Nghệ An, away from the traditional Red River Delta region. Unfortunately, the invasion of the Ming dynasty ended his dream.

After Chế Bồng Nga died in 1390, the fire went out of Champa aggression. Hồ Quý Ly took advantage of the situation and began to consolidate Đại Việt territorial gains at the frontier province of Hóa Châu by reinforcing fortifications and sending troops to secure the area. In 1391, he sent a contingent of the Đại Việt army, but the Chams ambushed them and captured its leader, though he eventually escaped. Hồ Quý Ly punished the failed expedition by ordering 30 of his officers beheaded.[18]

In 1396, Hồ Quý Ly ordered Commander Trần Tùng to attack Champa. During this campaign, Trần Tùng took a Cham general, Bố Đông, prisoner. Bố Đông then joined the Đại Việt army to defend its frontier against the Ming forces. A year later, in 1397, another Cham general, Chế Đa Biệt and his younger brother, Mộ Hoa Từ Ca Điệp, and their families defected to Đại Việt.[19] They were given Vietnamese names and allowed to settle in Hóa Châu to defend it against Champa.[20]

Before becoming senior king in 1400, Hồ Quý Ly sent a massive army, reportedly 150,000 strong, to invade Champa. The army was commanded by four generals, including the same Trần Tùng, who had now taken a Hồ surname, to lead the infantry column, and Đỗ Mãn, who led the navy. This time, Trần (Hồ) Tùng Trần Tùng took the mountain route, far away from the navy, which carried the necessary supplies. However, the expedition was disastrous. The infantry column got trapped in a flood, ran out of food, and had to resort to eating their body armour by roasting them over a fire. Eventually, the army had to retreat, and Trần Tùng returned in disgrace. Though he was demoted to a common foot soldier, his life was spared because of his past service in helping Hồ Hán Thương before he became king.[21] A few years later in 1404, Trần Tùng conspired against Hồ Quý Ly with Chế Sơn Nô, Chế Bồng

Nga's refugee son. The conspiracy was uncovered, and he was executed for his role in the plot.

That year, the lord of Champa, La Ngai, who was Chế Bồng Nga's general died, and his son Ba Đích Lại succeeded him.

'ONE THOUSAND-MILE ROAD'

The setback did not deter the Hồ family, and two years later, in 1402, Hồ Hán Thương ordered the construction of a road from Tây Đô to Hóa Châu and named it 'a thousand-mile (or 450 km) road' (*Thiên Lý*). Along the road, he established towns and communication posts. In Hóa Châu, a citadel, originally built by the Chams, was occupied by the Hồ army, and it is likely that the road ended there. On the current map, this road most likely follows Highway 1A, which spans approximately 550 km from Tây Đô to the Hóa Châu citadel.

LAND AND MORE LAND

In the seventh lunar month (or August) of 1402, Hồ Hán Thương led another large army to invade Champa, with Đỗ Mãn serving as one of the commanders. The Đại Ngu army reached Champa and engaged in battle, likely at present-day Quảng Nam province, south of Hải Vân Pass. The general of Đại Ngu, Đinh Đại Trung, and the Cham commander, Chế Tra Nan, were both killed at the first engagement. The death of Chế Tra Nan caused panic in the lord of Champa, Ba Đích Lại. He instructed his uncle, Bố Điền, to offer one white and one black elephant, plus local products, and most important of all, the land of Chiêm Động as a peace offering to Đại Ngu to allow him to retreat.[22] It should be noted SKTT may have mistaken in referring to the name of a member of the Cham royal family as *Bố Điền* as it explains elsewhere that *Bố Điền* was in fact a title, meaning 'great or crown prince'.[23]

When this Bố Điền arrived at the Đại Ngu camp to negotiate, Hồ Quý Ly pressured him into yielding even more land, including Cổ Lũy. He then established four provinces from the total land that he had acquired from Champa: Thăng (Sheng, 升), Hoa (Hua, 華), Tư (Si, 思) and Nghĩa (yi, 四).[24] These provinces covered the contemporary districts of Duy Xuyên, Quế Sơn, Thăng Bình, Tam Kỳ City, Bình Sơn, Sơn Tịnh, Tư Nghĩa, Mộ Đức, Đức Phổ, located between the Hàn and Thu Bồn Rivers of Quảng Nam province in the north, and the Trà Khúc and Vệ Nghĩa Rivers of Quảng Ngãi province immediately to the south. This campaign proved to be a resounding success for the Hồ clan; in one campaign, they had gained control of nearly 15,000 square kilometres—

an area larger than their home province of Thanh Hóa.²⁵ In 1402, Hồ Hán Thương built *Đàn Nam Giao* to offer prayers to heaven and earth and to thank the gods for the success in the south.

So, what were the Hồ dynasty planning to do with the land?

The first step they took was to establish a governing structure. The chief of Thăng Hoa (Thăng, Hoa, Tư, Nghĩa combined), an *An Phủ Sứ* (pacifying governor), was a Đại Ngu official. Meanwhile, the southern provinces of Tư and Nghĩa were overseen by a Cham marquis, Chế Ma Nô Đà Nan, Chế Bồng Nga's refugee son, who joined the Hồ dynasty as mentioned earlier. He was placed there to reassure the Cham people along the frontier. To ease the transition, Champa resettled some of their people in the newly ceded territory in the area south of Cổ Lũy, toward today's Bình Định province. Those who remained were incorporated into the military, presumably to keep them under control.²⁶

In 1403, once the governing structure was in place, Hồ Hán Thương began to implement a program of settlement for people from Đại Ngu, likely from Thanh Hóa and Nghệ An. He selected the people who did not own land but had some assets and settled them in Thăng Hoa. Their wives and children followed them in the following year, though many died when their ships were wrecked by storms, causing much discontent among the settlers. He also signed up the local people to provide water buffaloes to the southern colonists. Those who contributed were awarded with titles.²⁷ There is no official record of how many people eventually arrived between 1402 and 1407, but scholar Hồ Trung Tú estimated the figure to be around 10,000, although it could be as high as 20,000 to 30,000.²⁸

However, Hồ Hán Thương and his father were not satisfied with their previous gains and sought to expand their territory further. They gathered 200,000 men, including both infantry and navy, to invade Champa again that same year. This time, they aimed to capture the Cham capital at Vijaya. From there, they planned to march further south into Bạt Đạt Lang, Hắc Bạch and Sa Li Nha, eventually reaching the Cham border with Zhenla. Bạt Đạt Lang is the Vietnamese term for Panduranga which is today's Ninh Thuận and Bình Thuận provinces. Volume 3B tells the story of Panduranga, however, there is no information on the other two regions. I have not been able to locate Hắc Bạch and Sa Li Nha (Sha-li-ya). But in another context described further, Sa Li Nha could be around Mỹ Sơn/Trà Kiệu in Quảng Nam province.²⁹

Once again, Đỗ Mãn was one of the commanders, but the overall command fell to Phạm Nguyên Khôi, a relative of the Hồ family, probably on his maternal side. The Đại Ngu army reached Vijaya and surrounded it but were not able to breach the citadel walls. After nine months of fruitless campaigning, they ran out of food and withdrew.[30]

In response, Champa sought assistance from the Ming dynasty, which sent nine ships to aid them. The Ming fleet encountered Phạm Nguyên Khôi's flotilla at sea as they were returning to Tây Đô, advising them to withdraw from Champa immediately. When he returned to the capital, Hồ Quý Ly reprimanded Phạm Nguyên Khôi for failing to eliminate the Ming forces when they had the opportunity.[31]

3.3 - *The Ming is coming*

BUILDING UP TO THE INVASION

The Hồ dynasty's relationship with the Ming's first emperor, Hong Wu (Hồng Vũ) – Zhu Yuanzhang

The Trần dynasty (1226–1400) spanned the reigns of three dynasties of Imperial China, namely the Southern Song (1127–1279), the Mongol-led Yuan (1271-1368) and the Ming (1368–1644). Its decline almost matched the weakening of the Yuan dynasty, and unfortunately for the Hồ father and sons, their new reign began when the Ming dynasty was at its peak. As was the case of previous Đại Việt dynasties, when Imperial China was on the rise, it threatened Đại Việt.

The mid-14th century was a time of epidemics, famines, floods and rebellions in Imperial China, with many warlords and rebels.[32] One of these was the Red Turbans, and the man who successfully led them was Zhu Yuanzhang (1328–1398), who went on to found the Ming dynasty (officially the Great Ming or *Dà Míng*) and become Emperor Hongwu, its first ruler. In 1356, Zhu Yuanzhang and his army captured Nanjing (*Kim Lăng*), located east of present-day Shanghai, which later became the Ming dynasty's first capital.[33]

Before Zhu Yuanzhang was able to secure his reign, however, he had to deal with Chen Youliang (*Trần Hữu Lượng*) whom he defeated in 1363, and five years later in 1368, Zhu Yuanzhang formally became the first Ming emperor. In Thăng Long, Đại Việt kings followed these events with interest and in 1359, the Ming emperor sent a representative to the court of Trần Hạo to establish diplomatic relations. However, uncertain about who held true authority in Imperial China at the time, Trần Hạo dispatched an emissary to determine whether Zhu Yuanzhang or Chen Youliang was the legitimate ruler to whom Đại Việt should offer tribute.[34]

In 1361, Zhu Yuanzhang sought assistance from Trần Hạo while waging war against Chen Youliang near present-day Wuhan, but Trần Hạo declined the request.[35] However, as soon as Trần Hạo learned that Zhu Yuanzhang had successfully pacified the Two Guangs (present-day Guangxi and Guangdong provinces), he sent an envoy to establish relations and receive official seals. A year later, in 1369, Zhu Yuanzhang's representative arrived in Thăng Long to invest Trần Hạo as the King of An Nam State (*An Nam Quốc Vương*) and present him with a silver seal. Unfortunately, Trần Hạo had already passed away by then, and the Ming envoy refused to confer the seal on his successor, Chen Yijian (Trần Nhật Kiên or Nhật Lễ). They awaited instructions from the Ming emperor, who eventually invested Nhật Lễ in 1371.[36] It should be noted that the Ming court had always referred to Đại Việt (and later Đại Ngu) as An Nam (or Annan, 安南, a term dating back to its status as a protectorate under the Tang dynasty (618–907)). Following the Ming occupation of Đại Việt, the country was renamed Jiaozhi (or Jiao-zhi, *Giao Chỉ*). Thus, in the following text, Đại Việt = Đại Ngu = An Nam = Annam = Jiao-zhi = Giao Chỉ.

Not long after the investiture, Nhật Lễ was killed, as mentioned earlier. Trần Phủ sent elephants and other local products as tribute to the Ming court but the offerings were rejected because the signature tags were not in Nhật Lễ's name. However, the Ming emperor permitted Trần Phủ to manage affairs temporarily using the seal of the previous king.

Sending tributes, seeking investiture, and royal seals from the court of Imperial China were a tradition that Đại Việt kings had followed since the kingdom became independent in the 10th century. It is interesting to note the difference between how the compilers of the respective countries recorded these events. In Ming shi, Đại Việt kings, fearing punishment, sent their envoys and offered to accept any penalties at the Ming emperor's wishes, while at the same time requesting investiture.[37] On the other hand, SKTT barely mentioned these events, presenting them as routine formalities, rather than acts of submission.[38]

In 1384, Zhu Yuanzhang requested Đại Việt to provide supplies to the Ming troops during their campaign in Yunnan. This time, Đại Việt complied, and several officials leading the supply convoys died from disease.

This request from Ming was the first of many in the years that followed. In 1385, the Ming dynasty demanded 20 monks from Đại Việt after a Đại Việt official, who had been retained at the Ming court, claimed that Đại Việt monks were superior to Ming's counterparts in establishing Buddhist retreats (Bodhimaṇḍa or daochang (*đạo tràng*), a site for rituals). In 1386, Ming wanted seeds and plants of areca, lychee, jackfruit, and longan, though they perished en route due to the cold climate. Ming also demanded 50 war elephants and supply stations constructed from Nghệ An to Yunnan to supply forage for the elephants. Additionally, like the Mongols before them, the Ming court asked to use Đại Việt as a transit route for a campaign against Champa.[39]

In 1395, Ming demanded Đại Việt deliver 50,000 men, 50 war elephants and 50,000 *dan* of supplies to the border. Ming needed them to fight the rebels in present-day Guangxi province; however, the official who made the request secretly warned Đại Việt that Ming would likely use the excuse that the supplies delivered were insufficient to retain the men. In the end, Đại Việt did not bring any men or elephants to the border, only a small quantity of supplies.[40]

Ming then changed tacks and requested monks, masseuses and eunuchs instead. Đại Việt complied but only sent a few of each. I have included these examples to illustrate Ming's tactics of making unreasonable demands and using them against Đại Việt when they were not fully complied. Đại Việt was fully aware of such a tactic and would comply with the request, but only partially, with some justifications to mitigate negative consequences. On a separate note, in 1397, Ming sent two members of the defeated Yuan dynasty to reside in Đại Việt, reflecting the long-standing practice of Imperial China of using Đại Việt as a destination for political exiles.[41]

The Ming court did not approve Hồ Quý Ly's power grab following Trần Phủ's death in 1394. However, the emperor did not want to send his soldiers on a distant expedition and grudgingly accepted the tribute Hồ Quý Ly sent 1395.[42]

The Hồ dynasty's relationship with the Ming's second emperor, Yongle (Vĩnh Lạc) – Zhu Di

Zhu Yuanzhang died in 1398 and after his death, a three-year civil war followed between his son, Zhu Di (1360–1424), and grandson, Zhu Yunwen. Zhu Di triumphed and burned the palaces in Nanjing, including Zhu Yunwen and his family.[43] He became Emperor Yongle in the middle of 1402, moved his capital to modern Beijing (*Yên Kinh*), and the relationship between Ming and Đại Ngu began to change.

Hồ Quý Ly was adept at managing relations with Imperial China, and upon transferring the throne to his son in 1400, he promptly dispatched an envoy to the Ming court. The mission explained that the Trần dynasty had come to an end, and that Hồ Hán Thương—a maternal grandson of Trần Mạnh—was temporarily assuming authority.[44] However, the Ming court did not respond until the new emperor began his reign in 1403. That year Hồ Hán Thương sent an envoy and sought a seal of office and a title. The Ming emperor was suspicious and dispatched an envoy to Thăng Long to *inquire into the existence of the Trần heir and the sincerity of the Hồ clan's claim to power*.[45] At the end of 1403, the emperor's envoy returned and reported that all the male descendants of the former king of An Nam Chen Ri-kui (*Trần Ngung*) had died and that *We respectfully hope for Heaven's grace and that in accordance with the popular will, the title will be conferred upon him* [Hồ Hán Thương] *so that he can guard this state and the people in this corner of the ocean will all be in their place. We humbly dare, at the risk of our lives, to advise this.*[46] Early in 1404, the emperor enfeoffed (recognised) Hu Di (*Hồ Hán Thương/Quý Ly*) as the king of the country of Đại Việt.[47]

The emperor's recognition of Hồ Hán Thương provided the Hồ dynasty with a legitimacy they could not have attained if Hồ Quý Ly had remained on the throne. This need for legitimacy explains why Hồ Quý Ly never claimed the title of emperor or king himself but quickly abdicated in favour of his son, who, despite being of Trần lineage only through the maternal line, could strengthen their claim to rule.

Four events that marked a turning point in Đại Ngu's relationship with the Ming dynasty. The first was a border dispute in southern Guangxi province. Ming claimed that Đại Ngu had invaded and seized the territories administered by Siming—Lu prefecture (*Lu zhou, Lộc Châu*) and Xiping prefecture—which are around modern Longzhou and Ningming Counties in China, north of Lạng Sơn in Vietnam. This dispute dated back to 1377.[48] The emperor ordered their return but his instructions were ignored. The second was a complaint from Champa that Đại Ngu had invaded and plundered their lands. The emperor ordered Đại Ngu to behave but it had little effect. Not only did Đại Ngu disregard the emperor's orders, but they also seized items bestowed by the Ming court, presumably on Champa.

The third event involved claims from two Đại Ngu officials: Bùi Bá Kỳ (*Pei Bo-qi*), who served with Trần Khát Chân, killed by Hồ Quý Ly as mentioned earlier, and Trần Thiên (Thiêm) Bình (*Chen Tianping*). Bùi Bá Kỳ submitted to the Ming court that Hồ Quý Ly had usurped the Trần throne and requested that the Ming emperor send a punitive army. Trần Thiêm Bình claimed to be the son of Trần Vượng, brother of Trần Hạo, and thus a legitimate successor to the Trần lineage. The emperor tested Trần Thiêm Bình's claim by presenting him to the envoys sent by Hồ Quý Ly; they bowed before Thiêm Bình, some even wept.[49] When the story got back to Hồ Quý Ly, he had one of them beheaded upon his return to Đại Ngu.[50] The fourth event involved a complaint from Ningyuan district in Yunnan that Đại Ngu had invaded seven outposts.

Meanwhile, Hồ Hán Thương dispatched an envoy to the Ming court, who explained that Hồ Quý Ly did not usurp any king and that he welcomed Trần Thiêm Bình's return as lord and would return Ningyuan and Lu prefectures. In 1406, the emperor sent a deputy general from Guangxi with 5,000 men to escort Trần Thiêm Bình to travel to Đại Ngu. In the third lunar month, they reached Jiling Pass. As they were close to Qinzhan, Đại Ngu soldiers ambushed them and killed Trần Thiêm Bình. Jiling Pass could be today's Chi Lăng Pass, but I cannot locate Qinzhan.

SKTT records the event differently, with Trần Thiêm Bình captured and sentenced to death by a brutal method called *Lăng Trì (lingchi)* or *Tùng Xẻo* (dismemberment), where the executioner used a knife to cut off pieces of flesh from his body over a long period, eventually leading to death.[51] According to SKTT, the emperor sent 100,000 men.[52] I am inclined to adopt the Ming shi's version as described here for the reason that they did not need 100,000 men to accompany a throne's claimant. A later Vietnamese work mentions only 5,000 men.[53]

When the news reached Emperor Yongle, he was very angry, and on 11 May 1406, he summoned one of his best generals, Zhu Neng (*Chu Năng*, 1370–1406), to formulate a plan to invade Đại Việt.

SKTT records the events leading to this fateful decision differently, as summarised below.

During Emperor Yongle's reign, Ming envoys regularly came like a 'shuttle loom', making demands and asking questions, creating hard work for the Hồ court. By then, the Hồ court knew that Ming was planning to invade. One event that proved their suspicion was when they learned that the Đại Ngu eunuchs told relatives to raise golden banners with the eunuch's name when the northerners came. These eunuchs were sent by Đại Việt to Ming earlier and were retained to work in the Ming court. Hồ Quý Ly promptly put the eunuchs' relatives to death.[54]

In 1405, Ming demanded that Đại Ngu return Lu prefecture (*Lộc Châu*), near present-day Lạng Sơn. Much to the anger of Hồ Quý Ly, his representative, Hoàng Hối Khanh, agreed to return 59 hamlets, which was too many for him. Following the transfer, Hồ Quý Ly had the Ming-appointed heads of these hamlets poisoned.[55] Hoàng Hối Khanh passed a national examination in 1384 and later established a *Điền Trang* (private estates or farms), in what is now Lệ Thủy district in Quảng Bình province.[56]

Up to that time, Ming demands had been anything but land; this request for a return of land indicated that the invasion was imminent, and a year later, in the autumn of 1406, Ming amassed 800,000 men from present-day Guangxi and Yunnan provinces and invaded Đại Ngu.

3.4 - Relationship between Đại Việt, Champa and the Ming dynasty in the late 14th and early 15th centuries according to Ming shilu

THE VASSAL STATES

The four decades from 1370 to 1410 were a tumultuous period for both Champa and Đại Việt, marked by prolonged conflicts between the two kingdoms. Initially, Champa enjoyed a series of victories, but the tide turned in favour of Đại Việt until the Ming court intervened, which altered the balance of power. This era also coincided with significant changes in China, including the fall of the Yuan and the rise of the Ming dynasties.

To better understand the subsequent events between Đại Việt and Champa through the beginning of the 15th century, it is helpful to recount the key developments involving these three countries during these decades, as recorded in Ming shilu.

Once Zhu Yuanzhang, Emperor Hong Wu, the founding emperor of the Ming dynasty, consolidated his reign, he dispatched envoys in February 1369 to the countries of Japan, Champa, Java and Xi-yang (Western Ocean) to announce his imperial accession.[57] The emperor expected these countries to send envoys, submit memorials acknowledging themselves subjects and present tributes. The emperor also ordered *each country map its mountains and rivers, copy its inscriptions and record its population, and that these records be given to the* [Ming] *envoy to bring back*. The envoys were to offer sacrifices (animals and silk) to the spirits in the mountains and the rivers.[58]

In 1394, Ming shilu listed 17 countries including modern Korea (formerly Joseon) and Japan in the east, Siam (now Thailand), Champa, Cambodia, An Nam, Java and others in the south. The Ming dynasty considered them as feudatory countries of the *yi* [barbarians] *in the four directions*.[59] Ming shilu records Đại Việt was the first to present tribute, followed Korea and then by Champa.

However, the king of Champa, A-da-a-zhe (identified earlier as Chế Bồng Nga), sent his envoy, Hu-du-man, who arrived with gifts of tigers and elephants before the emperor's envoy even reached Champa. The emperor was greatly pleased by this gesture. It seems that Chế Bồng Nga sought to gain the emperor's favour to strengthen his position in his war against Đại Việt.

SILKS AND CALENDARS FOR ELEPHANTS

From 1369 to the end of Hongwu's reign in 1398, spanning nearly 30 years, Champa sent at least 22 tribute missions to the Ming court. These missions brought various local goods, including elephants, elephant tusks, rhinoceros horns, laka wood, sandalwood, and other products, which were primarily raw commodities. In exchange, the Ming emperor conferred upon Champa with patterned fine silks, silk gauzes interwoven with gold thread, clothing, Da (Jian) Tong Li calendars and paper money—manufactured items. This exchange highlighted the industrial strength and capabilities of the Ming dynasty compared to Champa. It was also representative of the Ming court's practice of gifting manufactured goods to vassal states in return for precious raw materials.

During this period, Ming shilu records the names of three Cham kings. From 1369 to 1390, the Cham ruler was A-da-a-zhe. In 1391, the emperor refused the tribute from the new Cham king, Ge-sheng, because he, as a Cham Minister, had killed the previous king, A-da-a-zhe.[60] However, according to SKTT, Chế Bồng Nga, the previous king, died in 1390, and his general, La Ngai, ascended to the throne. La Ngai ruled for a decade until he died in 1400, after which his son, Ba Đích Lại, succeeded him. Ming shilu later mentions a Cham king named Zhan-ba Di-lai in 1403, most likely the same as Ba Đích Lại. Zhan-ba Di-lai ruled for decades until his death in 1441.

DIPLOMATIC MANOEUVRES

Earlier, we learned that Champa sacked Thăng Long in April 1371. Later that same year, in September, Ming shilu records that a Cham envoy presented a memorial to the Ming court, claiming that Đại Việt had attacked Champa and sought help from the Ming emperor. If the timing of these two events is accurate, it would seem peculiar that, having burned the capital of Đại Việt, Champa would then report being under attack. This apparent contradiction suggests a diversion tactics from A-da-a-zhe, not only to mislead the Ming court but also to prepare it for the inevitable Đại Việt retaliation, which he anticipated would come.

The memorial was inscribed on a gold-leaf sheet over one *chi* (312 mm) long and five *cun* (156 mm) wide. It was written in the Cham language, which is most likely in Cham script rather than the earlier Sanskrit, and required translation. This document offers valuable insight into A-da-a-zhe's thoughts and strategies during that period. Below is the content of the memorial from Ming shilu.

> *The great Ming Emperor has ascended the throne and pacified all within the four seas. He is like the Heaven and the Earth which cover and contain all, and like the sun and moon which shed their rays on all. In comparison, A-da-a-zhe is like a piece of grass. The Emperor favoured me by sending an envoy to give me a gold seal and enfeoff me as the king of the country. I am grateful and elated, and will remain so forever. However, at present, Annam is using arms to attack our borders. They have killed and plundered officials and the people. I humbly pray that the Emperor will be compassionate and confer upon me military weapons, musical instruments and musicians. Thus, Annam will know that our Champa is a region to which [China's] culture extends and is a place which provides tribute to China. Thereafter, Annam will not dare to oppress or maltreat us.*[61]

In response, the Ming emperor politely declined the request for military weapons, as he did not want Champa to use them against Đại Việt. Likewise, he refused to provide musical instruments and musicians, reasoning that the Chams would require training in Chinese to use them properly. However, the emperor extended a tax exemption for goods carried on Cham ships and dispatched an order to Đại Việt, ordering an immediate cessation of hostilities.

Over the next ten years to 1380, as the war between Đại Việt and Champa raged on, both sides presented memorials to the Ming court, accusing each other of violating their borders. Emperor Hongwu adopted the role of an 'impartial' arbiter, admonishing both parties. He repeatedly urged them to end the conflict, secure their borders, and focus on the welfare of their people. Despite these admonishments, the Ming court refrained from direct interference in the ongoing hostilities.[62]

A CHANGE OF POLICY

Đại Việt and Champa continued their war sporadically in the last two decades of the 14th century, culminating in the occupation of the Cham territory south of Hải Vân Pass, encompassing present-day Quảng Nam and Quảng Ngãi provinces, in the early 15th century, as discussed earlier. However, Ming shilu was silent on this ongoing conflict during this period until the reign of Emperor Yongle, who no longer followed his father's policy of impartiality.

In response to the claims from Zhan-ba Di-lai, the new king of Champa, regarding the frequent attacks by Đại Việt, Emperor Yongle sent out a strongly worded memorial to Hồ Quý Ly in August 1403. He told them that *the people of Champa have been brought distress by your pernicious evil* and demanded an immediate cessation of hostilities and respect the emperor's will.[63] In February 1404, the Hồ court sent an envoy to the Ming court, admitting guilt and agreeing to stop the aggression.[64] Following this, the emperor reassured Champa that Hu Di (Hồ Quý Ly), the king of Đại Việt, had admitted his wrongdoing and would no longer infringe on Cham territory.[65] However, over six months later, in September 1404, Champa reported that the Hồ court had defied imperial orders, attacked Champa, and occupied Cham territory at Sha-li-ya (likely around Mỹ Sơn/Trà Kiệu in present-day Quảng Nam). The emperor was furious at this violation.[66]

Perhaps drawing from their previous dealings with Emperor Hongwu—characterized by frequent admonishments but no direct interference—the Hồ court may have misread Emperor Yongle's intentions. This miscalculation likely led them to dismiss the gravity of his warnings, inadvertently playing into his hands. Their continued defiance set the stage for the Ming invasion of Đại Việt, marking a significant turning point in the history of Đại Việt. On the other hand, one could argue that, regardless of the Hồ court's actions, the Ming court would have found a pretext to justify their invasion.

3.5 - The Ming invasion of Đại Việt

ĐẠI NGU'S PREPARATION

The three-year civil war among the successors of the first Ming emperor, which began following his death in 1398, gave the Hồ court some breathing space. Still, they knew that it would only be a matter of time before Ming sent their soldiers south.

In 1401, Hồ Quý Ly asked his officials how to raise a 1,000,000-strong army to resist the northerners. Hoàng Hối Khanh proposed taking a census of everyone in Đại Ngu, including vagrants, starting from the age of two.[67] After the work was completed, the number of people aged 15–60 increased significantly, allowing the Hồ court to recruit more soldiers from 1402. Unfortunately, the census record for 1401/02 is lost. In 1404, Hồ Hán Thương ordered the construction of iron-bolted boats disguised as rice transports.[68] In 1405, Hồ Quý Ly and his son spent a month travelling to assess defensive locations at the river crossings, river mouths and routes.[69] They followed up by having wood stakes planted at the strategic locations on the Cái River (today's the Red River), several sea gates and established four arsenals to produce weapons.[70]

By 1405, the Hồ court had the men, the ships, the weapons, defensive forts and lines constructed. After the interception and killing of Trần Thiêm Bình, Hồ Hán Thương dispatched two officials to the Ming court to seek a truce and to explain the role of Thiêm Bình. However, the Hồ court knew the Ming army would return, and in the autumn of 1406, they ordered the construction of wooden poles as barricades along the south bank of the rivers that crossed the route where they expected the Ming forces to take.

According to SKTT, the work extended from Fort Đa Bang to the Lỗ Giang (present-day Phong Vân to Tản Hồng), a distance of around ten kilometres, and from Lạng Châu to Trú Giang (present-day Lạng Sơn to the Thương River). The first line was to defend against the expected attack from Yunnan, while the second was to protect Thăng Long in the north-east direction against the Ming column from Guangxi via Lạng Sơn.

All they could do was wait for the invasion. Later that year, they summoned the governors to the capital at Tây Đô to consult with other officials at court as to whether Đại Ngu should seek a peaceful solution or fight the Ming army. Some wanted to fight, and others preferred a temporary truce. Hồ Quý Ly's younger son, Hồ Nguyên Trừng, stated that he was not concerned with fighting, but he worried that the people would not follow.

THE INVASION

The invasion is described with some details in Ming shilu, Ming shi and SKTT. The narratives in each work are broadly similar and can be generally summarised in three key phases. In the first phase, the Ming forces entered Đại Ngu in two separate columns from Guangxi and Yunnan in November 1406. They converged at the confluence of three rivers—Đà, Red and Lô, defeated Đại Ngu at a decisive battle at Fort Đa Bang (*Duo-bang*) and captured Đông Đô, two months later in January 1407. In the second phase, Đại Ngu counterattacked the Ming army at Hàm Tử on the Red River but failed, allowed the Ming forces to reach the coast and pursued the Hồ father and sons. In the following weeks, the Ming army took Tây Đô, and seized the Hồ family afterwards in southern provinces as they planned to flee to the Champa border. The whole campaign took about 12 months, from July 1406 and ended the Hồ dynasty. The relevant locations are shown in Figure 3-4.

THE HỒ DYNASTY (1400–1407)

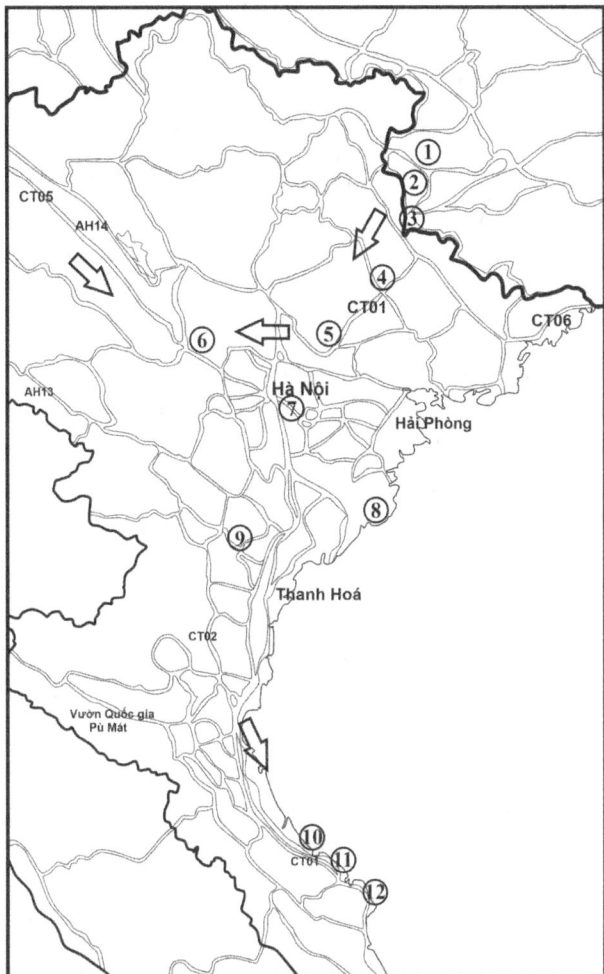

Figure 3-4: Map of the Ming's invasion of Đại Ngu, 1406–1407.

Key: 1. Longzhou County; 2. Pingxiang; 3. Friendship Pass; 4. Chi Lăng Gorge; 5. Thương River; 6. Old Fort Đa Bang (crucial battlefield); 7. Hàm Tử; 8. Giao Thủy District; 9. Hồ Citadel (Tây Đô), 10. Cửa Nhượng; 11. Cao Vong (Kỳ Anh); 12. Ngang Pass. White arrows illustrate the directions of the advance of the Ming forces.

The first phase – The battle of Fort Đa Bang, Ming enters Đông Đô

Around two months after Emperor Yongle summoned Zhu Neng, he had assembled a force of over 100,000 men, composed of 75,000 cavalry and infantry troops from Yunnan and 30,000 native soldiers from Guangxi province, plus an unknown number who accompanied him directly. The emperor ordered Zhu Neng to take on the seal of 'General for Subduing the Yi (barbarians)', as the commander of all Ming forces. Zhang Fu (*Trương Phụ*, 1375-1449) and Mu Sheng (*Mộc Thạnh*, 1368-1439) were his right and left deputy commanders, respectively. Zhu Neng, Zhang Fu and their men were to march from Guangxi, while Mu Sheng and his troops would come from Yunnan. Bùi Bá Kỳ, a throne claimant of the Trần descendant, was conferred a headwear and a belt, and was to travel with Zhu Neng.

The three men were in their 30s, and their fathers had served under the first Ming emperor. On Đại Ngu's side, Hồ Quý Ly, who had just turned 70, and his two sons, Hồ Hán Thương and Hồ Nguyên Trừng, both in their 30s. They were supported by Hồ Xạ, Đỗ Mãn, the veteran of the Champa expedition, and another commander, Hồ Đỗ. The commanders of both sides were experienced warriors, and the stage was set for a clash that would determine the fate of the Hồ family and Đại Ngu.

On 30 July 1406, the emperor offered sacrifices to all spirits and sent Zhu Neng and his men off, presumably from the capital Beijing. His order to Mu Sheng was specific; in about three months, Zhu Neng was to cross the border into Đại Ngu from Ping-xiang (today's Pingxiang) in Guangxi province to Po-lei and Ji-ling in the first ten days of the 10th month (11 to 20 November 1406). Around a month later, between 25 November and 4 December, they would cross the Fu-liang (Phú Lương) River (now Cầu River). The emperor instructed Mu Sheng to contact Zhu Neng before committing his troops to any major engagement. In return, Mu Sheng asked for another 10,000 troops as reserve and 220,000 *shi* or *dan* of grain.

The emperor was cautious; he knew about the failures of the Song and the Yuan dynasties in their previous efforts to subdue Đại Việt and warned his commanders *not to be greedy for riches and given to lust*. The emperor then advised them not to prolong the fighting as they would not be able to sustain it and not to waste time building boats and rafts to cross the rivers. Instead, they should keep Đại Ngu engaged while secretly finding a shallow river upstream to cross.[71]

Three months after they left Beijing, the Ming army arrived at the border with Đại Việt on schedule but Zhu Neng died of illness at Long-zhou (now Longzhou), in Guangxi province. Zhang Fu replaced him, and on 19 November 1406, they left Ping-xiang and passed through Po-lei (Pha Lũy) Pass (now Friendship Pass or Ải Nam Quan near Lạng Sơn).

They overcame Đại Ngu resistance at Ai-liu Pass and advanced to the Ji-ling (now Chi Lăng) Pass. Đại Ngu troops had fire guns (or tubes), spears, crossbows and set up stockades with numerous ditches with bamboo spikes. According to Ming shilu, Đại Ngu had 30,000 troops to guard the pass but abandoned the position after receiving bad news brought to them by the retreated troops from Ai-liu.[72] Five days later, the Ming army reached the Shi Bridge on the Chang River (today's Thương River), where they built a pontoon bridge. From there, they learnt that Mu Sheng had arrived at Bai-he (now Bạch Hạc).

From the end of November 1406 to the middle of January 1407, two wings of the Ming army fought several battles; Zhang Fu moved west and eventually joined forces with Mu Sheng to oppose Fort Đa Bang. It appeared that Đại Ngu had withdrawn their troops to the southern sides of the Red and the Đuống Rivers, effectively yielding the northern half of present-day North Vietnam to the Ming forces. The battle of Fort Đa Bang was a turning point in the Ming invasion and, as expected, was described differently by the combatants involved.

According to the entry on 19 January 1407 (Day 11 Month 12) in Ming shilu:

The palisades erected by the bandits [a derogatory term that the compilers of Ming shilu refer to Đại Ngu] *formed a line close to the river. Only the sandy areas below Duo-bang City* [Fort Đa Bang] *were broad enough to station the army on. The earth walls were lofty and steep and the bandits had dug successive trenches in front of the walls. Within these trenches they had placed bamboo spikes very closely together, while outside the trenches they had dug holes for men and horses to fall into. Above and within these holes there were also bamboo spikes. On the walls the defences were tight and the bandit troops were as numerous as ants. When the Imperial forces were ready to attack, an order was issued to the army as follows: "The bandits are depending on this city. Men of spirit should repay their country. The names of those who achieve merit will be recorded and those first on to the walls will be promoted and rewarded at the highest levels."*

At this, the troops were enthusiastic about carrying out the orders. On this day, [Zhang] Fu and so on took their troops on to the sand-flats and the division of troops for the attack on the bandits was discussed. Fu was to attack the South-west of the city while [Mu] Sheng was to attack from the South-east. With the division decided, some officers and troops were sent off about one li [around 450 m] distant from where the attack was to take place. Here they readied many implements for the surprise attack. At night, torches were given to the troops and it was agreed that when they stormed the walls, they would signal by lighting the torches and blowing trumpets.

> *In the middle of the night at the fourth drum Fu sent the Assistant Commissioner Huang Zhong and other with gagged troops [covering their mouths] carrying the implements for the attack. They passed the successive ditches and arrived at the bottom of the South-west wall. Here they placed scaling ladders against the wall and the Commissioner Cai Fu [Thái Phúc] and others were first on to the wall. They commenced striking quickly with their swords and the bandits soldiers cried out in alarm. Suddenly, on the walls torches shone brightly and the sounds of the trumpets competed one with the other. All of the officers and troops below the wall bravely mounted the wall and the bandit troops, having become greatly confused, did not fire their arrows or fling their stones. They all jumped off the walls and fled, following which our troops entered the city.*
>
> *Within the city, the bandit generals re-formed their troops to do battle, and drove elephants before them as their vanguard. Fu directed the Mobile Corps Commander Zhu Guang [Chu Quảng] and others to disguise their horses with paintings of lions, while the firearms commander Luo Wen and others advanced with firearms at the flanks. The elephants were frightened and some were injured by the fire-arrows, upon which they turned back and fled. The bandit troops scattered in confusion. The Imperial army progressed as it pursued the bandits, and killed the bandit commanders Liang Min-xian and Cai Bo-le. The bandits were pursued into the Mount San-yuan and they trampled each other to death in their frenzy. The dead were beyond count. Twelve elephants were captured and innumerable weapons were taken.*[73]

According to SKTT, before departing to Đại Ngu, Zhu Neng wrote a message detailing the crimes committed by Hồ Quý Ly and appealing for a Trần to restore the dynasty.[74] Mu Sheng and Zhang Fu copied the message onto wooden placards and floated them down the river. Many Đại Ngu troops picked up the placards and believed the message. They were already anti-Hồ due to their harsh regime, became demoralised and lost the motivation to fight. Some defected to the Ming army and were subsequently appointed to senior official positions.[75]

The battle escalated quickly with three major engagements over a week on the 10th, 15th, and 17th of January 1407. Đại Ngu won one fight on the 15th, but lost the other two on the 10th and 15th. The last defeat was a major blow to Đại Ngu since its commander was caught unprepared while girls entertaining him, which allowed the Ming army to cross the river. Đại Ngu forces retreated to the fort of Fort Đa Bang, and in the morning of 20 January 1407, the Ming forces commenced their assaults on the fort, described by SKTT as follows.

> *On the morning of the 12th day (20 January 1407), the Trương Phụ [Zhang Fu] led Admiral Hoàng Trung [Huang Zong] and Commander Thái Phúc [Cai Fu]*

to attack the north-west of the Đa Bang fort. Mộc Thạnh led Admiral Trần Tuấn's group to attack the southeastern part of the fort. Corpses were piled as high as the citadel wall, but the enemy continued to attack, and no one dared to stop. Nguyễn Tông Đỗ, the general commanding the Thiên Trường army, dug an opening in the fort wall to let the elephants out. The Ming army used fire rockets to shoot the elephants. The elephant retreated, the Ming troops followed the elephants and attacked. The fort was immediately defeated. The troops along the rivers were all broken up and retreated to the Hoàng Giang River.[76]

By retreating to the Hoàng Giang River, which is south of Đông Đô, Đại Ngu had abandoned it to the Ming forces. Sometime in early 1407, Mu Sheng and Zhang Fu entered Đông Đô and ordered a stocktake of food supplies, gathered all the refugees, and organised the officials to administer. They clearly planned for a long-term stay. According to SKTT, they also took girls, castrated young boys, collected all the coins and delivered them via road stations to Nanjing.[77]

Ming shilu's entry on 20 January 1407 mentions the capture of Đông Đô but says nothing about the castrated young boys.

Today, two roads close to the confluence of the Red and Đà Rivers by the Phong Vân commune in Ba Vì district are named the Đa Bang Fort Road (*Đường Thành Đa Bang*). Three kilometres north of these roads is a location named the Old Fort of Đa Bang (*Thành Cổ Đa Bang*), which appears to be in the middle of rice paddies. The actual site of the fort is most likely around this area.[78]

The numbers

Based on Ming shilu, the Ming army that invaded in 1406 numbered around 115,000 or more. On the other hand, SKTT reports a figure of 800,000 based on a different entry in Ming shilu.[79] Similarly, Ming shilu describes 900 *li* (450 km) of ramparts and palisades extended from Fort Đa Bang, guarded by two million people. Ming shilu further records that Đại Ngu forces on land and water totalled seven million.

One can understand why the compilers of these annals exaggerated the figures, as the invaders and the defenders have a tendency to overestimate each other's capabilities. However, it is difficult to believe that the Ming army had 800,000 men in the campaign; the supplies for such a large army would make the figure unrealistic. Similarly, 900 *li* is about the same distance from Hanoi to Ngang Pass, making it impossible for the Hồ court to mobilise the people to build such a long defensive line over a year or so. The two and seven million figures are also greatly exaggerated; 502 years later, in 1909, Tonkin (North Vietnam) had a population of only 6.9 million.[80]

The second phase – Đại Ngu counterattacks but fails
The record of what happened following the taking of Đông Đô in January until the Ming forces' capture of the Hồ family five months later was unclear, and below is my attempt to reconstruct the events.

For about a month after entering Đông Đô, the Ming army appeared to consolidate their positions, fight several battles, and accept surrenders from several counties and prefectures. However, to travel south to reach Tây Đô, they needed to get to the coast, which required sailing down the Red River.

Đại Ngu commander knew the Ming army's intentions and took a defensive position by the Hoàng (*Huang*) Giang River, which I believe is the present-day Châu Giang River in Hà Nam province.[81] Mu Sheng learned of Đại Ngu concentration of forces at the Mộc Hoàn (Mộc Phàm, *Mu-wan*) River, a tributary of the Red River, near the Hoàng Giang River, and on 21 February 1407, he led a contingent of infantry, cavalry and boats to confront Đại Ngu.[82] When the Ming army was near the Lu River (most likely todays' Luộc River), Đại Ngu attacked but their boats ran into shallow water and the Ming army defeated them, beheaded all prisoners. At that time, a local person who had long opposed the Hồ dynasty—Mạc Thúy (*Mo Sui*) of Nam Sách (*Nan-ce*), near present-day Chí Linh, led 10,000 men to join the Ming forces. The surrender of Mạc Thúy was hardly surprising as Chí Linh was a strong Trần dynasty's domain.

Unfortunately for the Hồ family, Mạc Thúy was not alone in surrendering and collaborating with the Ming forces. Other local leaders linked to the Trần dynasty or acting out of self-preservation also did. The collaborators gave the Ming army a justification to invade Đại Ngu and provided Zhang Fu with a significant political victory, as his progress appeared to be stalled for two months after the battle of the Mộc Hoàn. They were unable to reach the coast.

In early March 1407, Zhang Fu sent Mạc Thúy to pacify other prefectures and to seek out a male descendant of the Trần line to re-establish a Trần king. A month later, Mạc Thúy returned with 1,120 others from Bắc Giang (*Bei River*) and other prefectures, to report that *We respectfully have gone to the various places to promulgate the instructions of pacification and the officials, troops and people have been settled in their former post, units and occupations. However, as for the males of the Chen [Trần] line, the Li bandits eliminated all of them. There are no descendants and no one is left to inherit the throne... and all wish that the ancient prefectures and counties be re-established.*[83] Zhang Fu dispatched a report to Emperor Yongle and request that a regional military commission be set up in An Nam but the emperor refused, he wanted the Hồ father and sons captured first.[84]

The Ming army continued their advance down the Red River to reach the coast, and there were several battles around Cửa Muộn (*Men Sea-Port*), the estuary of today's Red River by the National Park of Xuân Thủy in Giao Thủy (*Jiao-shui*) district).

According to SKTT, the Hồ family consolidated their forces, raised money, manufactured canons, built ships and constructed barricades and ramparts. Both sides faced each other from their respective defensive lines and the day and night fighting was intense but appeared to reach a stalemate. The Ming forces suffering from the heat, the rain and diseases, decided to retreat to Hàm Tử (*Xian-zi*), some 30 kilometres south of Đông Đô by the Red River, a strategic location that was fought over several times during the Mongol-Yuan invasions in the 13th century.

By that time, officials and people from several provinces surrendered and joined the Ming forces. However, many from Đông Đô, angered at their treatments by the Ming army, came to the Hồ camps and volunteered to fight. The Hồ court assembled the generals, men, ships and weapons and decided to attack Hàm Tử. It appeared this decision was their last roll of the dice and on 20 April 1407, they commenced their assault.

Hồ Xạ, the commander at Chi Lăng Pass, advised against the attack as he knew the Ming army had staged an ambush, but his advice was overruled. Đại Ngu forces numbered around 70,000, but the Hồ court let it be known that they had 210,000 men, including infantry and navy. Hồ Xạ led the infantry on the south bank, while another column advanced on the northern bank of the Red River. Hồ Nguyên Trừng and Đỗ Mãn commanded the navy, with 100 warships in the river.

Unfortunately, Hồ Xạ was right. Đại Ngu troops marched into a trap and were forced to jump into the river; many died. The navy was also under heavy attack; they fared a little better and several managed to escaped but all the supply ships were sunk, drowning all on board. It was a massive defeat for the Hồ court, but Hồ Quý Ly, Hồ Hán Thương and other officers were able to reach the coast and return to Thanh Hóa (*Qing-hua*).[85]

Ming shilu records a similar event on 4 May 1407, but with a smaller number of troops of 10,000 but a long line of boats over ten *li* (4.5 kilometres) long. They attacked the Đại Ngu boats from the river and both riverbanks. It was a rout with Hồ Xạ (*Hu She*) losing his life during the battle and Nguyễn Phi Khanh (Ruan Fei-qing), a minister in the Hồ court, surrendering.[86]

The third phase – the capture of the Hồ family and the end of Đại Ngu
After the battle of Hàm Tử, the Red River was clear for the Ming forces to travel to the coast and pursue the remnants of the Hồ army. According to SKTT, at the end of May, on the 29th, they reached Lỗi Giang (a branch of the

Mã River near Vĩnh Lộc, possibly the Bưởi River), and the Hồ army crumbled without a fight.[87] The Bưởi River was near the Tây Đô, indicating that the Ming army had taken it.

The Ming forces were relentless in their pursuit of the Hồ family and other members of the Hồ court. A week later, in early June, they attacked the sea gate at Điền Canh (*Dian shi?*) in present-day Nghi Sơn of Thanh Hóa province and continued their pursuit. In the middle of June, they captured Hồ Nguyên Trừng on the 16th at the Cửa Kỳ La (*Qi-luo* sea-port or the contemporary Cửa Nhượng in Hà Tĩnh province). Hồ Quý Ly and his son had planned to flee to Tân Bình, in today's Quảng Bình province, but the Ming army caught him at Kỳ La. When he first got there, a local elder explained that the name of the location was Ky Lê (meaning tied up the Lê, Hồ previous surname) with a mountain called Thiên Cầm (meaning caught by heaven), and suggested that Hồ Quý Ly should not stay. It appears that the locals deliberately distorted the names as they did not want the Hồ family to stop in the village. Hồ Quý Ly had the poor man beheaded, but his counsel came true, as the Hồ family was captured soon after.

Ming shilu's entry of the event was dated 16 June 1407, with Zhang Fu and Mu Sheng leading the force that captured Hồ Quý Ly (*Li Ji-li*) and his son Cheng (Hồ Nguyên Trừng).

The day after, on 17 June 1407, they seized Hồ Hán Thương (*Li Cang?*) and his son, Prince Nhuế (*Li Rui?*) at Mount Cao Vọng (*Gao-wang?*) in Kỳ Anh (Võng Án, *Yong-an* sea-port), together with Hồ Đỗ (*Hu Du*), near Ngang Pass, the traditional border with Champa.

In summary, the Ming army left Beijing in late July 1406 and four months later crossed the border into Đại Việt on 19 November. They took two months to capture Đông Đô in January 1407 but were unable to reach the coast until May, which was four months later. The timetable illustrates the strong resistance by the Hồ court, however, despite their brave efforts, they were unable to stop the Ming advance. About a month later, in the middle of June 1407, the Hồ family was captured just north of Ngang Pass. Soon afterward, Mu Sheng and Zhang Fu ordered several of his commanders, including Liu Sheng (Liễu Thăng), to escort Hồ Quý Ly—along with his sons, Hồ Nguyên Trừng, Hồ Hán Thương, other close relatives, and several Đại Ngu generals, and the Hồ royal seals—to Beijing to submit to the emperor.[88]

On 5 July 1407, Emperor Yongle issued an imperial proclamation to justify the invasion. He formally established a Jiaozhi Regional Military Commission and a Provisional Administration Commission for An Nam. He also appointed Bùi Bá Kỳ as an assistant administration commissioner and instructed Zhang Fu and Mu Sheng to wait for the cooler weather and withdraw the troops.[89]

In early October 1407, Li Sheng arrived at the capital Beijing with the Hồ clan and about 20 others in caged-carts. According to Ming shilu, Emperor Yongle sent Hồ Quý Ly, his son, Hồ Hán Thương, and Hồ Đỗ to prison but pardoned the remainders including Hồ Quý Ly's second son, Hồ Nguyên Trừng. We do not know what became of Hồ Quý Ly and Hồ Hán Thương, presumably they died in exile. However, Hồ Nguyên Trừng went on to work for the Ming court as a secretary in the Bureau of Construction and was promoted to the vice minister of the right in the Auxiliary Ministry of Works in 1428. He was paid entirely in rice because *some of the eunuchs said that he was impoverished.*[90] He wrote *Nam Ông Mộng Lục* while living in exile, as cited earlier, and died in 1446.[91]

According to SKTT, Emperor Yongle was not as magnanimous as recorded in Ming shilu. A number of Đại Ngu prisoners were appointed to official positions in different provinces but were murdered en route.[92]

Champa retakes occupied land
Before the Ming invasion, Hồ Hán Thương appointed Hoàng Hối Khanh to govern the newly settled territory of Thăng Hoa, drawing on his prior experience managing a private estate in southern Quảng Bình—land formerly held by Champa. Thăng Hoa is corresponding to modern Quảng Nam and Quảng Ngãi provinces. During their retreat from the advancing Ming forces, the Hồ rulers instructed Hoàng Hối Khanh to take one-third of the earlier migrant settlers and combine them with local troops to form a loyalist army.

Meanwhile, the Cham king, Zhan-ba Di-lai, took advantage of the Ming invasion to raise an army to reclaim Thăng Hoa. The Cham offensive caused panic among the migrant settlers, who fled, likely heading north to Hóa Châu. Hoàng Hối Khanh retreated to Hóa Châu citadel in Huế, leaving Chế Ma Nô Đà Nan to resist the Cham forces. Isolated and outmatched, he was eventually killed. Champa regained Thăng Hoa and began launching raids into Hóa Châu. One of Hoàng Hối Khanh's officials, Đặng Tất, requested Zhang Fu to appoint him as administrator of Hóa Châu and successfully repelled the Cham forces. He then sent Hoàng Hối Khanh to Đông Đô. En route, Hoàng Hối Khanh committed suicide, but that did not stop Zhang Fu from having his head removed from his corpse and publicly displayed in Đông Đô marketplace.[93]

In summary, although the territory south of the Hải Vân Pass to the Vệ River was nominally under Đại Việt's control from 1402 to 1407, Champa soon recaptured it. They held it until the Ming forces suppressed the final Trần rebellions in 1414 and placed the region under direct Ming administration, as discussed in the next chapter.

CHAPTER 4

UNDER THE MING'S RULE – ĐẠI VIỆT FIGHTS BACK

4.1 - A six-year resistance, 1407–1413

As far as Emperor Yongle was concerned, An Nam was pacified and became part of his empire from July 1407. His imperial orders to Zhang Fu and others were clear.

> *The Li bandits [the Hồ family] of Annam killed their ruler, usurped control of the country and illegally changed the dynastic title and adopted a reign title. They acted cruelly without benevolence and caused pain and suffering throughout the country. They attacked and seized neighbouring territory, resisted the orders of the Court and did not fulfil their tribute obligations. I could not tolerate this and thus ordered you to go and punish their crimes. Through reliance on the secret assistance of Heaven and Earth, the ancestors and the spirits, the officers and the men carried out their orders. Wherever the power of the troops reached, there all was pacified. The rebel bandit Li Ji-li [Hồ Quý Ly], his son and their false ministers have been captured, the*

good and benevolent have been comforted and those who have surrendered have been received and cared for. They have not been subject to even the slightest injury... The summer is now at its height. You should select a high and cool place where to rest the troops. Await the cooler weather and then withdraw the troops.

You previously sent a memorial from the elder Mo Sui [Mạc Thúy] and others which noted that all the males of the Chen [Trần] line had been eliminated by the Li bandits and that there was no-one who could succeed, and which requested that the old system be revived and the former prefectures and counties re-instituted. I ordered you to pay special attention to investigating these claims. Your memorial has now been received noting that the Chen line has already been broken and that, as the prefectures and counties have to be governed, requesting the establishment of the three offices to administer and govern the military personnel and the civilians. All is approved as requested. Establish the Jiao-zhi Regional Military Commission with the Assistant Commissioner-in-chief Lu Yi [Lữ Nghị] in charge of matters and Huang Zhong [Hoàng Trung] as his deputy. You are also to select two other able commissioners-in-chief to act as their assistants. The provincial administration commission [Bố Chính] and the provincial surveillance commission [Án Sát] will both be headed by the Minister Huang Fu [Hoàng Phúc].[1]

In reality, Đại Việt was far from pacified; the Trần line was not completely eliminated, and the Ming army was not able to withdraw. Zhang Fu and Mu Sheng had to fight more battles to suppress the resistance, and it was not until March 1415 that their armies eventually returned to the capital in Beijing.[2]

GATHERING THE SPOILS

Late in July 1407, the emperor instructed Zhang Fu to seek out talented and virtuous people, retired scholars, people who are skilled in writing and calculations, experienced in official and military matters, knowledgeable in strategic planning, skilled in medicines and medical diagnosis *to send them to the capital they can be promoted and employed.*[3]

Three months later, in October, 7,700 Đại Việt tradesmen and artisans of all types who had been sent by Zhang Fu arrived at the capital.[4] The Emperor had them provided with cotton-padded clothing to keep warm. Not long after, Zhang Fu located 9,000 talented, virtuous people, retired scholars and so on, as specified above and sent them in groups to the capital.[5]

Emperor Yongle was clear in his intention of why he wanted some of these people. He wanted to train them so that *they can return to their original places to soothe and govern the people.*[6] As for the others, the explanations range from making up for a shortage of skilled workers in Beijing to destroying the ruling elites in Đại Việt as a deliberate policy. I am inclined to adopt the latter as the policy would weaken Đại Việt, making it dependent on the Ming administration and thus easier to govern.

The Ming officials found the people of Đại Việt venerated Buddha and wanted them to worship the Ming's spiritual practices, including *the spirits of the wind, clouds, thunder and rain, the mountains and rivers and the soil and grain.*[7] In February 1408, gold mining offices were established in seven commanderies, mostly in the west and north-west of Hanoi.[8]

The Ming administrators were making good progress, even SKTT acknowledged that the deputy commissioner, Huang Fu, was competent, *Phúc [Fu] was an intelligent person, good at improvising, talented in governing people, and people respected him as capable person.*[9] A year later, in July 1408, Zhang Fu and Mu Sheng returned to the capital and presented a map of Đại Việt showing the territory gained of 1,760 *li* (792 km) from east to west and 2,800 *li* (1,260 km) from north to south.[10] The east-west distance is comparable to the current straight-line measurement from Móng Cái, in the far east, to Điện Biên Phủ, in the far west, which spans approximately 550 km on Google Maps. However, the north-south distance is less accurate, as 1,260 km of road distance from Lạng Sơn to Quy Nhơn extends far beyond the areas reached by the Ming army in 1407, which never advanced that far south.

A few days later, the Ming ministries reported that *The Xin-cheng Marquis Zhang Fu and others have pacified Jiao-zhi and have established a total of 472 military and civilian offices. There is a regional military commission, a provincial administration commission, a provincial surveillance commission, ten guards, two battalions, 15 prefectures, 41 subprefectures and 208 counties, one maritime trade supervisorate, 100 police offices and 92 commercial tax offices. They have also built walls and moats in 12 cities and pacified 3,120,000-plus people. Further, they have obtained 2,087,500-plus man [man (蠻): barbarians in the south] persons, 13,600,000 shi of grain, 235,900-plus elephants, horses and cattle, 8,677 (Alt: 8,672) ships and 2,539,852 items of military equipment.*[11]

Based on this report, the population of Đại Việt at the time was over five million. By comparison, in 1909, Tonkin (North Vietnam) had a population of 6.9 million.[12] Other estimates, however, place the figure closer 1.8 million. I would suggest that figure of between three to five million would be reasonable.[13] Note the large share of the 'barbarians' of the total population as recorded by the Ming officials.

Despite the success, the emperor was impatient. Earlier, in late 1407, he wanted the army to withdraw, leaving a small contingent to support the civilian government and protect the supply route from Guangxi. He reminded Zhang Fu in the winter of 1406/07 and, again, at the beginning of the summer of 1408, when he believed the opportunity was gone because of the hot weather, and the dreaded miasmic vapours (bad air) were on the rise.[14]

However, Zhang Fu was not able to leave, instead in early 1408, he asked for an additional 22,700-plus troops to establish a further 15 battalions.[15] In August of that year, he requested that the 10,000 troops transported grain supplies be permitted to stay to provide defence duties.[16] Why could he not depart when Đại Việt was supposed to be pacified over a year earlier? The reason was because, contrary to Mạc Thúy's report, the Trần line did not end but continued with two kings.

1408 – ĐẠI VIỆT REGAINS LOST TERRITORY

The last Trần king

According to SKTT, Trần Phủ had a son named Trần Ngỗi (also known as Trần Quỹ (Quĩ) from other sources), who held the title Giản Định (*Jian Ding*) Đế.[17] When Zhang Fu compiled a record of Trần descendants, Trần Ngỗi fled to Trường Yên, near the ancient capital of Hoa Lư, in present-day Ninh Bình district. There, at Mô Độ (now Yên Mô), on 1 November 1407, a man from Thiên Trường—the Trần heartland of Nam Định province—rallied an army and declared Trần Ngỗi, the next Trần king. By this time, the Hồ family and their officials had already been captured by the Ming forces and taken to Beijing.

The Ming army promptly attacked the new king's camp and forced him to flee to Nghệ An (*Yi-an*) later that year. The news of a crowned Trần king soon spread throughout the land, and from Hóa Châu, Đặng Tất (*Deng Xi*) killed the local Ming mandarin, gathered troops and joined Trần Ngỗi. He was granted the title of Imperial Duke (*Quốc Công*) and, together, they planned a military campaign to restore the Trần.[18] They were joined by other groups who were loyal to the Trần and had taken arms against the Ming army.

In early 1408, Zhang Fu and Mạc Thúy led an expedition force against Trần Ngỗi in Diễn Châu, Nghệ An and drove the Trần south to beyond Ngang Pass to Quảng Bình province. Zhang Fu appointed a local man to be the governor of Tân Bình (north of Hóa Châu) and returned to Đông Đô. However, Trần Ngỗi and Đặng Tất survived and consolidated their forces in Hóa Châu and marched north. They killed the newly appointed governor and, by the end of 1408, had assembled a formidable army drawn from the southern provinces. Marching from south to north, they gathered forces from Thuận Hóa, Tân Bình, Nghệ An, Diễn Châu, and Thanh Hóa as they advanced toward Đông

Đô, killing the collaborators, brushing aside the Ming apposition and gained wide support from the local leaders as they went.

Emperor Yongle became alarmed. He did not expect this. He was concerned that the revolt would spread and become uncontrollable if the rebels were not eliminated, so he ordered the deployment of 40,000 troops to be despatched from Yunnan and other provinces and the preparation of 20,000 naval troops. Mu Sheng, now taking on the 'General for Subduing the Yi' seal from Zhang Fu, led the additional deployment or, in contemporary language, a 'troop surge'. The emperor also offered Trần Ngỗi and his followers official positions, forgiveness and return of land if they abandoned the rebellion.[19]

The battle of Bô Cô

However, the emperor's offer was ignored, and in early 1409, the two armies met at a place called Bô Cô, which is around present-day Ý Yên district, in Nam Định province by the Đáy River, near Hoa Lư. According to SKTT, Mu Sheng had 50,000 men from Yunnan, while Trần Ngỗi and Đặng Tất came up from the south with an unknown number of troops. Đại Việt anchored their boats and built the palisades on the riverbanks, while the Ming battle formation was similar. However, the rising tide and strong winds favoured Đại Việt as their boats moved upstream. Trần Ngỗi beat the drums and urged the troops forward. The battle lasted for five hours, from the hour of the snake (11 am) to the monkey (4 pm), and Trần Khỗi emerged victorious.[20] The Ming army was routed. Mu Sheng escaped to Cổ Lộng (Cổ Động? near present-day Giáo Xứ Bình Cách), but other senior commanders, including the recently-appointed Assistant Commissioner-in-chief Lu Yi (*Lữ Nghị*) and Liu Yu (*Lưu Vũ*), the administration vice commissioner of Jiao-zhi, were killed. When surrounded, the Minister of War Liu Jun (*Lưu Tuấn*), took his own life. Ming shilu dates the entry of this event as 9 January 1409, whereas SKTT records it as 30 December 1408.[21]

Based on the duration of the battle and the number of senior Ming commanders killed, it must have been a major engagement. The Ming army had suffered the greatest defeat since the invasion two years earlier.

A strategic mistake

According to SKTT, Trần Ngỗi wanted to pursue Mu Sheng and continued to Đông Đô but Đặng Tất advised the king to mop up the last pockets of the Ming army first. The hesitancy in the Đại Việt camp about which course of action to take allowed the Ming troops stationed in Đông Đô to reach Cổ Lộng and rescue Mu Sheng. To give this military decision a perspective, the straight-line distance between Bô Cô, where the battle took place, to Cổ Lộng is about 15 kilometres. In contrast, Cổ Lộng to Đông Đô is about 70 kilometres. In other words, Đại Việt would have reached Cổ Lộng long before the Ming reinforcements came down from Đông Đô to rescue Mu Sheng, the Ming's commander-in-chief.

For the next two months, Đặng Tất dispatched messages to various prefectures to mobilise locals against the Ming and begin the siege of the Ming strongholds. Đại Việt had their main camp at the Hoàng Giang River (present-day Châu Giang River), approximately 35 kilometres north as the crow flies.

The delay may have been a misjudgement; however, at the Hoàng Giang River, Trần Ngỗi made a terrible self-inflicting mistake. An eunuch advised the king that Đặng Tất and his military advisor, Nguyễn Cảnh Chân, were able to appoint and fire officials, thus, wielding too much power and should be removed. Trần Ngỗi agreed. He summoned the two men and had Đặng Tất strangled.[22] Nguyễn Cảnh Chân attempted to escape but was seized and killed. In one incomprehensible act, two most senior and competent commanders of the Đại Việt army were eliminated by their own king.

Unsurprisingly, the sons of these two men, Đặng Dung and Nguyễn Cảnh Dị, became extremely angry, raised an army and marched north from Hóa Châu to Thanh Hóa, rallied behind another Trần descendant named Trần Quý Khoáng, took him to Nghệ An and proclaimed him king. On 2 April 1409, Trần Quý Khoáng (*Chen Ji-kuo*), a nephew of Trần Ngỗi, became a second Trần king with the title of Trùng Quang (*Chong-guang*) Đế in a ceremony held at Chi Lai (present-day Đức Thủy district) by the Cả (or Lam) River, in Hà Tĩnh province.

Meanwhile, Trần Ngỗi was still up north at Ngự Thiên (around present-day Hưng Hà, where the Trần ancestor's tombs are), fighting with the Ming army. Trần Quý Khoáng and his generals may have believed that Đại Việt should not have two Trần kings and decided to kidnap him. They completed the operation and transported Trần Ngỗi to Hà Tĩnh. When Trần Ngỗi arrived, the dark sky suddenly brightened up with *golden clouds*, the men took this as a good sign and made Trần Ngỗi the Senior King, as was customary in the Trần dynasty.[23]

A united front with two Trần kings
Now, the Đại Việt army had two kings. Đặng Dung and Nguyễn Cảnh Dị appeared to have set aside their desire to avenge their fathers' deaths, and the army was ready to take the fight to the Ming forces. However, the Ming

high command was not idle at this time. A month after the defeat in January 1409, Emperor Yongle sent Zhang Fu to Đại Việt to replace Mu Sheng as the commander-in-chief along with 47,000 troops.[24] Zhang Fu arrived, and in an entry of 5 July 1409 noted the presence of the two kings and Đại Việt had taken the control of the rivers. He needed a flotilla of boats if they wanted success and ordered his troops to move to Mount Chi-lan (*Chí Linh?*) to procure materials and build boats.[25] Chí Linh was the Đại Việt naval headquarter in the 13th century.[26]

By the middle of 1409, Đại Việt had recaptured most of the territories that the Ming army had taken two years earlier, from present-day Thừa Thiên-Huế to Thái Bình provinces, which broadly speaking, covers the land south of the Châu Giang and the Luộc Rivers. However, the invasion had caused terrible suffering for its people. Aside from losing the skilled and educated, thousands more died as a result of starvation and pandemic-related illness.[27]

1409 – ĐẠI VIỆT RETREATS

The arrival of Zhang Fu and the additional Ming troops shifted the balance of power. Zhang Fu was a brutal commander and applied terror indiscriminately. He also made promises of rewards for voluntary surrenderers and ensured the Ming army had secured food supplies. According to SKTT, wherever Fu went, there was a lot of killing with *corpses piled up into mountains*.[28] Ming shilu confirmed the practice, recording a large number of beheadings.[29] The Ming army had established several granaries to store rice, received additional supplies from Yunnan and the southern provinces by roads and by sea. They also grew food in the areas under their control and prohibited harvesting in regions in the south. On the other hand, Đại Việt army was slowly running out of food and had to revert to raids and put their soldiers to the paddy fields to gather rice.[30] However, they had support from locals and several rebellions broke out in areas under the Ming control.

Two locations of strategic importance to both sides were Hàm Tử Pass and Bình Than (*Pan-tan*). The former is by the Red River, and Đặng Dung was holding it, blocking the Ming army from reaching the coast. The latter is near Mount Chí Linh. If Đại Việt secured it, they would stop the supplies from getting to the Ming army by sea and preventing them from travelling to the coast. In September 1409, Đại Việt attacked Bình Than, killing the Ming general defending the camp and burning many boats but was not able to hold it. Later in the same month, the Ming forces, led by Zhang Fu, Zhu Guang and Fang Zheng (*Phương Chính*) defeated Đại Việt at Hàm Tử Pass.[31]

Slowly, the Ming pushed Đặng Dung and his men out of the Red River Delta, and by early November, Zhang Fu was able to reach Thanh Hóa. In December, they captured Trần Ngỗi near Thiên Quan (*Tian-guan*), near today's Nho Quan, north of Tây Đô, and sent him to Kim Lăng (*Yên Lăng*, Beijing).[32] The capture of a Trần senior king was a major blow to Đại Việt. The prospect of expelling the Ming forces and restoring the Trần dynasty had become increasingly unlikely.

1410 – A STALEMATE

Both sides appeared to settle in for a quiet winter in 1409/10. In early February 1410, the emperor ordered Zhang Fu and his senior commanders and the 'surge' troops to return to Beijing. However, Zhang Fu explained that while he would return with some forces, the threat from Đại Việt remained and he asked most of the 'surge' troops be left behind under the command of Mu Sheng. According to Zhang Fu, Trần Quý Khoáng, the Trần king, and his commander, Đặng Dung, were in Diễn Châu, Nghệ An pressing Thanh Hóa, while another commander blocked the river port of Thần Phù (entrance to the Đáy River). Zhang Fu was concerned that the Ming army's successes since September 1409 would be reversed if Mu Sheng did not have enough troops.

The two sides fought several battles in the second half of 1410 around northern Thanh Hóa without any decisive victories from either side. While Ming shilu records several Ming victories, it also notes a defeat against Đặng Dung.[33]

1411 – THE TIDE TURNS

In January 1411, Đại Việt adjusted its strategy. Trần Quý Khoáng sent an envoy to the Ming court, offering to surrender. Emperor Yongle accepted the offer and appointed Trần Quý Khoáng as *provincial administration commissioner in Jiaozhi*. He also appointed Đặng Dung and other senior Đại Việt commanders as commissioners.[34] However, three weeks later, he sent Zhang Fu to join Mu Sheng and lead an additional force of 24,000 troops into Đại Việt.[35] In March, the emperor also dispatched imperial orders to Jiaozhi, extending pardon to all rebels until 18 March 1411, a three-year suspension of taxes, except for grain tax, and lifting the prohibition of gold, silver, copper and iron trades for the next three years.[36] It was a classic 'stick and carrot' strategy.

Emperor Yongle wanted to end the war and bring his troops home. However, his commander on the ground had different ideas. Zhang Fu did not trust the surrender offer and, in May, requested more troops to finish Trần Quý Khoáng and his forces on the battlefields. The decisive battle came in August at the Yue-chang River, in Jiu-zhen (*Cửu Chân*) subprefecture (likely to be the present-day Yên River in the Nghi Sơn district, south of Thanh Hóa City). According to Ming shilu, Zhang Fu arrived in boats and found that Đại Việt had erected stakes in the river for over 40 zhang (approximately 125 m) and palisades on both sides of the river mouth, stretching for 2 to 3 *li* (0.9 to 1.35 kilometres). In the river, Đại Việt had deployed 300 ships and had troops hidden on the hills to the right. It was a setup for an ambush.

However, it appears that Đại Việt was unaware of an infantry column led by Mu Sheng marching down from the north. Đặng Dung and his men were focusing on the river and left their backs exposed. Zhang Fu directed his boats to move forward and remove the stakes, while he led the infantry to attack the concealed troops on land. They broke down the palisades and drove Đại Việt troops to the river bank. In effect, the ambush backfired, and Đại Việt forces were caught in a pincer movement by the Ming army from the river and the land.

It was a devastating defeat for Đại Việt. Several senior commanders were captured alive, 400 heads were taken, and many soldiers drowned. Đặng Dung managed to escape, but he left his seal behind, suggesting the battle ended swiftly as the Ming army caught Đại Việt forces by surprise.[37]

Despite the loss, Đại Việt continued to resist the Ming occupation in other places, including cutting the floating bridge and blocking the road to the east of Đông Đô, in the north, near Từ Liêm (*Ci-lian*), while Zhang Fu and his main forces were in the south. The Ming army were able to suppress these activities, but the fighting suggests that Jiao-zhi was far from pacified. By the end of November 1411, the emperor was so frustrated that he sought an explanation for Zhang Fu's failure to report on progress and to rest the men when the resistance in Jiao-zhi was allegedly waning.[38]

1412 – THE WAR CONTINUES

The Ming army was gradually gaining ground as the war went on in 1412. At the end of 1411, there was a shortage of grain, but they were able to secure their supply channel and ship 10,000 shi (about 800 tonnes) of rice from southern China. In the meantime, Đại Việt persisted in raiding the northern Thanh Hóa coast and further north, in part to look for supplies and in part to probe the Ming defence's weak points.[39] Ming shilu documents a battle in the Shen-tou (*Thần Phù*, north of modern-day Sầm Sơn) on 6 September 1412. It was a brutal battle, and even taken into account the language's propaganda tone, the text paints a vivid picture of the war at the time.

> *Over 400 of the bandits' [Đại Việt] ships came out into the Shen-tou Sea and divided into three groups. At that time, there was a northerly wind blowing and [Zhang] Fu commanded the troops to directly attack the main force. The bandits were very spirited, but the government [Ming] troops bravely pushed ahead and locked ships with them. They fought with swords and lances and firearms (火器) were discharged in rapid succession. The bandits could not withstand this and immediately fled in their ships. The government troops pursued and caught up with them. Using grappling hooks, they drew the bandit ships to their own and engaged in mortal battle. Between the mao period (5-7 a.m.) and the si period (9-11 a.m.), the bandits were greatly defeated.*[40]

The text confirmed Zhang Fu's determination to extinguish Đại Việt resistance (he could have let them escape), and his method of using overwhelming forces (discharge of firearms rapidly).

By the end of 1412, the Ming forces had Thanh Hóa and the northern provinces under control. They now reached the Wu (*Cả*) River and attacked Đại Việt bases in Nghệ An, where a Đại Việt commissioner, Pan Ji-you (*Phan Quý Hữu*) and his son Liao (*Liễu*) surrendered to Zhang Fu.[41] According to SKTT, Zhang Fu was delighted. Ji-you died soon after, but his son told Zhang Fu details of the Đại Việt army and the terrain further south. Based on this information, Zhang Fu decided to attack Hóa Châu.[42]

1413 AND 1414 – THE LAST BATTLES AND THE END OF RESISTANCE

1413 was a quiet year based on the entries from Ming shilu. However, sometime in late 1413, Zhang Fu and his men crossed the Ngang Pass into the former land of Champa. In February 1414, they reached Zheng-ping (*Chính Bình*, or today's Quảng Trạch, Bố Trạch district around the Gianh River in Quảng Bình province) subprefecture. They chased Đặng Dung and his men to some hills in the west and attacked, and a fierce battle followed. Đặng Dung was injured, captured and the Ming troops decapitated him. His head was sent with his brothers to Beijing, where the brothers were later beheaded.[43] The grim severed heads provided the evidence to the court that Zhang Fu had completed his task.

A few days later, the Ming troops captured Nguyễn Súy (*Ruan Shuai*) (in Nan-ling (Nam Linh, today's Gio Linh in northern Quảng Trị province) and his family. Back in August 1408, Zhang Fu had named Nguyễn Súy as one of the four leaders of Đại Việt, aside from Đặng Dung and the two Trần kings.[44] Nearly six years later, three out four had been killed or captured and only the last Trần king, Trần Quý Khoáng, was still free. However, in March 1414, Trần Quý Khoáng was captured in Ai Lao and sent to Beijing with Nguyễn Súy. They arrived in August and were executed. The resistance was over.[45]

In October 1414, Zhang Fu and Mu Sheng left 5,000 imperial troops to defend Jiao-zhi, and led the remaining troops home, arriving on 25 March 1415.[46]

BECOMING SERVANTS

SKTT also documents events occurring during the last two Trần kings, from 1407 to 1414. Generally, some of its accounts are similar to those described in Ming shilu, however, several are not. To complete the picture of this important period of Vietnamese history, I have included some of the key stories as follows.

By 1412, based on Ming shilu, the Ming army controlled most of Đại Việt territory north of Thanh Hóa. Still, a rebellion in Lạng Sơn near the northern border threatened the supply route. The Ming commanders sent the collaborator Mạc Thúy to fight, but a poisoned arrow killed him.[47]

Around April of 1413, Trần Quý Khoáng was in Nghệ An. He had lost 60 to 70 per cent of his soldiers, so he then retreated to Hóa Châu, presumably to the Hóa Châu citadel, which Champa first built. Today, signs of the citadel ramparts and moats can be seen, as discussed in Volume 3B.

From Hóa Châu, Trần Quý Khoáng sent an envoy, Nguyễn Biểu, to Zhang Fu, in Nghệ An with gifts seeking a title. Zhang Fu kept the envoy who became indignant and told Fu that *Internally,* [you] *plan to attack and conquer. Externally,* [you] *claim to be noble, benevolent and righteous.* [You] *promised to establish descendants of the Trần family and then established prefectures and counties. Not only did* [you] *plunder wealth and treasure, but* [you] *also ruined and harmed the people.* [You] *are truly a ferocious enemy.*[48]

Zhang Fu got angry and killed the envoy. Later, in the middle of 1413, Zhang Fu met with Mu Sheng and other generals to plan an attack on Hóa Châu. Sheng suggested that it would not be easy to do that as the mountain there is high, and the sea is vast, but Zhang Fu was determined. He told the assembly *I can live because of Hóa Châu; even if I become a ghost, it would also be because of Hóa Châu. If Hóa Châu has not been taken yet, how can face my lord* [the emperor]*!*

Zhang Fu led a naval force south, taking 21 days to reach Thuận Hóa. In the ninth lunar month (around October), they engaged the Đại Việt forces, led by Nguyễn Súy and Đặng Dung, at the Sái Già Canal (also known as the Ái Tử River in Quảng Bình province). The battle initially ended without a decisive victor. That night, Đặng Dung launched a surprise attack on Zhang Fu's camp. He boarded Zhang Fu's boat, intending to capture him alive, but failed to identify the Ming commander, who escaped in a small boat. Although Đại Việt burned most of the Ming fleet, Nguyễn Súy refused to participate in the battle. Realizing that Đặng Dung's forces were small, Zhang Fu regrouped, counterattacked, scattered Đặng Dung's troops, and forced them to retreat into the mountains and groves.[49]

Two months later, Đặng Dung and Nguyễn Súy were captured. Trần Quý Khoáng fled to Ai Lao but was also seized by the Ming troops. In the summer of the following year, around May 1414, the Ming army transported the three men to Đông Đô and then to Yên Kinh (modern-day Beijing). During the journey, Trần Quý Khoáng ended his life by leaping into the water. Nguyễn Súy, meanwhile, befriended one of the guards and often played chess with him. One day, during a game, Nguyễn Súy used the chessboard to push the guard into the water, drowning him. He then followed suit, taking his own life by jumping in and drowning as well.

As for the members of the last court of the Trần king, most fled to Ai Lao or Champa with their families. From that time, SKTT comments that *all the people of Đại Việt became servants [thần thiếp] of the Ming occupiers.*[50]

Đặng Dung and his father, Đặng Tất, played a significant role in the resistance against the Ming forces. A poem attributed to Đặng Dung is still studied today in Vietnamese schools. It is a poignant poem and I have translated it as follows.[51]

> **Feelings in Remembrance** (*Cảm Hoài*)
> *Life's affairs grow tangled as old age nears,*
> *The boundless world feels like one drunken dream.*
> *Even the lowly rise when fortune smiles,*
> *While stumbled—the heroes have to swallow much bitterness.*
> *I longed to shoulder Earth to aid my lord,*
> *I longed to cleanse my weapons but there was no route to the river in the sky,*
> *The country's revenge has not yet been fulfilled, and already my hair has turned grey before its time,*
> *I have sharpened the precious sword many times under the shadow of the moon.*

The poem expresses a moving sentiment, but I am unsure if Đặng Dung wrote it. Since he and his father fought in the war against the Ming army, he was likely a young man in his 20s or 30s when he was captured and eventually executed. The tone and reflections in the poem seem more fitting for an older man, someone who may have survived the war and had the time to look back in contemplation.

4.2 - The Ming occupation, 1414–1417

AN ANALYSIS OF FAILURES OF THE HỒ DYNASTY AND THE RESISTANCE

The Ming army crossed the border into Đại Việt in November 1406, and within about 7 months, they captured the Hồ family, ending Đại Việt's independence and incorporating it into imperial territory. However, despite the emperor's proclamation of the country's pacification in July 1407, Zhang Fu, Mu Sheng and their soldiers spent the next six years fighting the resistance. It not until 1414, with the capture of the last Trần king, that the Ming forces were able to secure relative peace in the region.

Why did the Hồ dynasty collapse quickly while the resistance persisted for years? The primary reason lies in the Hồ family's lack of broad support from the Vietnamese population. The Trần dynasty had ruled Đại Việt for over 170 years, embedding its legitimacy in the eyes of the people. In contrast, Hồ Quý Ly failed to provide a convincing justification for his seizure of power and the transfer of authority to himself and his sons, leaving the new regime without the legitimacy to unify and rally the kingdom against the Ming invaders.

Despite their lack of legitimacy, given time, the Hồ family might have been able to build up greater support from regions north of their base in Thanh Hóa before the Ming army invaded. In the event, these regions quickly capitulated. To make matters worse, the Hồ family's introduction of unpopular policies—such as the use of paper money and the reduction in landownership size—alienated the population and those still loyal to the Trần dynasty, further undermining their ability to organise the fight against the Ming forces.

On the other hand, the resistance lasted longer for the opposite reason—it was led by the descendants of the Trần kings, which granted it legitimacy. Later Vietnamese historians recognised these men as the kings of the Later Trần (*Hậu Trần*) dynasty (1407–1413), even though they did not govern Đại Việt from Thăng Long as their forefathers had. During this time, Thăng Long was under the Ming occupation. The legitimacy was of such importance that Ngô Sĩ Liên, a 15th-century historian, suggested that the Hồ family deserved to die, even at the hands of the Ming soldiers.

> *The Hồ family killed Trần Thuận Tông [Trần Ngung] to seize the country; people like Trần Hãng and Trần Khát Chân tried to kill them but could not...* [The Hồ family] *believed that no one in the country would dare to try again. But anyone could have killed these deranged usurpers, and heaven would not forgo their punishment for even a single day under its gaze! If people in the country could not kill them, people from neighbouring countries could kill them. If people from neighbouring countries could not kill them, people from Di and Địch [barbarians] could kill them. That's why the Ming people were able to kill them.*

Even though the Ming forces effectively controlled Đại Việt from 1407, Vietnamese historians traditionally mark the start of Ming rule in 1414. This period lasted until 1418, when a man from Thanh Hóa province, named Lê Lợi, raised his banner of rebellion. Over the next decade, Lê Lợi successfully expelled the Ming occupiers, culminating in their defeat in 1427. He subsequently established the Later Lê (*Hậu Lê*) dynasty, which lasted in two phases: the Early or Initial Lê (*Lê Sơ*) dynasty (1428–1527) and the Restored or Revival Lê (*Lê Trung Hưng*) period (1533–1789) as mentioned earlier.

While the Later Trần kings had legitimacy and the support of many local leaders, they ultimately failed to drive out the Ming forces The main cause was their lack of a strong logistical foundation compared to the Ming army. While Đại Việt troops often had to scavenge and raid for food, the Ming army had granaries and a secured supply line from southern China. The situation worsened when the Ming army drove the Later Trần kings forces out of the Red River Delta, the most agriculturally productive region of Đại Việt at the time. Despite their bravery and occasional victories—defeating Mu Sheng and killing several senior Ming commanders—they could not overcome Zhang Fu. The latter's use of terror tactics, overwhelming forces, and substantial rewards for collaborators eventually prevailed.

THE MING COLONISATION POLICY

The process that the Ming court followed during the invasion of Đại Việt can be briefly summarised as follows:

a) Justify the invasion (cited 20 alleged crimes committed by the Hồ family, including claims of illegitimacy),

b) Defeat the resistance of Đại Việt and overthrowing its rulers (the Hồ family),

c) Install a puppet regime (restored the Trần dynasty under Ming control, though this step was merely a pretence, as the Ming court intended direct rule from the outset),

d) Establish a civilian government supported by a strong military presence (created military and civil commissions, established guards, and set up police offices),

e) Extract wealth from Đại Việt (setup granaries, tax offices, gold and silver mines, Salt Distribution Supervisorate, Maritime Trade Supervisorate),

f) Recruit and train local officials to administer local offices (identified and trained young and ambitious individuals in Beijing to ensure loyalty to the Ming emperor),

g) Implement Sinicisation policies (opened schools, built shrines and promoted Ming religious and cultural practices to assimilate the population),

h) Construct infrastructure (built bridges and roads to facilitate movements of goods and troops).

The Ming court aimed to fully integrate Đại Việt into its imperial system, effectively ending its existence as an independent state. Under the Ming dynasty, Đại Việt was renamed Jiao-zhi and governed by a commissioner based in Đông Quan. Beginning in July 1407, the Ming administrators established 15 prefectures (*phủ*), largely based on the administrative divisions of the Hồ and Trần dynasties. Each prefecture consisted of several subprefectures (*châu*), which in turn oversaw multiple counties or districts *(huyện)*, totalling 44 subprefectures across the region as shown in Appendix 1.

The numbers and names of administrative units changed as the Ming forces tightened their control over Đại Việt. A notable record from 1417, found in a 17th-century Chinese work, *An Nam Chí Nguyên* (Annan Zhiyuan, Original Record of Annam or Annam Chronicles, abbreviated as ANCN), provides data on the population and households in the country. According to the record, Đại Việt had 162,558 households and 450,288 people spread across 15 prefectures and five subprefectures. The majority of the population, approximately 81 per cent, resided north of present-day Thanh Hóa province. Thanh Hóa and Nghệ An prefectures accounted for 17 per cent, while the two southernmost prefectures, located between the Hải Vân and Ngang Passes—formerly part of Champa territory—contained only 2 per cent of the population. The land between these two passes has historically been sparsely populated, which may explain why the Chế Mân was willing to offer part of it as a wedding gift as mentioned earlier.

Given that the figure of 450,288 people is significantly lower than the earlier estimate of 5 million, it is reasonable to assume that the record is incomplete. It likely omits data from several subprefectures and excludes certain populations, such as tribal communities, children, and older people. These gaps suggest that the record provides only a partial snapshot of Đại Việt's total population at the time. The other explanation is that 5 million is an overestimation.

The six-year resistance that followed the capture of the Hồ family slowed the Ming administrators implementation of their policy, but from 1414, once the last Trần kings were killed, the Ming officials applied the direct rule more vigorously. Three years earlier, in 1411, Liu Ben, the administration commissioner in Jiao-zhi submitted a memorial advising the Ming officials should *bestow grace in order to pacify people's hearts*. He warned if changes were applied too quickly, the locals would likely join the rebellion. He also recommended that the Ming court should *select experienced, honest and careful people* to govern the people. He pointed out that quite a few of the Jiao-zhi people were literate and more schools should be established so that *the young men will become familiar with China's propriety and righteousness and will change their 'yi'* [barbaric] *ways*.[52]

The emperor approved Liu Ben's recommendations, and in 1416, the Ming administrators established 92 Confucian schools, 46 Yin-yang schools, 48 Medical schools, 75 Buddhist registries and 58 Daoist registries in Jiao-zhi. However, it appears that they did not build any of these institutions in the southern prefectures, including Nghệ An, Tân Bình and Thuận Hóa.[53]

As a footnote, the Confucian schools most likely focused on teaching the Confucian philosophy's Four Books and Five Classics.[54] On the other hand, the Yin-yang schools, also known as the School of Naturalists, would teach the concepts of yin (dark, cold, female, negative) and yang (light, hot, male, positive) and the Five Elements (water, fire, wood, metal, and earth).

Around 1419, the Ming court distributed books for use in schools across all prefectures, subprefectures, and counties. They also dispatched Buddhist monks to propagate Buddhist scriptures. They also confiscated all historical records and chronicles from the Trần dynasty and earlier, sending them to Kim Lăng (present-day Nanjing). The Ming occupiers took at least 33 titles comprising 94 volumes, some dating back to the Lý dynasty in the 11th century. They were never seen again.[55]

While Ming officials like Liu Ben saw their actions as bringing 'civilisation' to the 'barbaric' inhabitants of Jiao-zhi, the people of Đại Việt viewed the situation very differently, as exemplified by envoy Nguyễn Biểu's defiant words to Zhang Fu cited earlier. According to SKTT, in 1414, the Ming administrators ordered the construction of several cultural and religious structures, including the Temple of Literature (*Văn Miếu*, dedicated to Confucius), shrines to worship the gods of land and agriculture (*xã tắc*), and *the gods of wind, the gods of clouds, the gods of mountains, the gods of rivers, and other gods that no one prayed to for regular worship*.[56] The Ming officials also imposed cultural assimilation policies: boys and girls were forbidden from cutting their hair, and women were required to adopt northern customs by wearing short shirts and long pants.[57]

The ineffectiveness of the Confucian schools is evident in a memorial submitted by the Jiao-zhi Provincial Administration Commission a decade later, which requested that the Ming court appoint teachers and send them from China:

> *Since the Confucian schools were first established in the various prefectures, subprefectures and counties in the 13th year of the Yong-le reign (1415/16), no appointments have been made by the Court, and the teachers are mainly native people. Only a few of the instructors are familiar with the classics and very few of the students know how to read. Also, their language is coarse and their actions rude and, even those who have studied have not become versed in Chinese ways.*[58]

In fact, after a decade of education, in 1425, only 82 students, selected from various Confucian schools in Đại Việt, arrived in Beijing for further education.[59]

Similarly, in practice, local officials often circumvented Ming policies for personal gain. When Zhang Fu ordered servants and women who had fled to other counties to be brought to the army, local officials instead seized poor individuals and sent them instead. Similarly, when the Ming required the declaration of rice paddies and mulberry fields, they instituted a rule that any household with one *mẫu* (*mu* or 畝, approximately 614 to 667 m²) of land had to register it as three *mẫu*, thereby tripling the tax burden on those households.

From 1415, the Ming intensified their exploitation of Đại Việt resources by seizing control of gold and silver mines, hunting white elephants, searching for pearls, and imposing heavy taxes. These measures left the local population devastated. The Ming officials also established a strict monopoly on salt production and trade. Private salt trade was prohibited, and all salt had to be delivered to government-controlled stores. Merchants could only purchase salt from these stores if they possessed official papers issued by the government, allowing them to sell it on the market. Any salt trade without these papers was deemed smuggling. Additionally, travellers could only carry three bowls of rice and one bottle of fish sauce.[60]

The Ming occupation and practices would have continued for decades, but for the uprising by Lê Lợi in 1418, which will be covered in the next chapter.

RELATIONSHIP WITH CHAMPA IN THE EARLY 15TH CENTURY

After the last Trần king was captured in March 1414, the Ming army continued south and occupied the territories that Đại Việt had previously taken from Champa. However, instead of returning these lands to the Chams, Zhang Fu decided to establish four subprefectures—Sheng, Hua, Si and Yi—placing them under the jurisdiction of Sheng-hua (*Thuận Hóa*) prefecture in Jiao-zhi.[61] This arrangement essentially followed the policies instituted by the Hồ court. Understandably, Champa was upset. In 1415, the king of Champa, Zhan-ba Di-lai, launched multiple attacks against Sheng-hua prefectures. The Ming's Minister of War wanted to send troops to punish him, but the emperor disagreed. Instead, he dispatched an envoy with a stern warning to Zhan-ba Di-lai, *do not return the territory you have invaded, the occurrences in Annam can serve as a warning as to what will happen to you!*[62]

The warning may have worked, as the following year, Zhan-ba Di-lai offered tribute of elephants, rhinoceros and other products and admitted guilt.[63] However, two years later, in 1417, Champa attacked Thuận Hóa again but after this incident, the king may have decided to accept the Ming's rule.[64] He sent his grandson and nephew as envoys to the court of Ming, presenting various tributes regularly until he died in 1441.

CHAPTER 5

LÊ LỢI, A NATIONAL HERO AND THE LIBERATION OF ĐẠI VIỆT

A timeline

YEARS	NOTABLE EVENTS
1385	Lê Lợi's birth.
Nov-Dec 1406	Ming forces invaded Đại Việt.
June 1407	Ming forces captured the Hồ family and ended Đại Việt's sovereignty.
1407–1414	Resistance to the Ming occupation by the descendants of the Trần kings.
March 1414	Ming forces captured the last Trần king.
1414–1417	Ming forces fully controlled Đại Việt.
1418	Lê Lợi raised the banner of rebellion at the foot of the mountain west of Thanh Hóa.

The struggling years (1418–1423)	1418: Ming forces captured Lê Lợi's family, and he fled to Mount Chí Linh. 1419: Ming forces captured and likely executed Lê Lai, who disguised as Lê Lợi. 1423: Ming and Laotian forces coordinated an assault on Lê Lợi. He escaped to Mount Chí Linh again. 1423: Under severe pressure, Lê Lợi made a temporary peace with the Ming commanders to recover and rebuild.
The southern campaigns; regaining southern territories (1424–1425)	October 1424: Lê Lợi's forces marched east and captured Đa Căng. They continued south and took the Trà Long subprefecture. Winter 1424/1425: Lê Lợi's forces defeated the Ming forces at Khả Lưu Pass. February 1425: Lê Lợi arrived and began the siege of Nghệ An Fort. 1425: Some of Lê Lợi's forces continued further south and captured other Ming strongholds in today's central Vietnam.
The northern campaigns and final victory (1426–1428)	1425-1426: Lê Lợi's forces marched north to attack Đông Quan and other Ming forts. Feb 1426: Nghệ An fort surrendered. Oct 1426: Wang Tong, Ming's new Commander-in-Chief, arrived in Đông Quan and began a series of operations against Lê Lợi. Nov 1426: Lê Lợi's forces defeated the Ming forces at the battle of Tốt Động/ Ninh bridge. Dec/Jan 1427: Wang Tong retreated to Đông Quan, and sought a cease-fire while waiting for reinforcements. 1427: Lê Lợi's forces besieged Đông Quan while methodically captured the remaining Ming forts. Oct/Nov 1427: Lê Lợi's forces annihilated the Ming reinforcements from Guangxi and expelled the other reinforcements from Yunnan. Nov/Dec 1427: Wang Tong surrendered to Lê Lợi. Tây Đô fort (or the Hồ Citadel) surrendered. Jan 1428: Wang Tong and all Ming forces in Đại Việt returned to China. Ming's occupation of Đại Việt was over.
1428	Lê Lợi founded the Later Lê dynasty.
1434	Lê Lợi passed away.

Table 5-1: The timeline of Lê Lợi's liberation campaign.

5.1 - *Lê Lợi (1385–1433), a national hero*

THE POLITICAL SETTINGS

By the end of 1416, the Ming commanders, Mu Sheng and Zhang Fu, along with most of their troops, had returned to China. In early 1417, a new regional commander, Li Bin (*Lý Bân*), took on the seal of 'General for Subduing the Yi' and the post of regional commander to once again attempt to subdue Đại Việt. Even after a decade, Đại Việt remained unpacified. In his instructions to Li Bin, Emperor Yongle conveyed his deep concern, *I am worried about the pacification and concern myself about it day and night*. To ensure that Li Bin had the support he needed, the emperor also ordered Minister of War Chen Qia (*Trần Kiều (Hiệp)*) to accompany him and, in all likelihood, to provide a back channel report to the emperor.[1]

The emperor's concern soon materialised when Li Bin faced two rebellions shortly after his arrival. One uprising occurred in Lục Ngạn (*Lu-na*) county, in the Lang River subprefecture (present-day Hải Dương, Bắc Ninh), in the north of the country, while the other erupted in Thuận (*Shun*) Châu subprefecture near the southern border.[2] Li Bin was able to suppress both revolts and dealt with an attack from Champa later that same year. However, the new year brought a more significant threat. This time, the man who led the rebellion, Lê Lợi (*Li Li*), was to eventually end the Ming occupation of Đại Việt.

In his memorial to the emperor, Li Bin advised that Lê Lợi, a native police officer of Nga Lạc (*E-le*) county, in Thanh Hóa prefecture, had rebelled and adopted the title 'Ping-ding King (*Bình Định Vương*), meaning Pacification King)'. Li Bin dispatched his commander-in-chief, Zhu Guang, to suppress the revolt. Zhu Quang succeeded in capturing 100 and beheading 60, but Lê Lợi escaped. The entry in Ming shilu documenting this rebellion was similar to other records of rebellions in Đại Việt and did not cause undue alarm in the court of Ming. According to Li Bin, Lê Lợi had previously followed Trần Quý Khoáng's rebellion and had been appointed as a Jin-wu General—General of the Guards—but later worked for the Ming administration. Vietnamese historians have rejected this account, noting that no Vietnamese history texts corroborate such a claim.[3] The date of the entry was the 3rd day of the 1st lunar month (8 February) of 1418.[4]

Zhu Guang was an experienced commander who actively participated in the 1406 invasion, the capture of Hồ Quý Ly in 1407 and Trần Khối, when the latter came through Cự Lặc in 1409. According to historian Đào Duy Anh, Cự Lặc corresponds to Ngọc Lặc, located not far from Nga Lạc where Lê Lợi was based.[5] Therefore, Trần Khối and Lê Lợi may have crossed paths or, at the very least, were familiar with each other's reputation. Lê Lợi might have participated in the resistance, but was unlikely to be active. No records indicating that he moved out of his home base before 1418. As for claims that he worked as a police officer, it would be unlikely as his family was wealthy, and he had an estate to manage. According to contemporary records, his forefathers were local chiefs and he was a *phụ đạo* (chief) of the village of Khả Lam (*Ke-lan*, Lam Sơn).[6] Even if he did collaborate with the Ming officials in some capacity, it would likely have been a strategic move to keep them at bay and learn about their operations at the same time.

THE HISTORICAL AND PHYSICAL SETTINGS OF THANH HÓA

Thanh Hóa is a province rich in historical sites. Up to this point in our story, it has produced many prominent Vietnamese, including Lady Triệu in the 3rd century, Dương Đình Nghệ and Ngô Quyền in the 9th and 10th centuries, Lê Đại Hành in the 10th century, Lê Văn Hưu in the 13th century, and, of course Hồ Quý Ly in the 14th century.

It is an ancient land shaped by two branches of the Chu and the Nam Mã (also known as Mã) Rivers that flow into the sea at the Lạch Hối estuary. Numerous pre-historic bronze drums were found here, and the provincial museum holds the most extensive collection of these artefacts in Vietnam. Previous volumes of this book series tell the stories associated with these historical sites.

The Mã River Delta creates a rich and fertile agricultural land, which could explain why Thanh Hóa has the third-largest population after Hanoi and Ho Chi Minh City.[7] The rivers also provide access to northern Laos and a staging area for the most direct road access to Hanoi from the south. Until the advent of large ships and planes became available, controlling Thanh Hóa was crucial for dominating the southern lands.

Ming shilu mentioned Nga Lạc, where Lê Lợi resided. In the present setting, it is located somewhere along the Chu River, about 40 kilometres in a straight line in the west-northwest direction from Thanh Hóa City.[8] The location is near the edge of the Trường Sơn mountain range and, on the modern map, is close to the intersection of Highway QL47C, which follows the Chu River, and Highway QL16, which leads to northern Laos. Nearby is the Historic Complex of Lam Kinh, along with the tombs of Lê Lợi and the subsequent Lê kings. Visitors can spend a day exploring the complex, strolling through its ground, and enjoying the beautiful scenery of this 15th-century historic site, which is shown in Figure 5-1. I will discuss this site in Section 6-10 of the next chapter.

LÊ LỢI, A NATIONAL HERO AND THE LIBERATION OF ĐẠI VIỆT   117

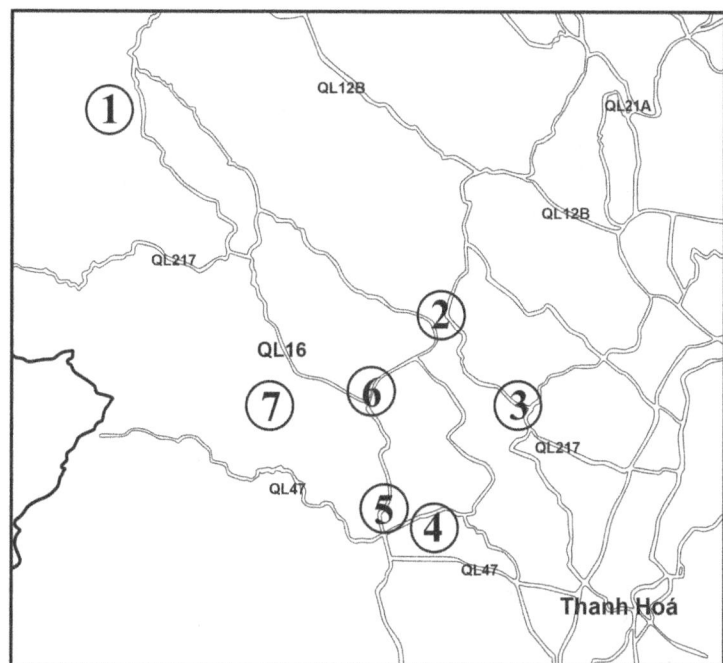

Figure 5-1: Map of historic Lam Kinh and other locations related to Lê Lợi's early years of the uprising.

Key: 1. Quan Hóa; 2. Cẩm Thủy; 3. Hồ Citadel (Tây Đô); 4. Thọ Xuân; 5. Historic Lam Kinh; 6. Ngọc Lặc; 7. Giao An (Mount Chí Linh?).

We know much about Lê Lợi, thanks to his counsellor, Nguyễn Trãi, who documented his life and deeds in records that have survived to this day. One such record is inscribed on the Vĩnh Lăng stele, shown in Figures 5.2, 5.3 and 5.4, located at the Historic Complex of Lam Kinh.[9] Nguyễn Trãi composed this inscription in 1433, shortly after Lê Lợi's death and burial at the site.[10]

THE VĨNH LĂNG STELE

The text inscribed on the stele consists of two parts. From the first part we learn that Lê Lợi passed away on 5 October 1433, and was buried nearly two months later, on 4 December 1433.[11] His death occurred in Đông Đô, while his burial took place at Lam Kinh, over 160 kilometres to the south. This distance likely accounts for the delay between his death and burial.

This part also reveals that his great-grandfather, Lê Hối, moved to Lam Sơn, a county south of the Vĩnh Lăng stele's location. He *observed a flock of birds flying near the foot of Lam Sơn, resembling a crowd of people gathering, so he knew this was a good land. On that occasion, he returned home and brought his* *whole family to settle there.*¹² Within three years, he cleared the land, prospered and grew his household with many children, grandchildren and servants. He was eventually appointed as the chief of the locality.

Lê Lợi's grandfather, Lê Đinh, inherited the family estate and expanded the enterprise to over 1,000 people. His paternal grandmother, a Nguyễn woman, had two sons. The younger son, Lê Khoáng, was Lê Lợi's father and his mother was Trịnh Thương.¹³ Lê Lợi, the youngest in the family, inherited the family fortune after his eldest brother, who had originally taken over, died young. Lê Lợi looked after the estate carefully and continued with agricultural activities but took time to study strategy.

The second part of the stele summarised Lê Lợi's campaign against the Ming army, which began in 1418 at Lạc Thủy station and ended in 1426 with his major victory at Tốt Động. This victory was followed by the siege of Đông Đô and his decisive defeat of the Ming reinforcements from China in 1427, culminating in the surrender of the Ming commander and his entire forces and personnel in Đại Việt in the final days of 1427. Before achieving these victories, in more than ten battles, Lê Lợi had engaged *ambush troops, attacked unexpectedly, avoided fortified places, attacked weak ones, employed less to fight more, and leveraged weaker positions to overcome stronger ones.* Lạc Thủy, where Lê Lợi's first camp was, is likely to be at present-day Ngọc Lặc, some 25 kilometres north of the Historic Complex of Lam Kinh.¹⁴

In contemporary setting, the region where Lê Lợi's family settled has a large population of the Mường people, who is the third the largest ethnic minority group in Vietnam, with an estimated population of 1.45 million.¹⁵ This has led to some speculations that perhaps Lê Lợi had some Mường ethic connections but that is yet to be proven.

The stele does not mention Lê Lợi's birthdate, but later records confirm he was born on the sixth day of the 8th lunar month (10 September) in 1385. This date means he was 21 when the Ming army invaded Đại Việt, 31 when he raised his banner, and spent nine arduous years liberating Đại Việt. He went on to establish the longest-lasting dynasty in Vietnamese history, which endure for over 350 years. He ruled for only five years and was 49 years old at the time of his passing.

For the remainder of this chapter, I will recount the incredible story of this remarkable man and his people—a journey marked by trials and tribulations. From their humble beginnings on the foot of a remote mountain, they rose to stand at the gates of Đông Đô, witnessing the final surrender of the Ming commanders, their soldiers, and their families as they departed for Imperial China nearly a decade later.

Figure 5-2: Vĩnh Lăng stele, Lam Kinh, Thanh Hóa, 1433, stone, H. 2.79 m, W. 1.94 m, D. 0.27 m.

Figure 5-3: The turtle base of the Vĩnh Lăng stele.

The dragon at the apex of the stele in Figure 5-2 represents the king, the son of heaven, as symbolled by the circle (the sun or heaven) within a square (the land or earth).[16]

Figure 5-4: Details of the dragons around the perimeter of the Vĩnh Lăng stele.

There are 18 dragons as shown in Figure 5-4 in total: six on each vertical edge and six at the top curved edge. The dragons are enclosed in half of the sacred fig (Ficus religiosa, also known as the bodhi tree)) leaves. Chrysanthemums fill the gaps between the leaves. These curled dragon dragons are typical of the Lý dynasty (1009–1226) design.

5.2 - Nguyễn Trãi (1380–1442), a scholar, a poet and a state counsellor

While Lê Lợi was the man who led the uprising that expelled the Ming occupiers from Đại Việt, Nguyễn Trãi played a critical role in securing the eventual victory. In addition to composing the inscription on the Vĩnh Lăng stele, Nguyễn Trãi wrote about the liberation campaign, documented Đại Việt geography and produced a substantial body of poetry. He was also responsible for drafting all the memorials and correspondence related to the military operations conducted under Lê Lợi's command.

We do not know for sure how many of such correspondence Nguyễn Trãi composed. Undoubtedly, some were lost over time due to the upheavals that Vietnam experienced. However, a significant number—69 in total—have survived. These documents, known as *Quân Trung Từ Mệnh Tập* (Compilation of Writings and Commands from the Military Camp, abbreviated as QTTMT), were later translated and included together with his other works in the volume entitled *Nguyễn Trãi Toàn Tập* (The Complete Works of Nguyễn Trãi).

NGUYỄN TRÃI'S BACKGROUND

As discussed in Chapter 2, Dương Nhật Lễ—a Trần king with no blood ties to the Trần royal lineage— was overthrown and killed. One of the key figures involved in this event was Trần Nguyên Đán (1325/26–1390), who later became Nguyễn Trãi's maternal grandfather.[17] Nguyễn Trãi's father, Nguyễn Phi Khanh—also known as Nguyễn Ứng Long, (?–1428)—was invited to tutor Trần Nguyên Đán's daughter. During his time in the household, he seduced her, resulting in a pregnancy. Fearing the consequences, Nguyễn Phi Khanh fled, but Trần Nguyên Đán recalled him and arranged their marriage.[18] Trần Nguyên Đán was a direct descendant of Trần Cảnh, or King Trần Thái Tông, the first king of the Trần dynasty.

The family came from the village of Nhị Khê in Thượng Phúc district, which is in present-day Nhị Khê commune in Thường Tín, some 20 kilometres south of Hanoi. Like his father, Nguyễn Trãi was a scholar, passed the triennial *Thi Hội* examination at 21 and went on to serve under the Hồ dynasty.[19]

In 1402, Nguyễn Phi Khanh joined the Hồ court and was appointed as an Academic Scholar (*Hàn Lâm Học Sĩ*).[20] When the Ming army invaded Đại Ngu, Nguyễn Phi Khanh and other officials surrendered to Zhang Fu in 1407.[21] Ming shilu also records the event.[22] The Ming army took them to China, where Nguyễn Phi Khanh presumably spent the rest of his life. However, according to a 19th-century work, Nguyễn Phi Khanh and Nguyễn Trãi were captured, but Nguyễn Trãi escaped and was later forced to surrender and held in Đông Quan.[23]

Nguyễn Trãi was 27 years old and reportedly accompanied his father to the border and bid the final farewell. Nguyễn Phi Khanh told his tearful son to stay behind and focus on avenging the kingdom's humiliation and his father's captivity. Most Vietnamese have learnt about this emotional scene as part of school history lessons.[24]

What Nguyễn Trãi did during the ten years between his father's capture in 1407 and Lê Lợi's uprising in 1428 remains unclear. According to some accounts, the Ming administrators held him in Đông Quan; others claim he went hiding with his father in Côn Sơn, in today's Chí Linh district, where his maternal grandfather retired.[25, 26] Yet another version suggests that Nguyễn Trãi concealed his identity and travelled widely during this period.[27] Ten years is a significant period, given his literary skills it seems unlikely that he remained under house arrest, or even freely in Đông Quan—the headquarters of the Ming occupation regime—for all that time. The Ming authorities would have employed him in some capacity, and his name would have appeared in the Ming shilu, as did those of other collaborators. Additionally, staying in Côn Sơn for an extended period would likely have drawn the attention of Ming authorities. The most plausible scenario is that he was held in Đông Quan but later escaped and moved from place to place, possibly including China, which is reflected in his poems and may also help explain his later geographical writings, such as *Dư Địa Chí* (Geographical Record).[28]

Sometime during this period Nguyễn Trãi met Lê Lợi, though the exact time and location of their first encounter remains unknown. Lê Lợi was active in the region near what is now the historic Lam Kinh site, roughly 150 to 170 kilometres south of Nguyễn Trãi's native village of Nhị Khê. While this distance was considerable by 15th-century standards, it could still be covered on foot within three to four weeks.

5.3 - *Lam Sơn Thực Lục [Veritable Records of Mount Lam]*'s account of the liberation campaign (1414–1428)

There are several records of the liberation campaign, including Vietnamese and Chinese sources. The primary Vietnamese source is *Lam Sơn Thực Lục* (Veritable Records of Mount Lam, abbreviated as LSTL). Lê Lợi instructed the compilation of LSTL in early 1432 (1431 in lunar calendar) and he wrote the introduction himself.[29] While SKTT does not mention it, Nguyễn Trãi was most likely the author of LSTL. The version that I have referred to in this book was translated from a copy made in the 17th century and published in 1956.[30] One can also find a copy of LSTL in *Nguyễn Trãi Toàn Tập*. The Chinese source used in this volume is Ming shilu, which is described in Appendix 2.

Apart from the introduction, LSTL consists of three separate 'books' (or chapters) within a single volume. Book 1 covers Lê Lợi's background and the campaign from 1418 to 1424; Book 2 deals with the events from 1425 to early 1428, culminating in the Ming withdrawal and the end of their occupation of Đại Việt. Book 3 briefly describes Lê Lợi's efforts after the liberation, his evaluation of Đại Việt's victory over the Ming forces, and includes the Great Proclamation upon the Pacification of the Wu (*Bình Ngô Đại Cáo*), which Lê Lợi ordered Nguyễn Trãi to write in 1428, shortly after the Ming army had withdrawn from Đại Việt.

While these accounts vary in details, the campaign can be broadly described in four stages: the struggling phase (1418–1423); a temporary peace (1423–1424); the southern campaign (1424–1425) and the northern advance (1426–1427). Each stage is detailed below.

In this volume, I have presented the campaign from both sources as each has details that the other does not. I will start with LSTL and follow by Ming shilu in Appendix 2.

The different stages of the liberation campaign, described in LSTL in Books 1 and 2 from 1414 to 1428 are summarised below.

1414–1417: KEEPING A LOW PROFILE

LSTL records that in 1414, the emperor of the Ming dynasty ordered Zhang Fu (*Trương Phụ*), Mu Sheng (*Mộc Thạnh*), Chen Zhi (*Trần Trí*), Shan Shou (*Sơn Thọ*), Ma Qi (*Mã Kỳ*), Li Bin (*Lý Bân*) and Fang Zheng (*Phương Chính*) to cross the border and invade Đại Việt.

However, as discussed previously, the Ming invasion of Đại Việt began in 1406, and 1414 marks the year when the Ming troops captured the last Trần ruler. Additionally, these seven figures did not arrive in Đại Việt simultaneously. Zhang Fu, Mu Sheng, and Fang Zheng were part of the initial invasion, while Chen Zhi and Li Bin arrived several years later. Zhang Fu returned to China in 1416, with no recorded return to Đại Việt afterwards.

Lê Lợi never fought against Zhang Fu, the first Regional Commander (also referred to as Commander-in-Chief) of Giao Chỉ. In the early years of the uprising, his main opponent was Li Bin, who succeeded Zhang Fu as Regional Commander in 1417. Li Bin died in 1422, and Wang Tong became the third

Regional Commander in 1426. During the crucial four years between 1422 and 1426, Lê Lợi primarily battled the two Assistant Regional Commanders, Chen Zhi and Fang Zheng. He also fought against and negotiated with Ma Qi and Shan Shou, both eunuch officials. They were first mentioned in Ming shilu around 1419 and 1424, respectively. As for Mu Sheng, he returned to Beijing in 1415, was appointed Regional Commander of Yunnan, and did not return to Giao Chỉ until 1426.

During the early years from 1414 to 1417, Lê Lợi recognized the overwhelming strength of the Ming forces, who built more than ten forts across the country.[31] He chose to bide his time, maintained a low profile, bribed Ming generals with gold, silver and other treasures, and waited for the right moment to strike back.

1416: An oath-taking ceremony at Lũng Nhai

At this point in the narrative, I will take a brief detour to discuss an event, which was not documented in LSTL or SKTT, but was a significant historical event that every Vietnamese schoolchild has learned in their history lessons. The event is the oath-taking ceremony at Lũng Nhai, which historians believe marked the beginning of Lê Lợi's uprising. The ceremony was first mentioned by Lê Quý Đôn (1726–1784)—an 18th-century poet, encyclopaedist and official—in his book, *Đại Việt Thông Sử* (Complete History of Đại Việt, abbreviated as ĐVTS), using local documents such as family lineage records.[32] Although ĐVTS does not specify the exact location of the ceremony, later historians have identified it as having taken place at Lũng Nhai (also known as Lũng Mi) in present-day Mé village, Ngọc Phụng commune of Thường Xuân district in Thanh Hóa, around eight kilometres in a straight line from the Historic Complex of Lam Kinh.

In the spring of 1426, over 11 days from 15 to 26 March, Lê Lợi and 18 men gathered at Lũng Nhai village to take a solemn blood oath before Heaven, Earth, and the divine spirits of rivers and mountains. They pledged to stand united in defending their homeland against invaders who had crossed the border to cause harm, vowing to the peace and safety of their villages.[33]

The 18 men included Nguyễn Trãi and others who would later rise to become senior commanders in Lê Lợi's army and founding ministers of the new kingdom, such as Lê Nhân Chú.[34] As expected, most of them were locals, but a few came from farther afield, including places like Đông Quan and Thái Nguyên—approximately 170 and 260 kilometres north of Lũng Nhai, respectively. Ranked 12th on the list, Nguyễn Trãi, who hailed from Đông Quan, was the most educated among them; the rest were mainly farmers and fishermen.[35]

One man was of Mường ethnicity.³⁶ While the composition of the group suggests a primarily local gathering, Lê Lợi must have already enjoyed a reputation beyond Lũng Nhai, attracting participants from more distant regions, especially a learned figure like Nguyễn Trãi.

Because the oath appeared late in the historical record, historian Hoàng Xuân Hãn undertook a detailed study to assess its authenticity, focusing on its date and stated purpose. He confirmed that the event occurred in 1416, despite some concerns regarding discrepancies in the document's era notation. He also concluded that the men took the oath to fight the Ming invaders, not the local chieftains with whom Lê Lợi had been in conflict.³⁷ If Lê Lợi had indeed participated in the rebellions led by the last Trần kings, as recorded by Ming shilu, it is likely that he continued to view the Ming occupiers as adversaries, even after those rebellions ended in 1414, two years before he took the oath.

The oath document analysed by Hoàng Xuân Hãn includes an interesting footnote stating that, on 31 March 1429, Nguyễn Trãi, as a *bồi tụng* (Deputy Chancellor, a minor clerical role according to Hoàng Xuân Hãn), produced multiple copies to be stored in separate chests. Over half a century later, on 15 March 1481, an official named Nguyễn Đôn made several copies for distribution among various ministers.³⁸

Swearing an oath before an altar dedicated to Heaven, Earth, and various spirits was a common practice at the time. As we will later see, even Lê Lợi and Wang Tong participated in such a ritual at the end of the war. Without modern legal contracts and enforcement mechanisms, oath-taking enables the participants to pledge solemnly to each other. Breaking such a pledge would be severely punished by the divinities.

1418: RAISING THE UPRISING BANNER AND LOSING THE FAMILY

Despite the oath-taking ceremony in 1416, Lê Lợi and his men adopted a low profile. However, Lương Nhữ Hốt (*Liang Ru-hu*), the prefect of Thanh Hóa prefecture, viewed Lê Lợi as a threat and urged the Ming commanders to eliminate him early before he could rise against them. A native of Đại Việt, Lương Nhữ Hốt governed the region where Lê Lợi resided.³⁹ He was well aware of Lê Lợi's efforts to build alliances and his generosity toward his soldiers, and he grew suspicious of his true intentions.⁴⁰

Lương Nhữ Hốt's suspicions may have forced Lê Lợi to act, and in 1418, at the age of 33, he raised a banner of rebellion against the Ming occupiers. What followed was a series of battles starting with the arrival of the Ming troops on 14 February 1418 and Lê Lợi's withdrawal to Lạc Thủy, where he waited. Four days later, Lê Lợi's soldiers defeated the Ming troops, killing many and seizing supplies and weapons. However, their fortunes soon reversed when one of Lê Lợi's servants betrayed him, leading the Ming army to launch a surprise attack on his position on 22 February. They captured his wife, children, and many of his servants. Among the captives was Lê Lợi's nine-year-old daughter, who was seized by Ma Qi and sent to serve as a maid in the imperial palace. A decade later, Lê Lợi wrote to the Ming court, inquired about her and requested her return, but was told that she had died of illness.[41]

The day before, a local man named Đỗ Phú had exhumed the remains of Lê Lợi's ancestors in an attempt to force him into surrender. One of Lê Lợi's servants, named Ái, had betrayed him and led Đỗ Phú and the Ming troops to the burial site. However, Lê Lợi's officers managed to retrieve the remains in time and reburied them.[42]

Lê Lợi's troops' morale suffered a severe blow after that defeat, losing the will to fight. Fortunately, his loyal lieutenants stayed by his side, taking refuge in Mount Chí Linh. They had no food for two months and only returned to Lam Sơn once the Ming troops had withdrawn. Lê Lợi gathered the remaining force of about 100 men. He also brought in the Mường troops and recruited boys and girls to serve as porters. According to historian Phan Huy Lê, Mount Chí Linh is in Giao An commune of Lang Chánh District, some 40 kilometres north-west of the Historic Complex of Lam Kinh, in Thanh Hóa province, as shown in Figure 5-1.

1419: A SACRIFICE AND A YEAR OF CONSOLIDATION

After winning a few more battles in 1418, LSTL records an event that can be described as a change in Lê Lợi's strategy. His army was small, while the Ming forces remained formidable. He needed time to hide, recover, and build up his forces. To achieve this, he devised a plan: one of his men would disguise himself as Lê Lợi, wearing a yellow battle robe, and lead 500 troops and two war elephants in an attack on Tây Đô. The goal was to draw the Ming's attention and allow himself to be captured, creating an opportunity for Lê Lợi to regroup.

When Lê Lợi called for volunteers, an officer named Lê Lai stepped forward. Before carrying out the plan, Lê Lai made one request—if Lê Lợi succeeded and became king, to remember his sacrifice and care for his descendants. Lê Lợi offered a solemn prayer to heaven, vowing that if he, his generals, or their descendants ever forgot this act of loyalty, then *palaces would turn to jungles, golden seals would become mere bronze and iron, and divine swords would be reduced to fighting blades.*[43]

Lê Lai led his troops and war elephants on horseback to the gates of Tây Đô, challenging the Ming forces inside the citadel. As the Ming troops poured out, Lê Lai, clad in the yellow battle robe, shouted, 'I am the Lord of Lam Sơn!' as he charged. Surrounded and swiftly captured, the Ming soldiers took him inside the citadel, where they subjected him to *extreme punishment far beyond the usual crimes.*[44] While LSTL does not record his exact fate, presumably, they executed him soon after.

The sacrifice by Lê Lai was recorded differently in ĐVTS. In this version, Lê Lai's sacrifice was not part of a premeditated strategy but an emergency act to allow Lê Lợi to escape when Ming forces surrounded them at Mường Một.[45] Lê Lợi fled to a remote location called Trịnh Cao, but all the escape routes were blocked. Lê Lợi called for a volunteer to dress up as him and Lê Lai stepped forward. The rest of the story follows a similar account to the version recorded in LSTL. Contemporary historians have widely accepted this later version, which I learned about at school.[46]

For his sacrifice, Lê Lai's name remains forever linked to Lê Lợi in Vietnamese history. To this day, he is widely remembered, and most Vietnamese continue to honour his legacy. Regardless of the various versions, Lê Lai's sacrifice achieved its purpose. For the rest of 1419, LSTL does not record any battles with the Ming army, allowing Lê Lợi and his generals to focus on building defensive forts, repairing weapons, and recruiting more troops.

1420–1423: WIDENING THE WAR, VICTORIES AND DEFEATS ALONG THE MÃ RIVER, A TEMPORARY PEACE

The Ming commanders soon realized they had captured a stand-in for Lê Lợi. In 1420, Li Bin and Fang Zheng led an army of over 100,000 troops to attack Lê Lợi's camp. A local official named Cầm Lạn acted as their scout. However, Lê Lợi's forces ambushed the Ming column, delivering a crushing defeat. Despite the losses, Li Bin and Fang Zheng managed to escape. Lê Lợi's troops pursued the retreating remnants for six days and nights before finally returning to camp.

The battles took place around Bồ Mộng and Bồ-thi-lang, which, according to historian Phan, corresponds to present-day Mộng Sơn commune in Cẩm Thủy district, Thanh Hóa—upstream from Tây Đô, on the southern bank of the Mã River. The locations suggest that the Ming expedition travelled by boat, horseback and on foot. However, the reported figure of 100,000 is likely an exaggeration compared with previous campaigns. After the defeat, the Ming troops withdrew to their forts at Nga Lạc, Quan Du and Tây Đô Citadel. Seizing the momentum, Lê Lợi advanced, set up camp at Ba-Lẫm, and defeated the Ming army near Quan Du, which historian Phan suggests may correspond to present-day Quan Hóa in Thanh Hóa, as shown in Figure 5-2. Lê Lợi's victories forced Ming general Huang Cheng (*Hoàng Thành*) to retreat to the forts at Nga Lạc, Quan Du, then the Tây Đô citadel, the strongest fort in the Ming defensive line in the area.

Recognizing the weakening Ming forces, Lê Lợi issued a call for uprisings in other regions to attack other Ming strongholds. Many heeded his call and joined the fight.[47]

In 1421, another Ming commander, Chen Zhi, along with ethnic troops, launched an attack on Lê Lợi's camp at Ba-Lẫm. However, Lê Lợi's forces ambushed them, forcing the Ming troops to retreat. Amidst this conflict, a Laotian army arrived, offering assistance. Trusting them—since he had no prior quarrel with Ai Lao—Lê Lợi accepted their support. However, that night, the Laotians launched a surprise attack on his camp. Lê Lợi was forced to fight personally, and after a fierce battle, his forces ultimately drove them off. The Laotians had been guided by Lộ Văn Luật (*Lu Wen-lu*), a native official who worked for the Ming army.

On 6 January 1423, the Ming and Ai Lao troops launched a coordinated assault on Lê Lợi's camp at Da-quan (Quan Du according to Phan), forcing him to withdraw to Khôi.[48] There, the Ming army encircled his forces on all sides. Facing a dire situation, Lê Lợi addressed his men:

The enemy is surrounding us on all four sides. Where can we run to? This is the place that the book of war calls 'dead land'. If we fight quickly, we will survive! If we don't fight quickly, we will die!

Lê Lợi and his troops fought their way out of the siege. In the intense battle, they killed the senior Ming general, Feng Gui (*Phùng Quý*) and secured a significant victory, but at a very high cost. Following this battle, they once again retreated to Mount Chí Linh. Lê Lợi and his men endured two months of severe hunger in the mountains, surviving on root vegetables and bamboo shoots. Lê Lợi had to sacrifice four war elephants and his own horse to feed his soldiers. As conditions worsened, some soldiers attempted to flee. To restore discipline, Lê Lợi was forced to behead an officer caught trying to escape, using him as an example.

Exhausted from relentless battle and hardship, his officers and soldiers urged him to negotiate peace with the Ming commanders. Though reluctant, Lê Lợi eventually agreed and sent an envoy to negotiate with Shan Shou and

Ma Qi. Having suffered significant losses themselves, the Ming commanders accepted his peace offer.[49] The peace appeared to hold and over four months later, on 19 May 1423, Lê Lợi and his men returned to Lam Sơn. The rest of 1423 and most of 1424, seem a quiet time for Lê Lợi as there is no record of any significant battles during this time in the LSTL.

While LSTL suggests that some form of negotiation occurred between the two sides, Letter 1 in QTTMT does not reflect this and reads more like a heartfelt plea for forgiveness. In early 1423, Lê Lợi sent a letter—drafted by Nguyễn Trãi—to the Ming authorities, explaining that he had only captured the relatives and neighbours of Đỗ Phú, the district chief, in retaliation for what Đỗ Phú had done to his family, and that he had no broader intentions. This letter, preserved as Letter 1 in QTTMT, accuses Đỗ Phú of harbouring personal animosity toward Lê Lợi and bribing Lương Nhữ Hốt to persuade Ma Qi to launch an attack on Lê Lợi's household. The letter states that the assault, which happened in 1418, resulted in the killing of elderly members and children, the scattering of his kin, and the desecration of his ancestral graves, ultimately forcing Lê Lợi to flee into the mountains, where he endured six years of hardship and hunger.

The letter served to express Lê Lợi's grievances, recount his suffering, and appeal for forgiveness.[50] It was also written to justify Lê Lợi's actions and dispel any suspicions that the Ming commander might have had of Lê Lợi's rebellious intentions. By presenting his actions as personal revenge rather than open rebellion, Lê Lợi may have deliberately led the Ming high command to downplay his threat to their authority.

The offer of surrender was more explicit in Letter 2, addressed to Assistant Regional Commander Chen Zhi and the commanders stationed in Thanh Hóa:

> *Now I point to Heaven and swear, making this pact with them, to surrender with a faithful heart and humbly beg the king (and father) to grant me a chance at rehabilitation.*

In the letter, Lê Lợi insisted he had been falsely accused, declared his innocence, and pledged to surrender. He appealed for his grievances to be addressed and for past mistakes to be forgiven so that he may be able to serve the Ming court.[51]

Around this time, a man named Cầm Quý, fleeing the Hồ regime, came to Lê Lợi claiming to be a descendant of the Trần kings. Lê Lợi made him king with an era name of Thiên Khánh. However, a few years later, Thiên Khánh fled the fort of Cổ Lộng, where he was stationed at the time, to Nghệ An. Lê Lợi's men soon caught him. When questioned by Lê Lợi about his escape, despite having been made king, Thiên Khánh replied that he had done nothing to earn the title and feared for his life as Lê Lợi was on the verge of driving out the Ming occupiers. *Who would plant a tree for others to eat its fruit?*, he asked. Lê Lợi was initially undecided, but his men reminded him that *heaven does not have two suns; the country cannot have two kings*, Lê Lợi then allowed Thiên Khánh to take his own life by hanging.[52]

However, Letter 21 of TQTMT explains that Lê Lợi found a Trần Mỗ (also known as Trần Cảo) in 1425, and according to Ming shilu, a Trần descendant named Trần Cảo did not appear until 1427.

1424: THE NEW EMPERORS

Emperor Yongle passed away on 12 August 1424.[53] He was succeeded by his eldest son, Zhu Gaochi (1378–1425), known as the Hongxi (*Hồng Hy*) Emperor. However, Hongxi's reign was brief; he died in May 1425, less than a year after ascending the throne. His son, Zhu Zhanji (1399–1435) became the next emperor, Xuande (*Tuyên Đức*). He was 26 years old.

Before his death, Emperor Yongle issued a general amnesty and demanded that sympathy and clemency are to be especially demonstrated in Jiao-zhi. He also instructed the eunuch Shan Shou to appoint Lê Lợi as the prefect of Thanh Hóa prefecture.

At the time of Emperor Yongle's death, the Ming forces had been in Đại Việt for 18 years without achieving lasting pacification, despite various military campaigns. The emperor had been exploring alternative strategies to suppress the rebellions.

The years 1424 and 1425 marked a period of transition for the Ming dynasty with the succession of emperors. Still, they were also remarkably successful years for Lê Lợi and his forces, who made significant progress. Records in Ming shilu indicate a turning point in Đại Việt's war efforts from the end of 1424.

1424: MARCHING SOUTH TO NGHỆ AN

Capturing the fort of Đa Căng
Based on LSTL, Lê Lợi's forces had around 20 months to recover and rebuild following their devastating defeat in early 1423. With his troops rested and replenished, he launched a renewed offensive at the onset of winter. On 12 October 1424, he attacked Đa Căng fort. According to Phan, Đa Căng is located in present-day Thọ Nguyên commune, in the Thọ Xuân district of

Thanh Hóa. The commune is approximately 30 kilometres north-west of Thanh Hóa City and is on the southern bank of the Chu River.[54]

The assault marked a significant shift in Lê Lợi's strategy. Up to this point, his operations had primarily taken place upstream of the Mã River, from Tây Đô citadel, to take advantage of the mountainous terrain and access to Ai Lao as an escape route. The Ming army had a strong presence in Tây Đô and launched their campaigns against him from there. But by going to Thanh Hóa, he could utilise the Mã River, bypass Tây Đô and avoid the confrontation with the Laotians.

Đa Căng fell, but the prefect of Thanh Hóa, Lương Nhữ Hốt, escaped. The peace agreement reached in 1423 was broken, but Lê Lợi had secured a major victory. His forces captured many weapons and supplies, burned the fort and defeated a Ming reinforcement contingent, forcing them to retreat to Tây Đô. However, instead of pursuing them, Lê Lợi gathered more men, war elephants, horses and weapons and marched south to the Trà Long subprefecture of Nghệ An.[55] His movement may have caught the Ming commanders off guard as they would have expected him to advance to Tây Đô in the northwest.

LSTL does not provide an explanation for this shift in strategy, but according to ĐVTS, one of Lê Lợi's generals, Lê Chích, also known as Nguyễn Chích, advised him that they should occupy Nghệ An first, and use it as a base before advancing northward toward Đông Đô.[56]

Up to this time—six years after raising his banner—Lê Lợi and his forces had remained largely within the vicinity of Lam Sơn. His key operational areas had been Lam Sơn, Mount Chí Linh, and Tây Đô, forming a triangular region with each side spanning roughly 40 kilometres in a straight line. They had ventured furthest around Quan Hóa, near the Laotian border. Reaching the centre of Nghệ An, in present-day Vinh, would require a longer march of at least 170 kilometres or over four times the distance that they were used to. Fortunately, Nguyễn Chích assured Lê Lợi that he knew his way around the province and could guide them.

LSTL does not detail the exact route Lê Lợi's forces took. However, based on modern maps and known battle sites, they likely followed the Hiếu River south to its junction with the Cả (or Lam) River, then sailed eastward toward Vinh. The river junction is by present-day Con Cuông, as show in Figure 5-5. Given that they had war elephants and horses, part of the army must have travelled by land alongside the rivers. However, they first had to make an overland journey from Đa Căng to reach the Hiếu River.

Victories at Bồ Lạp and Trà Long subprefecture

The Ming commanders, alarmed by Lê Lợi advance, dispatched a force of 5,000 men from Trà Long in the south and another force from Tây Đô in the north. They had planned to catch Lê Lợi in a pincer movement. The three armies met at a place called Bồ Lạp, which, according to Phan, corresponds to contemporary Bồ Đằng, in Châu Nga commune, near the Hiếu River—approximately halfway between Con Cuông (Trà Long) and Tây Đô.[57] The northern Ming column, led by Chen Zhi and Fang Zheng, arrived late in the afternoon, only to find Lê Lợi's war elephants and troops prepared for battle. He immediately launched an attack, breaking their formation, beheaded over 1000, captured more than 100 horses and routed the Ming forces.

The following morning, Lê Lợi assaulted the camp of the Ming's southern column, led by Sư Hựu, Cầm Bành (*Qin Peng*), and Cầm Lạn, and overwhelmed them. Cầm Bành escaped—likely to a fort in Trà Long, possibly somewhere in Con Cuông, near the river junction shown in Figure 5-6, where he held out for two months waiting for reinforcements. However, as some of his soldiers began to surrender and it became clear that no reinforcements were coming, Cầm Bành had no choice but to capitulate. Later, he tried to escape but was captured and executed.[58]

With Trà Long subprefecture now under his control, Lê Lợi focused on consolidating his position. He reassured the local tribal leaders and expanded his army by recruiting another 5,000 young men. His forces—now bolstered by war elephants and horses—rested and prepared for the upcoming campaign in Nghệ An.

During this time, a Ming delegation, led by a eunuch named Shan Shou, arrived, attempting to appease Lê Lợi. LSTL does not specify what Shan Shou offered to persuade him to abandon his campaign but notes that the event took place around the reign of the new Ming emperor, Hongxi (August 1424 – May 1425). Lê Lợi played along with Shan Shou's overtures and sent an envoy to Nghệ An—not for serious negotiations, but to gather intelligence for his forthcoming offensive. Once the Ming commanders realised his true intentions, they ended the talks.

Figure 5-5: The junction of the Hiếu and Cà Rivers. The Hiếu River is on the left and the Cà River is on the right, looking south.[59]

Figure 5-6: View of the Cà River, looking west from Cây Chanh Bridge.

Upon learning of Shan Shou's arrival in Đại Việt, Lê Lợi addressed him in Letter 3 of QTTMT, offering praise, recounting the personal hostility of Đỗ Phú, and appealing for a chance to make amends. The tone of this letter is formal, yet notably less submissive than Letters 1 and 2. By late 1424, when Shan Shou arrived, Lê Lợi had gained significant momentum in his campaign, which—likely contributed to this communication's more confident and measured tone.[60]

Victory at Khả Lưu Pass

Both sides knew they had to settle the war on the battlefield, and just before Lê Lợi began his campaign, he learned that the Ming army—having recovered from the recent defeat—was coming once again, both by boat and on land. Lê

Lợi told his men that they should not wait for the Ming troops to reach their current position at present-day Con Cuông but to choose a defensible location with natural obstacles and difficult access. They selected a place named Khả (Khá) Lưu Pass. According to Phan, this site was in present-day Vĩnh Sơn commune, Anh Sơn district, approximately 20 kilometres in a straight line from the Hiếu/Cả river junction. Today, this commune is next to a narrow valley, where a highway crosses the Cả River at the Tri Lễ Bridge, as shown in Figure 5-7.[61] It is likely that this valley was the historical Khả Lưu Pass.

Lê Lợi's forces likely took two to three days to reach Khả Lưu Pass from Con Cuông, travelling along the Cả River and the track running alongside it. To protect his position, Lê Lợi dispatched 1,000 men under the command of Lê Liệt to take a shortcut by land and secure Đỗ Gia district ahead of Khả Lưu Pass.[62] According to Phan, Đỗ Gia district was likely located near Mount Linh Cảm, close to present-day Tam Soa, where the Ngàn Phố and Ngàn Sâu rivers converge before flowing into the Cả River.[63] However, I doubt this position because, at around 110 kilometres, it is too far forward of Khả Lưu Pass and would have taken at least a week to ten days for Lê Liệt to get there.

What followed was a series of complex tactical manoeuvres by Lê Lợi that ultimately led to a decisive rout of the Ming forces. Based on LSTL and available maps, I have reconstructed the sequence of this crucial battle to demonstrate how masterful Lê Lợi as a field commander was:

- While stationed at Con Cuông, Lê Lợi received intelligence that the Ming army was marching from Nghệ An—likely from the fort of Lam Thành in modern-day Vinh—to confront him. In response, he immediately departed from Con Cuông and moved his forces downstream along the Cả River, establishing a defensive position at Khả Lưu Pass. The journey likely took two to three days. He positioned his troops on the high ground of the pass.

- Meanwhile, the Ming army travelled upstream along the Cả River, most likely from Vinh, which is approximately 60 kilometres in a straight line from Khả Lưu Pass. Compared with Lê Lợi's route, the Ming forces had to traverse a path nearly three times as long. According to LSTL, the Ming army arrived in three to four days, though a more realistic estimate would be five to six days, given the longer distance.

- Upon arrival, the Ming forces disembarked from their boats, established camps, likely on both riverbanks, and erected palisades on the lower ground of the pass on the northern bank of the Cả River. Meanwhile, Lê

Lợi's troops stationed above the pass beat war drums, waved numerous flags, and lit many torches at night to create the illusion of a much larger army. Unbeknownst to the Ming army, Lê Lợi had secretly dispatched a contingent of his best troops and four war elephants to the southern side of the river. These forces remained in well-hidden places, ready to attack the Ming flank and from behind.

- In the early morning, the Ming troops attacked Lê Lợi's camp with troops from both land and river. Lê Lợi, anticipating this move, ordered a tactical withdrawal, luring the Ming forces deeper into the pass. Once they were fully committed, he sprung the trap with his men attacking from all four sides, overwhelming the Ming soldiers, killing and drowning many in the river.

- The surviving Ming forces retreated behind their palisades, positioning themselves with the mountain behind them to hold out for a prolonged battle. They had ample supplies, whereas Lê Lợi's army only had provisions for about ten days. Realising they could not outlast the Ming army in a siege, Lê Lợi informed his troops that they would have to retreat. He ordered his men to burn their camp and simulate a withdrawal deeper into the pass to deceive the enemy. However, instead of retreating, they took a hidden shortcut and waited for the Ming troops, setting up their next ambush.

- The Ming commanders, who believed that Lê Lợi had retreated, moved their troops into Lê Lợi's burnt-out camp and began constructing palisades. The following day, Lê Lợi appeared in front of their fortification and openly challenged the Ming contingent. The Ming forces took the bait and poured out of their recently built fort to confront him. This move was precisely what Lê Lợi had planned, knowing he could not win in a prolonged siege. At that moment, his remaining forces, led by trusted commanders such as Lê Sát, Lê Lễ, Lê Vấn and Lê Nhân Chú, emerged and joined the battle.[64] The men he sent secretly to the southern side of the river may have participated in the attack, which may have explained the drowning of some of the Ming forces.

What followed was a complete rout of the Ming army, described by LSTL as follows:

The enemy broke up and fled, and countless were beheaded. The enemy's boat drifted aimlessly and drowned corpses clogged the river. A large number of weapons were abandoned in the mountains. Enemy general Chu Kiệt [Zhu Jie] was captured alive, and the enemy's vanguard commander, Hoàng Thành [Huang Cheng], was beheaded. Over a thousand enemy soldiers were tied up. The victory was followed by a long chase of the enemy, three days and nights, straight to Nghe An Citadel. The enemy entered the citadel, built more ramparts, and tried to hold it.

Zhu Jie and Huang Cheng were seasoned Ming officers stationed in Đại Việt. Ming shilu first mentioned them both as vice commander and guard commander in 1415.[65] They played a role in suppressing the Trần kings' rebellion, and Huang Cheng had engaged in battle against Lê Lợi on at least two occasions.

Based on the timing of Lê Lợi's arrival in Nghệ An, the battle of Khả Lưu Pass likely took place in the winter of 1424, around late 1424 to early 1425.

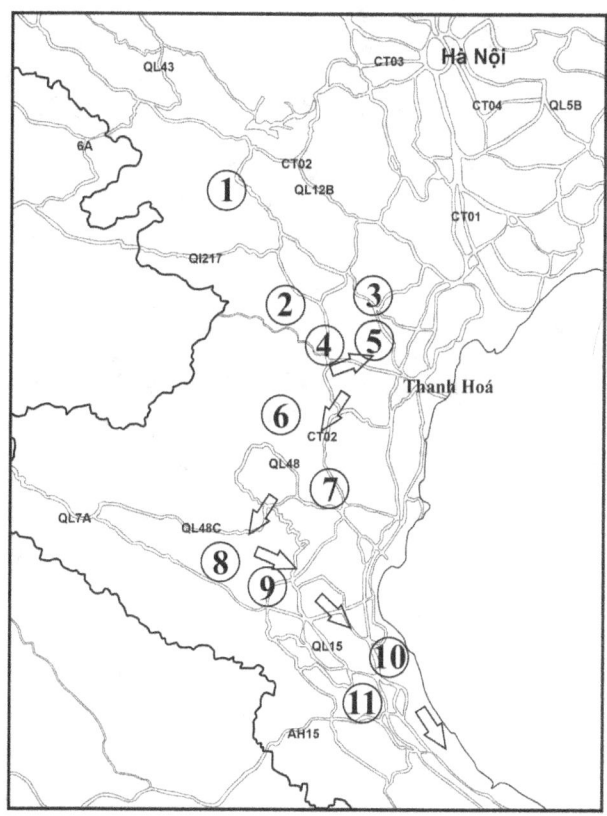

Figure 5-7: Map of Lê Lợi's southern campaign (1424–1425).

Key: 1. Quan Hóa; 2. Giao An (Mount Chí Linh); 3. Hồ Citadel (Tây Đô); 4. Lam Sơn; 5. Thọ Nguyên; 6. Châu Nga; 7. Thái Hòa; 8. Mỏ Cát Thúy (near Côn Cuông), 9. Tri Lễ Bridge; 10. Vinh; 11. Bến Tam Soa; Tân Bình and Thuận Hóa further south are not shown. White arrows illustrate the direction of Lê Lợi's advance.

1425: BESIEGING NGHỆ AN AND CAPTURING THE SOUTHERN FORTS

On 12 February 1425, Lê Lợi arrived in Nghệ An. The journey had taken him and his forces four months from Đa Căng Fort and likely just under six months from his base at Lam Sơn. Along the way, they had fought and won at least four battles, and now they stood at the gates of Nghệ An Fort. The fort is believed to be at present-day Mount Lam Thành, in Hưng Phú commune of Vinh City, near the junction of the Cả and La Rivers, as shown in Figure 5-8.

Figure 5-8: The Old Fort of Lam Thành (15th century).

According to a 19th-century work, the fort shown in Figure 5-8 was built by Zhang Fu, had three gates, with a circumference of 603 trượng (approximately 2.4 to 2.8 kilometres) and stone walls measuring 1.15 trượng (4.6 and 5.4 metres).[66] Today, the exact locations of the gates are difficult to determine, but based on an early 20th-century photograph, I have marked two possible gate sites in yellow crosses in Figure 5-8.[67] A green triangle marks the highest spot in the fort, where a hole for a flagpole can still be seen. Modern measurements using Google Maps estimate the fort's circumference at around 1.5 kilometres, covering an area of around ten hectares (0.1 square kilometres). Given the undulation of the hill, the 19th-century estimates are not too far from Google Maps. On the southern side, remnants of what appears to be a foundation—roughly square and measuring 110 meters on each side—are still visible. While the fort is unlikely to accommodate a garrison with more than 1000 men, its strategic position atop a hill overlooking the Cả River made it a formidable defensive stronghold in the 15th century.[68]

According to LTSL, the people welcomed Lê Lợi in Nghệ An with great joy. Eager to support his cause, they brought offerings of water buffalo meat and alcohol, Lê Lợi shared the provisions with his soldiers to celebrate; everyone danced and pledged their lives to the rebellion. With the Ming forces trapped inside the fort, Lê Lợi laid siege to Nghệ An. Meanwhile, the rest of the prefecture was firmly under his control, allowing him to train his troops, gather supplies, and prepare weapons for future campaigns.

About three months later, around 2 May 1425, a Ming relief naval force from Đông Đô led by Li An (*Lý An*) arrived, and on 14 May, the fort's gates opened as the Ming troops tried to break through the siege. Lê Lợi's troops lay in wait along the riverbank, allowing the Ming soldiers to reach halfway across the river before attack. They scored a decisive victory, with many Ming soldiers drowning in the battle. The Ming troops retreated to the fort, where their senior commanders, Li An and Fang Zheng, were trapped for nearly six months.

By this point, Lê Lợi had written at least four letters to Fang Zheng. The tone between them had become increasingly combative as Lê Lợi's forces advanced toward Nghệ An. The two exchanged taunts: Lê Lợi challenged Fang Zheng to lay down his arms and rest his troops, while Fang Zheng mocked Lê Lợi's army as mountain-dwelling rats too afraid to fight on open ground. When Fang Zheng eventually retreated into the fortress at Nghệ An, Lê Lợi seized the opportunity to remind him of his earlier bravado, ridiculing him for hiding behind walls 'like an old woman.' In Letters 4 through 8 of QTTMT, the language shifts noticeably—from the respectful *ngài* (sir) to the dismissive *mày* (a term used for those of lower status)—reflecting Lê Lợi's growing confidence and disdain for his rival.[69]

While the Ming senior commanders remained trapped, Lê Lợi told his men that other strongholds must be left vulnerable, that is, 'empty', with the enemy's best troops pinned down in Nghệ An. Seizing this opportunity, he dispatched 2,000 of his best soldiers, along with two war elephants, under the command of the veterans of the Khả Lưu Pass battle, Lê Sát, Lê Lễ and Lê Triện.[70] They marched day and night toward Tây Đô, and upon arrival, launched an attack, which defeated the Ming forces and forced them to retreat into Tây Đô Citadel. The people of Thanh Hóa, along with Lê Lợi's friends and relatives, rallied to join Lê Sát and his troops. Lê Sát reassured the populace, trained the new recruits, and prepared for a prolonged siege.

Realising that the Ming strongholds in Thuận Hóa, Tân Bình, Nghệ An, and Đông Đô had lost contact with each other for some time, Lê Lợi dispatched 1,000 men and one war elephant led by Lê Nỗ to capture Tân Bình to recruit additional soldiers. Lê Nỗ's forces crossed Ngang Pass, defeated a Ming contingent at Bá Chính (Bố Chính), and advanced to take Tân Bình (southern Quảng Bình province).[71] Meanwhile, another force, commanded by Lê Bôi and Lê Văn An—also veterans of the Khả Lưu Pass battle—embarked on a naval expedition with 70 ships. They sailed to Thuận Hóa, where they defeated the Ming forces and captured the forts. These two locations were likely to be the forts of Thuận Châu and Hóa Châu, as discussed in Volume 3B.

In a single campaign, by the end of 1425 or around then, Lê Lợi had driven the Ming army out of the southern region, from Nghệ An to Hải Vân Pass. This success was a remarkable achievement, especially considering that he and his men had been struggling to survive on Mount Chí Linh just two years earlier.

1425–1426: MARCHING NORTH

The plan

As previously mentioned, shortly after occupying Đại Việt, the Ming army built walls and moats in 12 cities in 1408. These forts became the backbone of their defence, commanded by guards, supported by battalions, and backed by police offices. In 1408, there were ten guards, 17 battalions and 100 police offices.[72] This number of forts is confirmed by LSTL, which notes that the Ming army built more than ten forts across the country. While Ming shilu does not list these forts, LSTL records the following 14 forts (*thành*), which I have arranged in the order from north to south with respect to Đông Đô: Ôn Khâu, Xương Giang (north-east); Tam Giang (north-west); Điêu Khê, Đông Đô (centre); Thị Kiều (Đáp Cầu), Chí Linh (east); Cổ Lộng, Phù Liệt (south-east); Tây Đô, Đa Căng, Nghệ An, Tân Bình, Thuận Hóa (further south), as indicated in Figure 5-9.

By 1425, Lê Lợi's forces had successfully captured Thuận Hóa, Tân Bình and Đa Căng. Meanwhile, Nghệ An and Tây Đô were under siege, with the Ming senior commanders and their best troops trapped inside. Evaluating the military situation, Lê Lợi decided to send his men north to capture the remaining forts rather than trying to assault the heavily fortified and well-defended fort of Nghệ An (likely at Lam Thành), which would have been a costly operation.

Lê Lợi deployed his forces northward in three separate directions: north-west, central, and north-east. The north-west column, with 2,000 men, was aimed at blocking any potential Ming reinforcements from Yunnan. The central force, also with 2,000 troops, was positioned to intercept Li An and Fang Zheng if they attempted to escape Nghệ An and to pose a direct threat to Đông Đô. This column marched through present-day Nam Định and Thái Bình provinces and quickly overwhelmed local Ming resistance. They, then, marched north-east with over 3,000 men from Thanh Hóa and two war elephants to prevent reinforcements from Guangxi via Ôn Khâu. Several commanders of these columns were veterans of the Khả Lưu Pass battle.[73]

Lê Lợi then dispatched a force of 2,000 men, led by two officials responsible for public works, agriculture, land and manufacture to march toward Đông Đô, Lê (or Đinh) Lễ and Lê Xý (or Nguyễn Xí). Their mission was not to engage in direct combat but to demonstrate the strength of the rebellion and also to keep the Ming forces confined to the citadel. These objectives may explain why Lê Lợi chose men responsible for administrative functions rather than battlefield generals to lead this column.[74] The strategy proved effective—along the way, local villagers welcomed Lê Lợi's troops with enthusiasm, offering water buffaloes, food, and alcohol to support the soldiers and their commanders.

These strategic manoeuvres illustrated Lê Lợi and his generals' remarkable grasp of geography and strategies—an impressive feat considering that before they rose against the Ming occupiers, most of them were farmers who had not travelled far from the remote foothills of northwestern Thanh Hóa.

The deployment and some of the associated locations are shown in Figure 5-9.

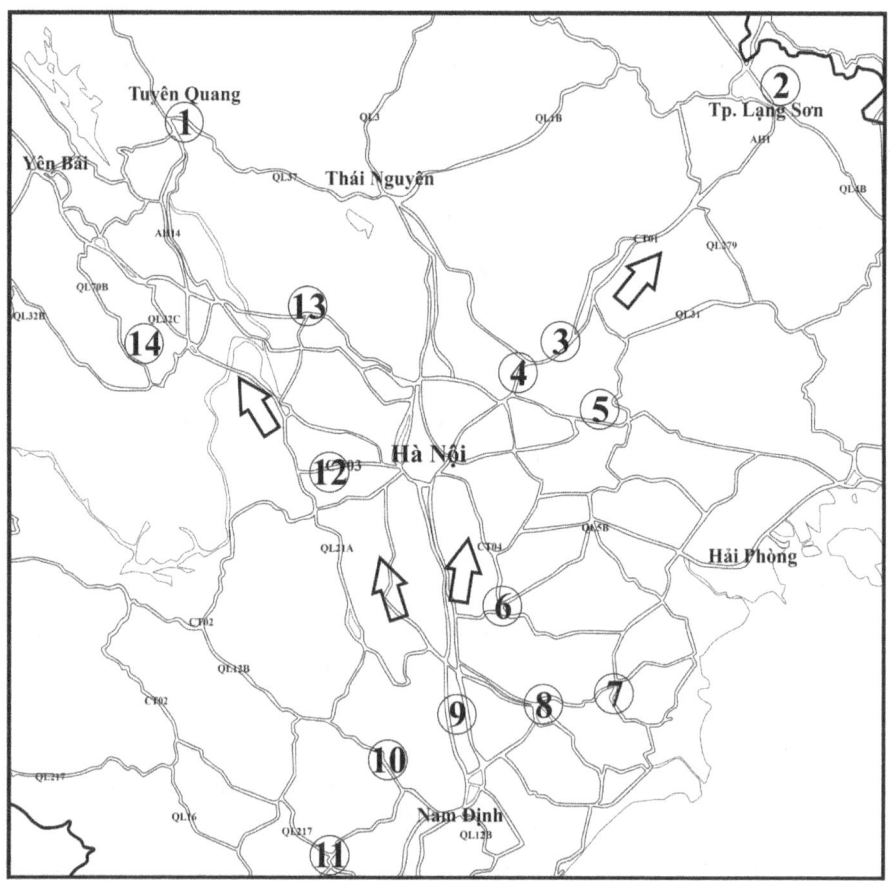

Figure 5-9: Map of Lê Lợi northern campaign (1425–1426).

Key: 1. Tuyên Quang; 2. Lạng Sơn; 3. Bắc Giang; 4. Đáp Cầu; 5. Chí Linh; 6. Hưng Yên; 7. Thái Bình; 8. Nam Định; 9. Giáo Xứ Bình Cách; 10. Nho Quan; 11. Hồ Citadel (Tây Đô); 12. Quốc Oai; 13. Vĩnh Phúc; 14. Phú Thọ province.

All these operations likely took place between late 1425 and early 1426, as Lê Lợi's forces expanded their control and put the Ming army on the defensive, confining them to various forts. The situation shifted in the autumn of 1426 when, on 21 September, a Ming force from Đông Đô moved out to confront Lê Lợi's north-western column. However, the column's commanders, Lê Triện and Lê Bí, ambushed the Ming army at Ninh Kiều, forcing them to retreat to Nhân Mục village. The Ming troops then fled back to Đông Đô and remained within the citadel for the rest of the war. Ninh Kiều corresponds to present-day Ninh Sơn in Chương Mỹ, about 20 kilometres south-west of Hà Nội, while Nhân Mục village is near Mọc village, close to the Cống Mọc bridge over the Tô Lịch River.[75]

Li An and Fang Zheng escaped from Nghệ An
From Đông Đô, the Ming commanders somehow were able to communicate with Li An and Fang Zheng, who were still trapped in Nghệ An, presumably requesting their urgent return. Around 26 October 1426, these two senior Ming commanders escaped under the cover of darkness and fled back to Đông Đô, leaving Cai Fu to defend it. Lê Lợi's men, while anticipating such a move, were unable to intercept them. Recognising the Ming forces were weakening, Lê Lợi seized the opportunity to advance with the bulk of his army toward Đông Đô, while leaving behind a contingent to continue the besiege at the fort. They travelled day and night, using land and river routes, following Li An and Fang Zheng. They reached Tây Đô and set up camp, where the people from Thanh Hóa came out to welcome Lê Lợi upon learning of his presence. Many eagerly volunteered to join the rebellion.

Ming reinforcements led by Wang Tong
By this time, Lê Lợi's forces in the north had grown beyond the original 9,000 recorded by LSTL. Assuming he brought an additional 3,000 men, his total figure would have been around 12,000. A month later, in November 1426, Ming reinforcements arrived from Imperial China. Led by Wang Tong (*Vương Thông*) and Ma Ying (*Mã Ánh*), the force consisted of 50,000 troops and 5,000 horses. The first 10,000 men advanced from Yunnan in the north-west and the rest entered from Ôn Khâu (Lạng Sơn) in the north-east, as Lê Lợi had expected.

One of the commanders of Lê Lợi's north-west column, Lê Khả (also known as Trịnh Khả), led a force from Ninh Kiều to intercept the Ming reinforcements from Yunnan. The two sides clashed at the Luội Bridge (also referred to as Xa Lộc, near present-day Tứ Xã, Lâm Thao district, Phú Thọ), where Lê Khả's troops decisively defeated the Ming troops, killing and drowning many. The surviving Ming forces retreated to the fort of Tam Giang, which may have been located near present-day Dục Mỹ, near Tứ Xã commune.[76]

The battle of Tốt (or Tố) Động
Meanwhile, Wang Tong and his troops arrived in Đông Đô and joined forces with other Ming commanders already stationed in the citadel, including Shan Shou, Ma Qi, Lu (Yuan?) Liang (*Lý Lượng*), Chen Qia (Xie?) (*Trần Hiệp*) and Fang Zheng, who had recently escaped from Nghệ An. In addition to the thousand troops who came with him, Wang Tong now commanded another 10,000 already present in Đông Đô. However, instead of taking time to settle

his forces properly and gathering intelligence for the upcoming campaign, he appeared to be in haste. Within just five days of arrival, he set out to seek battle with Lê Lợi's army.

They marched west toward Cổ Sở (present-day Yên Sở), approximately 25 kilometres west of Đông Đô, near the Đáy River, where the two commanders of Lê Lợi's north-west column, Lê Triện and Lê Bí, stationed. The third commander, Lê Khả, was likely further north, engaging the Ming reinforcement from Yunnan. This information, if correct, may explain Wang Tong's haste if he believed that Lê Khả was in Phú Thọ at the time. According to LSTL, the Ming camp stretched nearly 10 *li* (4.5 kilometres), with banners fluttering and soldiers' helmets and armour gleaming under the sun. Wang Tong was determined to crush Lê Lợi's forces in a single decisive campaign.

Lê Triện's troops were unable to halt Wang Tong's advance and sent an urgent request for reinforcements to the commanders of the central column, Lê Lễ and Lê Xí, who were stationed at Thanh Đàm (present-day Thanh Trì, Hanoi). In response, Lê Lễ and Lê Xí led 3,000 men and two war elephants to join the battle. While LTSL does not provide a detailed account of how the battle unfolded, it briefly states that the combined forces decisively defeated the Ming forces at Tố Động (present-day Tốt Động) and Ninh Kiều. They beheaded Lu Liang and Chen Qia, along with 5,000 Ming soldiers. The remaining Ming commanders, Wang Tong, Ma Ying, Shan Shou and Ma Qi, barely escaped and retreated to Đông Đô where they stayed, making no further offensives for the rest of the war.

LTSL describes the end of the battle as: *Many of the enemy soldiers drowned, and more than a hundred were captured alive. Weapons, horses, silver, gold, silk, and food carts were left behind* [on the battlefield] *in countless quantities.*[77] While the figure of Ming soldiers beheaded at 5,000 seems high relative to the 100 captured alive, the description of the battlefield indicates that the Ming army had suffered a massive defeat. Building on the momentum of the victory, the combined forces then advanced and laid siege to Đông Đô.

Lê Lợi's victory at the battle of the Khả Lưu Pass in early 1425 had shifted the war in Đại Việt's favour. Still, it was his men's decisive defeat of Wang Tong's army at the battle of Tốt Động and Ninh Kiều, later known as the Battle of Tốt Động – Chúc Động, nearly two years later, in late 1426, that signalled the beginning of the end of the Ming occupation. After this defeat, the Ming high command realised that victory over Lê Lợi was no longer possible and began seeking a face-saving exit.

Figure 5-10 shows the locations related to the Battle of Tốt Động – Chúc Động. Historian Phan provides a more detailed account of the battle, drawing from later works such as SKTT, ĐVTS, and CM, whereas my analysis is based primarily on LSTL and Ming shilu.[78] I have mainly referenced Phan's work for identifying locations, but the level of detail his book presents exceeds what is necessary for this volume. Furthermore, additional information would not significantly alter the overall narrative of the battle, and I prefer to rely on earlier sources that were nearly contemporaneous to the events.

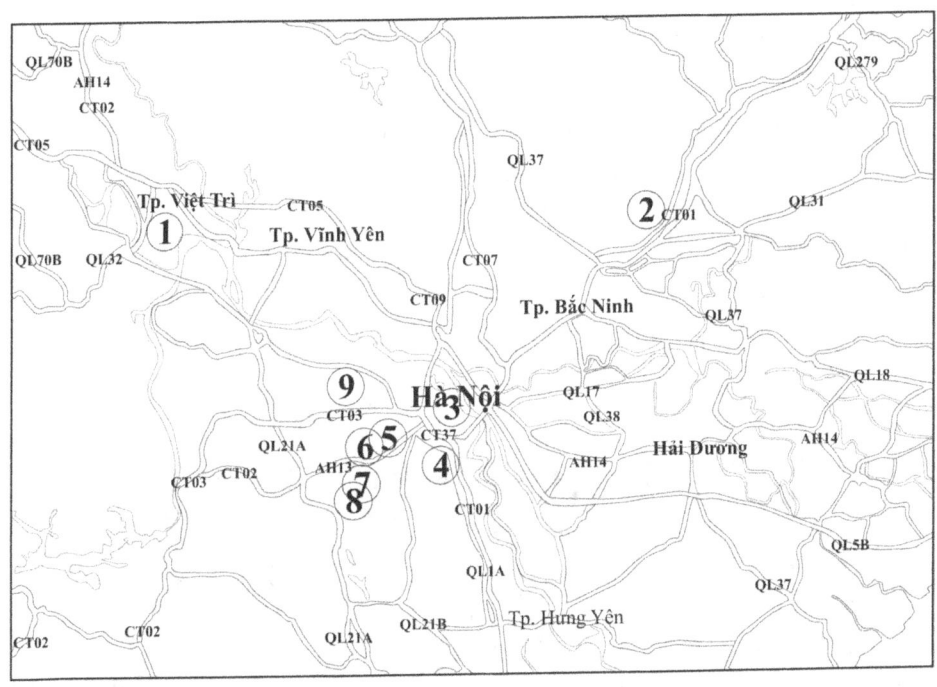

Figure 5-10: Map of the battle of Tốt Động – Chúc Động.

Key: 1. Tứ Xã; 2. Ancient fort of Xương Giang; 3. Cống Mọc Bridge; 4. Thanh Trì, 5. Mai Lĩnh Bridge, 6. Chúc Sơn Market; 7. Tốt Động Communal House; 8. Quán Bến Temple; 9. Yên Sở.

Despite its significance in Vietnamese history, there was no marker or memorial of the Tốt Động victory when I visited in February 2025. However, the locals have preserved the memory of the battle through the Quán Bến Temple and the Communal House of Tốt Động, as shown in Figures 5-11 and 5-13.[79]

Figure 5-11: Quán Bến, the temple for the battle of Tốt Động, viewed looking east.

Figure 5-12: The Đáy River by Quán Bến Temple, viewed looking north.

The Đáy River, shown in Figure 5-12, is a tributary and merges with the main Đáy River, near Phùng Xá, Mỹ Đức. Upstream, this tributary is known as the Tích Giang River. According to the information at the Quán Bến Temple, the bodies of the Ming soldiers who perished in the battle clogged up the river in this area. Temple records also mention that in 1866, King Tự Đức issued an edict for the remains of the fallen Ming soldiers to be collected and buried in a mound with a shrine. Although I could not locate this shrine, it is believed to have been near the Communal House of Tốt Động, as shown in Figure 5-14.

Figure 5-13: The communal house of Tốt Động village.

Figure 5-14: A shrine near the burial ground of the Ming soldiers.

This shrine or area around here could be where the remains of the Ming soldiers were buried.

The Battle of Tốt Động – Chúc Động is referred in Ming shilu as the Battle of Ninh Bridge, which took place at the end of 1426, during which Minister Chen Qia was killed. While the exact location of the bridge is not known, its proximity to Ninh Kiều on modern maps suggests it may have been near today's Mai Lĩnh Bridge on AH13, spanning the Đáy River, as illustrated in Figure 5-10.[80]

Figure 5-15: View of the Đáy River from Mai Lĩnh Bridge, viewed looking south.

Figure 5-16: Xương Giang historic site.

Besieging Đông Đô

When news of the victory at the battle at Tốt Động reached Lê Lợi in Thanh Hóa, he immediately gathered his commanders and led the bulk of his army with 20 war elephants, toward Đông Đô, taking both the land and river routes.[81] Initially, Lê Lợi established his headquarters at Tây (West) Phù Liệt before relocating to Đông (East) Phù Liệt shortly after, both places are located in present-day Thanh Trì, roughly 12 kilometres south of Hanoi. In the three days following his arrival, a large number of local warriors from Đông Đô region, residents from various prefectures and districts, and tribal leaders from the frontier regions flocked to his camp. They came with great enthusiasm, pledging to join the fight against the Ming strongholds across the country.[82]

In the 11th lunar month (around December) of 1426, Lê Lợi met with Lê Lễ, the commander of the central force. The combined forces launched a series of assaults on the Ming positions outside Đông Đô Citadel, forcing them to retreat behind its walls. Đại Việt forces captured many boats and weapons.

Having suffered multiple defeats and with no immediate reinforcements, the Ming commanders inside the citadel sent an envoy to Lê Lợi, requesting a cease-fire and permission to leave and take their army back to China. Lê Lợi considered the proposal and agreed, as it was what he would have wanted *to defeat the enemy's army without fighting is the best of all strategies!* He informed the envoy that he expected the Ming high command to notify their fellow commanders at other forts to regroup at Đông Đô, where he would provide horses, elephants and support troops for the journey, and facilitate the exchange of goods along the way.

Of the 69 letters (46 in the 1961 edition plus 23 found later and in the 1976 edition) preserved in TQTMT, nearly half—around 29—were addressed to Wang Tong, beginning with Letter 9, written around late 1426, and concluding with Letter 23 in late 1427 or early 1428. After Feng Zheng was demoted and replaced by Wang Tong in 1426, most of the subsequent correspondence following Letter 8 was directed to Wang Tong. Note that there are some similarities in letters found in the later edition to the previous one.[83]

Letter 9 was a reply to Wang Tong's ceasefire proposal and suggests that Wang Tong orders the Ming forces at Diễn Châu, Nghệ An, and Tân Bình to withdraw.[84] The Ming commanders accepted the terms and sent letters to their forces at these places and Thuận Hóa, instructing them to regroup at Đông Đô. They also set a departure date for their coordinated withdrawal from Đại Việt.

In any event, Lương Nhữ Hốt, Trần Phong and other natives of Đại Việt working for the Ming army warned their commanders about the fate of Omar Baghatur, a 13th-century Mongol-Yuan general who had surrendered to Trần Hưng Đạo, a Đại Việt general only to have his ship sunk by divers while returning to China.[85] This story, told in Volume 3A, made the Ming commanders suspicious of Lê Lợi's intentions and prompted them to reinforce the defences of Đông Đô Citadel, including melting large bronze bells and cauldrons to make fire tubes. Aware of their actions, Lê Lợi tightened security at the four citadel gates, capturing several Ming reconnaissance units and their horses as they attempted to slip out. After this, Lê Lợi ceased all envoy exchanges with the Ming commanders.[86]

Lê Lợi accused Wang Tong of breaking the trust in Letter 15. It is a classic Nguyễn Trãi's composed correspondence, and I have translated it in full as follows:

> *I have heard it said: 'Trustworthiness is the treasure of a kingdom. If people do not have trust, then what can they conduct their affairs with?'*
>
> *Recently, you sent a letter and envoys proposing a truce, and I have complied with everything accordingly. Yet now, I see that inside the citadel, trenches are still being dug, stakes planted, fences raised, and ramparts fortified; ancient relics are being destroyed to cast fire tubes and other weapons—so, are you planning to withdraw your troops? or hold the fort permanently? I honestly cannot tell. The Zhongyong* [Doctrine of the Mean] *says: 'Without honesty, nothing can be accomplished.' For when the heart is not sincere, all actions are false.*
>
> *If you genuinely honour the previous terms of the truce, then whatever you do, the advantages and disadvantages should be clear. If you want to withdraw, then withdraw. If you want to hold on* [defend the fort], *then hold on. Why outwardly talk about negotiating peace while inwardly plotting something else? Don't let the beginning and the end contradict or be outwardly and inwardly at odds like that.*
>
> *Although ordinary people are ignorant, they are very perceptive. Although I am ignorant and know nothing, as Confucius said 'Seeing the reason why, observing*

the cause, examine the comfort' [Observe what a person does, consider why they do it, and see if they are happy doing it.] *So, no matter how real or false human feelings are, they cannot be concealed in the slightest.*

A single letter cannot say it all.[87]

These letters followed a certain format, beginning with Nguyễn Trãi setting the tone by citing a famous saying, proverb, or historical precedent relevant to the issue he wished to address. He would then explain the events, present his rebuttals, and strengthen his arguments with examples drawn from Imperial China, showcasing both his knowledge and the legitimacy of his position. Each letter typically concluded with a warning about the consequences if the recipient failed to accept his proposals.

In Letter 23, Lê Lợi increased the pressure on Wang Tong by pointing out that he had 30,000 men plus 6,000 to 7,000 angry Ming soldiers, who came from various garrisons on Wang Tong's orders and promises of a safe return to China. They waited outside Đông Quan under the supervision of Lê Lợi's men. Furious at being deceived, they requested Lê Lợi's permission to launch an all-out attack against Wang Tong. Lê Lợi concluded the letter by warning that if Wang Tong failed to honour the terms of the truce, he would lead both his troops and the angry Ming soldiers in an assault on Đông Quan.[88]

1427: ATTACKING AND CAPTURING OTHER FORTS – PERSUADING WANG TONG TO SURRENDER

By late 1426 and early 1427, according to LSTL, Lê Lợi commanded more than 50,000 experienced troops, all eager to fight the Ming army.[89] Lê Lợi ordered his troops to capture the remaining Ming-held forts. The garrisons of Điêu Kê and Thị Cầu in the east surrendered in Feb/Mar 1427.[90] The Ming forces in Nghệ An and Diễn Châu forts also surrendered around the same time.[91] In the middle of 1427, his troops captured Tam Giang, in today's Vĩnh Phú, in the north-west and assaulted Xương Giang, which fell around September, according to TQTMT (or in April 1427 according to Ming shilu), and Ôn Khâu in the north-east, leaving only Đông Đô, Cổ Lộng, Tây Đô and Chí Linh under Ming control.[92] The last four forts held out until Wang Tong surrendered in November 1427.[93]

Xương Giang is approximately 60 kilometres north-east of Hanoi. It was a major fort on the supply route from Guangxi. Today, a memorial complex stands at the site, as shown in Figure 5-16, commemorating the victory of Đại Việt over the Ming army some five centuries ago.[94]

In early 1427, Lê Lợi moved his headquarters from Phù Liệt, near where Lê Lễ was, to Bồ Đề camp (present-day Gia Lâm), on the Red River's eastern bank, directly across from Đông Đô.[95] There, he trained his generals, recruited additional soldiers, prepared siege equipment, and deployed his troops to key mountain passes where he expected the Ming reinforcements to cross.[96]

Together with military actions, Lê Lợi also sent several letters in early 1427 to persuade the commanders of various garrisons close to Đông Quan to surrender, and they did. He sent Letters 30, 31 and 32 to the forts at Điêu Diêu (or Điêu Kê, likely to be in present-day Gia Lâm), Bắc Giang (or Thị-cầu) and Tam Giang warning them that their forts were weaker than those of other forts that had surrendered, and they lacked the manpower to withstand an onslaught from his forces. To heighten pressure, the letters even listed fallen forts, including some that had yet to be captured. The strategy proved effective, as these forts capitulated without a fight.[97]

His generals and troops urged him to assault Đông Đô Citadel but he told them:

> *Attacking the citadel is the lowest strategy [least effective]! We attack a strong citadel, and [we] may not take it for months or years. Our army will be exhausted and discouraged. If the enemy's reinforcements arrive, we will be attacked from the front and back, which is a dangerous situation! It is better to preserve our strength and wait a few days. When their reinforcements are defeated, the citadel will inevitably surrender. Doing one thing and achieving two [objectives]; that is the perfect strategy.*[98]

As a general military principle, defenders inside a besieged citadel may attempt a breakout when reinforcements arrive. However, in this instance, Lê Lợi likely assessed the Ming defenders were in no position to break out, and he had a better chance to defeat the reinforcements. Ultimately, his strategy proved correct, as events unfolded just as he had anticipated.

Lê Lợi was not rigid in his strategy of avoiding direct assault on forts, as he had earlier ordered the capture of the fort of Xương Giang to isolate Đông Đô completely from reinforcements, which proved to be one of the best decisions of his campaign.

While not assaulting Đông Đô, which they had surrounded since late 1426, and with other forts having surrendered, Lê Lợi stepped up the diplomatic pressure by sending several letters—33 to 37—to persuade Wang Tong to surrender.

In Letter 35, Lê Lợi outlined six reasons why Wang Tong's defeat was inevitable:[99]

- Floods destroyed defensive walls and fences, horses were dying, and soldiers were falling sick; supplies and forage were getting scarce.

- Lê Lợi's forces occupied all key strategic locations. They would defeat any reinforcements.

- The Ming's strong armies and good horses were stationed in the north to guard against the Mongols.

- Constant warfare had people worn out, restless and disillusioned.

- The Ming court was suffering from internal strife and political turmoil.

- Wang Tong's garrison troops were exhausted while Lê Lợi commanded an army of righteousness, united and well-trained.

As expected, Wang Tong did not share the same assessment of the situation. He likely believed that his best option was to hold out for reinforcements. In the meantime, he conducted several sorties to probe Lê Lợi's strength, during which the Ming soldiers killed two of Lê Lợi's top commanders: Lê Triện and Lê (or Đinh) Lễ. Wang Tong appeared to use these victories to boost his troops' morale. In response, Lê Lợi wrote to him in Letter 36, mocking Wang Tong that waiting for reinforcements and spreading rumours of their imminent arrival is like *talking about delusions in a dream. It's even more laughable!* In the same letter, Lê Lợi also claimed that his forces had taken Pingxiang and Longzhou, key locations inside Chinese territory likely intended as the staging areas for the reinforcements. Although the claim was false, it was a calculated move to demoralise Wang Tong further.[100]

Lê Lợi then challenged Wang Tong to come out of the fort and face him in open battle—whether by ships on the river or by infantry and cavalry in the paddy fields—and *not hide away in a corner of the fort, darting in and out to steal firewood and forage*. Lê Lợi followed up with Letter 37, taunting Wang Tong, calling Feng Zheng, Ma Qi 'defeated generals' and boasting even if a hundred Zhang Fus commanded the Ming forces, they would still be unable to defeat him. He claimed that, compared to the mere 2,000 half-staved men he had started with, his army now numbered at least 100,000 in the north and no fewer than 20,000 in the south.[101] His forces, he said, were armed with warships *reaching the sky*, gleaming armours, mountains of arrows and cannon balls, and enough captured supplies from the Ming forces to sustain them for 30 years. Against such a force, Lê Lợi argued Wang Tong could not hope to prevail and should instead follow the example of Cai Fu—surrender and retreat to China.[102]

The figure of 120,000 men that Lê Lợi claimed in Letter 37 was an exaggeration. LSTL notes in Book 2 that Lê Lợi commanded an army of 50,000 experienced soldiers; Book 3 presents a more modest and detailed account. It lists 35 military commanders—including Lê Thạch, Lê Lễ, Lê Sát, Lê Văn, Lê Lý, and Lê Ngân—alongside two civil officials, Lê Văn Linh and Lê Quốc Hưng. In terms of troops, he had 200 cavalry, 200 righteous warriors, 200 brave fighters, and 14 war elephants. The force was also accompanied by food porters and less able individuals who looked after families of around 2,000. According to LSTL, Lê Lợi only needed this force and other soldiers like sons, to fight the Ming army and expel the Laotians, winning over 100 battles.[103]

These figures, totalling less than 1,000 warriors, contradict the numbers given in LSTL (50,000) and TQTMT (30,000 and 120,000) and are likely significant underestimates. It would be implausible for Lê Lợi to have fought and won so many battles against the Ming army across such a vast territory with only 1,000 or even 10,000 men. I would suggest a more realistic figure for Lê Lợi's army would be 30,000 to 50,000.

1427: MING REINFORCEMENTS TO RESCUE WANG TONG

According to LSTL, the Ming emperor sent two waves of reinforcements as shown in Figure 5-19. The first, on 4 July 1427, was led by a Trần Viễn Hầu (*Zhen-yuan Marquis*), with 50,000 men and 1,000 horses from Guangxi. However, they were defeated by Lê (Trần) Lưu and Lê Bôi at Pha Lũy Pass, known today as Friendship Pass (*Ải Nam Quan*). Despite this failure, the Ming emperor ordered a second reinforcement, consisting of 200,000 men and 3,000 horses, led by Liu Sheng (a Marquis), Mu Sheng (a Duke), Liang Ming (*Lương Minh*, an Earl), Cui Ju (*Thôi Tụ*, an Admiral), Li Qing (*Lý Khánh*) (a Minister), and Huang Fu (a former Jiaozhi Minister), advancing from two directions: Liu Sheng from the north-east via Ôn Khâu and Mu Sheng from the north-west via Yunnan. Liu Sheng and his army reached the border on 8 October 1427.

Lê Lợi reassured his men, advising them not to fear the arrival of a large enemy force. He pointed out that the Ming troops would be exhausted from their rushed march to the rescue, whereas his forces could remain patient and well-rested. He told them, *we take our time and wait for their tired troops; there is no way we will not win!*

Lê Lợi then dispatched a force of 10,000 seasoned troops and five war elephants, led by Khả Lưu Pass veterans Lê Sát, Lê Lễ, and Lê Nhân Chú, to position themselves at Chi Lăng Pass, located south of Pha Lũy Pass.[104] Meanwhile, Lê Lợi remained at his headquarters outside Đông Đô, while the troops from his north-west column were still around the Phú Thọ region, ready to intercept the Ming reinforcements arriving from Yunnan.

After the Ming forces crossed the border, a series of battles ensued, resulting in devastating losses for the Ming army, with most of their commanders killed. These defeats culminated in the surrender of the Ming commanders trapped in Đông Kinh on 2 January 1428, bringing an end to the 20-year Ming occupation of Đại Việt. LSTL recounts these momentous events in just one page, which I have reconstructed as follows:

The north-east battles

- The first border fort at Pha Lũy Pass, commanded by Lê Lựu, fell to the Ming army under Liu Sheng's command shortly after they crossed the border.

- Lê Lựu withdrew to Truy Pass, but the Ming forces pressed forward, overwhelming his troops.

- Meanwhile, the bulk of Lê Lợi's forces were positioned at Chi Lăng Pass. As the Ming army approached, commanders Lê Sát and Lê Nhân Chú ordered Lê Lựu to launch an attack and then feign a retreat, luring the Ming troops into an ambush.

- Confident in his progress, Liu Sheng led the charge forward, only to fall into the trap. He, along with Li Qing and thousands of Ming soldiers, was killed in the ambush. He died on 10 October 1427.

- Lê Lợi then sent in additional troops with another veteran of the Khả Lưu Pass, Lê Văn An, who led an assault against Huang Fu and Cui Ju, driving them toward Mount Mã Yên, where the combined forces of Lê Sát and Lê Văn An routed them.

- The remaining Ming forces managed to break out of the trap and fled to Cần Trạm (modern Kép in Bắc Giang province, some 40 kilometres south-west of Mount Mã Yên) where Liang Ming was killed by a lance which pierced his armour, Li Qing also died in the same battle.[105] The survivors headed to the fort of Xương Giang, some 20 kilometres south-west of Cần Trạm, only to discover that it had already fallen to Lê Lợi's forces. Desperate, they built temporary palisades and sent firework signals to the Ming commanders inside Đông Đô for reinforcements, but Đông Đô was in no position to send assistance.

- Lê Lợi then ordered an all-out assault on the Ming positions while deploying troops to secure the key passes at Mã Yên, Chi Lăng, Pha Lũy and Bàn Quan (Pingxiang?). Trapped between Lê Lợi's forces, Huang Fu and Cui Ju found themselves in a dire situation—unable to retreat to China or advance to Đông Kinh. They requested a ceasefire but Lê Lợi refused and intensified the attacks. The Đại Việt forces captured Huang Fu and Cui Ju and inflicted heavy casualties on the Ming troops. LSTL vividly describes the aftermath of the battle: *Spears, lances, donkeys, horses, gold, silver, silk, brocade, and rattan, each box and each pile, piled up like mountains, beyond counting!*

The Ming reinforcement column from the north-east was completely annihilated. Following the victories, Lê Lợi wrote to Wang Tong in Letter 42 to inform him of the news and once again urged him to have his forces *remove their armours, open the gates of the citadel,* and return to China as had been agreed nearly a year earlier.[106]

Mã Yên (meaning 'horse saddle')—also known historically as Đảo Mã—is a small mountain marked by a stele beside Highway 1A connecting Hanoi and Lạng Sơn.[107] The site is approximately 2.6 kilometres south-west of the Chi Lăng Museum.[108] The pass is marked by another stele on the old road, DT234B, about 800 metres north of the museum, as shown in Figures 5-17 and 5-18.[109]

Figure 5-17: Chi Lăng Pass, viewed looking south.

Figure 5-18: A painting of the beheading of Liu Sheng in the Chi Lăng Museum. The caption reads *The bandit general Liễu Thăng [Liu Sheng] beheaded on the 20/9 lunar calendar or 10/10/1427 at the base of Mount Mã Yên.*

The modern map shows a stream flowing between the pass and Mount Mã Yên, running alongside Highway 1A. In the 15th century, this stream could be the river that Liu Sheng and his forces crossed.

The north-west battles

The Ming reinforcement column, led by Mu Sheng and Liang Minh, arrived and camped at Lê Hoa market, near the present-day Lào Cai border.[110] Lê Khả, the commander of Lê Lợi's forces in the north-west, prepared to attack, but Lê Lợi instructed him to wait. He anticipated that being old and cautious, Mu Sheng would hold off advancing until he had learned the fate of Liu Sheng's campaign.

Once Liu Sheng was killed and his forces defeated, Lê Lợi sent Liu Sheng's seal, along with a captured Ming commander and three guards to Mu Sheng's camp.[111] Upon receiving the seal, Mu Sheng immediately ordered a retreat. Seizing the opportunity, Lê Khả's troops surged forward on the retreating Ming army, inflicting heavy casualties and capturing many horses.

Note that according to Ming shilu, Liang Minh travelled with Liu Sheng, as mentioned previously.

1427–1428: THE END OF THE WAR AND MING OCCUPATION

By this time, the Ming commanders in Đông Đô and other forts had learned that both reinforcement columns had been decimated. However, some forts remained defiant, unwilling to believe the news. To convince them and prevent further bloodshed, Lê Lợi sent Huang Fu and Cui Ju, along with Liu Sheng's seal, captured weapons, flags, military records, horses, and Ming soldiers, to present evidence of the defeat. Upon seeing this, the remaining Ming forces abandoned their armour and promptly surrendered.

Around this time, Nguyễn Trãi intercepted a wax-sealed letter from Wang Tong in which the Ming commander expressed doubts about the viability of continuing the war. Even with a large army led by six or seven, or even eight capable generals like Zhang Fu, Wang Tong admitted that they would not be able to hold the territory in the long run, even if they achieved military victories. Based on this insight, Nguyễn Trãi counselled Lê Lợi to seek a peaceful settlement.[112]

However, it had taken over a month after the death of Liu Sheng in mid-October 1427 for events to reach a turning point. During that time, Lê Lợi sent at least five letters to Wang Tong following Letter 42. In these, he responded to Wang Tong's concerns, challenged his claims, and proposed terms for negotiation, including an exchange of hostages and a safe passage for the Ming forces. Lê Lợi offered his own son and Nguyễn Trãi—whom he referred to as his military advisor (*mưu sĩ*)—in exchange for Shan Shou and Ma Qi. However, there is no record that Nguyễn Trãi was ever handed over as a hostage.[113] However, according to the foreword, written in 1480, of one of Nguyễn Trãi's works, he undertook five dangerous trips to the Đông Đô Citadel about that time.[114]

To facilitate the withdrawal, Lê Lợi even proposed relocating his headquarters from Bồ Đề to Ninh Kiều, about 30 kilometres to the south-east, allowing Wang Tong to evacuate Đông Quan without pressure. In Letter 18, Lê Lợi firmly asserted that, *it is clear that Jiaozhi has never been part of China since ancient times*.[115]

Eventually, with no other options left, Wang Tong capitulated. Over 13 days from 19 November to 12 December 1427, Wang Tong, as the General-in-Chief, alongside Ma Ying, Li An, Chen Zhi, Ma Qi, Shan Shou, Fang Zheng and other Ming officials met with Lê Lợi, as the Principal Chieftain (*Đại Đầu Mục*) of An Nam, and his senior commanders, including Trần (Nguyên) Văn Hãn, Lê Nhân Chú, Trịnh Khả and others (notably Nguyễn Trãi was not among them). Together, they solemnly swore an oath before an altar dedicated to *the August Heaven, Generous Earth, Sacred Mountains, Great Rivers, and Local Spirits of All Regions*. The terms declared that Wang Tong would lead his troops back to China without delay, while Lê Lợi's forces would ensure their safe departure without obstruction or harm.[116]

Within three weeks of the declaration, on the 16th day of the 12th month of 1427 (2 January 1428), the Ming commanders in Đông Đô—Wang Tong, Ma Ying, Li An, Chen Zhi—along with Ma Qi, Shan Shou, Fang Zheng and

Yi Qian? (Dặc Khiêm), the commander of Tây Đô Citadel, He Zhong? (Hà Trung), and Chí Linh fort, Gao Xiang? (Cao Tường) gathered all the Đại Việt officials who had served the Ming administration and the local people the Ming officials forced to work inside the forts. Wang Tong only requested that Lê Lợi allowed him, his officials, officers and soldiers to return to China. There was no mention of local collaborators.

Lê Lợi's generals and soldiers, along with the local people who had long suffered the brutalities of Ming's rule, appealed to him to execute all the Ming personnel. They implored him to do so *to relieve the anger of Heaven, Earth, Gods, and People; to honour the loyal subjects and righteous men* [who had perished at the hands of the Ming occupiers]; *to comfort the innocent souls who had suffered injustice; and to wash away the immense humiliation of the kingdom!*[117]

Lê Lợi, while recognising the desire for revenge from his people, explained that it would be evil to execute those who had surrendered. Though it might bring temporary satisfaction, the stain of betraying accepted terms of surrender would last for eternity. Instead, he argued that sparing them would bring a true end to the war between the two countries and ensure that history would forever remember this act of mercy.

Having made his decision, Lê Lợi ordered 500 boats to be prepared with sufficient provisions for Wang Tong and his men. He released the captured commanders, Huang Fu and Cui Ju, along with Liu Sheng's seal. Additionally, he handed over more than 20,000 newly arrived troops and over 30,000 fort guards, men, women, and children, allowing them to return to China by either land or water, whichever route they preferred. Ming shilu records a higher figure of 86,640 and dates the departure of Wang Tong and his entourage as 3 January 1428.

LSTL does not specify the exact routes Wang Tong and his people took to return to China. Since 500 boats would not have been enough to transport 50,000 people, plus provisions and belongings, Wang Tong's convoy must have taken both the land and water routes. According to Minh shilu, Wang Tong, other commanders, clerks, and their families took the land route. They likely travelled via Chi Lăng and Pha Lũy Passes—the same path they had taken three months earlier in October 1426. Shan Shou, Chen Zhi and others travelled by the water route, which was likely by the Red River to the sea, and continued to the port at Beihai or Guangzhou.

In the winter of 1428, around February or March, Wang Tong and his men crossed the northern border into Longzhou, in present-day Guangxi province. As soon as they arrived, the Ming emperor issued an edict ordering the commanders to bring their soldiers home and return the land to An Nam.

An Nam was to resume sending tributes to the Ming court, as it had under the reign of Hong Wu. According to LSTL, the emperor realised that he had little choice but to formally acknowledge the fait accompli.

The war had come to an end, and LSTL concludes with a clear statement that *from the time of the uprising until the time of pacifying the enemy and restoration of the kingdom, the king had all the documents for military operations prepared by the civil servant Nguyễn Trãi.*[118]

Interestingly, LSTL notes that Lê Lợi sent an envoy with a letter of apology to the Ming court. However, to keep up the pretence, the letter was sent under Trần Cảo's name.[119] One might wonder why he chose to do so when the Ming dynasty had invaded and occupied Đại Việt for 20 years and thus should owe him an apology. The most plausible explanation is that Lê Lợi understood the delicate diplomacy required for a smaller country to preserve its sovereignty, while coexisting alongside a more powerful neighbour.

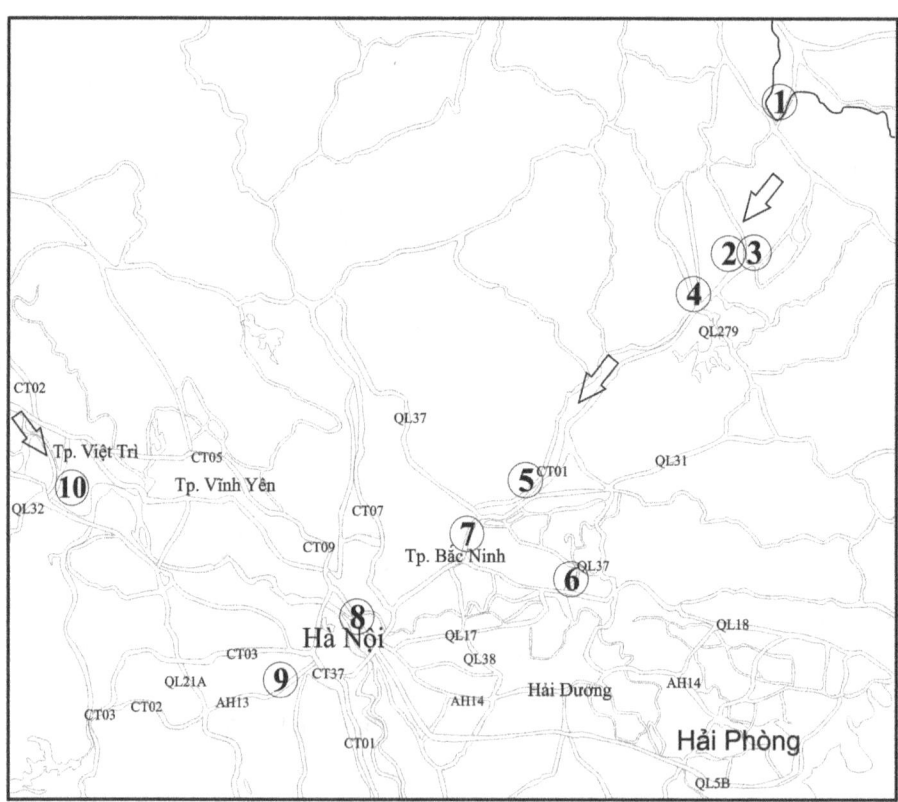

Figure 5-19: Map of Ming reinforcements at the end of 1427.

Key: 1. Friendship Pass (Ải Nam Quan); 2. Mai Sao; 3. Nhân Lý; 4. Chi Lăng Gorge; 5. Ancient fort of Xương Giang; 6. Chí Linh; 7. Đáp Cầu; 8. Gia Lâm Station; 9. Mai Lĩnh Bridge; 10. Tứ Xã. White arrows illustrates the direction of Ming reinforcements.

5.4 - Bình Ngô Đại Cáo (Great Proclamation upon the Pacification of the Wu)

Book 3 of LSTL briefly describes Lê Lợi's efforts after the liberation, his evaluation of Đại Việt's victory over the Ming forces, and includes the *Bình Ngô Đại Cáo* (Great Proclamation upon the Pacification of the Wu, abbreviated as BNĐC), which Lê Lợi instructed Nguyễn Trãi to write in 1428, shortly after the Ming army had withdrawn from Đại Việt.[120]

Up to this point in history, BNĐC is one of the most important documents in Vietnamese history, along with other foundation texts such as the poem *Nam Quốc Sơn Hà* (Southern Country's Mountains and Rivers, 10th–11th centuries), the declaration *Chiếu Dời Đô* (Edict to Transfer the Capital, 11th century), and the *Hịch Tướng Sĩ* (Proclamation to Military Officers, 13th century); the last three of which are discussed in Volume 3A.

The version of BNĐC that I refer to contains 145 lines, which can be divided into five paragraphs.[121] In the opening, comprising 20 lines, Nguyễn Trãi outlines the guiding principles of Lê Lợi's leadership—upholding humanity and justice, caring for people, punishing wrongdoers and eradicating cruelty. Nguyễn Trãi also affirms that Đại Việt had long been a sovereign country, with its territory and customs since ancient times dating back to Zhao Tuo in the 3rd century BCE, distinct from its northern neighbour. He concludes this section with a strong assertion: *Although the strengths and weaknesses may sometimes vary, there has never been a shortage of heroes!*[122] He cited the deaths of Omar (*Ô Mã Nhi*) Baghatur and Sodu (*Toa Đô*) as examples of foreigners who had previously attempted to conquer Đại Việt. However, he emphasized that it was the harsh and oppressive policies of the Hồ dynasty, combined with the actions of local collaborators willing to betray the country to the Ming dynasty, that ultimately enabled the Ming invasion and occupation of Đại Việt.[123]

In the following 20 lines, Nguyễn Trãi vividly portrays the atrocities committed by the Ming occupiers over 20 years—their oppressive taxation, the enslavement of the population, and the ruthless exploitation of the land's resources. The suffering was so severe that, as he wrote, *Even worms, bugs, grass, and trees do not know there will be a day of joy!*[124]

The next 30 lines recount Lê Lợi's early struggles and hardships during a time when Ming forces were powerful, and when he lacked capable allies to support his cause. Nguyễn Trãi captured this sense of isolation with the lament, *Unfortunately: outstanding men are* [rare] *like morning stars! Talented individuals are* [scarce] *like autumn leaves!*[125] Yet Lê Lợi remained undeterred. He viewed adversity as a test from heaven, pushing himself harder and firmly believed that righteousness would ultimately triumph over cruelty and that compassion would prevail over violence. He also embraced the strategy of surprise attacks to catch the enemy was off guard. He also believed the weak could overcome the strong and that through a well-planned ambush, a few could defeat the many.

Then the tide of battle turned, but BNĐC does not explain what triggered the shift in Lê Lợi's fortunes, as detailed in the following 60 lines of his military victories. These begin with the battle of Trà Lạn (Trà Long), followed by ten days of successive defeats suffered by Liu Sheng's army, between the 8th and 18th of October 1427, and culminating in the decisive rout of Mu Sheng's forces at Cần Trạm.[126] The paragraph concludes with an act of clemency: Lê Lợi provided 500 ships to ensure the safe return of the Ming commanders, their officials and their families to China.

This 4th paragraph is also full of contemptuous depictions of the Ming high command, from the mocking remark that *the brat* [Emperor] *Xuande ordered his generals to bring oil to extinguish the fire!* to *Admiral Cui Jui knelt and presented gifts* and *Minister Huang Fu shamelessly surrendered himself!* These disdainful portrayals starkly contrast to the deferential tone of Lê Lợi's memorials to the Ming court, as recorded in Ming shilu. Similarly, Ming shilu records that the people of Jiaozhi regarded Huang Fu as a father figure, while dismissing Lê Lợi as nothing more than a common bandit. While such contrasting perspectives are not surprising, they highlight how deeply the Ming court misjudged the strength of Lê Lợi's forces and his appeal to the local people.

The final 15 lines close with a tone of pride, optimism, and gratitude to heaven:

> *Not only is the strategy extremely profound!*
> *But it is also unprecedented in history!*
> ...
> *To lay the foundation for ten thousand generations!*
> *To wash away the shame for a thousand ancient years!*
> *It was through the spirits of Heaven, Earth, and the sacred ancestors, who silently and secretly bestowed their protection, that this has come to be!*[127]

The last three lines of BNĐC reads:

> *Peace now reigns across the four seas.*
> *Thus, this proclamation of renewal is issued*
> *To be announced far and wide, so that all may hear and know.*[128]

THE SCHOLARS' DEBATE

Scholars have offered various interpretations of BNĐC and I have summarised the key points as follows:

Firstly, there are different views on the meaning of the term *Ngô/Wu* in the title. One interpretation suggests that *Ngô* refers to the ancestral homeland of Zhu Yuanzhang, the founder of the Ming dynasty, who once held the titles Duke of Wu and King of Wu.[129] In this context, Nguyễn Trãi could have deliberately chosen the term as a form of diplomatic subtlety, avoiding a direct reference to the pacification of the Ming occupiers. However, given the document's contemptuous description of the Ming high command, this is unlikely. The opposite may be the case where *Ngô* could be a disdainful term used to describe the Ming people at the time. The compilers of SKTT refer to the Ming people as *giặc Ngô* (Wu Bandits) several times.[130]

In contrast, other scholars argue that *Ngô* refers to the Sino-Vietnamese coastal communities in the lower Red River Delta—regions that Lê Lợi, coming from the mountainous Thanh Hóa region, had to subdue.[131] In this interpretation, *Ngô* also encompasses internal rival factions, including remnants of the Trần and Hồ dynasties.[132]

Along with these interpretations are different views on the meaning of North (*Bắc*) and South (*Nam*) in BNĐC.[133] Did Nguyễn Trãi refer to Imperial China as *Bắc*, or was he discussing *Bắc* as the lower delta of the Red River and *Nam* as the Thanh Hóa region?

Secondly, another scholar mentions that BNĐC represents a second declaration of independence, the first being the poem *Nam Quốc Sơn Hà* mentioned above.[134] However, other disagrees and suggests that BNĐC was written for a domestic audience and not aimed at China.[135]

Having studied the whole episode of the Ming invasion, occupation and eventual forced departure from Đại Việt, I believe Nguyễn Trãi composed BNĐC primarily for a domestic audience. It was not a declaration of independence, as he made it clear that Đại Việt had long been a separate country founded by the *Triệu, Đinh, Lý, Trần* dynasties. Likewise, the terms *Ngô, Wu* and *Bắc, North* refer to the Ming and Imperial China, while *Nam, South* signifies Đại Việt. It would be doubtful that he meant otherwise, especially given that the entire liberation campaign as described in BNĐC centred on expelling the Ming occupiers. Letter 16 of QTTMT makes this distinction very clear. In response to Wang Tong's proposal to the Ming emperor—to pardon An Nam and to restore a Trần descendant to the throne—Nguyễn Trãi wrote, *If that truly comes to pass, then from now on, there will be peace between the North and the South*.[136]

In writing BNĐC, Nguyễn Trãi may have adopted a practice of Imperial China where emperors issued proclamations to publicly announce major events, for example, Emperor Yongle's proclamation on 5 July 1407 announcing that An Nam had been pacified.[137]

5.5 - *The aftermath*

THE PUNISHMENTS

Wang Tong

Back in Nanning in Guangxi, Wang Tong, needing to justify his decision to surrender Đông Quan to Lê Lợi's forces, submitted a memorial to the Ming court in early 1428. As expected, the memorial portrays Wang Tong in a favourable light, but it still offers valuable historical insights despite some inconsistencies. I have summarised the key points of his memorial below:[138]

- When Lê Lợi's forces surrounded Đông Quan in 1427, Wang Tong led and won several battles, killing Lê Triện (*Li Zhi*) and Đinh Lễ (or Lê Lễ, *Dinh Li*), and temporarily relieved pressure on the citadel.

- But Lê Lợi's forces regrouped, installed a pretender king (Trần Cảo) and crossed the river (the Red River) to continue their offensive.

- Wang Tong awaited reinforcements but learned of the deaths of three senior commanders, Liu Sheng, Liang Ming and Li Qing. Meanwhile, Lê Lợi's forces attacked Cui Ju's troops at the Chang River and halted Mu Sheng's advance.

- Lê Lợi, fearing further Ming reinforcements, sent an envoy to Wang Tong's headquarters requesting permission to surrender. Lê Lợi also admitted guilt and offered tribute, including two human figures, one in gold and the other in silver, representing Trần Cảo and himself, along with different gifts.

- Lê Lợi sent his son and nephew to Wang Tong's headquarters with tribute and an expression of his willingness to submit to the Ming court, and a request that the Ming army be withdraw. The request was approved, and both sides agreed that the Ming army would withdraw on the first day of the 12th lunar month, corresponding to 18 December 1427.[139]

In response:

- Wang Tong dispatched Cai Fu and Lu Zeng (*Lỗ Tăng*), along with 13,391 people and 1,200 horses and mules, back to the capital (Beijing) with a request that the army withdraws.

Negotiation broke down:

- Lê Lợi then intensified his attacks and captured several key positions by land and water.

- Wang Tong, low on troops and without reinforcements, wanted to continue fighting but, after consultation with his officers, agreed to withdraw from Đông Quan and regroup in Guangxi, while awaiting the emperor's orders.

- He proposed that the court send officials to assess whether Trần Cảo was indeed a descendant of the Trần royal line. If not, the emperor could launch another expedition, with Wang Tong and his men ready to rejoin the campaign—pledging, if they failed again, to face execution.

The emperor was not persuaded by Wang Tong's justification. In June 1428, he approved the recommendation from five military commissions that Wang Tong, Chen Zhi, Ma Ying, Fang Zheng and Yi Qian be sent to prison, with the charges being: *violated the Court's orders and took it upon themselves to make peace with the bandits* [Lê Lợi's forces], *abandon the city and return*. Shan Shou was also imprisoned for *protected rebellious bandits*, and Ma Qi was jailed *for provoked rebellion in the region*. The property of their families was also confiscated.[140] Wang Tong was eventually released over a decade later, in 1439, and lived as an ordinary citizen. His status and property were restored in 1450, and he passed away in 1452.[141]

Cai Fu

Other Ming senior commanders were not as fortunate; they paid the ultimate price for failures. A month after Wang Tong and his colleagues were sentenced to prison Cai Fu, Zhu Guang, Xue Ju (*Tiết Tụ*), Yu Zan (*Chu Tán*), Lu Gui (*Lỗ Quý*) and Li Zhong (*Lý Trung*) were executed.[142]

While Zhang Fu was ruthless, Wang Tong and Chen Zhi were timid, and Liu Sheng was reckless, Cai Fu was a brave but complex figure among the Ming commanders. He was among the first over the wall at the battle of Đa Bang Fort in 1407 and was involved in fighting against the later Trần kings in 1409. Nearly two decades later, in 1426, tasked to defend the fort of Nghệ An after Li An and Fang Zheng escaped. He chose to abandon the fort and retreat to Đông Quan, citing the lack of supplies.

However, Letter 11 of TQTMT offers a different account, stating that Lê Lợi was so pleased with Cai Fu's surrender to Trần Cảo in front of the Nghệ An fort that he sent 15 ships to transport Cai Fu and his family, along with other Ming officials to Đông Quan.[143] The event happened around February 1427.

Nevertheless, according to Ming shilu, on their retreat from Nghệ An, Lê Lợi's forces intercepted the Ming forces and captured Cai Fu. Lê Lợi's men then marched Cai Fu to other forts and urged the defenders to surrender. At the battle of Chiang River Fort, Cai Fu approached the walls and called on Li Ren, the fort commander, to surrender. From the top of the rampart, Li Ren spat and cursed him: *You, a senior minister, cannot kill bandits and instead are employed by them. You are not even the equal of a dog or a pig!* He then fired the cannons at Cai Fu. As the fort fell, Li Ren took his own life by slitting his own throat.[144]

Cai Fu was also accused of trying to talk the defender of the city of Thanh Hóa into surrendering. After Wang Tong entered negotiations with Lê Lợi in 1427, he sent Cai Fu, presumably released by that time, together with a large contingent of people, back to China, where he was sentenced and executed within a year in 1428. Like Wang Tong, Cai Fu may have come to believe that the war was lost and that continuing the occupation of Đại Việt was futile. Alternatively, as a middle-aged man, he may have simply hoped to return home safely, but that was not to be. Similarly, Cai Fu's comrade-in-arms, Zhu Guang, was executed for the crime of opening the gates to allow Lê Lợi's forces to enter.[145]

Interestingly, before Cai Fu returned to China at the end of 1427, Lê Lợi had offered him a position at the court of Đại Việt in Letter 38 in TQTMT.[146] We do not have his reply, but he must have declined the offer and returned to China, where he was later investigated and executed by the imperial commission, as previously noted.

Mu Sheng

The five military commissions and other officials also recommended the impeachment of Mu Sheng and his two subordinates, Xu Heng and Tang Zhong. They were accused of deliberately stalling their advance, taking three months to reach the border between Yunnan and Đại Việt, and then withdrawing instead of proceeding to relieve Đông Quan after learning of Liu Sheng's death. This decision had allowed Lê Lợi's forces to attack the retreating army, inflicting heavy casualties and loss of weapons. The commissions may have been justified in the charges. On today's map, the distance from Kunming—the provincial capital of Yunnan—to Hekouzhen at the border is roughly 400 kilometres. Taking 90 days to cover that distance suggests that either Mu Sheng spent an extended period preparing his troops before marching, or that their pace was extremely slow, with frequent stops and plenty of rest along the way. However, the emperor told the officials not to investigate Mu Sheng and to wait for Heng and Zhong's return. The matter was then dropped.[147] I suspect the emperor was reluctant to remove Mu Sheng from his post in Yunnan, given its strategic importance to the dynasty. As it turned out, the Mu family continued to govern the region for another two hundred years, lasting into the 17th century.[148] Mu Sheng had made the right decision to retreat from Đại Việt after all.

Lương Nhữ Hốt, Trần Phong and Đỗ Duy Trung

In the final days of 1428, Lê Lợi ordered the execution of eight collaborators, including his nemesis, Lương Nhữ Hốt, the prefect of Thanh Hóa prefecture, Trần Phong, a military commander and Đỗ Duy Trung, a prefect of Hóa Châu and later, Tam Giang.[149]

AN UNEASY TRANSITION

Despite reprimanding Wang Tong, Emperor Xuande had already agreed to his recommendation. Upon receiving the letter from Lê Lợi and a memorial from Trần Cảo in 1427, he dispatched Vice Minister Li Qi (*Lý Kỳ*) to Giao Chỉ, as previously mentioned. However, once Wang Tong and his forces returned to Guangxi, the emperor seemed to realise that Ming had indeed lost the war. During the first three months of 1428, the Ming court issued a series of imperial orders admonishing various commanders for their failures, ordering troops to their original barracks, and strengthening the borders.

At the end of March 1428, the envoy from Đại Việt, Lê Thiếu Dĩnh (*Li Shao-ying*), arrived at the Ming court. He presented a second memorial from Trần Cảo, and the gold and silver human figures mentioned earlier to the emperor. The tone of the memorial was deferential, seeking the emperor's formal approval for Trần Cảo to: *inherit the wilds of the southern border and bring tribute to the Heavenly Court.*[150]

Two weeks later, in mid-April 1428, Lê Thiếu Dĩnh departed for Đại Việt, carrying an imperial order addressed to Lê Lợi, along with gifts of fine silks and paper money. The emperor approved the request that: *A descendant of the Chen* [Trần] *family be enthroned*. Still, he instructed that Lê Lợi and other chieftains and elders must first verify the legitimacy of the claimant and report the findings. Only then, would the court consider formal enfeoffment. Trần Cảo's name was not mentioned in the order.

The emperor also reproached Lê Lợi for his actions, stating: *You hurriedly discussed peace with Wang Tong and induced him to withdraw the government troops. You then occupied the city. This was presumptuous and improper in the extreme.* But despite recommendations from the military ministers to punish Lê Lợi, the emperor chose instead to pardon him. He also demanded that Lê Lợi return all the people and weapons which he had retained.[151]

In June 1428, Li Qi returned from Jiaozhi accompanied by envoys from Lê Lợi. They informed the Ming court that Trần Cảo had died early that year, on 26 January 1428. The envoys also conveyed that the people of Đại Việt had chosen Lê Lợi to lead the country.[152]

Nearly nine months later, in March 1429, Luo Ru-jing returned to the Ming court with another envoy from Lê Lợi. The envoy reported that no descendant of the Trần dynasty could be found. He also advised that all the people and weapons requested by the court had already been returned with Wang Tong in late 1427. However, the emperor remained unconvinced. In May 1429, he dispatched Li Qi back to Jiaozhi with an imperial order, instructing the search for a Trần descendant to continue and demanding that all weapons—wherever found, except those abandoned in the hills or swamps—be returned.

The diplomatic back-and-forth dragged on for the next two years. The Ming court continued to press for the discovery of a Trần descendant and the return of all captured people and weapons. Meanwhile, Đại Việt showed little interest in finding a Trần heir or surrendering the Ming weapons they had seized. Instead, their priority was to obtain formal recognition of Lê Lợi as the legitimate ruler of the country. They also reminded the Ming of the emperor's earlier suggestion to repatriate students and officials who had remained in the capital after the war. In April 1430, Lê Lợi's envoy reported that Đại Việt had located and was preparing to return an additional 280 military officials,

157 civil officials and clerks, 15,170 soldiers and 1,200 horses to be returned to Guangxi—but notably, no weapons.[153]

Eventually, the emperor relented. In July 1431, he agreed to send special envoys bearing an official seal and instructed Lê Lợi to take charge and govern An Nam temporarily.[154] Three years later, Ming shilu's entry on 17 April 1434 states that Lê Lợi had died.[155]

Barely a year later, on 31 January 1435, Emperor Xuande died. His elder son, Zhu Qizhen, succeeded him as Emperor Yingzong (1427–1464). In 1437, the emperor formally granted Lê Lợi's son—Lê Nguyên Long, or King Lê Thái Tông—the title of the King of An Nam State (*An Nam Quốc Vương*).[156]

Mu Sheng died in 1439 at 71 in Yunnan.[157] His fellow commander, Zhang Fu, died a few years later in 1449, at 74 in northern China.[158]

CHAPTER 6

THE EARLY LÊ (LÊ SƠ) DYNASTY (1428–1527)

6.1 - Lê Lợi (King Lê Thái Tổ, r.1428–1433)

A DISCIPLINARIAN KING

In early January 1428, Wang Tong, along with his military and civilian officials, their soldiers, and their families, evacuated Đông Quan. Several months later, around May, Lê Lợi and his entourage departed their temporary camp in Bồ Đề—located in present-day Gia Lâm—crossed the Red River, and entered Đông Quan. By then, Wang Tong and his forces had returned to China, and Lê Lợi's men had made ample preparations to welcome him as the new king of Đại Việt and the founder of the Later Lê dynasty.

Later that month, on 28 May, Lê Lợi was formally crowned. He renamed Đông Quan back to Đông Kinh and restored the name of the kingdom to Đại Việt—a name that had existed since 1054 before being changed to Đại Ngu by Hồ Quý Ly, and later to Giao Chỉ under Ming occupation. However, even before this official coronation, Lê Lợi had already exercised authority as the Principal Chieftain. When he first approached the outskirts of Đông Quan in 1426 and camped at Phù Liệt, crowds had gathered to welcome him. From that position, he began governing by establishing four circuits covering present-day northern Vietnam, issuing orders to military and civilian officials to patrol the river estuaries, arrest collaborators, seize their families and assets, and recruit talented individuals. He also imposed strict rules forbidding his troops from cutting down trees, picking fruits or taking property from locals without consent.[1]

In early 1427, Lê Lợi moved his headquarters to Bồ Đề. Champa, astutely predicted a Lê Lợi victory over the Ming army, sent tribute. In response, Lê Lợi received the Cham envoys with honour, gifting them edible birds' nests, silks, horses, and instructing them to return home. While at Bồ Đề, when the war was still ongoing, he issued at least 45 edicts covering a wide range of matters—from opening foundries for iron production, manufacturing weapons, to establishing shrines, recruiting talented individuals, and resettling those displaced by the war.[2] Among these was a strict set of ten military regulations for his commanders and troops. These rules addressed offences such as causing disorder, spreading false rumours, hesitating in battle, disobeying commands to retreat, deserting posts, indulging in women, accepting bribes, favouritism, quarrelsomeness, and theft. Violators faced harsh punishment.[3]

These laws demonstrated Lê Lợi's firm belief in military discipline, which he upheld even after ascending the throne. The edict that he issued in the first year as a king in 1428 illustrates his governing philosophy:

From ancient times to the present, governing a country must have laws; without laws, there will be chaos. Thus, studying the past shows that laws were established to educate generals, officials, and down to the ordinary people, so they could understand what is good and what is evil, to do good and avoid evil things, so as not to end up violating the law.

Under Lê Lợi's reign, the laws were strict and unambiguous. For example, activities such as gambling, playing chess, and drinking in groups were strictly forbidden. Violators faced harsh penalties: gamblers had five fingers severed, chess players had a centimetre of their fingers cut off, and those caught drinking in groups were subjected to 100 strokes with a staff.[4]

Figure 6-1 depicts a statue of Lê Lợi in Thanh Hóa City, standing with a sword in his left hand and a turtle at his left foot. He is dressed in what appears to be a breastplate adorned with two dragons flanking a sun.[5]

Front view · Side view

Figure 6-1: The statue of 'National Hero Lê Lợi' at Thanh Hóa City.

The stature was installed on 29 November 2004. It was carved from blue stone, and stands approximately 16 metres in height and weighs 480 tonnes.[6]

GOVERNING WITH HIS WAR-TIME COMMANDERS

Unlike the Lý and Trần dynasties before him, Lê Lợi did not have many family members to appoint to senior positions in his government. Many of his close relatives had been captured by the Ming soldiers or scattered during the war. So when he became king in 1428, he turned to those who had commanded his army to help him govern. Many of these were among the original 18 men who had taken the blood oath with him in Lũng Nhai 12 years earlier, in 1416.

In 1429, he conferred the title of 'meritorious official' (*công thần*) on 93 individuals, granting them the noble rank of marquis (*hầu*) across nine hierarchical tiers, in recognition of their roles in the liberation campaign and the founding of the Later Lê dynasty. Among them were 11 of the 18 men who had taken the blood oath at Lũng Nhai, at least two had died during the war, and the remaining five were not listed. Interestingly, the top three recipients were not among the original 18, and Nguyễn Trãi, despite his prominence as the compiler of Lê Lợi's letters and documents, was ranked at the sixth tier, the lowest among those from the Lũng Nhai oath group. His relatively modest placement may reflect Lê Lợi's preference for rewarding military figures over civilian officials.[7]

One of the top three honourees was Lê Văn, originally Phạm Vấn, who had already been recognised in 1428 as one of the gunners in Lê Lợi's army. That year, 1428, Lê Lợi rewarded 121 fire-tube operators or gunners (*hỏa thủ*) and their troops for their contributions to the resistance effort dating back to Lũng Nhai. As a further mark of honour, he also granted them the right to adopt his royal surname, Lê.[8] Lê Văn was later appointed as a *Nhập nội kiểm hiệu bình chương sự* (Inner Court Acting Chancellor) and became a *Đô Đốc* (Admiral). The second honouree, Lê Sát, was named *Nhập nội tư khấu* (Inner Court Grand Marshal or Minister of War). The third, Lê Văn Xảo, originally Phạm Văn Xảo, was granted the title of *Thái Bảo* (Grand Protector).[9]

All three men were among Lê Lợi's most trusted military commanders during the resistance against the Ming occupiers. Lê Văn had fought alongside him during the desperate battles of early 1423, and both he and Lê Sát were key figures in the decisive Khả Lưu campaign in late 1424. Lê Sát, a native of Lam Sơn, joined Lê Lợi in the early stages of the uprising and quickly distinguished himself as a courageous and effective field general. He secured major victories at Quan Du in 1420 and Xương Giang in 1427, and was the principal strategist behind the successful campaign against Liu Sheng that same year. After the war, he was appointed *Đại Tư Đồ* (Grand Minister over the Masses or Prime Minister of Civil Affairs), acting as regent during the early reign of Lê Lợi's successor.[10]

While Lê Văn and Lê Sát hailed from Lương Giang (modern-day Thiệu Hóa, located downstream from Thọ Xuân) and Lam Sơn, respectively, the third commander, Phạm Văn Xảo, was from the vicinity of Đông Quan. He likely joined Lê Lợi early in the resistance and rose to become a leading general in the northern campaigns, particularly in the battles against Mu Sheng and Wang Tong in 1427.

Lê Văn died peacefully in 1435, but Phạm Văn Xảo met a more tragic end. Within a few years of appointing him as a *Thái Bảo*, Lê Lợi became suspicious of Xảo's intention and had him executed around 1430 on the advice of minor court officials.[11] Lê Sát survived a few years longer, but his fate was similarly grim, when Lê Lợi's successor forced him to commit suicide at home in 1437.

Lê Lợi also forced the death of another general, Trần Nguyễn Hãn, who had played a key role in driving out the Ming forces from the north-central provinces of present-day Thừa Thiên-Huế, Quảng Trị and Quảng Bình in 1425.[12] In his final years, Lê Lợi grew increasingly anxious about securing his succession, and Phạm Văn Xảo and Trần Nguyễn Hãn, being from outside the Lam Sơn region, were seen as a potential threat.[13] Before his death, Lê Lợi reportedly expressed regrets at having these two men killed, but by then, it was too.[14] Notably, neither of the men participated in the Lũng Nhai oath-taking ceremony. If they did, Lê Lợi might have hesitated as the oath takers had pledged *live or die together, never forget the heartfelt blood oath*.[15]

Trần Nguyên Hãn was of the Trần Nguyên Đán lineage and was a cousin of Nguyễn Trãi. This connection could explain Nguyễn Trãi's brief imprisonment—an experience he reflected upon in his poem, *Than Oan*, (Lamenting Justice).[16] It might also shed light on why he was ranked only sixth out of ninth on Lê Lợi's list of meritorious officials.

The jostling for power among Lê Lợi's commanders after the war also led to the death of Lê Nhân Chú, originally named Lưu Nhân Chú from Thái Nguyên, and one of the 18 oath takers at Lũng Nhai. Although they had fought side by side in numerous campaigns, Lê Sát did not like Lê Nhân Chú and had him poisoned.[17]

I have included these events to highlight the political turbulence in the early years of the Later Lê dynasty and to illustrate the recurring pattern of 'meritorious officials' eliminating each other as they competed for influence and as the Lê royal family worked to consolidate its hold on power.

ADMINISTRATION

Lê Lợi named his reign *Thuận Thiên* (In Accord with Heaven) and expanded the administrative structure by adding a fifth circuit to the four he had established in 1426. At that point, Đại Việt was divided into five circuits arranged in a clockwise direction: West, North, East, South, and Western Sea (*Hải Tây*). Centred around Hanoi, the first four circuits encompassed the northwest, north, east, and southeast regions. The Western Sea circuit covered the area stretching from Thanh Hóa to just north of the Hải Vân Pass.[18] Beyond that pass, Champa still controlled territory extending as far south as present-day Bình Thuận province.

A *Tổng quản* (a Governor General or Chief Manager) headed each circuit, and in the early years of the Later Lê dynasty, Lê Lợi typically filled these roles with those selected from among the 18 Lũng Nhai oath-takers, such as Phạm (Lê) Bôi for the Eastern Circuit and Lê Văn An for the Northern Circuit.[19] Under the previous dynasties, these positions would have been filled by close relatives of the kings.

Lê Lợi maintained a simple administrative structure. Below him were Left and Right Generals and a combination of 'Three Ministers': Grand Tutor (*thái phó*), Grand Commandant (*thái uý*), Grand Protector (*thái bảo*), and their deputies (*thiếu phó, thiếu uý, thiếu bảo*). These positions were accompanied by key ministerial roles such as the Minister of War (*tư mã*), Minister of Works (*tư không*), and Minister of Justice (*tư khấu*). Several of these senior positions were held by the original Lũng Nhai oath-takers; for example, Lê Nhân Chú served as the Minister of Works, while Lê (Bùi) Quốc Hưng held the post of Deputy Commandant.

Beneath this upper tier were the operational branches of government, divided into military and civil sectors. For the administrative side, Lê Lợi appointed Nguyễn Trãi as *Hành khiển* (Chief Administrator), entrusting him with the drafting of royal edicts and administrative orders and other duties such as compiling LSTL.

THE ARMY, WEAPONS AND TACTICS

By 1427, Lê Lợi had built a formidable military force that included infantry, cavalry, elephantry, and a small naval fleet. He ordered the establishment of foundries to produce weapons, including swords, knives, spearheads, arrowheads, and other iron tools. Meanwhile, naval yards constructed warships capable of carrying up to 50 soldiers—likely narrow, shallow-draft vessels designed for riverine operations and coastal transport.[20] His forces built vehicles to assault forts, but they also used weapons captured from the Ming army, particularly fire tubes and small cannons.[21]

The Hồ and late Trần kings frequently battled the Ming troops along rivers, but Lê Lợi's forces primarily fought on land. Their tactics centred on ambushes, sieges, and occasional assaults on Ming fortifications, with little emphasis on flanking manoeuvres or direct frontal attacks. While soldiers on both sides would use ranged weapons like fire tubes, bows, and arrows, combat often devolved into close-quarters fighting with swords, lances, and other melee weapons. In general, the Ming army relied on cavalry, whereas Đại Việt forces typically deployed war elephants on the battlefield.

According to ĐVTS, Lê Lợi reportedly had 350,000 troops before he reached Đông Đô. He intended to discharge 250,000 and retain 100,000 for active service after the war. However, this figure seems doubtful, as most of his campaign directives typically involved forces ranging from a few thousand to ten thousand men at most.[22]

6.2 - A reflection on Lê Lợi – An analysis of success

On 5 October 1433, Lê Lợi passed away peacefully in his bed at the palace in Đông Kinh. The old war horse finally found rest, just two years short of his 50th birthday.[23]

Up to this point in Vietnamese history, there had been many heroes, but it would be difficult to find someone who had achieved as much as Lê Lợi in the near-impossible task of expelling a powerful foreign invader, particularly when such an invader had occupied Đại Việt for 20 years.

Unlike earlier military leaders such as Ngô Quyền, Lê Hoàn, Lý Thường Kiệt, and Trần Hưng Đạo (my previous volumes cover their stories), who had commanded established armies with trained soldiers, seasoned commanders, weapons, logistical support, armoury, horses, war elephants, and boats, Lê Lợi began his resistance with almost nothing. He had no formal army, only a handful of local commanders and villagers who picked up whatever makeshift weapons they could find: spears, knives, swords—often homemade. While a few may have had prior experience from earlier Trần rebellions, most were simple farmers. Though they started with some elephants and horses, Lê Lợi's forces were quickly decimated by Ming suppression campaigns, forcing the remnants to retreat into the mountains, where they barely survived.[24]

From this humble beginning, how did Lê Lợi and his followers accomplish such an extraordinary feat?

Lê Lợi's views

Historians have offered various explanations to this question, but perhaps it's best to begin with Lê Lợi's own words. When they had a quiet moment, Lê Lợi often discussed with his ministers the causes of the rise and decline, the success and failure of past regimes. A few years before his death, during one of those lulls in his busy schedules, his ministers asked him why the Ming invaders failed and why the king succeeded.

His ministers suggested that the Ming forces had lost because their brutality and corrupt rule, which alienated the people and ultimately cost them the war. In contrast, Lê Lợi had replaced cruelty with compassion and chaos with order, earning the people's trust and securing victory.

While Lê Lợi agreed with this reasoning, he offered a more personal and detailed perspective, as recorded in LSTL. I have summarised his response as follows:

a) Lê Lợi did not initially intend to rebel; the uprising was born out of necessity. Despite his efforts to please the Ming commanders, they did not let him live in peace, leaving him no choice. He had no thought of seizing the realm.

b) He and his family suffered terribly at the hands of the Ming occupiers. His family was scattered, he and his followers did not have enough to eat and clothes to wear, and, at one point, eight or nine out of ten deserted him but he never wavered. He saw these trials as Heaven's way of testing his resolve and each time the Ming commanders tried to weaken him, his determination grew.

c) With each victory over the Ming forces, Lê Lợi's forces seized valuable supplies, weapons, gold, and silver. Many who had once deserted him returned, often bringing with them former Ming soldiers who had switched sides. These growing successes, along with his survival through years of hardship, only strengthened his convictions that Heaven had abandoned the Ming army and favoured his cause.

d) Even the Laotians, who had once been allies, turned against Lê Lợi. However, he was able to anticipate their actions, turning their territory into a base for his troops and using the region's rugged terrain to trap his enemies.

e) Lê Lợi believed in dealing with others sincerely, treating his followers like family. He learned to restrain his anger, entrusting others with confidence, which was why he was able to win people's hearts and support.

f) Ultimately, Lê Lợi attributed his success to Heaven's blessing and the virtue of his ancestors.

g) He concluded his reflections by telling the ministers:

Remember that the Mandate of Heaven is not always guaranteed; one must consider the difficulties when planning easy things. Great endeavours are difficult to build but easy to ruin; one must be careful at the beginning and plan for the future. Guard against the seeds of disaster, which often grow during times of peace. Check the rise of arrogance and luxury, sometimes, comfort and happiness can cause trouble. Only by doing so can the legacy be preserved.

Reading his response, one cannot help but be moved by Lê Lợi's unwavering resolve to drive out the Ming occupiers and his deep convictions that Heaven supported his cause. Notably, he made no mention of superior strategy, advanced weaponry, or the unification of the Đại Việt people as reasons for his victories.

THE EARLY LÊ (LÊ SƠ) DYNASTY (1428–1527)

Views of Later Lê dynasty's historians

The compilers of SKTT—officials of the Later Lê dynasty—offered additional, specific reasons for Lê Lợi's military success. They highlighted his use of ambush tactics, his strategy of avoiding well-defended positions while targeting weaker ones, and his ability to defeat larger forces with smaller ones through careful planning. They commended his strict discipline, his avoidance of indiscriminate violence, and his remarkable capacity to overcome strength with gentleness, meet might with humility and subdue the enemy by persuasion. In their view, Lê Lợi embodied the saying: *One who possesses benevolence has no rival in all the world.*[25]

They praised the accomplishments of his brief reign, noting his establishment of laws and decrees, the codification of rituals and court music, the introduction of civil service examinations, the organisation of a structured bureaucracy, the creation of administrative regions, the collection of books, and the promotion of education. However, they also criticised him for his excessive suspicion and his propensity for killing. Their criticism contradicts the earlier portrayals of Lê Lợi's benevolence and may relate to the deaths of Trần Nguyễn Hãn and Phạm Văn Xảo.

In the 18th century, Lê Quý Đôn attributed Lê Lợi's success to his military prowess, political skills, administrative abilities and respect for Confucianism.[26]

Views of contemporary historians

Modern Vietnamese historians have described Lê Lợi's uprising as a war of national liberation with widespread popular support over a long period of time utilising guerilla warfare tactics.[27] Its success is attributed to the active response of the people, the participation of the country's elite, and the leadership of resolute and wise leaders.[28] Others points to the abandonment of the Jiao-zhi project by Emperor Yongle's successors, because it cost the empire more than the benefits it brought. as the primary cause for its rapid collapse after 1424.[29]

Author's contribution

A comprehensive evaluation of these differing perspectives falls beyond the scope of this volume. A dedicated work, such as a complete biography of Lê Lợi, would be a more appropriate place for such an analysis. Here, I offer a summary of my key findings and interpretations.

a) *The population is discontented*: Undoubtedly, the Ming's policies in Đại Việt during the occupation provoked widespread resentment and anger among the local population. Despite the good deeds of the first Ming commissioner in Đại Việt, Huang Fu and the initial cooperation of regional leaders such as Mạc Thúy, the corrupt and arrogant conduct of many Ming officials ultimately alienated most of the Đại Việt people. Among these officials, the eunuch Ma Qi, the first of Lê Lợi's enemies was likely the worst. During one of the early campaigns against Lê Lợi, Ma Qi took Lê Lợi's nine-year-old daughter and took her to China, where she later died. Even Ming shilu notes Ma Qi's maltreatment, abuses and the corruption, extravagant of another official, Feng Gui, citing their actions as the key causes of the growing unrest.

The exploitation of Đại Việt's resources and the Ming administrators' attempts to impose Sinicisation enriched certain Ming officials and their local collaborators, but left the broader population impoverished and disgruntled.

b) *The environment is rebellious*: When Lê Lợi raised his banner of uprising in 1418, he followed the footsteps of the rebellions initiated by the last two Trần kings. While Lê Lợi criticised them as weak and distracted by indulgence in wine and women, their six-year rebellions from 1407 to 1414, had ignited a strong spirit of defiance among the population, particularly in Thanh Hóa, Nghệ An and the southern region.[30] At one point, their efforts came close to expelling the Ming occupiers, but were ultimately crushed by reinforcements from the imperial court and the brutal suppression, led by Zhang Fu. Lê Lợi was not the only rebel at this time; numerous uprisings broke out across many prefectures, including present-day Lạng Sơn, Thái Nguyên, Bắc Ninh, Hải Phòng and Nghệ An.[31] While most of these revolts were eventually suppressed, many of the surviving rebels with experience in fighting the Ming army likely joined Lê Lợi as his movement gathered momentum from late 1424 onward. Regardless, the widespread resistance prevented the Ming commanders from claiming that Đại Việt had been fully pacified and prompted Emperor Yongle to begin considering alternative strategies.

c) *Victory is not guaranteed*: There is little doubt that Emperor Yongle's desire to find an honourable exit from Đại Việt in 1424 significantly affected the morale of Ming commanders and troops on the ground. However, the Ming forces in Đại Việt were far from expended—fresh reinforcements arrived in May 1426 and again in October 1427. Had these troops succeeded, they would have fulfilled Emperor Xuande's aim of restoring a

Trần descendant to power and returning Đại Việt to its previous status as a vassal state under Emperor Hongwu. In other words, despite the internal turmoil at the Ming court from late 1424 to mid-1425—when Lê Lợi was scoring spectacular victories in the south—there was no guarantee that he could defeat the reinforcements led by Wang Tong and later by Liu Sheng once the court stabilised under Emperor Xuande.

d) *The Commanders are competent*: The decisive victories against the Ming reinforcements were primarily achieved under the leadership of Lê Lợi's senior commanders rather than by Lê Lợi himself. In the early years of the uprising, until the siege of Nghệ An in 1425, Lê Lợi was directly involved in combat, at times likely participating in hand-to-hand fighting. However, after he ordered the army's advance northward in three columns, he shifted to a more strategic role, directing operations from a central command post. Given the delays inherent in relaying messages over long distances, it is unlikely that field commanders depended on him for real-time tactical decisions or battlefield intelligence. Their ability to defeat the Ming forces independently is a testament to their military and leadership skill. Two of these commanders, Lê Triện and Lê Lễ, the victors of the battle of Tốt Động, died during the fighting against Wang Tong in 1426. Yet, their contributions and those of Lê Sát, Lê Nhân Chú, who defeated Liu Sheng, are often underappreciated in assessments of Lê Lợi's success against the Ming forces.

e) *The leader is dedicated, charismatic and capable*: Lê Lợi was unwavering in his conviction that Heaven was on his side in the fight against the Ming occupiers. The Ming emperor's effort to bribe him with an amnesty and a position as the prefect of Thanh Hóa did not undermine his resolve. His determination to drive out the Ming occupiers was deeply personal; they had taken his daughter, his family, desecrated his ancestors' graves, and drove him and his followers into starvation in the mountain. One could easily imagine that he would never forgive them.

Yet Lê Lợi was more than a determined patriot; he was a charismatic leader who inspired loyalty among a circle of talented followers, many of whom, including his nephews, remained by his side through years of adversity. He also enjoyed widespread support among the populace. His victory at Khả Lưu Pass demonstrated his ability as a masterful tactician, and his decision to march south and capture the southern provinces proved his strategic brilliance. The Ming army maintained only a limited presence south of Thanh Hóa, building just three forts out of fourteen for the whole of Đại Việt. These provinces also provided Lê Lợi and the Trần kings before him, with many recruits. His decision to bypass the heavily fortified forts of Nghệ An, Tây Đô and instead threaten Đông Đô from the west, where the Ming army did not have any fort, was a master stroke. Similarly, his decision to concentrate forces on capturing the Xương Giang fort, thereby isolating Đông Đô, stands as another testament to his strategic acumen.

Lê Lợi was a capable military leader and a shrewd and ruthless political strategist. Aware that the Ming court sought a political resolution to end the war and withdraw from Đại Việt, he devised a plan to meet their expectations. In 1425, he located a man named Trần Cảo, in Ai Lao, claiming he was a descendant of the former Trần dynasty. Lê Lợi kept him in reserve and, in late 1426, installed him as king of Đại Việt in a bid to present a legitimate ruler that might satisfy the Ming court and avert further conflict. Finding the man in Ai Lao, and not Đại Việt, was another clever move. It would be harder to verify Trần Cảo's identity in Ai Lao than in Đại Việt.

Despite this manoeuvre, the Ming commanders were not persuaded to withdraw peacefully. Ultimately, it was the decisive military victories of 1427 that compelled their retreat. However, the presence of Trần Cảo provided the Ming court with a face-saving exit, they could claim they were leaving Đại Việt in the hands of a Trần heir, not Lê Lợi, the rebel leader. Once the Ming forces departed, however, Lê Lợi quickly dispensed with the political fiction. Trần Cảo was eliminated, forced to take poison.

The roles of Nguyễn Trãi

Bình Ngô Sách (The Book of Pacifying the Wu)
Trần Khắc Khiệm, an official of the Later Lê dynasty wrote a foreword in 1480 to *Ức Trai Thi Tập* (A Collection of Ức Trai's Poems—Ức Trai being Nguyễn Trãi's pen name), in which he mentioned that Nguyễn Trãi authored a now-lost treatise titled *Bình Ngô Sách* (The Book of Pacifying the Wu) and presented this work to Lê Lợi during their first meeting at Lỗi Giang in Thanh Hóa.[32] However, Trần Khắc Khiệm did not elaborate on the content of this work.

In the early 19th century, historian Phan Huy Chú (1782–1840) describes Nguyễn Trãi as *He was a man of letters and strategy; upon meeting the king, he helped manage state affairs and stabilise the realm, becoming the foremost (first) meritorious official in founding the country.*[33]

In another foreword written in 1833 for the *Nguyễn Trãi Toàn Tập*, Nguyễn Năng Tĩnh, a scholar of the Nguyễn dynasty, explained that Nguyễn Trãi's initial strategy did not focus on the capture of citadels (*Do not speak of attacking the city*) but rather on a core principle: 'win the people's hearts' (*But be skilled in attacking the heart/mind*). According to this account, this approach eventually inspired people from 15 circuits across Đại Việt to rise and join Lê Lợi's cause.[34]

Later Vietnamese historians built upon these sources, treating *Bình Ngô Sách* as the ideological foundation of the Lam Sơn uprising. They interpreted the notion of 'winning the people's hearts' as a reliance on the populace's vast, invincible latent strength. This principle, they argued, shaped the entire course of the resistance. They depicted Nguyễn Trãi as the chief strategist behind Lê Lợi's victory. In this portrayal, Nguyễn Trãi and Lê Lợi are seen as the very soul of the insurgent army and the brains of its general staff.[35]

However, other historians take a more restrained view. They see Nguyễn Trãi primarily as a distinguished scholar, *an erudite writer of letters and proclamations, a knowledgeable administrator, an expert on court music and rituals, and a voice of moderation*, whose contributions to Lê Lợi's military tactics and strategic planning were limited.[36]

Judging from the merit-based rewards and high-ranking court appointments that Lê Lợi bestowed upon his closest lieutenants after he became king, as previously discussed, it seems unlikely that he regarded Nguyễn Trãi as his second-in-command or principal military advisor. Nevertheless, the belief that Nguyễn Trãi was Lê Lợi's right-hand man and the second most important figure in the Lam Sơn uprising is firmly rooted in today's Vietnamese historical consciousness and merits closer examination.

LSTL and the compilers of SKTT do not refer to 'win the people's hearts' strategy or *Bình Ngô Sách*. As previously noted, in early 1427, Lê Lợi relocated his headquarters from Phù Liệt to Bồ Đề—named for the two sacred fig (Bồ Đề or a ficus religiosa) trees within the camp—situated in present-day Gia Lâm district, on the eastern bank of the Red River, directly opposite Đông Đô. There, he had a tower constructed near the riverbank. This Bồ Đề Tower was as tall as the famed Báo Thiên Tower and stood approximately 80 to 85 meters tall. Each day, Lê Lợi ascended to the upper levels of the tower to monitor activities within Đông Quan. On the second level, Nguyễn Trãi would be stationed, receiving Lê Lợi's instructions and drafting official correspondence.[37] In the 18th century, Lê Quý Đôn recorded the same event in his book, ĐVTS, and added that while there, Nguyễn Trãi also deliberated on strategies in service of Lê Lợi.[38]

At that time, Lê Lợi appointed Nguyễn Trãi as *Triều liệt đại phu, Nhập nội hành khiển, Lại bộ thượng thư kiêm hành Khu mật viện sự* (Senior Official for the Imperial Court, Inner Court Secretariat, Minister of Personnel concurrently managing affairs of the Bureau of Military Affairs—a military-administrative role), a very senior and influential position in Lê Lợi's inner circles. Prior to that, the compilers of SKTT refer to Nguyễn Trãi as *văn thần* (civilian or literary official) as opposed to *võ thần* (military official), and *Hàn Lâm* [Hanlin] *viện thừa chỉ học sĩ* (Scholar of the *Hàn Lâm* [Hanlin] Academy Recipient of Imperial Edicts).[39]

Note that while Nguyễn Trãi managed the all-powerful Bureau of Military Affairs, he was not the head of the bureau. Phạm Văn Xảo filled that position until he became a *Thái Bảo* (Grand Protector) in 1428, as mentioned earlier. Lê Lợi appointed Nguyễn Trãi as a *Quan Phục hầu* (Master of Ceremonial Attire) at the same time.[40]

A conclusion

SKTT clearly indicates that Nguyễn Trãi worked closely with Lê Lợi, who entrusted him with the drafting of all official documents. At the Bồ Đề camp, they likely interacted daily as Nguyễn Trãi compiled a flurry of letters addressed to Wang Tong and other Ming commanders. One notable piece of advice that Nguyễn Trãi offered, and Lê Lợi agreed, was to allow Wang Tong and his troops to withdraw from Đông Quan without interference.[41] Undoubtedly, they discussed other political issues while dealing with the Ming court. According to Trần Khắc Khiệm, Nguyễn Trãi was responsible for peace negotiations, handling diplomatic missions, and overseeing the withdrawal of the Ming troops.[42] However, it seems unlikely that Lê Lợi sought Nguyễn Trãi's counsel on military strategies, such as his southern campaign to seize the provinces, his approach to Đông Đô from the west, or his decision to besiege Đông Đô but to take Xương Giang. Lê Lợi was known for his discipline, which likely maintained a clear distinction between civil and military affairs. Moreover, he had many capable and trusted military commanders to counsel him.

Regarding Nguyễn Trãi's purported 'winning the people's hearts' strategy, I have not found any specific reference to it in the various letters that he drafted for Lê Lợi, as compiled in TQTMT. However, his writings consistently reflect a foundation in Confucian values. In Letter 8 to Feng Zheng, Nguyễn Trãi asserts that success in great undertakings must be grounded in benevolence and righteousness.[43] In Letter 15 to Wang Tong, Nguyễn Trãi describes trustworthiness as a national treasure.[44] Letter 31 emphasises that right action requires adherence to proper rituals, guided by wisdom, the will of Heaven, and the people's wishes.⁴⁵ These virtues—*ren* (benevolence, humanness, *nhân*), *yi* (righteousness, justice, *nghĩa*), *li* (propriety, ritual, *lễ*), *zhi* (wisdom, knowledge, *trí*), and *xin* (trustworthiness, sincerity, *tín*)—are core Confucian virtues and collectively form the ethical framework underlying Nguyễn Trãi's political and diplomatic thought.

In other words, as a Confucian scholar, Nguyễn Trãi's political philosophy was likely rooted in the teachings of Confucius, particularly the emphasis on aligning governance with the people's will. Lê Lợi was an educated man, and likely to have a fair knowledge of Confucian philosophy. He demonstrated more than once the Confucian virtue of *ren* (benevolence) in his compassionate treatment of the populace, which earned him widespread popular support. Yet, this benevolence may have also stemmed from another key Confucian ideal—that the ruler is the parent of the people. Reflecting this belief, Lê Lợi once told his generals: *I am the people's father and mother; how could I not think of their hardships and dare to cause them suffering?*⁴⁶

In conclusion, it is possible that the treatise *Bình Ngô Sách* did exist, and Nguyễn Trãi likely advocated the strategy of winning the people's hearts to Lê Lợi. While Nguyễn Trãi is unquestionably one of the most distinguished scholars in Vietnamese history, portraying him as the chief architect of the Lam Sơn uprising, and Lê Lợi's second-in-command remains open to debate, given the available historical evidence and the prevailing political ideology of the period.

The poems of Nguyễn Trãi

Nguyễn Trãi was a prolific writer; in addition to the works already mentioned, he composed numerous poems in both Chinese and Nôm scripts. *Ức Trai Thi Tập* includes 99 poems in Chinese script, which translators have categorized as follows: 17 written before he succeeded; 31 during his time serving at court; 22 composed during a period of disheartening when he considered resigning; 17 after he withdrew from public life to Côn Sơn; and the final 12—perhaps the most intriguing—were reportedly written while he was in China.⁴⁷

Nguyễn Trãi's *Quốc Âm Thi Tập* (A Collection of Poems in the National Pronunciation, or National Language) contains 254 poems and is regarded as the oldest known collection of poems in Chữ Nôm. The compilation is organised into 192 untitled poems, 21 related to seasonal changes, 32 focusing on flowers and trees, and 7 themed around birds and beasts.⁴⁸

Although BNĐC and the letters in QTTM are attributed to Nguyễn Trãi, they were written on behalf of Lê Lợi. Determining how much of their content reflected Lê Lợi's direct instructions versus Nguyễn Trãi's own thoughts is difficult without detailed analysis of Nguyễn Trãi's independent writings—particularly his poetry. Such a study is beyond the scope of this volume, but it would offer deep insights into his philosophy and shed light on his strategic role in the Lam Sơn uprising.

Some of his poems were translated into English and edited by Nguyen Do and Paul Hoover in *Beyond the Court Gate: Selected Poems of Nguyen Trai*. I have reproduced one of them:[49]

> PAINTING OF CON SON
> Half of my life I've had to forget the joy of climbing mountains.
> After the chaos of war, I've wasted my dreams in returning home.
> Wind from the pines whistles on stone stairs; no one enjoys hearing it.
> Plums wave beside the creek; I can't take joy in singing of them.
> Seeing this silent scene wrenches my heart; witnessing
> The desolation of gibbons and ciconia creates emotions
> Too strong to be stopped, so, please, won't some talented
> Artist in this world make a painting of my feelings?[50]

Nguyễn Trãi likely wrote this poem after the war when he returned to Côn Sơn in Chí Linh.

Words on leaves

At the turn of the 18th to the 19th century, two Vietnamese scholars compiled a collection of stories in classical Chinese, which was not published until nearly a century later and translated in the 20th century.[51] The work, titled *Tang thương ngẫu lục* (*Incidental Records Amid Life's Upheavals*), contains 89 stories, one of which depicts Nguyễn Trãi under the name Lê Trãi.[52] I recount this tale not only because it is a familiar story taught to most Vietnamese schoolchildren, but also because it has long been invoked to affirm Nguyễn Trãi's position as the second most important figure after Lê Lợi in the struggle against the Ming occupation.

According to the tale, a fairy appeared in Nguyễn Trãi's dream and foretold that Lê Lợi would become king, while he himself would serve as his subject. This vision seemed to confirm what Trần Nguyên Hãn—then an oil seller passing through the village—had already told him. Together, Nguyễn Trãi and Trần Nguyên Hãn made inquiries and soon discovered Lê Lợi's whereabouts. When they visited him, they found the future king living as a simple farmer, dressed in a short brown shirt and carrying a hoe to drive his cattle. They stayed for several days, and on the occasion of an ancestral anniversary, Lê Lợi slaughtered a pig to prepare a feast. Entering the kitchen to cook, he was seen by Nguyễn Trãi holding a knife to cut the meat and eat at the same time. Disheartened, Nguyễn Trãi confided to Trần Nguyên Hãn that the fairy had deceived him and demanded the return of his gold. But that very night, the fairy reappeared in his dream, assuring him that Lê Lợi's destiny as king had already been ordained by Heaven, and that he must wait. Around this time, Lê Lợi came into possession of a military strategy book and a divine sword. Each night, he would lock his door and study the text. Curious, Nguyễn Trãi and Trần Nguyên Hãn once crept into his room; startled, Lê Lợi drew his sword, but the two men knelt before him, declaring that they had journeyed far in search of the one destined to rule. It was then that Lê Lợi began to speak of raising an army.

Nguyễn Trãi urged Lê Lợi to proceed with caution. He erected a hut and began teaching the village children. In the forest, he used animal fat to trace the words 'Lê Lợi will be king' and 'Lê Trãi will be his servant' on leaves.[53] In time, worms and ants consumed the fat, leaving the characters carved upon the leaves. Villagers gathering firewood came across them and regarded the markings as a heavenly portent. From then, word spread, and an ever-growing number of followers gathered under Lê Lợi's banner.

Historical records such as SKTT, ĐVTS, and CM make no mention of this tale. Yet, if true, Nguyễn Trãi's act of inscribing words upon forest leaves would have been a masterstroke in rallying popular support for Lê Lợi—and for himself. The story recalls similar legends, such as the prophecy said to appear on a lightning-struck, charred tree, foretelling the rise of Lý Công Uẩn as the founder of the Lý dynasty in the 10th century, as noted in Volume 3A.

6.3 - *Three kings over 30 years*

LÊ NGUYÊN LONG (KING LÊ THÁI TÔNG, R. 1433–1442)

Succession planning

By 1432, the Ming forces had long gone from Đại Việt, and most of Lê Lợi's troops had been discharged and returned to their villages.[54] Yet, Lê Lợi was far from retiring from military campaigns. That same year, he personally led a campaign to suppress a rebellion in the north-west, followed later by an invasion into Ai Lao. One might wonder why he did not assign another commander to lead the expedition; perhaps it had something to do with the Laotians' betrayal in 1423, when they joined forces with the Ming army to attack him.

However, at 47—considered an advanced age at the time—Lê Lợi was in declining health and increasingly preoccupied with securing the royal succession, and the long and gruelling years of warfare against the Ming had taken a heavy toll on him.

Lê Lợi had two sons from different wives: Lê Tư Tề and Lê Nguyên Long. While Tư Tề's birth date is unrecorded, his active role in the war against the Ming forces suggests he was already a teenager when the rebellion began in 1418—likely born around 1402, making him about 30 years old in 1432, ready to succeed his father. However, Tư Tề became increasingly violent, reportedly killing concubines and servants without cause. Such behaviour deeply concerned Lê Lợi, a strict and disciplined leader. After consulting with Lê Khôi—a Deputy Commandant and a fourth-tier 'meritorious official'—Lê Lợi demoted Tư Tề around September 1433 and named his younger son, Lê Nguyên Long, as heir to the throne.[55] Shortly after Lê Nguyên Long ascended the throne, he issued a decree forbidding anyone at court from visiting Tư Tề. In 1438, he stripped Tư Tề of his titles, reducing him to the status of a commoner. Tư Tề died not long afterwards.[56]

Lê Nguyên Long was born in 1423, making him just ten years old when he was named heir to the throne. Naturally, Lê Lợi sought to protect his son until he reached maturity. To secure the throne for Nguyên Long, Lê Lợi appears to have pursued at least three strategies:

a) eliminating potential rivals to remove threats to the succession,

b) appointing a trusted and senior commander as regent to oversee the transition, and

c) maintaining a strong and loyal base of supporters to deter challenges.

Strategy a) was implemented earlier in Lê Lợi's reign, as previously mentioned, with the forced death of Trần Nguyên Hãn and the execution of Phạm Văn Xảo in 1429 and 1430, respectively. In 1433, Lê Lợi appointed Lê Sát as the Grand Minister, and he relied on his Lũng Nhai oath-takers as a loyal base of support. On 5 October 1433, Lê Lợi passed away and two weeks later on 20 October 1433, Lê Nguyên Long succeeded him as King Lê Thái Tông.

The purges
Lê Nguyên Long was still young when he ascended the throne, and during the early years of his reign, he was supported by two of Lê Lợi's most senior

commanders: Lê Sát and Lê Ngân. However, in mid-1437—about a year before he stripped his brother of all titles—Lê Nguyên Long accused Lê Sát of abusing his power and of orchestrating the death of fellow commander Lê Nhân Chú.[57] As a result, Lê Sát was dismissed from office and allowed to die at home. His house and possessions were seized, and his belongings were sold off to other court officials. His daughter, Lê Ngọc Dao, once a principal consort, was demoted to commoner status, and his son-in-law was exiled.[58] At the same time, Lê Văn Linh—a third-tier meritorious official—was stripped of this title. He and his fellow commander during the war, Lê Thụ, were told to wait for trials. Both survived the ordeal, and Lê Văn Linh died as Grand Tutor in 1448 at 72.[59]

Meanwhile, Lê Ngân—the only second-tier 'meritorious official' after Lê Sát —was elevated to the highest noble-military rank, with sweeping administrative and military authority. He was regarded as a pillar of the state and granted the rank of top marquis.[60] His daughter, Lê Nhật Lệ, became a top-ranking consort. Despite these honours, Lê Ngân's fortune was short-lived. By the end of that same year, he was arrested on dubious charges involving prayers to Quan Âm Buddha. He met the same end as Lê Sát—permitted to die at home, stripped of assets, and his daughter's status reduced to that of a commoner.[61]

One might wonder what motivated Lê Nguyên Long to purge such senior officials—men who had fought alongside his father in the war against the Ming army—when he was only around 14 years old. One possible explanation is that he had become aware of his authority and chose to assert it simply because he could. The compilers of SKTT note that Lê Nguyên Long had matured and begun making decisions independently, yet Lê Sát failed to recognize this shift and continued to wield power as if nothing had changed.[62]

SKTT also records multiple instances in which Lê Nguyên Long ignored advice from senior court officials or responded with silent resentment when corrected.[63] Lê Sát had made many enemies at court, and as they detected the young king's growing displeasure with him, they seized the opportunity to whisper against him and hasten his fall. By this time, Lê Nguyên Long already had several royal consorts, and his harsh treatment of these older officials—many of whom were in their 50s—may well reflect the impulses of a rebellious adolescent asserting control in a world dominated by men far more experienced than himself.

According to ĐVTS, Lê Nguyên Long's mother, Phạm Ngọc Trần, died when he was just three years old—offered as a human sacrifice to become the consort of a local deity. In 1425, while Lê Lợi was campaigning in Nghệ An, the spirit of this deity reportedly appeared to him in a dream, promising victory over the Ming army in exchange for one of his wives. The next day, Lê

Lợi asked for a volunteer, and Phạm Ngọc Trần stepped forward. She knelt and offered herself, asking only that Lê Lợi care for her son if he triumphed. It is a haunting and tragic story, one that may explain Lê Nguyên Long's later behaviour. One could imagine that he might have made different decisions had his mother lived to guide him.

However, subsequent Lê kings also executed or imprisoned these 'meritorious officials', so these acts were not unique to Lê Nguyên Long. The application of removing potential threats by the Lê royal family could explain this.

Death of Nguyễn Trãi and his family

The deaths of Lê Sát and Lê Ngân— the two most senior officials at the Lê court—in 1437 likely instilled a sense of fear and uncertainty among senior officials in the capital and throughout the provinces of Đại Việt. As a high-ranking figure himself, Nguyễn Trãi might have sensed the growing danger and sought permission to retire. In 1439, at 60, he retired to his home village of Côn Sơn, in today's Chí Linh district. Three years later, in early September 1442, Lê Nguyên Long visited Chí Linh, a traditional naval base of Đại Việt, to observe a military parade. Nguyễn Trãi welcomed the king during his visit and invited him to tour a pagoda close to his residence.[64]

The visit might have remained a routine royal occasion were it not for the dramatic events that followed. On his return journey from Chí Linh, the king fell ill and died at a place called Lệ Chi Viên (or Garden of Vải), located in what is now Gia Lương, Bắc Ninh province. According to historical records, he stayed up all night at Lệ Chi Viên with Nguyễn Thị Lộ, one of Nguyễn Trãi's wives. Two days later, on 9 September 1442, his body was secretly brought back to Đông Quan by a small entourage of officials and servants. The court soon blamed Nguyễn Thị Lộ for the king's death. Within six days, the king's young son, Lê Bang Cơ, ascended the throne, and just ten days later, on 19 September 1442, the court ordered the execution of Nguyễn Thị Lộ, Nguyễn Trãi, and their children and grandchildren, using a form of severe punishment called *Tru di tam tộc* (execution of three generations).[65] Nguyễn Thị Lộ was renowned for her beauty and literary talent. Before the tragic incident at Lệ Chi Viên, she had been invited to the palace by the king, who openly admired and flirted with her.[66]

When Lê Sát was accused, several 'meritorious officials' defended him. In contrast, no one stepped forward to defend Nguyễn Trãi. In fact, some of them, like Trịnh Khả and Nguyễn Xí, might have been behind the court's harsh sentence. One could conclude that it was either because they disliked Nguyễn Trãi. After all, he came from Đông Kinh and a civilian, making him an outsider among the Thanh Hóa military elite, or they were fearful of being seen as Nguyễn Trãi's allies. Another possible explanation for the brutal and unjust treatment of Nguyễn Trãi and his family could be jealousy from one of Lê Nguyên Long's wives. Nguyễn Thị Lộ, being young and likely of child-bearing age, may have been viewed as a threat if she were to bear the king a son, competing against their own.[67] Eliminating her—and, by extension, Nguyễn Trãi and their descendants—may have been seen as a way to remove that risk entirely.

Nguyễn Thị Lộ may have also made many enemies at court. According to SKTT, it was her slander resulted in the demotion of Lê Lễ, a 4th-tier 'meritorious official'; she was also said to have advised the king to imprison concubines who were deemed disobedient or defiant.[68] Adding to the mystery, two court eunuchs were also killed after reportedly remarking that Nguyễn Trãi had expressed regret for not listening to them before his execution.[69] Ultimately, the whole truth behind Nguyễn Trãi's tragic end remains lost to history.

Compilers of CM in the 19th century were critical of Nguyễn Trãi.[70] According to them, Nguyễn Trãi brought the execution of his entire family upon himself, because he allowed his younger wife to act in a way they deemed promiscuous and shameless.[71] In the 18th century, Lê Quý Đôn reportedly referred to Nguyễn Trãi as a 'treacherous official and unscrupulous individual'.[72] In his work, ĐVTS, Lê Quý Đôn included biographies of Lê Lợi, other Lê kings, their immediate family members, most of the 'meritorious officials', and even known traitors. Notably, he omitted any biography of Nguyễn Trãi.

However, such views remain in the minority. Contemporary Vietnamese perspectives are more sympathetic to Nguyễn Trãi. After all, he and Nguyễn Thị Lộ were unlikely to have a choice against Lê Nguyên Long's unwanted advances toward her. In any event, this dramatic episode has since become deeply woven into Vietnamese folklore, inspiring numerous books and plays.

Nguyễn Trãi is commemorated in several temples in Hanoi and Chí Linh, and many streets across Vietnam are named after him. Visitors can pay tribute to him at the Nguyễn Trãi Temple located in Nhị Khê, approximately 20 kilometres south of Hanoi.[73]

Nguyễn Trãi was a complex and multifaceted figure. He came of age during the final years of the Trần dynasty, passed the national examination, and served under the Hồ dynasty—until the Ming invasion upended his world. Captured by the Ming troops, he may have escaped and wandered, possibly even travelling as far as China, before eventually joining Lê Lợi. He likely remained by Lê Lợi's side through much of the resistance war against the Ming occupiers.

Shortly after Lê Lợi's ascension, Nguyễn Trãi was briefly imprisoned and became entangled in the political intrigues that followed. His life ended in tragedy, but his legacy is that of a truly remarkable man. The account in this book cannot do him justice fully, and I will always remember him, above all, as a wonderful poet.

LÊ BANG CƠ (KING LÊ NHÂN TÔNG, R.1442–1459)

Lê Nguyên Long died at the young age of 19, but during his brief reign, he had several wives who bore him three sons. His first son, Lê Nghi Dân, was born in 1439, followed by Lê Bang Cơ in 1441 and Lê Tư Thành in 1442. Initially, Lê Nghi Dân was named crown prince at the age of one, with a clear path to the throne. However, his mother, Dương Thị Bí, grew increasingly arrogant due to her status as the king's consort and mother of the future ruler. This behaviour displeased Lê Nguyên Long, who demoted her and changed his succession plan, appointing Lê Bang Cơ as crown prince instead. Upon the king's death, the infant Lê Bang Cơ, barely a year old, was crowned the next Lê king by five 'meritorious officials': Lê Liệt (4th-tier) and Lê Thụ, Lê (Trịnh) Khả, Lê Bôi, and Lê (Nguyễn) Xí (5th-tier).

However, within a few years of Lê Bang Cơ's accession to the throne, Lê Liệt and Lê Thụ were imprisoned, though both were released several years later.[74] Lê Khả and his son were executed in 1451, but Nguyễn Xí and Lê Bôi managed to survive such a fate and lived out their lives, eventually passing away due to illness.[75] Court intrigues, involving high-ranking officials and the king's mother, were likely the key factors behind these purges.[76]

During Lê Bang Cơ's reign, Đại Việt endured consecutive years of natural disasters, including droughts, infestations, poor harvests, floods, breached dykes, thunderstorms, and even sleet and earthquakes. Troubled by these events, the king issued multiple edicts, questioning whether his governance had not been in harmony with Heaven above and had not satisfied the needs of the people below, thus bringing about such calamities.[77] In response, he offered prayers at pagodas and shrines, proclaimed a general amnesty, and reduced taxes. Among those granted amnesty were the families of Lê Sát, Lê Ngân, and Lê Khả, all of whom received land as a compensation. All except for Nguyễn Trãi.[78]

The content of these edicts reflects a core Confucian principle of governance: moral accountability over mere power. In essence, a ruler's legitimacy depends on possessing the Mandate of Heaven (天命, *Tiānmìng*, *Thiên Mệnh*), which is granted only to those who govern with virtue, show compassion for the people, and uphold the rituals that ensure both social order and cosmic balance. Natural disasters and social unrest were traditionally interpreted as signs of Heaven's disapproval and a warning against poor or immoral leadership.

LÊ NGHI DÂN (R.1459–1460)

Lê Bang Cơ's reign ended abruptly in 1459. On the night of 28 October, his elder brother, Lê Nghi Dân, who had been stripped of the crown prince title years earlier, led a coup with the support of over 100 men and the palace guard commander. They scaled the walls of the Forbidden Palace and assassinated the king, his mother, and several attendants. Four days later, Lê Nghi Dân declared himself king. However, his reign only lasted 8 months. On 24 June 1460, two 'meritorious officials', Nguyễn Xí and Đinh (Lê) Liệt, rallied support from other high-ranking officials and staged a counter-coup. They forced Lê Nghi Dân to commit suicide. Two days later, the officials installed Lê Tư Thành, Lê Bang Cơ's younger brother, as the new king.

THE SLOW DECADES

Nearly three decades had passed since Lê Lợi's death, yet the Later Lê dynasty court had made limited progress in the development of Đại Việt. There were few notable achievements in palace or temple building, canal and infrastructure construction, educational institutions, territorial expansion, trade policy, or legal reforms. The SKTT entries from this period are dominated by accounts of court intrigues, the purging or imprisonment of 'meritorious officials,' reports of corrupted practices by officials, natural disasters, the king's self-reflection in edicts, military drills, the suppression of rebellions, and minor border conflicts.[79]

Despite the political turbulence, some educational and administrative efforts continued. In 1434, the court held a national examination, and over 1,000 candidates passed.[80] Those achieving first and second grades were admitted to *Quốc Tử Giám* (Imperial Academy) in Đông Kinh, while those passing the third grade were appointed to provincial posts. In 1442, one of the *Tiến Sĩ* (Doctoral degree) graduates was Ngô Sĩ Liên, who would later become the chief compiler of SKTT, the most significant historical chronicle of Vietnam, as discussed elsewhere.[81] That same year, the names of these doctoral graduates were inscribed on stone stelae at *Văn Miếu* (Temple of Literature), a practice that continued until 1779.[82] In 1455, under King Lê Bang Cơ's order, official

Phan Phu Tiên (1370–1462) compiled *Đại Việt Sử Ký* (Historical Records of the Great Việt), which chronicled the period from King Trần Thái Tông (r. 1226–1258) to the expulsion of the Ming forces in 1428.[83] *Đại Việt Sử Ký* is now lost but historians believe that Ngô Sĩ Liên incorporated much of its contents into SKTT.

When the Ming army withdrew from Đại Việt in 1428, not all returned to China; some remained behind. In 1438, the king issued an edict requiring them to adopt local customs, including cutting their hair short and wearing Vietnamese-style clothing.[84] However, these measures were largely superficial. The Lê court continued to follow many Ming administrative and cultural practices left behind after two decades of occupation. They looked to the Ming dynasty for models in court dress, music, and even religious observances. For example, in 1449, the king ordered the construction of altars dedicated to the City God and the gods of wind, cloud, thunder, and rain—deities introduced by the Ming administrators as part of their policy to supplant popular Buddhist beliefs, as previously discussed.[85]

The slow progress during these three decades is understandable. The two kings who ruled for most of this period both died before reaching the age of 20. While their consorts may have influenced them privately, the real power often rested with the mother, in the case of Lê Bang Cơ, and 'meritorious officials'—veterans of the war against the Ming forces, primarily from Thanh Hóa. These were military leaders, not scholars, and their governance reflected that background. SKTT frequently notes military drills and campaigns, underscoring their priorities. Intellectuals like Nguyễn Trãi were largely sidelined, tasked with drafting official documents, including mundane matters such as court music, dance instructions, and ceremonial attire.[86] It was not until the long reign of Lê Tư Thành that Đại Việt entered a period of real growth and development, as will be explored in the following pages.

6.4 - One king over nearly 40 years – Lê Tư Thành (King Lê Thánh Tông, r.1460–1497)

REWARDS AND REHABILITATION

A few months after ascending the throne, Lê Tư Thành instructed the two 'meritorious officials', Nguyễn Xí and Đinh (Lê) Liệt, to compile a list of those who had taken part in the June 1460 counter-coup, so he could reward them. The list consisted of nearly 60 people.[87] In recognition of their service, Lê Tư

Thành conferred the noble title of Duke on Nguyễn Xí and Đinh Liệt and appointed another official, Lê Niệm, grandson of Lê Lai, as Grand Tutor.[88] He also granted them parcels of land as part of their rewards. However, two years later, Lê Tư Thành had Grand Commandant Lê Lăng, Lê Triện's son, executed for suspected treason.[89]

In 1464, more than twenty years after Nguyễn Trãi's death, Lê Tư Thành declared that he had been wrongfully condemned. To rectify this injustice, the king posthumously restored Nguyễn Trãi's honour by conferring upon him the title of *bá* (Earl), appointing his surviving son—whose mother fled to Bồn Man—to an official position, and granting the family a parcel of land.[90] Most of Nguyễn Trãi's writings scattered after his death, but some survived and came to the attention of Lê Tư Thành. As a literary-minded ruler who composed many poems himself, Lê Tư Thành admired Nguyễn Trãi's work. In 1467, he ordered his officials to search for any remaining manuscripts. Thanks to these efforts, much of Nguyễn Trãi's literary legacy has been preserved to this day.

The title of Duke was based on the Confucian 'five ranks of nobility', listed in descending order as: *Công* (*gong*, Duke), *Hầu* (*hou*, Marquis), *Bá* (*bo*, Earl), *Tử* (*zi*, Viscount) and *Nam* (*nan*, Baron).[91] Although they were prestigious and highly coveted, the material benefits they conferred were modest compared to those enjoyed by members of the royal family. For example, a Duke received an annual allowance of just 120 *quan*, while a Crown Prince received 500 *quan* and a Royal Prince 200 *quan*. In comparison, the highest-ranking mandarin earned 80 *quan* per year, and a 4th-ranked civil servant earned 44 *quan*.

Land distribution followed a similar pattern: the king granted a Royal Prince 1000 *mẫu* of rice paddies compared to 400 *mẫu* for a Duke, 100 *mẫu* for a top mandarin and just 15 *mẫu* for a 4th-ranked official, (1 *mẫu* = 666.7 m2 under the Ming dynasty).[92]

I have presented these figures to highlight the disproportionately large share of the economy reserved for the royal family—benefits gained through inheritance rather than through merit or productivity.

NATIONAL EXAMINATIONS

Followed the tradition established under the Lý and the Trần dynasties, in 1434, Lê Tư Thành's father, Lê Nguyên Long, issued an edict to the royal court affirming his view that, *To obtain men of talent, one must first select scholars, and the method of selecting scholars must prioritize examinations.*[93] Following the edict, he established the regulations governing the examination cycles. From 1438 onward, *thi hương* (provincial examination) were to be held in all circuits, followed by *thi hội* (metropolitan examination) at the capital in 1439. Thereafter, major examinations would be held every three years as a permanent institution.[94] In the same year, a national examination was held and over 1,000 candidates passed as mentioned earlier.

The provincial examinations consisted of four rounds, with candidates required to pass each round in sequence to advance. Those who successfully completed all four rounds were awarded the title *Cử nhân* (Bachelor), qualifying them to take the metropolitan examination. Candidates who passed this stage received the degree of *Tiến sĩ* (Doctor), granting them access to the *thi đình* (palace examination), which was presided over by the king himself. Based on their final scores, the top three were conferred the prestigious titles of *Trạng nguyên* (First Laureate), *Bảng nhãn* (Second Laureate), and *Thám hoa* (Third Laureate).[95]

Figure 6-2 summarises the national examination process as established under the Later Lê dynasty, a structure that remained largely unchanged until the Nguyễn dynasty in the 19th century. The pass rates were extremely low. In 1448, only eight candidates advanced to the metropolitan and palace examinations.[96] Likewise, in 1475, just 43 out of 3,200 successful provincial candidates (*Cử nhân*) progressed to the metropolitan level; the figures in 1499 were 55 out of 5,000.[97] On average, the pass rate for the metropolitan examination was around 1 per cent.

The first round of the examination involved writing essays on topics drawn from the Chinese classics of Four Books and Five Classics. In the second round, candidates were required to composed poetry and prose following specific stylistic rules. The third round tested their ability to draft formal documents such as royal edicts. Occasionally, the second and third rounds were conducted in reverse order.[98] In the final round, candidates had to write a policy essay on strategies.[99]

The structure of the examination suggests a progressive increase in difficulty, with later rounds demanding higher levels of analytical thinking and originality. Interestingly, mathematics was excluded from this elite examination system, though it was a required subject in other types of exams—such as those used to recruit lower-level officials from commoners or to evaluate the children of existing officials.[100]

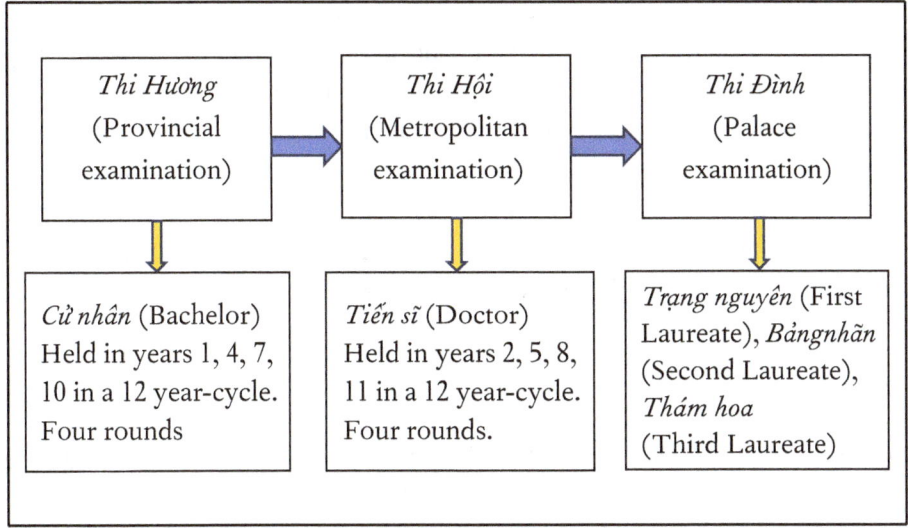

Figure 6-2: National examinations under the Later Lê dynasty.

SEVEN PROPOSALS

Around 1462, there was a calamity involving hailstorms and thunderstorms, so Lê Tư Thành issued an edict seeking forthright advice. An official named Hoàng Thanh submitted a memorial presenting seven proposals:

1. *Harmonize yin and yang to welcome favourable energies.*

2. *Prioritize [attend] the imperial lectures to uphold proper learning.*

3. *Carefully select the heir to secure the foundation of the state.*

4. *Practice fiscal restraint to ensure sufficient resources.*

5. *Appoint prefects and magistrates prudently to govern the people well.*

6. *Conduct regular military drills to strengthen defence.*

7. *Establish military-agricultural colonies to stockpile grain for the border regions.*

The king accepted all of them.[101]

    I have included this episode to highlight the contrasting ways Lê Tư Thành and his older brother, Lê Bang Cơ, responded to natural disasters, which were traditionally seen as signs of Heaven's dissatisfaction with the ruler. While Lê Bang Cơ issued self-reproaching edicts, Lê Tư Thành took a different approach by consulting his officials for advice. The response reflected Confucian principles, focusing on restoring the balance of yin and yang, promoting education, ensuring orderly succession, practising frugality, and strengthening national defence. However, judging by modern standards, the recommendations lacked any practical measures for mitigating the impact of natural disasters or enhancing economic and community resilience.

THE MILITARY

Like his grandfather, Lê Tư Thành was a warrior king. He believed in having a strong army. Shortly after ascending the throne, he issued an edict to the commanders at the five circuits, telling them:

> *Wherever there is a country, there must be military readiness. During free time from farming, all non-urgent tasks must be suspended. On the 15th day of every lunar month, [men] must assemble for roll call. Assign troops to duties such as guarding homes and posts, gathering thatch for roofing, or tending elephants. One or two days prior, [commanders] must follow the tactical drill manuals issued by the state, right in the area of their stationed garrison. [They] must organize ranks and instruct soldiers in the methods of sitting, standing, advancing, and retreating. Train them to recognise drum and gong signals, ensuring troops accustomed to bows and arrows, and never neglect military preparedness. Only from the fourth day onward may they be assigned to miscellaneous tasks. If any official does not pay attention to discipline, train, and drill the troops and dares to order them to perform miscellaneous tasks, they shall be demoted or dismissed from office.*[102]

In 1466, Lê Tư Thành reorganized the military structure, replacing the five military circuits (*quân năm đạo*) established under Lê Lợi with five military commands (*quân năm phủ*). Each command consisted of six guards or regiments (*vệ*), and each guard comprised five or six battalions (*sở*), with each battalion numbering 400 soldiers.[103] Based on this structure, Đại Việt had between 60,000 and 72,000 troops under arms by the mid-15th century. While not a particularly large standing force, Lê Tư Thành could quickly mobilize additional troops, thanks to a system that regularly trained rice farmers, as discussed earlier.

A year earlier, he issued a comprehensive set of regulations for naval and land battle formations. These included nine tactical naval formations with vivid names like Fish-Scale and Flying Goose formations, and three formations for land combats.¹⁰⁴ In addition, Lê Tư Thành promulgated military codes consisting of 32 articles on naval formulations, 22 on elephant units, 27 on cavalry tactics and 42 governing capital guard infantry.¹⁰⁵

Around 1478, Lê Tư Thành organised a military examination in which all nobles and officers in command positions must participate. Each candidate had to shoot five arrows, throw four javelins, and perform a combat drill using a shield and weapon.¹⁰⁶

ĐOAN MÔN GATE AND KÍNH THIÊN PALACE

Visitors to the Imperial Citadel of Thăng Long would pass through an imposing gate, called *Đoan Môn* (端門, Duān mén) or the Main Gate as shown in Figures 6-3 and 6-4. Archaeologists believe the original gate was first constructed in the 11th century during the Lý dynasty. However, they suggest the current structure was built in the 15th century, during the Early Lê Dynasty, possibly under the reign of Lê Tư Thành, and later restored in the 19th century by the Nguyễn kings.¹⁰⁷ The gate is U-shape in plan, with five front-facing openings, as shown in Figure 6-3.¹⁰⁸ The central opening was reserved for the king, while various officials used the others. Two outermost openings follow tunnel-like corridors that form the arms of the U shape, turning sharply at a 90-degree to connect with the central courtyard as shown in Figure 6-4.¹⁰⁹ Constructed from stone blocks and bricks, the gate's design bears notable architectural resemblance to that of the Hồ Citadel, as shown in Figure 3-1.

Figure 6-3: Đoan Môn Gate, viewed from the outside; viewed looking north-east.

Figure 6-4: Đoan Môn Gate, inside view from above; viewed looking south-west.

In 1428, after Lê Lợi relocated to Đông Quan, he ordered the construction of several palaces, including the Kính Thiên (meaning 'Revering Heaven') Palace.¹¹⁰ However, the project may have faced delays or involved mostly repairs to an existing structure, as nearly four decades later, in 1465, Lê Tư

Thành commissioned the construction of a palace with the same name. This new construction took eight months and was completed in December of that year alongside with another palace named Cần Đức.[111]

The Kính Thiên Palace served as the royal court, a reception hall for foreign envoys, and the site of key state ceremonies. While the original structure may have stood in some form until the 19th century, it was likely damaged and reconstructed over time. In 1886, the French colonial administration demolished what remained to build an artillery command centre.[112, 113] Today, only the front and back stone steps and intricately carved stone dragons, as shown in Figures 6-5 and 6-6—dating from the 15th century—survive. The palace was also known by other names throughout its history, including Càn Nguyên and Thiên An.[114, 115] Volume Two discusses the Imperial Citadel in more detail.[116]

Figure 6-5: The dragons at the Kính Thiên Palace (southern steps), Hanoi, 15th century, stone.

Figure 6-6: Head of the Kính Thiên dragon (southern steps).

Each dragon shown in Figure 6-5 was carved from a single block of stone. Measuring approximately 5.3 metres in length, the dragon coils in seven sinuous curves. It features four legs, each with five clawed toes, and its body is covered with carved scales.[117] As depicted in Figure 6-6, the dragon's head is adorned with bulging eyes, a large nose, and small ears. It bears fangs, curved horns, and flowing manes—lion-like features characteristic of dragon sculptures from the Đinh, Lý, and Trần dynasties, as discussed in Volume 3A.[118] A pearl rests in its mouth, and the head is currently supported by a modern stylised element, shown in white, which was added in recent times. Unfortunately, this supporting section is partially buried, making it difficult to determine the original design. However, based on northern dragons shown in Figure 6-6, it is likely that the dragon's head was originally supported by a chin beard anchored at the base by another set of claws, as depicted in Figure 6-19.

Figure 6-7: The dragons at the Kính Thiên Palace (northern steps), Hanoi, 15th century, stone.

Figure 6-8: Detail of the side of the Kính Thiên dragon (northern steps).

The dragons on the northern steps, shown in Figure 6-7, were constructed later in the 15th century. Each dragon was carved from a single stone block and measures approximately 3.4 metres in length, with six to seven curves along the body. The neck is partially buried, making it difficult to fully reconstruct the original form. The dragons have two visible hind legs, and the head design closely resembles that of the dragons on the southern steps, though the horns are more clearly defined.

As illustrated in Figure 6-8, the side of the dragon features an intricately carved scene of a stylised lotus pond, complete with blooming lotus flowers, buds, clusters of waves, a mandarin duck, and the motif of a carp transforming into a dragon. Stylised clouds floats above the pond.[119]

SIGNIFICANT ACHIEVEMENTS

Maps

In the early 11th century, a Song dynasty official presented the emperor with a map detailing both the maritime and overland routes from Ung Châu (modern-day Nanning) to Giao Châu (northern Vietnam). He recommended launching a military campaign to conquer Giao Châu. However, the emperor rejected the proposal, citing the danger of diseases and poisonous vapours would likely result in heavy casualties for the Song forces.[120]

In the 12th century, Lý Thiên Tộ (King Lý Anh Tông, r. 1138–1175) of the Lý dynasty conducted tours of the islands located near neighbouring states to the north and south. He created maps and documented local products during his travels.[121] While these efforts show that map-making was not unfamiliar in

Đại Việt, none of the maps from that era have survived. The earliest known maps of Đại Việt that still exist today date from the reign of Lê Tư Thành.

In 1467, Lê Tư Thành issued an edict instructing the twelve circuits of Đại Việt to gather detailed information on rivers, mountains, and local legends to create annotated maps.[122] These were to be submitted to the Ministry of Revenue (*Bộ Hộ*) to compile a comprehensive geographic atlas. By 1469, the administrative divisions—defining which districts and communes belonged to which provinces—were formalized for inclusion in the maps for 12 circuits.[123] The project appears to have reached a significant milestone in 1471 when Lê Cảnh Huy, the Minister of Revenue and a prince, son of Lê Tư Thành, submitted a new set of regulations regarding the format of maps and land deeds to the king. These regulations were to take effect in early 1472.[124] Nearly 20 years later, on the 4th day of the 4th lunar month (23/4) of 1490, the Minister of Revenue, which was also responsible for land and agriculture, confirmed the maps for 13 circuits as listed below.[125]

The five circuits of Đại Việt under Lê Lợi's reign had remained unchanged for nearly four decades until 1466 when Lê Tư Thành expanded the number to 12.[126] Following the conquest of Champa, he added Quảng Nam as the 13th circuit. From north to south approximately, these circuits were: Lạng Sơn, Tuyên Quang, Hưng Hóa, Thái Nguyên, Kinh Bắc, Sơn Tây, Hải Dương, Sơn Nam, An Bang, Thanh Hóa, Nghệ An, Thuận Hóa, and Quảng Nam.[127] Trung đô phủ refers to the capital Đông Đô.

The original maps have been lost, but they were likely reproduced in a 17th-century atlas titled *Hồng Đức Bản Đồ* (Atlas of Hồng Đức), named after the second-era of Lê Tư Thành's reign, which spanned from 1470 to 1497.[128] The atlas also includes a section from the early 19th century, suggesting that the surviving version was compiled or copied around that later time. While a detailed analysis of the Atlas of Hồng Đức falls outside the scope of this volume, one map of particular relevance is the map of Đại Việt, dated the 6th day of the 4th lunar month in 1490.[129] This date corresponds closely with the completion of the 13-circuit mapping project, as previously discussed. This map, a 17-century copy, is shown in Figure 6-9 and includes the locations of the 13 circuits.[130]

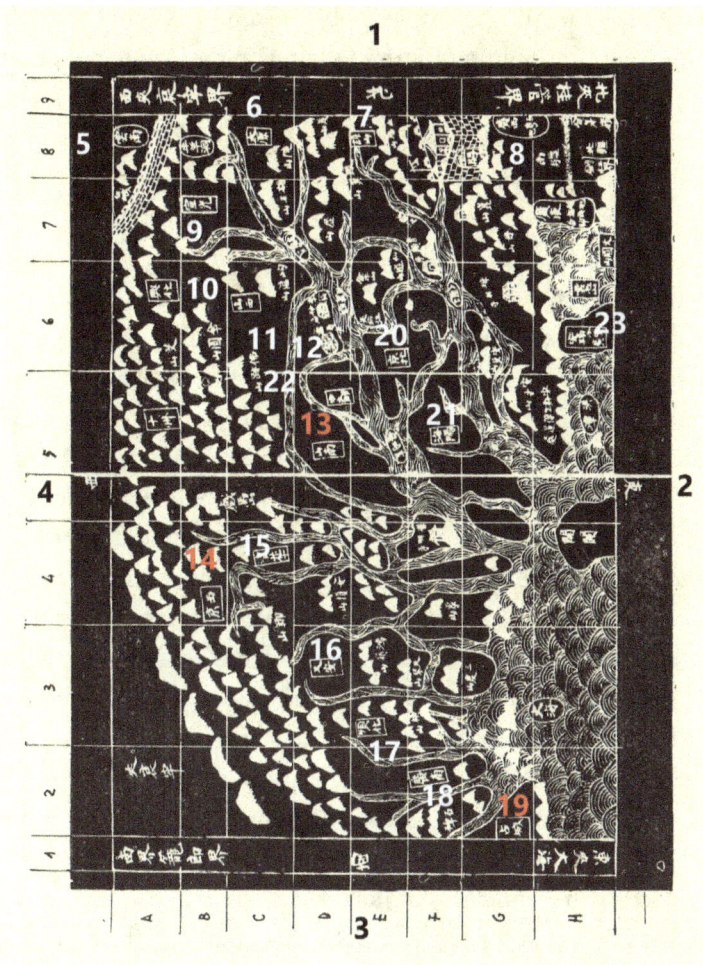

Figure 6-9: Map of An Nam reproduced from *Hồng Đức Bản Đồ* (Atlas of Hồng Đức).

Key: 1. North; 2. East; 3. South; 4. West; 5. Yunnan; 6. *Thái Nguyên*; 7. *Lạng Sơn*; 8. Ải Quan (border gate); 9. *Tuyên Quang*; 10. *Hưng Hóa*; 11. Mount Tản Viên; 12. West Lake; 13. Trung Đô (Hanoi) - *Sơn Nam*; 14. Tây kinh (Hồ Citadel); 15. Na-Sơn-*Thanh Hoa*; 16. *Nghệ An*; 17. *Thuận Hóa*; 18. *Quảng Nam* - Thạch Bi (stone stele); 19. Champa; 20. *Kinh Bắc*; 21. *Hải Dương*; 22. *Sơn Tây*; 23. *An Bang*.[131] Names in italics refer to the circuits. Notably, Champa is depicted as being south of Thạch Bi in modern Phú Yên.

Rivers, mountains, pagodas, and the sea are prominently depicted in Figure 6-9, though no roads are shown. Considering the cartographic knowledge of the period, the relative placement of key features is reasonably accurate: the mountain ranges appear in the west, the sea to the east, Champa lies to the south, and Yunnan to the northwest. Notably, three rivers, shown in the top left corner of the map, converge into the Red River before flowing into the sea. It is difficult to imagine that Lê Lợi and his generals planned their military campaigns against the Ming army without the aid of maps. If they did indeed rely on simple maps resembling Figure 6-9, it would be quite remarkable, given the effectiveness of their operations.

Legal Code

As previously mentioned, Lê Lợi believed in the importance of law in governance and issued a series of legal codes and regulations. Nearly twenty years later, in 1449, his grandson Lê Bang Cơ added 14 articles on land ownership chapter to the *Bộ Hình Luật* (Penal Code).[132] Although the original versions of these articles have been lost, scholars believe they were later copied and compiled in the 18th century, around 1767 or 1769, into the *Quốc Triều Hình Luật* (Penal Code of the Royal Court or National Dynasty Criminal Law), commonly referred to as the Hồng Đức Code or Lê Code.[133] Since many of the articles predate the Hồng Đức era (1470–1497) and others were added afterwards, the term 'Lê Code' is generally considered more accurate.[134]

The *Quốc Triều Hình Luật*, as translated into Vietnamese from manuscript A. 341 in 2006, consists of 13 chapters compiled into six volumes, with a total of 722 articles. The 13 chapters are General Provisions, Palace Security, Administrative Offenses, Military Discipline, Household and Marriage, Land and Property, Adultery, Theft and Treason, Fighting and Litigation, Fraud and Deception, Miscellaneous Laws, Escaped Criminals, and Trials and Imprisonment.[135] Some of these provisions in the Chapter on Household and Marriage are still reflected in present-day Vietnamese laws.[136]

As the legal code was produced in the 18th century, which falls beyond the time frame covered in this volume, I will discuss it in greater detail in a later volume.

Đại Việt Sử Ký Toàn Thư (Complete Book of the Historical Records of Great Viet)

Nearly 25 years after Phan Phu Tiên began compiling historical records of Đại Việt, Lê Tư Thành instructed Ngô Sĩ Liên to compile 15 volumes of the *Đại Việt Sử Ký Toàn Thư* (SKTT), chronicling Vietnamese history from the Hồng Bàng era (2878–256 BCE) up to the Ming withdrawal in early 1428.[137] For this work, Ngô Sĩ Liên drew heavily on earlier records written by Lê Văn Hưu (1230–1322) and Phan Phu Tiên.[138] His original contributions include the earliest period, from the Hồng Bàng era to the reign of An Dương Vương (257–208 BCE), focusing on the Hùng kings, who are now considered the founders of the Vietnamese kingdom.[139] Volume One recounts the stories from this era.[140]

Ngô Sĩ Liên is regarded as one of Vietnam's most distinguished historians after Lê Văn Hưu, and both men have streets named in their honour across the country. Lê Văn Hưu was discussed in Volume 3A.[141] Ngô Sĩ Liên was originally from Chúc Lý village, in Chương Đức district, now part of Ngọc Sơn commune, Chương Mỹ, Hanoi. His exact birth and death dates remain uncertain. However, some sources claim he was born in 1400, lived to the age of 98, and took part in the Lam Sơn uprising.[142] These details are difficult to verify—especially considering that if he were born in 1400, he would have been 42 years old when he passed the national examination, which would have been considered relatively late at the time.[143] Today, he is commemorated at a temple in Chương Mỹ, situated beside two scenic semicircular lakes.[144]

6.5 - Đại Việt invasions and the breakup of Champa

BUILDING UP THE FINAL CONFRONTATION

As discussed previously, the aggressive southward expansion of the Hồ dynasty had extended the southern border of Đại Việt as far as present-day Quảng Ngãi province. However, when the Ming army invaded and annexed Đại Việt, they chose not to return the territory seized by the Hồ dynasty to Champa, much to the disappointment of the Cham king.

After expelling the Ming occupiers, Lê Lợi was too preoccupied with governing Đại Việt to make any significant changes to the territorial status quo. By the mid-15th century, Đại Việt maintained a strong military presence in Hóa Châu Citadel, in modern Huế, but the region south of Hải Vân Pass remained largely under Cham control for nearly five decades, with a mixed population of Chams and remnants of earlier Vietnamese settlers, who came south at the turn of the century. Later historians have speculated that during this period, the two ethnic groups coexisted peacefully with frequent intermarriages between them.[145]

During this period, the king of Champa, Zhan-ba Di-lai, maintained a cautious and deferential policy toward Đại Việt, similar to the approach he had taken with the Ming court—paying tribute while avoiding provocation or military conflict. However, following the death of Lê Lợi, the situation along the southern border began to shift. According to SKTT, in 1434, the Cham lord Bố Đề personally led troops to the border and dispatched boats into Cửa Việt in present-day Quảng Trị province to capture several people.[146] Champa later sent tributes, and, when asked about the raids of Hóa Châu, explained that the incident had been the fault of a local commander, who was subsequently punished.[147] It should be noted SKTT may have mistaken in referring to a

Cham ruler named Bố Đề, as it explains elsewhere that *Bố Đề* was in fact a title.[148]

By this time, Đại Việt had begun paying closer attention to its southern frontier with Champa. In 1435, the Vietnamese court questioned the Cham envoy as to why Champa had not resumed its annual tribute payments and had failed to address the matter of returning Thổ Lũy (Chiêm Động and Cổ Lũy), territories seized under the Hồ dynasty. The Cham envoy responded that the king of Champa was old and senile, deeply distrustful of others, and suggested that Đại Việt should send a representative to raise the matter directly with the monarch.[149]

Within six years of being questioned about returning Thổ Lũy, Zhan-ba Di-lai died in 1441. The following year, Lê Nguyên Long, king of Đại Việt, also passed away. Champa's new ruler, Bí Cai, abandoned Zhan-ba Di-lai's cautious approach and adopted a more aggressive stance. In 1444 and 1445, Bí Cai launched repeated raids into Hóa Châu, upsetting the fragile peace between the two kingdoms. Lê Bang Cơ sent an envoy to the Ming court with a memorial protesting about these raids. In response, the emperor advised him (recorded in Ming shilu as Li Jun) to strengthen his defences and not to seek revenge. At the same time, he instructed Champa to cease its aggression and refrain from further attacks against Đại Việt.[150]

Despite the Ming court's warning, Đại Việt mounted a series of military expeditions in 1444 and 1445, deploying up to 100,000 troops under seasoned commanders who had fought in the war against the Ming army—such as Lê Khả, Lê Bôi, Lê Xí, and Lê Thụ.[151] The decisive campaign came in 1446, when Lê Bang Cơ sent Lê Thụ south with a force of 60,000 men. Earlier that year, Đại Việt had begun recruiting young men and stockpiling provisions in Hà Hoa, present-day Hà Tĩnh province. On 17 February 1446, the king issued formal orders to his generals, and two weeks later, dispatched envoys to notify the Ming court of the impending offensive. Over a month later, by 20 March 1446, Đại Việt forces had reached Ly Giang, Đa Lang, and Cổ Lũy (or Gu-lei, in modern-day Quảng Nam and Quảng Ngãi). They built fortifications, cleared and opened water routes, and fought the Cham forces.[152]

Đại Việt forces eventually prevailed and advanced to Vijaya.[153] They reached the city two months later in the summer of 1446, on 20 May, and defeated the Cham army. Lê Thụ captured King Bí Cai along with his consorts, retainers, horses, elephants, weapons, and other generals, then withdrew. The number was reportedly 33,500 as cited in Ming shilu.[154] Ma Ha Quý Lai (recorded as Mo-he Gui-lai in Ming shilu), a grandnephew of the former Cham king (likely Zhan-ba Di-lai), who had previously surrendered, sent his representatives to the Đại Việt court to pay tribute, declare vassalage, and request permission to be installed as king. Quý Lai also sought the enfeoffment from the Ming emperor, who approved his request in 1447.[155]

In the sixth lunar month (around July 1446), Lê Thụ presented Bí Cai in a victory ceremony at the ancestral temple. The king then declared a general amnesty across the realm. He ordered that Bí Cai and three of his consorts remain in the capital. However, he wanted other Cham people who had previously been living in the capital to be located and handed over to the attendants of the Cham king, along with other Cham officers, for repatriation.[156] While Lê Bang Cơ did not want any Cham people residing in his capital, he did not attempt to settle Vietnamese in the Cham territory that Lê Thụ forces seized during the 1446 campaign. In effect, Đại Việt seemed to return to the pre-campaign status quo following Bí Cai's capture. Later in 1448, the Ming emperor instructed Lê Bang Cơ to escort Bí Cai back to Champa, but SKTT does not record whether Đại Việt ever complied with this directive.[157]

Meanwhile, the new king of Champa, Ma Ha Quý Lai, was content to maintain a vassal relationship with Đại Việt until he was imprisoned by his younger brother, Quý Do (recorded as Mo-he Gui-you in Ming shilu), three years later in 1449.[158] However, Ming shilu records that Ma Ha Quý Lai had died.[159] When Quý Do later sent tribute, Lê Bang Cơ refused to accept it and, at some stage, even considered invading Champa, though he ultimately took no action. For the next 20 years, relations between the two kingdoms remained largely peaceful, aside from a few minor Cham raids into Hóa Châu.

In 1470, Champa experienced another bloody upheaval when a new king came to power. Bàn La Trà Duyệt, the son of a nursemaid, killed his lord, Bí Điền, took the throne and handed it over to his brother, Bàn La Trà Toàn.[160] According to SKTT, Trà Toàn was an arrogant, violent and reckless man. He was also the son-in-law of the former king, Bí Cai.[161] Notably, the name *Bí Điền* may have originally been *Bố Điền*, a title denoting a crown prince or high-ranking noble, as discussed elsewhere. In any event, in the eighth lunar month of 1470, Trà Toàn personally led over 100,000 land and naval troops, along with elephants and horses, in a surprise attack on Hóa Châu. The frontier general stationed there, Phạm Văn Hiển and his men, were unable to withstand the assault. They had to gather the populace into the citadel and send an urgent message for reinforcements.

Trà Toàn's actions set in motion a chain of events that ultimately led to his downfall and the breakup of Champa, as detailed below.

1471 INVASION OF CHAMPA

The preparation

The last time a Cham king successfully invaded Đại Việt and seized substantial territory was nearly a century earlier, when King Chế Bồng Nga sacked Thăng Long in 1371. Trà Toàn may have aspired to follow in his predecessor's footsteps. However, circumstances had changed. Đại Việt was now far stronger militarily and led by a capable and energetic ruler, the 29-year-old Lê Tư Thành.

Within three months of Trà Toàn's invasion, on 28 November 1470, Lê Tư Thành summoned 260,000 elite troops and issued a royal edict declaring that he would personally lead the expedition against Champa. The edict was lengthy, and I have summarised the key points as follows:[162]

Lê Tư Thành emphasised that his grandfather, Lê Lợi, had established and defended Đại Việt, securing its borders, honouring powerful states, and protecting smaller ones. These lesser states, in turn, paid tribute and acknowledged Đại Việt's authority. However, Champa defied this order, claiming seniority over Đại Việt's rulers, aiming to extend its territory as far north as Hoành Sơn (modern-day Ngang Pass), and falsely accusing Đại Việt of plotting to conquer China and seizing tributes meant for the Ming court.

He went on to portray Champa rulers as liars, criminals and illegitimate usurpers who imposed harsh taxes and brutal punishments on their people while enslaving Đại Việt citizens. He condemned their prohibition on meat slaughter, alcohol brewing, and the abandonment of traditional sacrificial rites to the gods. He also denounced their misguided faith in false Buddhas and demons, the construction of temples for these deities, and the cruel practices inflicted on widows and orphans, including body burning and nose mutilation.

Lê Tư Thành concluded the edict with a declaration that he would personally command the expedition and destroy Champa for nine generations. He promised that the campaign would be swift and he would end the Cham threat, cleanse the ancient hatred and protect future generations from the evil of Champa.

Through the edict, Lê Tư Thành was making a clear justification for the invasion. He described the Cham rulers and their people in dehumanising terms—likening them to venomous bees, rabid dogs, crows, foxes, termites, and ants burrowed at Cổ Lũy and Vijaya. In contrast, he portrayed Đại Việt soldiers as tiger-like warriors, brave troops with unwavering resolve. To him, the looming war was not merely a military campaign but a moral confrontation between the evil Chams and the righteous Vietnamese.

On the same day, he ordered the Grand Preceptor (*Thái Sư*) Đinh Liệt and Grand Tutor (*Thái Bảo*) Lê Niệm to lead a naval force of 100,000 troops drawn from the Eastern, Southern, and Northern military commands to depart ahead of the main army. He also issued 24 directives to various army units on the coming campaign. A month earlier, he had already dispatched envoys to inform the Ming court of the Cham invasion. The following day, he presented a memorial at the Imperial Ancestral Temple. Taken together with his royal edict, these actions highlight Lê Tư Thành's thorough planning and strategic foresight before launching the expedition. Then, on 8 December 1470, he personally led an additional naval force of 150,000 men to Champa.[163]

While the total figure of 250,000 may be exaggerated, considering Đại Việt's standing army at the time was estimated to be around 70,000, the speed with which such a large force—even at a lower figure of, perhaps around 25,000—was mobilised within ten days suggests the country was in a high state of military readiness. Notably, the 19th-century compilers of CM also expressed scepticism about the inflated figure.[164]

The campaign

Fighting in Quảng Nam and Quảng Ngãi Provinces
Over two weeks later, on 24 December 1470, Lê Tư Thành's forces departed from Thiết Sơn in modern Hưng Nguyên, near Vinh City of Nghệ An province. While encamped there, he admonished several officials for submitting absurd proposals. He ordered them to urinate into their official hats as punishment.[165] Three weeks later, on 8 January 1471, Đại Việt's naval forces reached Cham territory. Two weeks after that, Lê Tư Thành ordered local troops of Thuận Hóa to conduct naval training exercises. On 26 January, they captured the Cham official guarding the Cụ Đề river entrance, just south of Hải Vân Pass.

These events suggest that Đại Việt forces may have stopped in Hóa Châu, in present-day Huế in January 1471, before crossing the Hải Vân Pass at the end of the month. They also indicate that up to 26 January 1471, the Chams still maintained control over the territory south of the pass. Around that time, Lê Tư Thành issued a tactical manual titled *Bình Chiêm Sách* (The Book of Pacifying Champa) outlining ten obvious winning factors and three points of concern to his troops. He had the book translated into the national language, which was likely to be *Chữ Nôm*—a Vietnamese language using Chinese characters—so that the soldiers could understand.[166] He also ordered a local chieftain from Thuận Hóa to produce a map detailing the strategic topography of Champa. This use of maps in a military campaign was first recorded in SKTT, and mentioned in a paper by historian John Whitmore.[167]

Over a month later, on 24 February 1471, Trà Toàn sent his brother, Thị Nại, along with six high-ranking officials, 5,000 troops, and war elephants, to secretly approach the king's encampment. The following day, the king quietly ordered vanguard generals, along with their forces, to lead over 500 ships and 30,000 elite soldiers to depart from the Áp and Toạ estuaries. Under cover of night, they sailed south along the coast and landed at the Sa Kỳ estuary. There, they built ramparts and fortified walls to block the enemy's retreat. The Champa forces were completely unaware of these manoeuvres.

Once the blocking forces were in place, on 26 February 1471, the Đại Việt king personally led over 1,000 ships and what SKTT claims to be more than 700,000 elite troops —an inflated and erroneous figure—through the Tân Áp and Cựu Toạ estuaries. They raised the imperial banner, beat the war drums, and advanced with loud battle cries. Earlier, the king had secretly ordered an infantry column along hidden mountain paths on the west. Caught between this infantry column and the king's forces from the coast, the Cham army fell into disarray and fled toward Vijaya further south. Upon reaching Mount Mộ Nô west of the Sa Kỳ estuary, they encountered Đại Việt blocking forces. Shortly after, the king arrived at Mễ Cần and ordered a full assault. What followed was a decisive and complete rout of the Cham forces.

According to SKTT, the Chams suffered 300 beheaded and 60 captured alive, with one general slain. These reported casualties appear inconsistent with the earlier figures of 5,000 Cham troops and 250,000–260,000 Vietnamese soldiers. Even if the Chams had suffered losses of 30%, their force likely numbered no more than 1,000, casting further doubt on the scale claimed in official chronicles, including the 100,000 Cham troops that SKTT claimed to have invaded Hóa Châu five months earlier.

His grandfather, Lê Lợi, often relied on ambush tactics during his campaigns against the Ming forces due to limited manpower and resources in the face of a far superior enemy. In contrast, Lê Tư Thành commanded a well-equipped and fully mobilised army, enabling him to employ large-scale blocking and pincer movements to effectively encircle and crush the Cham forces. According to historical records, the major battles likely occurred along the 100-kilometre stretch between the Thu Bồn River —flowing into Cửa Đại (Đại estuary) near the tourist town of Hội An (corresponding to the historical Áp or Tân Áp and Toạ or Cửa Tọa estuaries)—and the Trà Khúc River, just south of the present-day Sa Kỳ estuary.[168]

Lê Tư Thành referred to two Cham citadels in his edict, Cổ Lũy and Vijaya as targets of his campaign. With the victory, he had captured the first Cham fort.

Fighting in Bình Định Province - The fall of Champa's capital, Vijaya

Upon hearing the news of his brother's defeat, Trà Toàn sent an envoy to Lê Tư Thành's camp to offer to surrender. The king responded by dispatching his representative but these diplomatic activities did not slow his advance toward Vijaya. On 18 March 1471, the king's forces reached the harbour of Thị Nại, in modern Quy Nhơn, and stormed the Thị Nại Citadel, reported beheading over 100 Cham defenders. It had taken the army 20 days to travel roughly 300 kilometres from Cửa Đại, moving by both land and along the coast by ships—a pace that suggests the earlier battles against Trần Toàn's brother were swift and decisive. Figure 6-10 shows the locations mentioned.

Having taken the citadel near the harbour, the king advanced inland and laid siege to Vijaya Citadel the following day. On 20 March, his forces surrounded the city in multiple layers. Trà Toàn, demoralised by his brother's defeat and the loss of Thị Nại Citadel, offered little resistance. He sent gifts daily to Lê Tư Thành's camp and repeatedly pleaded to surrender. However, the king ignored these overtures and continued preparations for a full assault, ordering the construction of siege equipment. Just two days later, on 22 March, he launched a coordinated assault. The vanguard troops raised ladders, facing little resistance, quickly scaled the walls and took control of the parapets. Around that time, at the signal of three cannon shots, the royal guards commander led the main force in storming the eastern gate. Vijaya fell soon thereafter.[169]

The king issued strict order prohibiting any burning or looting within the citadel. All treasures were to be sealed and kept secure, and Trà Toàn was not to be harmed. During the occupation, Đại Việt troops discovered a silver box shaped like a sword, which they presented to the king. The Cham explained that it was an ancient royal artefact of Champa, traditionally passed down through generations of their kings.

According to SKTT, Đại Việt forces captured over 30,000 Cham prisoners, beheaded over 40,000 and took Trà Toàn alive. As with earlier claims, these figures are questionable, given that the same forces only killed 100 a few days before. How they could physically and emotionally slaughter 40,000 soon afterwards is difficult to believe.[170] Nevertheless, such inflated figures have sometimes been cited to argue that Lê Tư Thành pursued a genocidal policy against the Chams.[171] This, however, seems unlikely. Vijaya fell quickly, but Lê Tư Thành forbade the sacking of the citadel. He seized treasures, captured the Cham king and royal family, divided Champa into several states (see below), and then withdrew. Many Cham elites fled south, and Đại Việt did not attempt to pursue or eradicate them entirely.

SKTT describes the scene of Trà Toàn kneeling before Lê Tư Thành—a powerful image that underscored the stark imbalance between the two kingdoms.

> *The soldiers of Thuận Hoá captured Trà Toàn alive and brought him before the king. Trà Toàn bowed his head and knelt. The king asked through an interpreter: "Are you the lord of Champa?"*
>
> *Toàn replied: "Yes."*
>
> *The king asked: "Do you know I am the king?"*
>
> *Toàn answered: "I saw your noble demeanour and already recognised Your Majesty."*
>
> *The king asked: "How many children do you have?"*
>
> *Toàn replied: "I have more than ten children."*
>
> *Đỗ Hoàn* [a Đại Việt officer] *interjected: "He has pleaded to become your subject and begs Your Majesty to spare his life."*
>
> *The king said to Toàn:*
>
> *"Amidst the swords and spears, I feared you might be harmed. Now, fortunately, you are alive and here before me, and I am truly relieved."*
>
> *He then ordered a small house to be built for Toàn to stay. The officials led Toàn away somewhat hastily. The king said:*
>
> *"Take him away gently. He was the king of a country—why do you force him like this?"*[172]

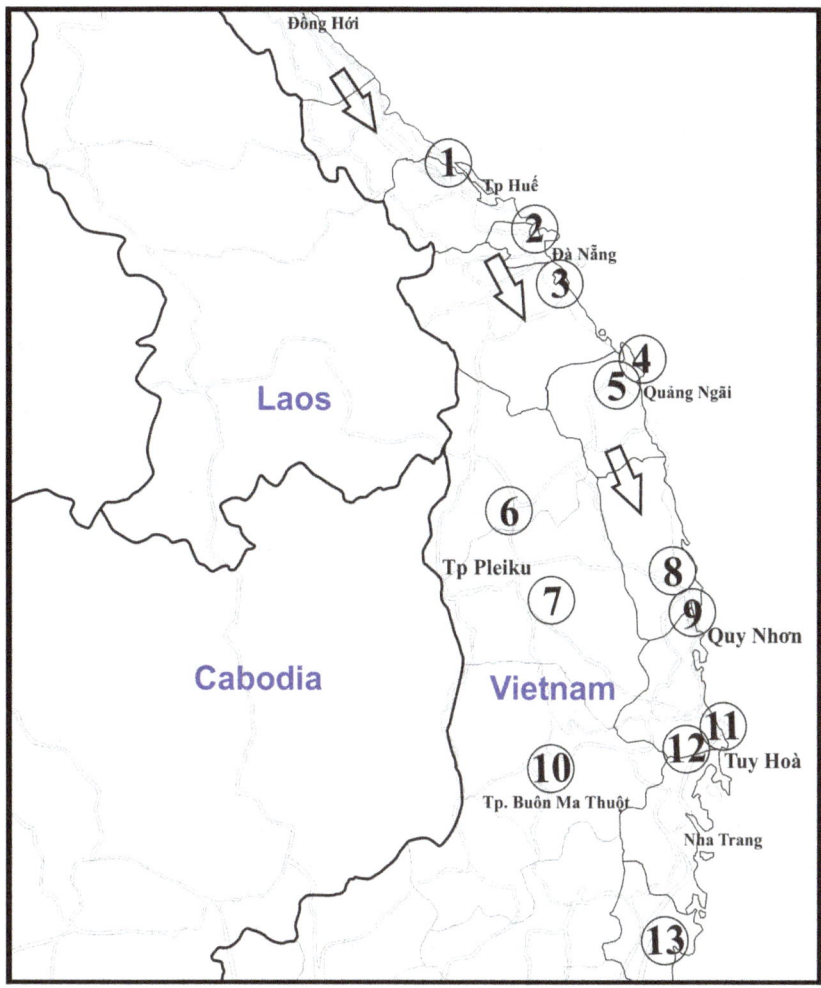

Figure 6-10: Map of the 1471 invasion of Champa.

Key: 1. Hóa Châu Citadel; 2. Cụ Đê Estuary; 3. Cửa Đại; 4. Sa Kỳ Port; 5. Châu Sa Citadel; 6. Kontum; 7. Gia Lai; 8. Vijaya Citadel; 9. Cù Mông Pass; 10. Đắk Lắk; 11. Mount Đá Bia; 12. Cả Pass; 13. Phan Rang-Tháp Chàm. White arrows illustrate the direction of the Đại Việt invasion.

The aftermath and the break-up of Champa

Although Trà Toàn was captured, one of his generals, Bô Trì Trì, escaped south to Phan Lung— around Phan Rang-Tháp Chàm, located in present-day Ninh Thuận province, roughly 300 kilometres from Vijaya—and declared himself ruler of Champa. According to SKTT, Bô Trì Trì retained control over one-fifth of Champa's former territory.[173] He soon sent envoys to Đại Việt, acknowledged vassalage, and offered tribute. In response, Lê Tư Thành granted him the title of *vương* (king).

However, instead of restoring him to Vijaya—the traditional Cham capital since the 11th century—Lê Tư Thành allowed Bô Trì Trì to remain in Phan Lung and created two more separate vassal states: Nam Bàn and Hoa Anh.[174] According to CM, Nam Bàn later became known as Thủy Xá and Hỏa Xá under the Nguyễn dynasty in the 19th century, encompassing parts of today's Central Highlands, including Kon Tum, Gia Lai, and Đắk Lắk.[175] Given the vast size of these provinces, it is likely that 15th-century Nam Bàn referred to a smaller portion of what is now Gia Lai and Đắk Lắk.

As for Hoa Anh, contemporary scholars suggest that it corresponded to present-day Phú Yên province, stretching from Cù Mông—just south of Quy Nhơn—to the Cả Pass.[176] According to CM, following the victory in 1471, Lê Tư Thành designated Mount Đá Bi near the Cả Pass as the northern boundary of Champa.[177] This border suggests that under Bô Trì Trì's rule, Champa was reduced to the historic kingdoms of Panduranga and Kauthara, as discussed in Volume 3B.[178]

Lê Tư Thành then appointed several Cham and Vietnamese as civil and military governors in the newly conquered regions under Đại Việt's control, before departing. He did not remain in Vijaya for long, and by 1 April 1471—about ten days later—he was back in Thuận Hóa. His short stay indicated that the battle for Vijaya was over quickly. Nearly a month later, on 27 April, the royal entourage reached Thanh Hóa, where Trà Toàn reported fallen ill from anxiety and died. The king ordered his corpse be beheaded, the body burned, and the ashes cast into the river. Around a month later, on 11 May, the king presented the severed head—along with the ear lobes of other fallen Chams—at the Ancestral Temple in Lam Kinh.

The expedition marked a major triumph for Đại Việt. Within just five months, Lê Tư Thành had pushed the kingdom's southern frontier nearly 500 kilometres further south, from Hải Vân Pass to Mount Đá Bia, and effectively dismantled Champa as a unified polity. Despite this, he made no apparent effort to establish large-scale Vietnamese settlements in the newly conquered territories or to exploit their mineral or natural resources. Instead, the administration of these lands was entrusted to a mix of local Cham and Vietnamese officials, and it was not until 1485 that he issued an order to collect taxes in Quảng Nam.[179] The last recorded attempt by Đại Việt to resettle vagrants for land reclamation occurred in 1467, and it took place in Bố Chính district of Quảng Bình province—south of the Ngang Pass but still far north of Quảng Nam.[180]

At the end of that year, on 19 December 1471, Đại Việt invaded Champa again, capturing its ruler, Trà Toại, and bringing him back to Đông Đô. This episode suggests that Đại Việt maintained its control over Champa primarily through military dominance from afar, rather than through direct colonisation or settlement.

Although Lê Tư Thành created Đại Việt's 13th administrative circuit, Quảng Nam, and incorporated it into the official map of the realm, the population in the area remained predominantly Cham. A mid-16th-century text records the existence of a Cham village where the Cham language was still spoken, and in Điện Bàn district in Quảng Nam province, local women continued to wear skirts made of traditional Cham fabric.[181] In short, for at least a century after the conquest, the region south of the Hải Vân Pass was likely to remain culturally and demographically Cham in character.[182] Intermarriage between Cham and Vietnamese appears to have been common enough to raise concern at the Lê court. In 1499, Lê Tư Thành's son—who had succeeded him as the next king—issued an edict prohibiting Vietnamese men, from the royal princes to the commoners, from marrying Cham women.[183]

In 1998, a bronze seal dated to 1471 was found at the site of the ancient Châu Sa Citadel (see Figure 6-11). The find confirmed the Quảng Nam circuit at the time extended to include present-day Quảng Ngãi province.[184] Volume 3D describes the citadels of Châu Sa and Cổ Lũy nearby.

6.6 - *The Cham records of the 1471 event*

Đại Việt's invasion of Champa in 1471 was a momentous event in the histories of both kingdoms. To date, however, I have found no direct reference to it in any Cham sources. The 15th-century Cham inscriptions that survive predate 1471, while 19th-century handwritten Cham records make no mention of the invasion.[185] One exception is the legend of Princess Po Sah Inư, reported in Volume 3B, which refers instead to a Yuen (i.e., Đại Việt) invasion in 1440. In this account, Yuen defeated Champa and compelled the Cham king to abdicate after a 37-year rule, while Yuen's ruler, Lê Thánh Tông (Lê Tư Thành), seized Princess Po Sah Inư and made her his wife.[186] Notably, the legend contains no reference to any genocide of the Chams.

Figure 6-11: Seal, History Museum of Ho Chi Minh City, 1471, bronze.

The seal was found at Phú Bình village, Tịnh Châu commune, Sơn Tịnh district, where the site of Châu Sa Citadel is in 1998.[187] The face of the seal is engraved with 12 script characters arranged in three lines from left to right: *Quảng Nam Đẳng Xứ - Tán Trị Thừa Tuyên - Sử Ty Chi Ấn* (Seal of the Commissioner of the Quảng Nam and associated regions' Administrative and Pacification Office, 廣南等處贊治承宣 使 司之印).[188]

6.7 - The court of Ming and Champa

Like Đại Việt, Champa regularly sent envoys and paid tribute to the Ming court. As noted elsewhere, both kingdoms lodged complaints with the emperor over each other's border raids, often presenting conflicting accounts. Faced with contradictory evidence, the Ming emperor typically waited for his envoys to return from both courts before making any substantive decisions. However, the diplomatic missions took months to travel between Beijing, Đông Kinh, and Vijaya, and by the time reports arrived, the immediacy of the situation had usually passed.

With limited options short of military intervention, the emperor's typical response was to issue admonitory memorials, urging both sides to cease hostilities—directives that were often ignored by both Đại Việt and Champa.

The 1471 invasion that led to the collapse of Champa was a major geopolitical event, yet the Ming emperor's response was notably restrained. This reaction was likely due to Đại Việt portraying the conflict as the result of internal Cham strife—family members vying for the throne—rather than an act of its aggression. Although the Ming's Ministry of War expressed scepticism and recommended punitive measures, the emperor remained indecisive and ultimately took no concrete action to reverse Đại Việt's annexation. Instead, he ordered strengthened border defences and issued additional admonitory edicts. His inaction was likely shaped by other pressing concerns, including the Jingxiang Rebellion (1465–1476) and ongoing threats from the Mongols at the time. Additionally, the memory of the Ming army's defeat by Đại Việt five decades earlier may have also influenced his reluctance to intervene.

In 1481, the new king of Champa sent a memorial to the Ming court and requested that the emperor order Đại Việt to return all of Champa's former lands. The emperor agreed and instructed Đại Việt accordingly, but the directive was ignored. Despite ongoing diplomatic appeals, by the end of the decade, Đại Việt's occupation of Champa had become a firmly established reality.

Further details of the interactions between the Ming emperor, Đại Việt and Champa are provided in Appendix 2.

6.8 - Wars in the west with Laos

BORDER SKIRMISHES

Like Ngưu Hống, the Later Lê dynasty regarded the Tai principality in Bồn Man (west of Nghệ An) as a vassal state. In 1448, Bồn Man sought to become a dependency of Đại Việt rather than Ai Lao. Lê Bang Cơ approved the request and established it as Quy Hợp prefecture.[189] However, soon after Lê Tư Thành ascended the throne in 1460, the chieftain of Bồn Man, a man with a Cầm in his name, refused to pay tribute to the Lê court. The new king of Đại Việt, perhaps wanted to assert his authority, dispatched an army led by three of the court's most senior ministers—Lê Liệt, Lê Lựu, and Lê Lăng—to launch a punitive campaign.[190] The campaign appeared to be successful as for the next 20 years, SKTT records no campaign against Bồn Man, aside from a brief skirmish, led by Lê Tư Thành, in 1469.

In 1467, Ai Lao occupied a grotto named Cư Lộng near the border of Đại Việt. In response, Lê Tư Thành dispatched a force of 1000 soldiers under the command of Khuất Đà, joined by 300 local troops from Mộc Châu and surrounding areas in Việt and Mỗi Châu—present-day Yên Châu and Thuận Châu in Sơn La province. The combined force camped for half a month along the upper reaches of the Mã River (Mã Giang) to secure the border routes. To intimidate the enemy, their commander spread word among the troops and local population that they intended to launch an all-out attack to eliminate the invaders. The ruse proved effective, frightening the Ai Lao soldiers into surrender. Based on the geographical clues, the incident likely occurred near Loóng Sập, along the current Laos-Vietnam border. Khuất Đà and his men probably marched up highway AH13, turning off at Mộc Châu to reach the area. The return trip of the whole operation took 18 days.[191]

In 1479, Bồn Man's new chieftain, another Cầm, allied with Lão Qua. With their support, Cầm Công began launching raids into Đại Việt territory.[192] In response, Lê Tư Thành once again launched another punitive campaign, employing a strategy similar to the one used in his 1470–1471 expedition against Champa.

WAR EDICTS

Lê Tư Thành issued two edicts declaring war—one against Bồn Man on 26 June 1479, and another against Lão Qua over a month later on 9 August 1479. Both echoed the tone and themes of the edict issued nearly a decade earlier during the campaign against Champa in 1470–1471. The language was similarly dehumanising, describing Đại Việt's enemies as beasts, pigs, dogs, bees, and caterpillars. The edicts outlined the alleged 'crimes' committed by Bồn Man and Lão Qua, including the Laotian attacks on Lê Lợi during the early years of his rebellion, and framed the military campaign as a righteous and justified response. Lê Tư Thành specifically targeted Cầm Công and Lão Qua, his supporter, as the central focus of the campaign.[193]

The man who led the expedition was Lê Thọ Vực, who was the first man to scale the walls of Vijaya nearly a decade earlier. Now holding the rank of Grand Commandant and the title 'General of the Western Expedition', Lê Thọ Vực led the main force along the Trà Lân (also known as Trà Long) route, following what is now Highway QL7A into Bồn Man. His task was to seize the strategic stronghold of Trấn Ninh or present-day Xieng Khoang province.[194]

FIVE ARMIES

As in the Champa campaign, Lê Tư Thành took no chances and employed a massive force of 180,000 troops, divided into five armies, to strike both Bồn Man and Lão Qua.[195] The five armies resembled five arrows moving from east to west, converging on the Plain of Jars and Luang Prabang, as illustrated in Figure 6-12. From north to south, the first army, commanded by Trịnh Công Lộ—a marquis and royal son-in-law—consisted of 2,000 elite troops from the Eastern Military Command and advanced the northernmost route via An Tây, in present-day Điện Biên and Lai Châu, most likely toward Luang Prabang, the capital of Lan Xang.[196] This route likely corresponds to today's AH13. The second army, led by cavalry deputy general Lê Lộng, advanced towards Thuận Mỗi prefecture to block the enemy's retreat. Thuận Mỗi also known as Gia Hưng, was located in the southern part of today's Sơn La province. This force likely took the turnoff at Mộc Châu from AH13 toward Sam Nuea of Houaphan province and onto the Plain of Jars or they could have continued on AH13 to support the first army.

Deputy General Lê Nhân Hiếu commanded the third army, advancing along the Thanh Đô route—present-day Thọ Xuân in Thanh Hóa province—to strike at the enemy's weak points. They likely marched north following highway QL16 and crossed the border into Houaphan province. The fourth army served as the main force as described earlier. The fifth army, under the command of General Lê Đình Ngạn, approached the Plain of Jars from the south, via the Ngọc Ma area, near present-day Viengthong in Bolikhamxai province. Their mission was to cut off the enemy's retreat, likely following the route of today's AH15.

Based on the commanders' titles and their assigned objectives, the first and fourth armies appear to have been the primary forces, while the remaining armies served mainly in supporting roles, such as flanking or cutting off enemy retreat. Nevertheless, the scale of the expedition was considerable, especially given the long distances and rugged mountainous terrain the troops had to traverse. Unlike the Champa campaign, where ships were heavily used to transport troops and supplies along the coast, this western expedition moved primarily on foot, horseback, and possibly war elephants.

The first army faced the longest march—over 800 kilometres—with roughly half that distance just to reach the modern-day border from Đông Kinh. In contrast, the fourth army, which formed the main force, had the shortest route: approximately 140 kilometres from the present-day border to the Plain of Jars, a journey that likely took 10 to 15 days on foot. The remaining armies covered intermediate distances ranging from 300 to 400 kilometres from the border.[197]

Given these distances, the logistical challenges involved, and the recorded figure of 2,000 troops in the first army, the reported total of 180,000 soldiers seems highly exaggerated. A more plausible estimate would place the actual number of troops involved in all five armies at around 8,000 to 12,000.

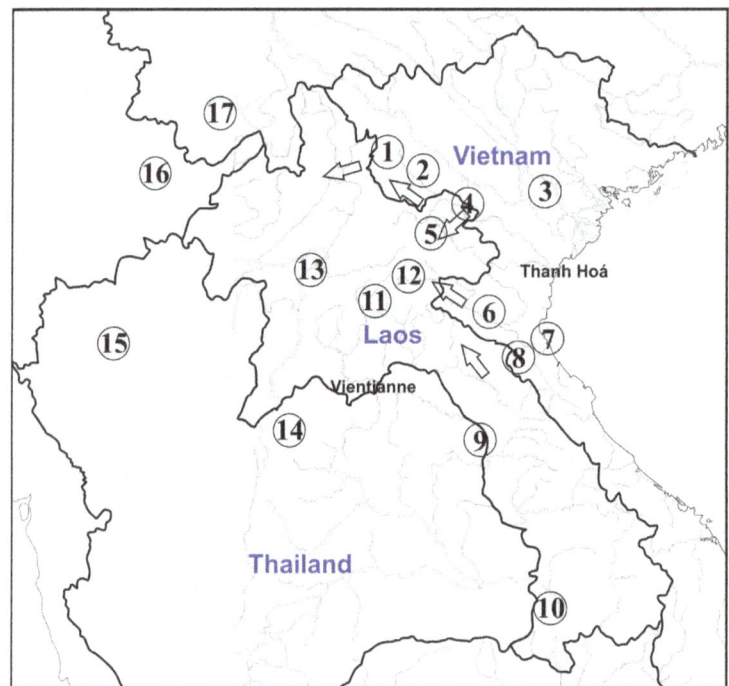

Figure 6-12: Map of the western campaign against Bồn Man and Lão Qua.

Key: 1. Điện Biên Phủ; 2. Sơn La; 3. Hanoi; 4. Mộc Châu; 5. Sam Nuea; 6. Bia Ma Nhai; 7. Vinh; 8. Nam Phao International Checkpoint; 9. Thakhek; 10. Muang Champasak; 11. Phonavan; 12. Plain of Jars; 13. Luang Prabang; 14. Loei; 15. Chiang Mai; 16. Keng Tung; 17. Jinghong (Xishuangbanna Dai Autonomous prefecture). White arrows illustrate the direction of the Đại Việt invasion in 1479, the first army is at the top, and the fifth army is at the bottom.

THE BATTLES

Approximately a month after the edict was issued, the armies set out on 8 September 1479. According to SKTT, they crushed Ai Lao, reached the capital of Lão Qua, and seized a vast number of treasures and riches. The king of Lão Qua fled in defeat. Đại Việt forces captured many Laotians, occupied their territory, and advanced as far as the Trường Sa River, reaching the southern border of Myanmar (Burma). After receiving a letter from the Myanmar court, the Đại Việt troops withdrew, returning home in triumph.

The translators of SKTT identify the capital of Lão Qua as Luang Prabang, which is accurate. However, they inaccurately equate the Trường Sa River with the Irrawaddy River. The Irrawaddy lies too far to the west of Luang Prabang, making this identification unlikely. A more plausible interpretation is that the Trường Sa River refers to the Mekong River, which flows past Luang Prabang and was the same river that Đoàn Nhữ Hài once planned to sail down to reach Cambodia, as mentioned previously.

Meanwhile, Lê Tư Thành prepared to lead the expedition to Lão Qua, as he had declared in his second edict. On 1 December 1479 he set out with his army to march to Ai Lao. On 18 December, the king sent his officials to go ahead to prepare food supplies in Trấn Ninh prefecture and also dispatched 1,200 additional troops to the headquarters of Lê Thọ Vực, the commander of the fourth army. He also issued order requiring the first and the fifth army commanders to send progress report to him at Chiềng Vang on 2 January 1489. On 19 January, the king and his entourage reached Châu Bồ and camped there for four days before turning back. They arrived in Đông Kinh on 8 February 1480.

By the time the king reached Châu Bồ, Lê Thọ Vực and the fourth army had already been in Laotian territory for nearly four months. They had captured the Plain of Jars and advanced as far as Luang Prabang. With news of this victory reaching him, the king—still far behind—may have concluded there was no need to proceed further and instead chose to return to the capital. SKTT does not specify the route taken by the king and his entourage in this campaign, but based on the events of 1467, it is likely they travelled westward to Mộc Châu via Hòa Bình on AH13. The return journey took 16 days, and at an estimated travel speed of 13 kilometres per day, the total distance covered would have been around 208 kilometres. This supports the likely scenario that the king travelled westward toward Mộc Châu, as the distance from Hanoi to Mộc Châu is approximately 188 kilometres. While the exact location of Châu Bồ remains unknown, Chiềng Vang is likely a hamlet in Lạc Sơn District, Hòa Bình Province.

Shortly after returning to the capital, Lê Tư Thành ordered Duke Lê Niệm to lead a force of 300,000 troops in a renewed attack on Bồn Man, using the loss of a letter from Lê Thọ Vực reporting the victory, while transiting through Bồn Man, as a pretext. The Đại Việt army crossed the border, destroyed forts, and seized various treasures. Cầm Công fled but died soon after. According to SKTT, Bồn Man had once consisted of 90,000 households, but famine had decimated the population, leaving only about 2,000 survivors. Those remaining surrendered to Đại Việt, and the king appointed Cầm Đông as the new local chieftain.

The figure of 300,000 soldiers was clearly exaggerated for reasons explained elsewhere. Likewise, the claim of 90,000 households for a remote mountainous region is also highly inflated when compared with the total population of Laos in 1910, which was only around 600,000.[198]

THE LAOTIAN RECORDS

While SKTT portrays the invasion of Bồn Man and Lão Qua as a major triumph, Laotian historical accounts tell a different story—one in which Đại Việt forces suffered heavy losses and were ultimately driven off. At the time, modern-day Laos was ruled from Luang Prabang by King Chakkaphat Phaen Phaeo (1415–1481), the 11th monarch of the Lan Xang kingdom.[199]

According to several sources, the invasion was triggered by an incident involving a diplomatic gift. Lê Tư Thành had learned of a white elephant in Lan Xang and requested that it be sent to Đông Kinh. The Laotians instead sent a gold casket containing the elephant's nails and hair, but the contents were swapped at the last moment with the animal's dung. While different versions of the tale vary in terms of who made the switch and where the elephant came from, the outcome remained the same. Upon receiving the offensive gift, Lê Tư Thành was incensed and ordered a military campaign against Lan Xang.[200]

King Chakkaphat was taken by surprise when the news of the invasion reached him. However, rather than panicking, he granted the full military authority to one of his sons, the Chief Minister, Chao Kon Keo and the Prince of Chienglaw (Sen-Luang-Xieng-Lo) to defend the capital. The prince quickly mobilised a force of 200,000 men and 2,000 elephants, dividing them into three armies of roughly equal size: one under him and the others led by senior commanders. They took up defensive positions at Thongna-Khao-Chao (now the site of Visul-Viharn or Wat Visunarat) in Luang Prabang, on the east bank of the Mekong River.

Once his forces were in position, the prince dispatched a contingent of 4,000 soldiers under the command of his four top lieutenants to stage an ambush near Mount Mung. The Đại Việt troops fell into the trap and suffered heavy casualties. The fighting lasted three full days, but on the fourth day, the Vietnamese managed to break through and forced the Laotian forces to retreat to a second defensive position.

There, another fierce battle broke out. Both sides sustained heavy losses, but the Đại Việt continued their advance until they encountered the main body of the Laotian army at Thongna-Khao-Chao. Outnumbered, the Laotians fought bravely, but in the ensuing battle, their two senior commanders were killed. The four lieutenants were captured and later executed.[201] The Vietnamese also suffered losses, with ten generals reportedly killed. The prince himself was wounded and drowned while attempting to escape in a canoe. King Chakkaphat and members of the royal family fled down the Mekong River to Vientiane. The battered Đại Việt army entered Luang Prabang shortly afterward.

However, their hold on the city was short-lived. Prince Chao Then-Kham, another son of King Chakkaphat and governor of Muong Dan Sai—located in what is now Loei Province in Thailand, approximately 350 kilometres south of Luang Prabang—mobilized his forces and launched a counterattack. Catching the exhausted Vietnamese off guard, he drove them out of Luang Prabang and relentlessly harassed their retreat back to the border. By the end of the campaign, only 600 of the original 4,000 Đại Việt soldiers survived.[202]

The story involving the elephant's dung is likely apocryphal, as it is difficult to believe that Lê Tư Thành would launch an invasion on another country over such a trivial insult. Historical accounts in SKTT depict him as a deliberate and strategic leader, not someone prone to rash decisions. In any case, Laotian sources suggest that the campaign against Lão Qua was far more challenging than the one against Champa. The Laotians put up strong resistance, and although the reported number of soldiers and elephants appears greatly exaggerated—especially when compared to the estimated population of Laos in 1910, which was only about 600,000—it is notable that Laotian records acknowledge they were outnumbered, with Đại Việt forces estimated at just 4,000.

Although I have been unable to pinpoint the location of Mount Mung on modern maps, it was likely situated somewhere along route 13, that connects with route 7 leading to the Plain of Jars in Phonsavan. It is plausible that the Đại Việt's fourth army advanced along this route to reach Luang Prabang. The mountainous terrain, with its winding paths and narrow passes, would have provided numerous locations well-suited for an ambush.

As for the other defensive positions, they were likely situated closer to Luang Prabang, given that Laotian records suggest that the Vietnamese reached the city within days rather than weeks or months. The final line of Laotian defence, located at what is now Wat Wisunarat, stood just in front of Phousi Hill, which today overlooks the Royal Palace and the National Museum by the Mekong River. If King Chakkaphat's palace was located in the same area during the 15th century, the positioning of Laotian forces to protect it would have been tactically sound.

Prince Chao Then-Kham's army had to travel approximately 350 kilometres to reach Luang Prabang and attempt to relieve it from Vietnamese control. Given that they likely marched on foot alongside elephants, the journey would have taken at least three to four weeks. This timeframe should have allowed the Đại Việt forces ample opportunity to recover. However, they were ultimately driven out of the city—possibly because their numbers had been severely depleted by then, or because they were already in the process of withdrawing.

REACTION FROM THE MING DYNASTY

In February 1480, Lê Tư Thành returned from his campaign against Lão Qua, although he never set foot in the country. By that time, news of the Đại Việt invasion had reached the Ming court, which responded with concern. Reports of Đại Việt military activity in northern Laos, near the Yunnan border, alarmed officials, especially given the potential threat to the kingdom of Bát Bách Tức Phụ (meaning Eight Hundred Wives, 八百媳婦). This kingdom corresponds to the kingdom of Lanna, spanning part of present-day Yunnan, Myanmar, and Thailand, including areas such as Jinghong (in Xishuangbanna), Keng Tung and Chiang Mai.

In September of that year, Lê Tư Thành received a memorial from the Ming court instructing Đại Việt forces to withdraw from Lão Qua. In response, Lê Thọ Vực, the commander of the fourth army—now back in Đông Quan—advised Lê Tư Thành to inform the Ming court that Đại Việt only chased 13 people fleeing to Lão Qua to the border and there was no invasion. The information about the invasion and intention to attack Bát Bách Tức Phụ was false.[203]

However, according to Ming shilu records, Li Hao (Lê Tư Thành) personally led 90,000 troops through the mountain along three separate routes. They attacked and destroyed Ai Lao, killing the local pacification superintendent Dao Ban-ya Lan-zhang, along with his two sons. His youngest son, Pa-ya Sai, fled and sought refuge in Ba-bai (Bát Bách). Li Hao then seized grain supplies, trained his troops, and even forged imperial orders directing the Che-li pacification superintendency (in present-day Xishuangbanna Dai Autonomous prefecture) to join the planned assault on Ba-bai. However, disaster soon struck: several thousand of his troops were reported to have died suddenly, said to have been struck by lightning. Seizing the opportunity, Ba-bai forces launched a counterattack, cutting off the Vietnamese retreat and killing 10,000 troops. The Jiao (Đại Việt) army suffered a devastating defeat and was forced to withdraw.[204]

The locations referenced in both SKTT and Ming shilu suggest that these events were primarily the result of the movements of Đại Việt's first—and possibly second—army, which advanced as far as the southern border of present-day Myanmar. According to Laotian records, the fourth army, after briefly occupying Luang Prabang, was forced to retreat. It appears that the third and fifth armies saw little to no action, likely due to the vast distances they needed to cover.

In summary, while Đại Việt may have succeeded in securing Bồn Man, the broader campaign against Lão Qua ultimately ended in failure. The combination of difficult mountainous terrain, inadequate maps and determined Laotian resistance proved insurmountable, effectively halting Lê Tư Thành's ambitions in the region.

6.9 - Six kings over 30 years of chaos and decay

THE DEMON KING

On 3 March 1497, Lê Tư Thành passed away at the age of 55, having ruled Đại Việt for 27 years. He had fallen ill about a year earlier with *phong thũng* (風腫疾), a 'wind-swelling illness' characterised by swelling, possibly edema or urticaria, an allergic skin condition. According to the compiler of SKTT, the illness may have been aggravated by poison applied to his skin by one of his wives, the mother of Lê Tranh, who would later succeed him.[205]

The king left behind 14 sons and 20 daughters. His eldest son and crown prince, Lê Tranh, proclaimed a three-year mourning period. During this time, officials and palace guards let their hair grow and wore white garments. Commoners, however, observed mourning by growing their hair and dressing in white for only 100 days. All weddings were postponed for three months.[206]

Less than a week after the king's death, the 38-year-old crown prince Lê Tranh ascended the throne on 9 March 1497. Around a year later, Lê Tư Thành's coffin was brought to Lam Kinh for the final burial, and Lê Tranh ordered the release of several hundred court ladies. Known posthumously as King Hiến Tông, Lê Tranh reigned for a relatively brief period of seven years. In 1504, he passed away from illness. According to SKTT, the king was endowed with brilliant and profound wisdom, presiding over an era of prosperity and peace.

Lê Tranh was succeeded by his third son, Lê Thuần (King Túc Tông). Though he reigned for less than a year and died at the young age of 17 without a son; he was reportedly a good ruler. However, his half-brother, Lê Tuấn, who succeeded him, committed so many terrible acts that he came to be known as *Quỷ Vương*, the Demon King. SKTT described him as *addicted to alcohol, fond of killing, debauched, and liked to flaunt his power. He persecuted members of the royal clan, secretly murdered his grandmother, and allowed his maternal relatives to run rampant.*[207]

After ascending the throne at the age of 17, Lê Tuấn was said to spend his nights indulging in revelry and heavy drinking with his concubines, sometimes even killing them in drunken fits.[208] His mother, Nguyễn Thị Cận, came from a poor background and was orphaned at a young age. In desperation, she sold herself into servitude in the household of an official. When that official was later convicted of a crime, she was seized as state property and assigned to work in the palace, eventually entering the service of Lê Tranh's mother. At the time, Lê Tranh was crown prince. Struck by her beauty, he took her as a consort.[209]

Lê Tuấn inherited the throne from his half-brother, Lê Thuần, who died without an heir. However, his paternal grandmother disapproved of his succession, disliking the fact that he was born to a commoner and a maid. Once he came to power, Lê Tuấn orchestrated her death and began a systematic purge of the royal family, having relatives executed or exiled under questionable charges.[210]

Among these victims were the family of his uncle, Lê Dinh, a grandson of Lê Tư Thành. Lê Dinh managed to escape to Tây Đô, where he raised an army and marched to Đông Đô at the end of 1509. After fierce fighting, Lê Dinh forces broke through and entered the capital. A guard captured Lê Tuấn, who committed suicide by taking poison on 10 January 1510. He was 22 years old.

Enraged over Lê Tuấn's earlier brutal killings of his parents, siblings, and relatives, Lê Dinh ordered a savage act of revenge. His men placed the king's corpse into a large cannon's muzzle and fired, reducing his body to ashes. Only a few charred fragments were recovered and later buried in his mother's native village.[211] Most Vietnamese have heard of Lê Tuấn's posthumous name as King Lê Uy Mục.

THE KILLING OF THE CHAMS

The Cham people in Đại Việt suffered terribly during the reign of Lê Tuấn. As previously mentioned, toward the end of 1471, Đại Việt invaded Champa, captured its ruler, Trà Toại and his family, and brought them back to Đông Kinh. Trà Toại lived there in exile and died around 30 years later. In 1508, his son, Trà Phúc, secretly exhumed his remains, leaving behind his sister— presumably to avoid arousing Vietnamese suspicion— and fled to Champa. At the same time, other Cham servants working in the households of wealthy families and officials at the private estates also fled back to their homeland. The Cham exiles in Đông King likely formed a close-knit community, and Trà Phúc's action did not go unnoticed. Around this period, Lê Tuấn's senior official, while on an inspection tour in Quảng Nam, sent a courier to report that the Cham people were rebelling. Later, a group of Cham people, including one named Ma Mạc, were captured while adrift at sea and imprisoned. Under interrogation, they confessed that the previous year, Trà Phúc had returned to Champa and sent his son, Ma La, to seek aid from the Ming dynasty. The Chams, they revealed, had also begun to build many ships and stockpile provisions in preparation for conflict.[212]

In response, around September 1509, the king ordered a near-total massacre of the Cham, including prisoners. He was unaware that the actual instigators were the Chế Mạn faction of Champa, who had allied with a Đại

Việt rebel in Tây Đô. Later that same year, Lê Tuấn also ordered the execution of all Cham individuals serving at the royal court.[213] Trà Phúc's sister was one of the victims. By the time of his death in early 1510, the Cham population in Đông Kinh and the surrounding areas had been almost completely wiped out. The killing was unlikely to spread beyond these regions, because soon after the execution order was issued, the rebellion from Tây Đô had escalated, culminating in the downfall of the king.

THE ROAD TO RUIN

Lê Dinh was the son of one of Lê Tư Thành's 14 sons.[214] After avenging himself by having his half-brother's corpse blasted from a cannon, he ascended the throne of Đại Việt in 1510, at the age of 15. According to SKTT, he initially promoted moral education and enforced the law.

In 1512, Vũ Quỳnh (1452–1516), then serving as the Minister of War, Academic Director of the Imperial Academy and Chief Editor of the Historiography Institute, submitted a historical work entitled *Đại Việt Thông Giám Thông Khảo* (Comprehensive Historical Mirror and Reference on Đại Việt or Comprehensive Study of the History of Đại Việt). Comprising 26 volumes, it covered Vietnamese history from the legendary Hùng kings until the enthronement of Emperor Lê Thái Tổ in 1428. Later, Lê Dinh instructed Lê Tung (dates of birth and death unknown), then serving as the Minister of Personnel and the Earl of Đôn Thư, to summarise this work into *Đại Việt Thông Giám Tổng Luận* (Overall Commentary on *Đại Việt Thông Giám*).[215] Unfortunately, these works have since been lost but believed to have been incorporated into SKTT. Vũ Quỳnh also wrote the foreword for *Lĩnh Nam Chích Quái* (A Collection of Strange Stories from Lingnan), a famous work compilation of folklore and legends that has survived to the present day.[216]

However, like his half-brother, Lê Dinh soon gave in to excessive indulgence and launched numerous construction projects. These burdens impoverished the people, sparking widespread banditry and rebellion—developments that ultimately led to the kingdom's downfall.[217] One particularly bizarre act attributed to him was the construction of warships rowed by naked court ladies across West Lake—a spectacle he reportedly took great pleasure in.[218]

Ming envoys often reported their observations during their visits to Đại Việt. In 1507, they expressed dismay that, despite Đại Việt's 400-year history, Heaven had produced a ruler as monstrous as Lê Tuấn. Their remarks were even harsher in 1513, when they spoke of his half-brother, Lê Dinh, with open contempt, noting that the king of An Nam had a handsome face but a deformed body and a lecherous nature—'a true swine of a monarch,' they said. They predicted that his reign, marked by chaos and ruin, would not last long.[219]

Two rebellions threatened his reign. The first was led by Trần Tuân in Sơn Tây, west of Đông Kinh. Trần Tuân was a nephew of a previous Minister of Personnel of the Lê court. His forces threatened the capital at one stage, but the rebellion collapsed after he was killed by Marquis Trịnh Duy Sản, a grandson of Trịnh Khả, one of the original oath-takers at Lũng Nhai and a meritorious official.[220] Trịnh Duy Sản had been a key commander who helped Lê Dinh overthrow his half-brother. He went on to suppress additional rebellions and rose to become a Duke and a powerful figure at Lê Dinh's court.

The second major rebellion erupted in 1516, led by a man named Trần Cảo, who claimed descent from Trần Cảnh, the founder of the Trần dynasty, King Trần Thái Tông. With the support of a Cham associate and several others, Trần Cảo launched a swift uprising and seized control of two districts in Hải Dương province. Dressed in black and with shaved heads, he and all his followers marched westward toward Đông Kinh. Lê Dinh personally led a force against them and quickly defeated the rebels, but Trần Cảo escaped.

The rebellion might have ended there if not for the treachery of Trịnh Duy Sản. Weeks earlier, Lê Dinh had made the mistake of flogging Duy Sản after the Duke tried to stop him from making an unwise decision. A seasoned warrior and high-ranking noble, Trịnh Duy Sản took the humiliation bitterly and began plotting to overthrow the king.

On the night of 7 May 1516, he and his co-conspirators led 3,000 troops through the citadel gates, spreading false rumours that they were mobilising to fight the rebels. Upon hearing the commotion and suspecting an attack, the king rode out to investigate. He encountered Trịnh Duy Sản and asked where the enemy was. Duy Sản said nothing, turned away, and burst into laughter. Sensing danger, the king spurred his horse sideways, but Duy Sản ordered a warrior to spear him, knocking him from his horse and killing him. Lê Dinh was just 21 years old.[221]

Trịnh Duy Sản then installed Lê Y, a 13-year-old son of Lê Dinh's elder brother, as the new ruler. Lê Y was a great-grandson of Lê Tư Thành. However, the transition did not bring stability. The killing of Lê Dinh plunged the country into months of infighting between rival factions, creating an opportunity for Trần Cảo to occupy Đông Kinh briefly. During the intense battles that followed between the rebels and forces loyal to the new king, Trịnh Duy Sản was captured and killed. Ironically, Trần Cảo survived, became a monk and died peacefully years later.

The civil war devastated Đông Kinh, as vividly described in SKTT: *By then, the city had already fallen, the altars of the land abandoned. The people rushed into the city, scrambling for gold, silver, and treasures—sandalwood, musk, silks, and fine linens piled high among the crowds. Books, pepper, spices, and other goods were discarded on the streets, piled up to 1.2 tấc [≈4-12 cm], beyond counting. The strong fought fiercely for gold and silver; some seized three to four hundred taels [≈15 kg], while even the weak managed over two hundred taels. Thus, the palaces and treasuries were utterly emptied.*[222]

During the campaign to drive Trần Cảo out of Đông Kinh, Đại Việt forces were led by four commanders: Trịnh Duy Sản, Nguyễn Hoằng Dụ, Trịnh Tuy and Trần Chân—each holding noble titles as marquises or earls of the court. As previously noted, Trịnh Duy Sản was killed later in the conflict. Shortly after Trần Cảo's defeat, tensions erupted among the remaining commanders: Nguyễn Hoằng Dụ and Trịnh Tuy turned on each other, while Trần Chân, adopted son of Trịnh Duy Sản, seized control of the capital and drove Nguyễn Hoằng Dụ off.

In response, the king and Trịnh Tuy conspired to deceive and kill Trần Chân. To suppress the remaining followers of Trần Chân, the king called upon another commander, Mạc Đăng Dung. Mạc successfully carried out the task and, in 1521, was elevated to the rank of Duke and placed in command of the military across all 13 circuits.

As Mạc Đăng Dung's influence grew, King Lê Ý grew increasingly uneasy and turned to Trịnh Tuy for support. In 1522, Trịnh Tuy forcibly escorted the king to Thanh Hóa. Meanwhile, Mạc Đăng Dung installed Lê Ý's younger brother, Lê Xuân, as a rival monarch in Đông Kinh in September of that year. Đại Việt was now divided between two kings: Lê Ý in Thanh Hóa and Lê Xuân in Đông Kinh.

Two years later, Mạc Đăng Dung defeated Trịnh Tuy, and soon after, his forces captured Lê Ý and had him executed in early 1527.

By mid-1527, Mạc Đăng Dung forced Lê Xuân to abdicate and placed him under arrest. He later compelled both Lê Xuân and his mother, Trịnh Thị Loan, to commit suicide. Shortly thereafter, Mạc Đăng Dung declared himself emperor, formally founding the Mạc dynasty.

For the next two and a half centuries—until the dawn of the 19th century—Đại Việt remained fractured. The seeds of this long division were sown during the turbulent years that saw Mạc Đăng Dung rise from a humble fisherman in a coastal village near present-day Hải Phòng to the throne of Đại Việt. The full story of this transformation will be explored in Volume Four of this series.

THE QUEENS

The Early Lê dynasty spanned approximately 100 years with the reign of 11 kings. The list of the Early Lê kings is shown in Table 6-1. Their familial relationships are illustrated in Figure 6-13. This figure also includes the names of the queens—both wives and mothers of various monarchs—who are often overlooked in traditional history books. Yet these women played significant roles, wielding considerable influence over key events and enduring the same trials and tragedies as their husbands and sons.

As previously mentioned, Phạm Ngọc Trần died as a human sacrifice to become the spiritual consort of a local deity. Nguyễn Anh effectively ruled the realm when her son became the king at the age of three. Dương Thị Bí's behaviour cost her son the chance to become king. Ngô (Thị Ngọc) Dao was a virtuous queen who lived to the age of 76. Nguyễn Huyên was deceived by an official and later killed by her grandson—the infamous Demon King—who also murdered Trịnh Thị Tuyên. In retaliation, the Demon King and his mother, Nguyễn Cẩn, were executed by Lê Dinh. Nguyễn Ngọc Hoàn died young, while Trần Tùng hanged herself at a pagoda. Nguyễn Đạo took her own life by jumping into a fire after her husband was murdered. The final two kings, along with their mother, Trịnh Thị Loan, were put to death on the orders of Mạc Đăng Dung.

Many of the queens bore the surnames Trịnh and Nguyễn, likely reflecting ancestral ties dating back to Lê Lợi, whose paternal grandmother was a Nguyễn and mother a Trịnh.[223] The queens of the early Lê monarchs were primarily from Thanh Hóa, consistent with the dynasty's original power base, while those of later kings came from a mix of Thanh Hóa and the areas surrounding Đông Kinh—reflecting the court's geographic shift.

Most queens were daughters of high-ranking officials at the Lê court, though some rose from humble origins, including palace maids who caught the king's eyes. While there was a formal process for selecting royal consorts, in practice, the choice of concubines ultimately rested with the king himself. One notable example is Nguyễn Quý Phi, a young girl from Kim Trà district, in what is now Hương Trà, Huế. During Lê Tư Thành's campaign against Champa in 1471, he noticed her as she was carrying water in two buckets suspended from a pole across her shoulder. He took a liking to her, and brought her back to Đông Kinh, where she was elevated to the rank of royal consort.[224] Note that 'Quý Phi' was not her real name, it means 'treasured concubine'.

THE EARLY LÊ (LÊ SƠ) DYNASTY (1428–1527)

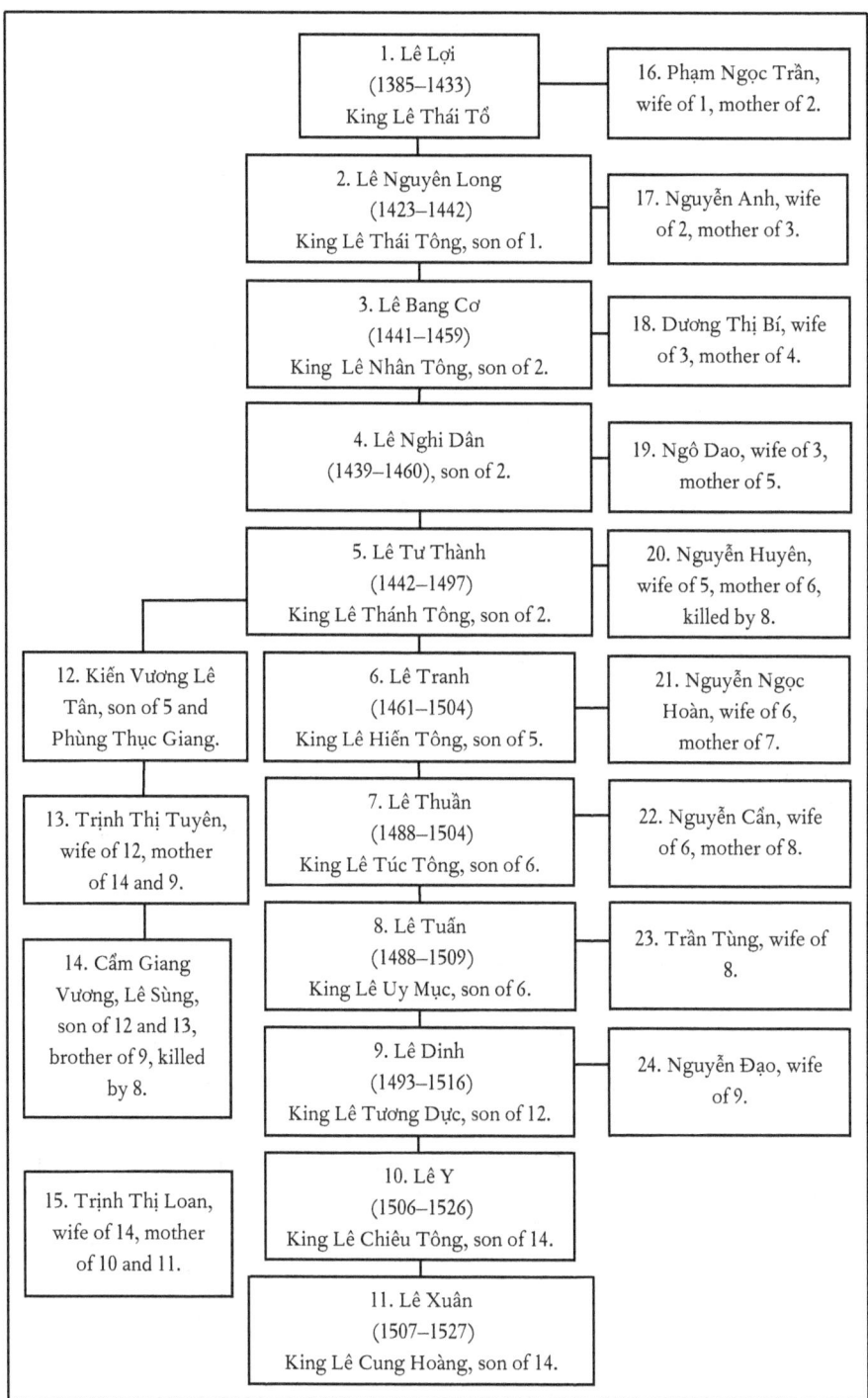

Figure 6-13: The Early Lê family tree, 14th–16th century.[225]

KINGS OF THE EARLY LÊ (LÊ SƠ) DYNASTY

	NAMES (BIRTH–DEATH)	TEMPLE NAMES (MIẾU HIỆU) (R=REIGN)
1	Lê Lợi (1385–1433)	Lê Thái Tổ (r.1428–1433)
2	Lê Nguyên Long (1423–1442)	Lê Thái Tông (r.1433–1442)
3	Lê Bang Cơ (1441–1459)	Lê Nhân Tông (r.1442–1459)
4	Lê Nghi Dân (1439–1460)	Lê Nghi Dân (r.1459–1460)
5	Lê Tư Thành (1442–1497)	Lê Thánh Tông (r.1460–1497)
6	Lê Tranh (also Sanh and Huy, 1461–1504)	Lê Hiến Tông (r.1497–1504)
7	Lê Thuần (1488–1504)	Lê Túc Tông (r.1504)
8	Lê Tuấn (also Huyên) (1488–1509)	Lê Uy Mục (r.1504–1509)
9	Lê Dinh (also Trừu and Oánh) (1493–1516)	Lê Tương Dực (r.1509–1516)
10	Lê Y (also Huệ) (1506–1526)	Lê Chiêu Tông (r.1516–1523)
11	Lê Xuân (also Khánh) (1507–1527)	Lê Cung Hoàng (r.1522–1527)

Table 6-1: Kings of the Early Lê (Lê Sơ) dynasty (1428–1527).[226]

6.10 - The final resting place – Lam Kinh

As mentioned earlier, Lê Lợi was buried at Lam Kinh, near his native village of Lam Sơn by the Chu River. His son, Lê Nguyên Long, and grandson Lê Tư Thành, were also laid to rest there, along with Lê Tư Thành's mother, Ngô (Thị Ngọc) Dao. Lê Tư Thành's son Lê Tranh and grandson Lê Thuần were also buried in the same ground. The tombs of Lê Bang Cơ and Nguyễn (Ngọc) Huyên are yet to be located.[227] This burial site, now known as Historic Lam Kinh, as shown in Figures 6-14 to 6-22, lies approximately 50 kilometres west of Thanh Hóa City.[228] The complex has been restored and renovated, offering visitors a tranquil setting to explore the grounds and pay their respects at the tombs of Lê Lợi and his descendants.[229]

Interestingly, an article from the Vietnam National Museum of History suggests that Lê Lợi's actual tomb may not lie within its current location in the main complex, but rather beneath a well situated just before the main entrance, as depicted in Figure 6-15. The article also notes that the tomb's structure follows ancient Mường burial traditions, further reinforcing Lê Lợi's ties to the Mường people. However, without additional archaeological investigation, this claim remains difficult to verify.[230]

Figure 6-14: Main entrance to Lam Kinh with the Main Hall building located behind.

Figure 6-15: The well before the main entrance, Lê Lợi's actual tomb?

Figure 6-16: *Nghê*, a mythical animal, 19th century? painted wood.

Figure 6-17: *Nghê*, 17th-19th century? stone.

Nghê is a uniquely Vietnamese mythical creature that combines the features of a lion and a dog. Traditionally, it is placed at entrances to provide protection and ward off evil spirits.

Figure 6-18: Dragon at the steps to the Main Hall.

Figure 6-19: Head of the dragon at the Main Hall.

The dragon shown in Figures 6-18 and 6-19 closely resembles those found at Kính Thiên Palace (see Figures 6-5 and 6-7). The dragon was carved from a single block of stone. It features four legs and coils in seven sinuous curves. Its head is supported by a chin beard anchored at the base by another set of claws.

Figure 6-20: The tomb of King Lê Thánh Tông (Lê Tư Thành).

Figure 6-21: The tomb of Ngô Thị Ngọc Dao, mother of King Lê Thánh Tông.

Figure 6-22: A rare statue of a female attendant at the tomb of Ngô Thị Ngọc Dao, Lam Kinh, stone, 17th-19th century?.

Figure 6-23: Small figures of an elephant, a rhinoceros and a horse, 15th century, stone.

The small figures (around 55 cm long) of the animals depicted in Figure 6-23 were displayed at the Vietnam National Fine Arts Museum (*Bảo Tàng Mỹ thuật Việt Nam*). These were found at Lam Kinh.

CHAPTER 7

CONCLUSION

A turbulent time

The two centuries between the mid-14th and mid-16th century were a turbulent and difficult period for the people of Đại Việt and Champa. Prolonged wars between the two kingdoms brought widespread devastation, at least to the people who lived in the respective capitals. Champa suffered the greater loss—its territory was fragmented and significantly reduced. In Đại Việt, the Ming occupation and the subsequent wars of resistance and liberation in the early 15th century resulted in years of bloodshed and destruction. Even after peace was restored, the kingdom was plagued by internal purges of senior court officials and bitter power struggles among rival royal factions. The only notable period of stability and prosperity during this time was the four decades under the reign of Lê Tư Thành (King Lê Thánh Tôn), who ruled for a relatively long 37 years.

However, just seven years after Lê Tư Thành's death in 1497, his legacy began to unravel. In 1504, his grandson—later known in history as the

Demon King—took a series of reckless action that plunged the kingdom into civil war, ultimately leading to the dynasty's collapse less than two decades later.

Lê Tư Thành was a learned and capable monarch; so, why did he not anticipate this outcome and take measures to reduce the risk? The answer is complex but can be explained by several key factors.

A risky royal succession

First, the system of royal succession—where the throne typically passed from father to crown prince, typically the eldest son of the first queen, appointed at a young age—was haphazard at best. The future king's fitness to rule often remained untested until he assumed the throne. To reduce this risk, the Lý dynasty began to groom their heirs more thoroughly. They arranged for them to live among the general population outside the palace, sent them to fight rebels and provided them with the finest education from the top scholars at court. The Trần dynasty went a step further, they generally avoided early designation of a crown prince and established a dual-king structure: a senior, retired king who acted as an adviser, while the reigning king handled governance—similar to today's chairman-CEO model. The Hồ dynasty adopted a similar approach, partly to lend legitimacy to their rule in the eyes of both the Ming dynasty and the local population.

The Later Lê dynasty, however, did not follow this precedent. While the king had the authority to demote an unfit crown prince and appoint another son, doing so in practice often triggered resentment, factional strife, and violence within the royal family, leading to instability and bloodshed. Lê Lợi did not have a senior king above him, and he saw no need to have one. This was partly due to the brevity of his reign, but also because he was a firm believer in established rules. Once the succession order was decided, he expected it to be respected. Moreover, with many capable military commanders serving him, there was little reason to train his heir apparent by sending him into battle against rebels and endangering his young life. Lê Lợi set a precedent, and after he died, none of his immediate successors became senior kings.

A challenge of unity

In the 10th century, the founders of the Đinh and Former Lê dynasties were based in Hoa Lư, in what is now Ninh Bình province. By the 11th century, the Lý dynasty emerged from today's Bắc Ninh province, while the 13th-century Trần dynasty had its roots in present-day Nam Định and Thái Bình. The Hồ and Lê dynasties both began in Thanh Hóa. Each dynasty brought their extended families, kin networks and regional followers—their 'tribes'—into the royal court. To secure their rule, the Lý and Trần kings ensured that key positions at court and across the kingdom were held by family members. The Trần went even further, discouraging marriage outside the clan to preserve internal unity. The Hồ family changed their surname from Lê and actively looked for other Hồ in Thanh Hóa to serve them at the capital in Tây Đô.

Lê Lợi, however, lacked a large family network. Instead, he granted the Lê surname to his most trusted allies and established a class of 'meritorious officials' to reward loyalty and service. But, as these men began to compete for influence, the cohesion of the court began to unravel. Later Lê kings responded with harsh purges to safeguard their authority, further weakening the foundation of the new regime. This internal strife was compounded by regional rivalries, particularly between officials from Thanh Hóa and those from the Red River Delta with ties to former dynasties. The divide was sharpened by the military orientation of the Thanh Hóa leaders, such as Lê Sát, in contrast to the more scholarly outlook of figures from the Delta like Nguyễn Trãi. The long reign of Lê Tư Thành managed to hold these tensions in check, but after his death, they quickly resurfaced. The five young kings who succeeded his son were barely in their twenties and lacked the authority or experience to unify the court. Unable to rein in competing factions, they failed to prevent a civil war from erupting among rival officials.

The scholar-officials

Despite these challenges, the Early Lê dynasty succeeded in laying down lasting foundations in law, the civil examination system, bureaucratic procedures, cartography and, most notably, territorial expansion at the expense of Champa. These accomplishments were largely achieved during the long and stable reign of Lê Tư Thành, under whose leadership the court was managed by officials who had entered through the examination system.

Although these scholar-officials ranked lowest in the hierarchy of rewards—beneath members of the royal family and aristocracy—they carried out the essential functions of the state. They oversaw tax collection, compiled historical records, organised examinations, drafted royal edicts, received foreign envoys, planned court rituals and educated royal children etc. More significantly, they shaped the political and moral ideology of the dynasty, grounding it firmly in Confucian principles, notably Nguyễn Trãi.

In contrast to the Lý and Trần dynasties, which were deeply influenced by Buddhism, both the Hồ and Lê dynasties adopted a more secular, Confucian outlook. While they built ancestral temples to honour their lineage and various gods, they constructed few pagodas—perhaps a lingering effect of the Ming occupation, which had generally discouraged Buddhist patronage.

These scholar-officials also contributed significantly to Vietnamese literature, producing their own works while painstakingly recovering every surviving text they could find. This effort followed a series of devastating losses: books in the capital were burned by the Chams, trampled upon by looters during the Trần Cảo rebellion, and later by the Ming occupiers who confiscated the writings of earlier scholars.[1] Thanks to them, the Vietnamese people have been able to preserve their history, and authors like myself have access to the necessary sources to tell these stories today.

The innovators

After spending years at the Trần court and witnessing its decline firsthand, Hồ Quý Ly sought a fresh beginning. He not only changed his family's surname but also renamed the kingdom, relocated the capital, introduced paper currency, limiting land ownership etc. and devised an ambitious plan to resettle people further south deep into the land of Champa. A long new road was even constructed to support the transport of migrants.

However, the Hồ dynasty had little time to realize these reforms, which might have steered Đại Việt in a new direction. Their ambitions were cut short by the Ming invasion, bringing an abrupt end to their rule. Yet, the seeds of southern expansion they planted would later be taken up and implemented by the Later Lê dynasty.

Contemporary historians hold different views on the successes and failures of the Hồ dynasty.[2] The full extent of its impact on Vietnamese history warrants a separate in-depth study, which is beyond the scope of this volume.

A militaristic regime

Lê Lợi was first and foremost a warrior, and many of his meritorious officials were seasoned military commanders who went on to occupy high-ranking positions at court and within the aristocracy. Their descendants inherited this legacy, and the militaristic spirit remained strong throughout the Early Lê dynasty. This martial culture shaped the kingdom's expansionist outlook, fuelling campaigns against Champa in the south and Ai Lao in the west. While the Chams were swiftly overwhelmed, the western expedition produced mixed results. Yet this imbalance of power between the two kingdoms had not always existed. In the final years of the Trần dynasty, Champa had successfully launched an invasion of Đại Việt, even sacking its capital. However, like Đại Việt, Champa was plagued by succession struggles. After the death of King Ba Đích Lại, who ruled from 1400 to 1441, the kingdom descended into internal conflict as rival factions vied for the throne. This prolonged instability weakened Champa to the point that, within three decades, it succumbed to Đại Việt's military advances.

Although one might argue that Champa provoked Lê Tư Thành into launching the invasion, it is more plausible that Đại Việt's expansion was inevitable. Rising population pressure in the north and a persistent fear of invasions from Imperial China created a powerful incentive to push southward—regardless of immediate provocations.

Could Champa have stopped this advance? It seems unlikely for several key reasons. First, unlike Ai Lao, Champa lacked strong natural defences. Although mountain passes running from west to east—such as Ngang, Hải Vân and Cù Mông—offered some protection against overland attacks from north or south, Cham fortresses and coastal settlements remained vulnerable to seaborn invasions. Second, Đại Việt had adopted 'advanced' military technology, such as cannons (acquired through fighting against the Ming army), whereas Champa was unlikely to have access to similar weaponry. Third, Champa's relatively small population—relative to Đại Việt's—meant it could not raise an army large enough to counter Đại Việt's military strength. Lastly, Champa's political structure, which revolved around the king, his close relatives and other religious figures, likely lacked the administrative depth—compared to Đại Việt's—needed to systematically recruit, organise and train a professional army.[3]

Some scholars argue that the drier conditions of the Little Ice Age, beginning in the late 13th and early 14th centuries, led to a decline in Champa's agricultural output, weakening its economy and political institutions. In this view, a weakened Champa became vulnerable to Đại Việt aggression. However, others propose an alternative explanation: that Champa was not economically weakened, but instead lost militarily to a stronger Đại Việt amid growing competition for trade during this period.[4]

An era of economic hardship?

As previously noted, it took the Lê kings decades to construct their palaces in the capital. In the early years, some officials supplemented their income by purchasing goods during diplomatic missions to Imperial China and reselling them upon returning to Đại Việt.[5] These signs suggest that the kingdom was less prosperous than it had been under the Trần and Lý dynasties. Prolonged warfare, invasions of Champa and Ai Lao, and the economic drain caused by the Ming occupation were major factors. Additionally, the stark disparity in rewards—where royal family members received generous privileges despite doing little, while the general population was expected to labour—did little to stimulate economic productivity. During the Trần dynasty, royal family members and nobles were expected to manage and often clear vast tracts of land for agriculture, this policy, however, was abandoned under the Hồ dynasty.

However, this observation is not supported by concrete economic data, as such records do not exist. Nevertheless, I have included it here in the hope of encouraging further discussion among historians.

A travel plan

This period of Vietnamese history features several fascinating sites worth visiting. The Hồ Citadel, a UNESCO World Heritage site, at Tây Đô, the royal tombs at the Historic Lam Kinh complex, and the scenic Chi Lăng Gorge are among the most striking. Sadly, beyond these landmarks, few grand structures or exquisite artefacts remain from the Hồ and Early Lê dynasties. Decades of warfare, resulting artefacts looted or destroyed by the Ming occupiers. In addition, limited resources coupled with perhaps a lack of artistic focus among the monarchs may explain this scarcity.

Even so, exploring the 15th-century battlefields has been a deeply rewarding experience. The view of the Cà River from Cây Chanh Bridge will stay with me for years, as I imagined Lê Lợi and his men sailing down its water centuries ago to confront the Ming forces. With this journey complete, I now look forward to exploring and reporting on the next chapter of Vietnamese history—when the kingdom's fragmentation became a lasting reality for more than two centuries.

Long Bay, August 2025

Tan Pham (Phạm Lương Tấn)

APPENDIX I

PREFECTURES, SUBPREFECTURES AND COUNTIES UNDER THE MING OCCUPATION

The 15 prefectures are 1. Jiao-zhou (Giao Châu, 5); 2. Bei River prefecture (Bắc Giang, 3); 3. Liang River prefecture (Lạng Giang, 3); 4. San River prefecture (Tam Giang, 3); 5. Jian-ping prefecture (Kiến Bình, 1); 6. Xin-an prefecture (Tân An (Yên),3); 7. Jian-chang prefecture (Kiến Xương, 1); 8. Feng-hua prefecture (Phụng Hóa, 4); 9. Qing-hua prefecture (Thanh Hóa, 3); 10. Zhen-man prefecture (Trấn Man, 4); 11. Liang-shan prefecture (Lạng Sơn, 7); 12. Xin-ping prefecture (Tân Bình, 2); 13. Yan-zhou prefecture (Diễn Châu, 1); 14. Yi-an prefecture (Nghệ An, 2); 15. Shun-hua (Thuận Hóa , 2). The figures in brackets are the number of subprefectures.[1]

Ten years later, in 1417, ANCN records an interesting breakdown of the number of households and people for each prefecture, as shown in Tables A1-1, A1-2 and A1-3.[2]

	PREFECTURES (PHỦ)	NAMES IN CHINESE	PRESENT LOCATIONS (APPROXIMATELY), BASED ON FOOTNOTES FROM ANCN AND UPDATED FROM NGHIENCUULICHSU.[3]	HOUSEHOLDS (HỘ)	MOUTHS/ PEOPLE (NHÂN KHẨU)	NO. OF PEOPLE PER HOUSEHOLD
1	Giao Châu	Jiao-zhou 交州	Hà Nội/Hà Nam, Hà Tây	19,586	65,219	3.33
2	Bắc Giang	Bei-jiang 北江	Bắc Giang, Bắc Ninh	10,073	35,667	3.54
3	Lạng Giang	Liang-jiang 涼江	Hải Dương, Bắc Ninh	8,136	17,087	2.10
4	Tân An (Yên)	Xin-an 新安	Hải Phòng/Quảng Ninh/Thái Bình	20,647	74,226	3.60
5	Kiến Xương	Jian-chang 建昌	Thái Bình/Hưng Yên	5,915	20,061	3.39
6	Trấn Man	Zhen-man 鎮蠻	Thái Bình/Hưng Yên/Nam Định	3,255	13,209	4.06
7	Phụng Hóa	Feng-hua 奉化	Nam Định/Thái Bình	3,500	11,564	3.30
8	Kiến Bình	Jian-ping 建平	Ninh Bình/Nam Định	4,618	19,267	4.17
9	Tam Giang	San River 三江	Phú Thọ/Hà Tây	8,583	41,505	4.84
10	Tuyên Hoá	Xuan-hua 宣化	Tuyên Quang/Vĩnh Phú	7,197	28,390	3.94
11	Thái Bình	Tai-ping	Thái Bình	4,332	62,084	14.33
12	Thanh Hóa	Qing-hua 清化	Thanh Hóa	7,660	67,071	8.76
13	Nghệ An	Yi-an 乂南	Nghệ An/Hà Tĩnh	7,660	16,066	2.10

14	Tân Bình	Xin-ping	Quảng Bình/Quảng Trị	2,132	4,738	2.22
15	Thuận Hóa	Shun-hua 順化	Quảng Trị/Thừa Thiên-Huế	1,470	5,662	3.85
	Average no. of people per household excluding Thái Bình					3.80
Total				120,418	500,264	100%

Table A1-1: Household records from some prefectures under the Ming occupation.

	SUBPREFECTURES (CHÂU)	NAMES IN CHINESE	PRESENT LOCATIONS (APPROXIMATELY), BASED ON FOOTNOTES FROM ANCN, UPDATED FROM NGHIENCUULICHSU.[4]	HOUSEHOLDS (HỘ)	MOUTHS/PEOPLE (NHÂN KHẨU)	NO. OF PEOPLE PER HOUSEHOLD
1	Quảng Oai	Guang-wei 廣威	Quảng Oai/Sơn Tây	1,526	5,301	3.47
2	Quy Hóa	Gui-hua 歸化	Phú Thọ/Yên Bái	1,577	5,230	3.32
3	Gia Hưng	Jia-xing 嘉興	Phú Thọ	1,019	4,509	4.42
4	Ninh Hóa	Ning-hua 寧化	Ninh Bình/Hòa Bình	933	2,238	2.40
5	Diễn (Diễn Châu)	Yan-zhou 演州	Diễn Châu/Quỳnh Lưu	599	1,170	1.95
	Average no. of people per household of all prefectures and subprefectures					3.11
	Total of all prefectures and subprefectures as the sum of the above figures			120,418	500,264	4.15
	Total as recorded in ANCN			162,558	450,288	2.77

Table A1-2: Household records from some subprefectures under the Ming occupation.

PREFECTURES (PHỦ)	HOUSEHOLDS (HỘ)	MOUTHS/PEOPLE (NHÂN KHẨU)	% OF TOTAL
North of Thanh Hóa, 1 to 11 inclusive, plus 1 to 5 of subprefectures	101,496	406,727	81%
Thanh Hóa + Nghệ An (12+13)	15,320	83,137	17%
Hải Vân to Ngang Passes (14+15)	3,602	10,400	2%
Total	120,418	500,264	100%

Table A1-3: A summary and comparison of households between regions under the Ming occupation.

APPENDIX 2

MING SHILU'S RECORDS

The war against Lê Lợi (1418–1428)

Ming Shilu offers a valuable perspective on the war against Lê Lợi. While it is naturally written from the Ming point of view, it contains important details not found in LSTL, such as internal court debates between the emperor and his advisers, as well as reflections from the Ming high command on the conduct of the campaign. From reading the account, it is clear that the Ming court significantly underestimated Lê Lợi's military capability and political strength. What follows is a summary of the key events as described in Ming shilu.

1418–1420: TIME TO REBEL

After the entry in February 1418 as mentioned in Chapter 5, Lê Lợi's name did not appear in Ming shilu until over a year later, in May 1419. This time, he occupied Khả Lâm and Li Bin sent the Vice Commissioner-in-chief Fang Zheng to suppress and capture him, some of his men were caught but he escaped to Laos, only to appear later and killed local police officers. The commissioners Zhu Guang and Huang Cheng were left to the Khả Lâm fort to guard it. Summer was coming and the Ming commanders wanted to wait until the autumn (around September) before continue their operations, as they were concerned about the raising miasma with the rain.[1]

However, the miasma did not appear to deter Lê Lợi. Three months later, in August 2019, he plundered Lỗi Giang (Lei River).² In response, Huang Cheng attacked and forced Lê Lợi to retreat to Laos. However, Lê Lợi soon returned to Lỗi Giang in early 1420 and erected palisades but the Ming troops destroyed them.³ This pattern of warfare continued: the Ming army maintained control of the forts with the support of locally-recruited troops while Lê Lợi and his men roamed the countryside, striking local police posts.⁴ Whenever the Ming soldiers came out with overwhelming forces, Lê Lợi would seek sanctuary in Laos.

Lê Lợi was not the only rebel at this time; numerous uprisings occurred across many prefectures, including present-day Lạng Sơn, Thái Nguyên, Bắc Ninh and Hải Phòng, Nghệ An.⁵ Emperor Yongle, growing increasingly frustrated, reprimanded Li Bin in March 1420:

> *I ordered you to pacify the area and desired that the military personnel and civilians all be in their proper place. However, the bandits have become numerous. How can the generals avoid taking the blame for this?*⁶

Three months later, he followed up with another rebuke:

> *The rebellious bandits Phan Liêu, Lê Lợi, Xa Tam, Nông Văn Lịch (Pan Liao, Li Li, Che San and Nong Wen-li) have still not been captured and still not been subject to judgment. When will the troops be rested?*⁷

To address the worsening situation in Đại Việt, the emperor sent reinforcements from Yunnan and Sichuan and in May 1420, appointed Chen Zhi (*Trần Trí*) to assist Li Bin to suppress the rebellions.⁸ Under pressure from the emperor and with the help of reinforcements, the Ming army had some successes in the following months but two of their senior commanders, Hou Bao (*Hầu Bảo*) and Feng Gui, the Administration Vice Commissioner Right and Left, were killed by the rebels in the middle of 1420.⁹ They were the highest-ranking Ming officers who were killed in the war since the Assistant Commissioner-in-chief Lu Yi was killed in over a decade ago in 1409, as cited earlier.

LSTL also mentions rebellions in various regions during this period but does not specify the names of the rebels or the locations. It also records the presence of Ming commanders Li Bin, Huang Cheng and Fang Zheng at the time while noting the death of Feng Gui in 1423.

1421–1423: WIDENING UNREST

The unrest continued for the rest of 1420 into 1421, and the Ming commanders were stressed by the grain supply situation. Li Bin submitted a memorial to the emperor, seeking permission to establish local military farms to grow food. The Ming army in Jiaozhi consisted of native and imperial troops, and Li Bin proposed allocating a portion of each to farming duties. While the memorial was about farming, his proposed division of forces shed light on the security in Đại Việt and the distribution of the imperial troops by the middle of 1421. Li Bin expressed reservations about the reliability of the native troops, stating that, *during fighting they are in two minds and often their full fighting abilities cannot be brought into play.*[10] In the battalions of Diễn Châu (Yan-zhou), Nam Tĩnh (Nan-jing) of contemporary Nghệ An/Hà Tĩnh province and Tân An (Xin-an), he recommended that no imperial troops be engaged in farming. However, in the three guards of Nghệ An (Yi-an), Tân Bình (Xin-ping) and Thuận Hóa (Shun-hua), he suggested that 30 per cent of imperial troops and 60 per cent of the native troops could be assigned to farming. It indicates that Li Bin did not anticipate significant unrest near Nghệ An and in the areas near Champa's northern border, away from where Lê Lợi and other rebels operated.

In February 1422, Li Bin died from illness and was succeeded by Chen Zhi. Despite Li Bin's efforts, the Ming commanders still did not have enough grain to pay the rice salaries and rations for officials and soldiers, which amounted to nearly 692,400 *shi* per annum in 1422. The deficit had to be supplemented by supplies transported from southern China. By the end of that year, the emperor severely castigated Chen Zhi, for Lê Lợi was still at large.[11]

In March 1423, Chen Zhi caught up with Lê Lợi in Ninh Hóa subprefecture (present-day Ninh Bình/Hòa Bình) but failed to capture him.[12] The rebellions continued, and 18 months later, in September 1424, Chen Zhi informed the emperor that the Laotians had driven Lê Lợi out of their territory. He claimed that Lê Lợi had offered to surrender along with 480 men and women, but in reality, Lê Lợi had remained in Nga Lạc county, secretly manufacturing weapons. Chen Zhi proposed deploying troops to eliminate him. In response, the emperor suggested a shift in strategy. He declared a general amnesty to pardon Lê Lợi if he wanted to surrender, in the emperor's view:

> *I have heard that this bandit* [Lê Lợi] *was originally forced into his plight by pressure from officials and taxation and, in the end, he had no option but to become a*

> bandit. Now, a general amnesty has been announced for all under Heaven. All is to begin anew. Sympathy and clemency are to be especially demonstrated in Jiao-zhi.

but the emperor also cautioned Chen Zhi:

> The bandit [Lê Lợi] is wily in his plans and skilled at laying ambushes at strategic places. They must send scouts far forward to make observations, so that they do not fall into his traps.[13]

1424–1426: HIGH NOON

By September 1424, Emperor Yongle had already passed away. He died on 12 August 1424, but the peace offering mentioned above likely reflected his approach to dealing with the situation. At the time of his death, the Ming forces had been in Đại Việt for 18 years without achieving lasting pacification despite various military campaigns. The emperor had been exploring alternative strategies to suppress the rebellions.

Emperor Yongle was succeeded by his eldest son, Zhu Gaochi (1378–1425), known as the Hongxi (*Hồng Hy*) Emperor. However, Hongxi's reign was brief; he died in May 1425, less than a year after ascending the throne. His son, Zhu Zhanji (1399–1435), then became the next emperor, Xuande (*Tuyên Đức*). He was 26 years old.

The years 1424 and 1425 marked a period of transition for the Ming dynasty with the succession of emperors, but they were also remarkably successful years for Lê Lợi and his forces, who made significant progress. Records in the Ming shilu indicate a turning point in Đại Việt's war efforts from the end of 1424.

In September, the emperor approved Chen Zhi's plan to pursue Lê Lợi. Fang Zheng led the troops to seek out Lê Lợi, and the two sides fought at Trà Long (*Cha-long*) subprefecture (in present-day Tương Dương district) in Nghệ An prefecture, where one of the Ming's senior commander, Wu Yun (*Ngũ Vân*), was killed in the fighting.[14] Trà Long lies over 170 kilometres south of Lê Lợi's base around Thọ Xuân and up to this time, Lê Lợi had not operated this far south, signalling a significant expansion of his campaign's scope.

In October 1424, two more senior Ming commanders, Chen Zong (*Trần Tống*) and Gao Fu (*Cao Phúc*) died in battle against Lê Lợi. The Ming court stepped up their diplomatic offerings and dispatched the eunuch Shan Shou (*Sơn Thọ*) with an imperial order to pardon and appoint Lê Lợi as the prefect of Thanh Hóa prefecture.[15] According to Ming shilu, Lê Lợi was waiting for the cooler Autumn of 1425 before taking up his post.[16] However, as events unfolded, Lê Lợi had no intentions of doing so, he was only playing for time. Interestingly, in Letter 21 to the emperor, written around early 1427, Lê Lợi addressed himself as the prefect of Thanh Hóa prefecture even though there was no evidence of him moving the fort of Thanh Hóa to take up his post.[17] The offer could be seen as a rebuke to Lương Nhữ Hốt, Lê Lợi's nemesis and prefect of Thanh Hóa at the time. Alternatively, it could reflect how the emperor viewed the natives as interchangeable pawns to be moved at his direction.

In early 1425, the Ming dynasty had a new emperor, Hongxi, who wasted no time in charging the Ming senior commanders in Đại Việt, Chen Zhi and Fang Cheng, for *being tardy in achieving success and thereby assisting the bandits*.[18] The emperor sent two more senior commanders, Li An and Dai Lun, to assist them but bad news kept coming. In August that year, the Ming high command reported that Lê Lợi and his forces had besieged the Trà Long subprefecture for seven months, i.e. since the beginning of 1425. The local native commander and prefect, Qin Peng (Cầm Bành), had exhausted the grain supplies and one-third of his troops had been killed.[19]

In October 1425, Chen Zhi reported to the emperor that 11 rebels and their families, soldiers and followers had expressed a desire to surrender. The Ming's new policy had proved effective; the emperor then granted them pardons and reinstated them to their former positions.[20] However, Lê Lợi was not among the named rebels. His forces were still surrounding Trà Long, and in early 1426, they killed its prefect, Qin Peng and gathered many more followers. In response, the emperor ordered Chen Zhi and Fang Cheng to command the troops to counterattack, and he demanded that they succeed by the spring of 1426.[21]

Chen Zhi and Fang Cheng duly complied with the emperor's wishes but only to march into a disaster when they advanced to Trà Long in April 1426. There, Lê Lợi and his forces decisively defeated them at Ải Khả Lưu (Ke-liu Pass) and Trà Long. Chen Qia reported that while Zheng was brave, Zhi was timid, and they could not agree on tactics. To make matters worse, Shan Shou, favouring a peaceful negotiation with Lê Lợi, remained in Nghệ An and withheld the 1000 troops under his command from aiding the campaign. Enraged by the debacle, the emperor harshly reprimanded all four senior commanders.

The new emperor, Xuande, directed the most severe rebuke at Shan Shou:

The rebellious bandit Li Li [Lê Lợi] *was originally a minor poor bandit. If great efforts had been made earlier to capture him, it would have been as easy as catching a fledgling chick. You foolishly held to your own ideas and repeatedly memorialized that we should try to bring him to negotiated pacification. This only led to the breeding of evil and the spreading of calamities.*[22]

However, Shan Shou was only following the thinking of the Ming emperors since the final days of Emperor Yongle, which was to seek an exit from the unsustainable situation the Ming dynasty faced in Đại Việt. An entry in Ming shilu from January 1426 records a confidential conversation between Emperor Xuande and his ministers, in which the emperor contemplated finding a descendant of the Trần family and restoring the Trần dynasty. This move would return Đại Việt to its former tributary relationship with the Ming court, as it had been during the reign of Emperor Hongwu.[23]

The dates provided in LSTL and Ming shilu do not always align. According to LSTL, Lê Lợi's southern campaign began when his forces attacked the fort of Đa Căng on 12 October 1424. From there, they went to Trà Long subprefecture and won a decisive victory at Khả Lưu Pass sometime in late 1424 or early 1425—relatively soon after departing from Lam Sơn. In contrast, Minh shilu records that Trà Long subprefecture was under siege for seven months and did not fall until late 1425, with Ming reinforcement being defeated at Khả Lưu Pass in April 1426, more than a year after LSTL's date.

Based on later entries in Ming shilu, including the timing of Wang Tong's appointment, it appears more consistent that the Battle of Khả Lưu Pass occurred in 1426 rather than late 1424 or early 1425 as recorded in LSTL.

1426: SITUATION DETERIORATES, LOOKING FOR A WAY OUT – THE BATTLE OF THE NINH BRIDGE

April 1426 also saw other revolts, notably the so-called 'red clothes' rebels, in the north-west prefectures close to Yunnan in Tuyên Hoá and Gia Hưng prefectures, north-west of Hanoi. Despite his earlier considerations about restoring the Trần dynasty, the emperor decided to send reinforcements to Đại Việt to address the escalating military crisis. By the end of April, imperial orders were issued across the empire, requiring the deployment of 20,000 cavalry, infantrymen and archers to Đại Việt. At the same time, the emperor issued a decree prohibiting Laos from providing refuge to the rebels.[24]

In May 1426, the emperor appointed Wang Tong as the new commander of Đại Việt and directed three local offices to select 30,000 native (Vietnamese) troops to serve under his command. The firearms division with 510 men were also dispatched to Đại Việt.[25] The emperor's instructions were unequivocal:

Military affairs must take precedence. All other tasks are to be suspended.[26] The stage was set for a showdown between the Ming imperial army and Lê Lợi's rebellious forces.

As for Chen Zhi and Fang Cheng, they were stripped of their offices and titles and posted as advance guards in Wang Tong's army. They were in the front line and were warned: *If, in going into battle, you do not act in a martial way, you will indeed be executed!*[27] Alongside the military deployment, the emperor continued his policy of granting of pardons and restoring positions to rebels willing to surrender.

However, despite sending a new general and additional troops, Emperor Xuande remained uncertain about his decision. His advisers were divided in two camps. One advocated for sending more troops to subdue the rebellions, arguing:

The Tai-zong [Yongle] Emperor battled hard to pacify that region. Now some minor wretches are engaged in evil. How can we suffer this and not subdue them! If, in an instant, we give up 20 years of great efforts, how can this fail to do injury to Imperial prestige?

The other camp counselled abandoning Đại Việt, reasoning:

Since the Han and the Tang dynasties, although Jiao-zhi has at times been administered through commanderies and counties, it has alternated between rebellion and submission. The soldiers who have been killed and the funds expended are incalculable. Yet, have we obtained the use of another coin or another soldier?... What gains are there in struggling for generations with these jackals and pigs?[28]

It is noteworthy that both camps invoked historical precedents to bolster their arguments. They understood that Emperor Xuande would be reluctant to take any actions that might later be seen as contradicting the legacy of his ancestors.

In Đại Việt, the fighting now centred around Nghệ An prefecture in the south and Tuyên Hóa in the north-west. Lê Lợi's forces attacked Nghệ An in June but were repelled. The Ming local commanders requested reinforcements; however, by September, Lê Lợi had renewed his offensive, threatening Nghệ An City and besieging it. Two months later, in November, Lê Triện (*Li Shan*), one of Lê Lợi's lieutenants, seized Quảng Oai (*Guang-wei*), to the west of present-day Hanoi. The location suggests that Lê Triện was able to link with the 'red clothes' rebels operating in the region. It also highlights the strength of Lê Lợi's rebellion that he could tie down Ming's forces in Nghệ An while conducting operations in the north that posed a direct threat to Đông Đô, the headquarters of the Ming occupation forces.

Chen Zhi, now demoted and fighting on the frontline, was keen to redeem himself. Shrewdly, he assigned the recently arrived Ming commander, Yuan Liang (*Vi Lượng*), to engage the rebels. Eager to prove himself, Liang ignored a warning from a native commander of the likelihood of an ambush on the far side of a river and proceeded to cross. As predicted, Liang's forces were ambushed in the ensuing battle. Liang was captured and several of his commanders, along with 500 native soldiers, were killed.[29]

The opening battle of a long awaited offensive from the Ming army ended in failure for the Ming commanders, and the victor, Lê Triện pressed on, launched a three-pronged attack on Jiao-zhi City (Đông Quan). However his forces were repelled. Seizing the momentum from this victory, Wang Tong led his army out of the city in separate columns. One column reached Quảng Oai, where they defeated a contingent of Lê Triện's forces, and then proceeded to Thạch Thất (*Shi Shi*) to rendezvous with Wang Tong. From there, the combined forces proceeded to Ứng Bình (*Ying-ping*) county and set up camp at Ning Bridge (*Ninh Kiều*).

Despite warnings from his generals against further advancement, Wang Tong chose to cross the bridge. What followed was a decisive battle, though Ming shilu recounts the events in a brief paragraph that fails to capture the significance of the encounter. The Battle of the Ninh Bridge marked the beginning of the end of Ming occupation in Đại Việt. Given the importance of this battle, I have included the relevant entry dated 4 December 1426 from the Ming shilu below.

> *The road was all mud and slush and the men had to crawl along it with their horses. The bandits* [Lê Lợi's men] *then launched their ambush and the Imperial army was defeated. The Minister Chen Qia was killed, while the Commander Li Teng* [Lý Đẳng] *and others fell into the bandits' hands. Tong was wounded and withdrew. When Li Li* [Lê Lợi] *heard of this in Yi-an* [Nghệ An], *he personally led his forces to Qing-tan* [Thanh Đàm] *to attack Bei River* [Bắc Giang] *and other areas. Subsequently, he surrounded Dong-guan* [Đông Quan].[30]

The Battle of the Ninh Bridge, referred to in LSTL as the Battle of Tố (Tốt) Động, is documented in both LSTL and the Ming shilu as taking place at the end of 1426, during which Minister Chen Qia was killed. While the exact location of the bridge is not known, its proximity to Ninh Kiều on modern maps suggests it may have been near today's Mai Lĩnh Bridge on AH13, spanning the Đáy River, as illustrated in Figure 5-10.[31]

As winter set in and the weather grew colder, Wang Tong retreated to the safety of Đông Quan's fortified walls. The heavy losses suffered by the Ming army at Ninh Bridge, including the death of the Minister of War, seemed to have unnerved him. According to the Ming shilu, Wang Tong *had not regained his firmness*. Acting without authorisation, he issued a notice instructing all officials, clerks, military personnel, and civilians in cities south of Thanh Hóa to abandon their positions and relocate to Đông Quan. These cities left behind were to be placed under the command of Lê Lợi. In one stroke, Wang Tong had abandoned nearly half of the territory of Đại Việt that the Ming forces had occupied since they invaded 20 years earlier.[32]

One could only speculate as to why Wang Tong took that decision. Perhaps he knew that the Ming army was on the verge of defeat and that the war was unwinnable, and it would best to save himself and as many others as possible. Alternatively, the mixed signals from the court—such as granting pardons to rebels and appointing Lê Lợi as the prefect of Thanh Hoá—may have left him uncertain about the broader strategy and justified his decision to hand over the territory south of Thanh Hoá to Lê Lợi. Ming shilu also records that despite Wang Tong's order, the commander of Thanh Hóa City refused to obey and held it until the war was over.[33]

Meanwhile, Huang Fu, who had been appointed the first Ming commissioner in Đại Việt nearly two decades earlier, was summoned back. According to the Ming shilu, Huang Fu had successfully maintained peace in Đại Việt through his benevolent policies, earning the affection of the local population. However, after his departure to China, his successors made numerous errors in *soothing and pacification*, fuelling widespread unrest and rebellion. The emperor hoped that Huang Fu's return to Đại Việt would help restore order and quell the ongoing uprisings.

1427: THE FINAL THROW OF THE DICE

Ming reinforcements
News of the disaster at the Ninh Bridge and Wang Tong's decision to abandon cities reached the Ming court in early 1427. The situation in Đại Việt had become a crisis for the Ming court. Wang Tong and his forces were besieged in Đông Quan, while the Ming army still held several forts scattered across the north and east of the city, particularly along the vital supply route from Guangxi through Lạng Sơn.

In mid-January 1427, Lê Lợi's forces attempted to cut off this supply route. They surrounded and launched an assault on Ài Lưu (*Ai-liu*) Pass, located between present-day Nhân Lý and Mai Sao communes, in Chi Lăng district with 10,000 men, but were repelled.[34]

At the end of January and early February 1427, the emperor issued a flurry of orders in response to the escalating crisis in Đại Việt. He appointed Liu Sheng as the new Regional Commander (the fourth appointment) to lead an expeditionary force, aiming to restore control after the failures of previous commanders, Chen Zhi/Fang Zheng and Wang Tong, to suppress the rebellions. Liu Sheng was instructed to advance from the north-east via Guangxi, while Mu Sheng, a veteran of the 1406 invasion, was tasked with leading troops from Yunnan in the north-west, supported by Xu Heng (*Từ Hanh*) and Tan Zhong (*Đàm Trung*).[35]

The Minister of War, Li Qing (*Lý Khánh*), was to accompany them together with clerical and administrative personnel selected from the various offices in Nanjing.[36] Huang Fu was also ordered to return to Đại Việt to assume the roles of administration (*bố chánh*) and surveillance (*án sát*), the same positions he had held 20 years earlier.

Liu Sheng and Mu Sheng were to command a combined force of 70,000 troops. While the number of survivors from the 20,000 men who had accompanied Wang Tong to Đại Việt a year earlier remains unknown, the Ming high command had once again assembled a formidable army, nearly matching the size of the original invasion force of over 100,000 soldiers from two decades prior.

Before their departure, members of the expedition were rewarded with paper money, with the amounts varying based on rank. Regional Commanders received the largest sums, while native soldiers and civilians received the smallest. This distribution offers insight into the hierarchy of ranks within the Ming army at that time. I have copied the ranking structure below for reference.

> *Regional commissioners 500 guan; guard commanders 400 guan; battalion commanders, guard judges and chiefs 300 guan; company commanders, battalion judges and local commanders 200 guan; platoon commanders 150 guan; squad commanders 120 guan; troops, native soldiers and native civilians 100 guan.*[37]

As previously noted, Emperor Xuande had been consulting his ministers regarding the occupation of Đại Việt. However, by early 1427, he had made up his mind. He sought a military victory before installing a Trần successor and restoring Đại Việt to its status as a tributary state. His orders were issued, the generals and soldiers were in place, and the logistical support was prepared. All that remained was to await the outcome of the impending confrontation between the imperial forces and the 'Jiao-zhi bandits'.[38]

Meanwhile, Lê Lợi was not idle. In March, his forces, which had surrounded Đông Quan since January, launched an assault on the city but suffered a heavy defeat. According to Ming shilu, *Li Li* [Lê Lợi] *was startled and lost his bravado*. Wang Tong's generals and officials urged him to capitalise on the momentum of their victory by crossing the river, likely the Red River, to launch a counterattack. However, Wang Tong hesitated, preferring to wait. He knew Liu Sheng and the reinforcements were coming, and as a timid commander, he would rather not risk losing more men. Three days later, Lê Lợi regrouped his remaining forces and launched another coordinated attack on the city again from all sides.[39]

Later in March, the emperor dispatched another 45,200 troops from various military commissions in the dynasty. In total, the Ming army by then had approximately 150,000 men in their latest efforts to eliminate Lê Lợi and pacify Đại Việt.[40]

In early April, Lê Lợi continued with his plan to disrupt the supply line from southern China. His forces circled and attacked Ôn Khâu (also known as Khâu Ôn, *Qui-wen*) near present-day Chi Lăng district in Lạng Sơn but they were driven off and the fort was held.

Lê Lợi's strategy and troop deployments reveal his anticipation that the Ming offensive would originate from Yunnan and Guangxi. He correctly assessed that the primary thrust would likely come from Guangxi, advancing along the northwest axis. His plan focused on securing control over the key Ming strongholds in that direction. In early March, he attempted to defeat the local Ming forces under Wang Tong in Đông Quan before reinforcements arrived but was unsuccessful.

Capturing of Chang River fort
On 28 April 1427, Lê Lợi's forces achieved a significant victory by capturing the fort at Chang River (*Xương Giang*), in present-day Bắc Giang province. The battle was ferocious and bloody, with the Ming defenders putting up stiff resistance. Lê Lợi's troops repeatedly attempted to breach the gates, scaling the city walls, digging tunnels, and hurling spears from high earthen mounds constructed outside the fortifications. Supported by war elephants, they eventually broke through and overwhelmed the defenders. In the aftermath, the

commissioners Li Ren (*Lý Nhiệm*) and Gu Fu (*Cố Phúc*) committed suicide by slitting their throats, while other senior commanders chose to hang themselves. Many other officers, men and women died at the same time.⁴¹

Xương Giang was a major fort on the supply route from Guangxi and Liu Sheng's army must pass through here to relieve Đông Quan. Today, a memorial complex stands at the site, as shown in Figure 5-16.

The fall of Xương Giang left Đông Quan virtually encircled, and at the end of May, Wang Tong decided to withdraw all his troops into the city, where they remained. Ming shilu notes that *since his defeat at Ning Bridge, Tong's spirit had been greatly weakened*. During this time, Lê Lợi extended a peace proposal to Wang Tong, which Wang Tong was prepared to accept, despite opposition from some of his generals, worrying about acting without authorisation from the emperor. Wang Tong reasoned that Liu Sheng's reinforcements were still months away, and negotiating peace with Lê Lợi in the interim might allow the Ming forces to leave Đông Quan and potentially recapture it later.⁴²

In July, the Ming court received a secret report that Xương Giang was surrounded and in dire conditions—though by then, the fort had already fallen. The emperor issued urgent orders to Liu Sheng and Mu Sheng to relieve Xương Giang immediately. However, both commanders appeared to proceed at a leisurely pace, and it was not until 1 October that Liu Sheng reached Ải Lưu Pass.

At that time, Lê Lợi and other local chieftains sent a representative to the Ming headquarters, proposing that the Ming troops withdraw and a descendant of the Trần dynasty be installed as Đại Việt's rule. Liu Sheng, however, did not break the seal but forwarded it to the Ming court instead.⁴³ Perhaps he did not want to be involved in a political decision and opted for a military solution instead. Meanwhile, Đại Việt put up defensive palisades, but the Ming army easily destroyed them as they advanced right up to Trấn Di (*Zhen-yi*) Pass.

TQTMT portrayed the event surrounding Liu Sheng's arrival differently. According to this account, Lê Lợi sent two letters to Liu Sheng. The newly discovered Letter 6, written under Trần Cảo's name, explained that by late 1426, the officials and soldiers from various garrisons in Đại Việt had laid down their arms and reconciled with Lê Lợi. The letter urged Liu Sheng to set up camp at the border and submit a report to the Ming court detailing the situation. Meanwhile, Trần Cảo would present a golden statue and other local products as tribute. Essentially, Lê Lợi was advising Liu Sheng not to advance further, pointing out that the local Ming forces had surrendered, even if Wang Tong still held out. In return, he offered tribute to the court.

Liu Sheng did not reply to Letter 6, and Lê Lợi followed with Letter 7, written under his name. The tone of Letter 7 is direct and defiant:

And again, even bees and insects have stingers, let alone the people in a country. Do I not have anyone brave and resourceful [with strategic skills]*? You should not look down on my country because it has few people. When the time comes, our loyalty to the great empire may falter, and by then, your regret will be too late.*

However, Liu Sheng did not take much notice of Lê Lợi's letters, and within ten days of receiving them, he was killed on the battlefield as described below.

Deaths of Liu Sheng and other commanders
Liu Sheng, a veteran of the 1406 invasion, had fought alongside Zhang Fu and played a key role in capturing the Hồ father and sons. According to Ming shilu, *Sheng considered this an easy mission.* He was confident of victory. However, some of his officials were less optimistic. They saw Liu Sheng as haughty, and the ease of their advance raised concerns and warned the Minister of War, Li Qing, that Lê Lợi's forces, *wily and deceitful,* might feign retreat to lure them into a trap. Li Qing cautioned Liu Sheng to proceed with greater caution.

Liu Sheng acknowledged the warnings, made some assurances, but ultimately took no serious precautions. When the Ming army arrived at Đảo Mã (*Dao-Ma Po*), Liu Sheng crossed a bridge with over 100 cavalrymen. Ming shilu vividly describes what happened next: *as soon as they had crossed, the bridge was suddenly destroyed and the rear force could not advance. Those with Sheng got bogged in the muddy ground and the ambushing bandit* [Đại Việt] *troops rose from four sides. Sheng was killed by a sword and all those who had accompanied Sheng were also killed.* Ming shilu comments that *although Sheng was brave, he was lacking in tactics.*[44]

Đảo Mã, also known today as Mã Yên (meaning 'horse saddle') is a small mountain marked by a stele beside Highway 1A connecting Hanoi and Lạng Sơn.[45]

Liu Sheng's deputy-on-the-left, Liang Ming, and the Minister of War, Li Qing, both died from illness within a day of each other. However, according to TQTMT, Liang Ming and Li Qing were killed during battles as previously stated. Nevertheless, their deaths, and Liu Sheng's, did not halt the Ming army's advance. Liu Sheng's deputy-on-the-right, Cui Ju, assumed command and led the troops forward.

About two days after Liu Sheng's death, Cui Ju's forces reached Xương Giang. They did not have many men with them and were swiftly overwhelmed by Lê Lợi's troops. Covering a distance of 60 kilometres in two or three days suggests that Cui Ju and his men likely travelled on horseback, which may explain why only a small contingent reached the destination. Cui Ju was captured, several of his senior commanders were killed, and the remaining troops either fled or perished.⁴⁶

The two major engagements at Mount Mã Yên, Cần Trạm and Xương Giang involved only a small portion of Ming's forces, likely fewer than 3,000, including their top commanders, over barely a week. These figures seem disproportionate compared to the expedition's recorded size, which included at least 70,000.

The death of all four top Ming commanders marked the end of the reinforcement mission, and by then, Wang Tong had abandoned any hope of rescue. On 12 November 1427, Wang Tong, along with his military and civil officials, met Lê Lợi on the bank of the Xia-shao River (Hạ Thiệu?, likely the Red River). In a ceremonial setting before an altar, they made a pact to withdraw the Ming army. The meeting concluded with a feast and an exchange of gifts.⁴⁷ We do not know where this pact-signing ceremony was held, but according to LSTL, Lê Lợi was in present-day Gia Lâm at the time. So, it is likely that he and Wang Tong met somewhere on the riverbank of the Red River east of the Hanoi Citadel, likely to be close to Lê Lợi's camp.⁴⁸

Two days later, Ming shilu records the arrival of Mu Sheng's army at Gao Stockade (Lào Cai?) in Jiao-zhi.⁴⁹

The appearance of a Trần descendant – Trần Cảo (Chen Hao)
In November 1427, Ming shilu documents a letter that Lê Lợi sent to the Ming court, via Mu Sheng, stating that he had a found a Trần descendant named Trần Cảo, who had been living in Laos for the past 20 years, and that he was seeking the emperor's approval to restore the Trần dynasty.⁵⁰ Later that month, following the peace agreement between Wang Tong and Lê Lợi, a memorial arrived—this time by Trần Cảo—formally requesting the reinstatement of Jiaozhi as a vassal state.⁵¹ The emperor granted the request.

In Letter 21 to the emperor, Lê Lợi — as the prefect of Thanh Hóa prefecture — explained that in 1425, he and other elders found Trần Mỗ (also known as Trần Cảo) in Laos. The letter sought his enfeoffment and a return to the previous tributary relationship. We have no information on the response from the Ming court, but Lê Lợi raised the issue again in Letter 44, together with Trần Cảo as a co-author. This letter reached the Ming court via Mu Sheng, as discussed above.⁵²

The emperor then issued a general amnesty for all military personnel and civilians in Jiaozhi, ordering Wang Tong to lead the troops back to their original garrisons. He also instructed all soldiers, officials, civilians, and their families stationed in Jiaozhi to return home. He further tasked the elders and local chieftains in An Nam with verifying Trần Cảo's claim and reporting their findings. He was to send an envoy to reinstate the previous tribute system from An Nam.[53] Vice Ministers Li Qi (*Lý Kỳ*) and Luo Ru-jing (*La Nhữ Kính*) were to take the proclamation to An Nam.

Throughout most of November, the emperor continued to issue orders to his commanders in Jiaozhi and officials at court as if he still held control over the situation—seemingly unaware of the actual developments on the ground. That illusion was shattered on 25 November when news of Liu Sheng's death reached the court. To make matters worse, Huang Fu — the man with whom the emperor had placed great hope to reverse the tide of battle—was captured by Lê Lợi's forces at Chi Lăng (*Zhi Ling*) Pass as he attempted to retreat to Guangxi. According to Ming shilu, Huang Fu tried to take his own life but was prevented as the men considered him to be the parent of the Jiaozhi people. Lê Lợi held him in high regard and arranged for an escort to return him safely to China.[54]

1428: THE END OF THE OCCUPATION

On a cold winter's day, on 3 January 1428, without waiting for authorisation, Wang Tong led his troops out of Jiao-zhi City (Đông Quan) with other military officials, commanders, clerks and their family members and returned to Guangxi by the land route. Shan Shou, Chen Zhi and others returned by the water route. The total number of returnees was 86,640 but some were retained by Lê Lợi. The Ming occupation of Đại Việt was over.[55]

The locations of the key battles: Ninh Bridge, Chang River and Dao-Ma Po are shown in Figures 5-10 and 5-19.

Ming - Champa - Đại Việt relations in the mid to late 15th century

According to SKTT, in 1470, Bàn La Trà Duyệt (槃羅茶悅), the son of a nursemaid, killed his lord, Bí Điền, seized the throne and then passed it to his brother, Bàn La Trà Toàn. However, Ming shilu presented a different account; it records that a figure named Pan-luo Yue (*Bàn La Duyệt*) became king of Champa after his elder brother, Mo-he Gui-you (*Quý Do*) died in 1457.[56] He died in less than four years and his younger brother, Pan-luo Cha-quan (*Bàn La Trà Toàn*, 槃羅茶全), succeeded him in 1460. This different account suggests that Trà Toàn ascended the throne a decade earlier than recorded in SKTT. In 1469, Ming shilu records a tribute mission from a ruler named Pan-luo Cha-yue (*Bàn La Trà Duyệt*).[57] This name may have been a clerical error, possibly intended to refer to Pan-luo Cha-quan. Nonetheless, the records suggest that between 1460 and 1470, Champa consistently maintained tribute relations with the Ming court and continued to lodge protests against Đại Việt's incursions.

In 1471, the Ming court received a memorial from Li Hao (the name for Lê Thư Thành in Ming shilu) stating that he had considered sending troops against Champa in response to attacks on his southern territories but ultimately refrained so as to comply with imperial instructions. The Ming emperor, however, was sceptical of this explanation and warned Lê Thư Thành not to use the unrest as a pretext to annex Cham territory. The entry documenting this exchange is dated 15 June 1471—by which point Đại Việt had already conquered the territory referenced in the memorial, and more.[58]

A year later, in June 1472, Champa submitted its memorial to the Ming court, reporting that Đại Việt forces had attacked their capital, captured Pan-luo Cha-quan, along with more than 50 members of his family, seized official seals, burned buildings, and killed or abducted countless soldiers and civilians, both men and women. It added that the king's younger brother Pan-luo Cha-yue had assumed temporary control of state affairs. In response, the Ming's Minister of War recommended punitive action against Đại Việt and proposed sending an envoy to An Nam to demand the return of the Cham king, his family, and the official seals. However, the emperor chose not to act immediately, instead opting to wait for an envoy from An Nam.[59]

Three months later, Ming shilu records that the envoy from An Nam arrived and presented a letter from the king stating that as Champa attacked the frontier districts, troops were raised and the people rebelled, leading to its defeat.[60] Nearly three years later, in early 1475, Ming shilu records that their envoys to Champa were refused entry to the country when they reached Xin-zhou Port (present-day Quy Nhơn). They learned then that An Nam had occupied the territory and that Champa's territory had been re-named Jiao-nan subprefecture.

Later that year, the Ming court received a memorial from Li Hao reporting that Pan-luo Cha-quan had been assassinated by his younger brother Pan-luo Cha-yue, who was then killed by his son Cha-zhi-tai-lai. Following these events, the country fell into chaos and there was much killing on all sides. At the emperor's request, Li Hao had sent back over 740 men and women who had been taken. The explanation sowed doubt in the emperor's mind that the destruction of Champa was the result of their own actions. His instruction to Li Hao states:

> *In the past, Pan-luo Cha-yue of Champa memorialized that you had captured their king Pan-luo Cha-quan and that Champa was without a ruler. He thus requested*

that he be enfeoffed. In manifesting Heaven and Earth's love for all living things, I granted this request and sent and envoy to go to enfeoff him. When the envoy returned, he memorialized claims that Champa's territory had been occupied by your country and that you had instituted your own administrative divisions (州邑). I was doubtful and did not believe this. Now I have received your memorial stating that Champa raised troops, engendered enmity and attacked neighbouring states and that their own deaths and the destruction of their country are all the result of their own actions. Although the events are not clearly known, this does seem possible.

It is possible that the emperor did not fully believe Li Hao's explanation, but it offered a convenient justification for not intervening or punishing Đại Việt.

Li Hao kept up the narrative in another memorial recorded in Ming shilu in 1478, claiming that Champa had nothing of value for Đại Việt to occupy and converted the territory into subprefectures and counties—despite the evidence to the contrary. According to Li Hao, Champa had few animals, little stored grains, no gold or precious stones, and even the surrounding seas yielded little fish or salt.[61] Later that year, the emperor enfeoffed Zhai-ya-ma-wu-an as the king of Champa. In a subsequent memorial, Zhai-ya-ma-wu-an informed the emperor that An Nam had returned to him an area on the Southern border of Champa for him to govern.[62]

In 1481, following the death of Zhai-ya-ma-wu-an, his brother Gu-Lai sent an envoy to the Ming court with a memorial requesting formal enfeoffment. In his petition, Gu-Lai explained that the Jiao people (i.e., Đại Việt) had returned only five territorial areas to Champa, stretching from Bang-du-lang (i.e., Panduranga) to the Cambodian border. He noted that historically, Champa comprised 27 administrative units, including four prefectures, one subprefecture and 22 counties. Its territory, he asserted, extended eastward to the Eastern Sea, south to Cambodia, west to Mount Li-ren, and north to A-mu-la-bu, covering over 3,500 *li* (1,575 kilometres). Gu-Lai requested that the emperor order Đại Việt to return all of Champa's former lands. The emperor agreed and instructed Li Hao accordingly, but once again, the directive was ignored. Despite ongoing diplomatic appeals, by the end of the decade, Đại Việt's occupation of Champa had become a firmly established reality.[63]

A-mu-la-bu is likely a reference to Amavarati, which corresponds to present-day Quảng Nam and Quảng Ngãi provinces. However, the claimed distance of 3,500 *li* is likely to be wrong. In modern terms, the road distance between Đà Nẵng (located in former Amavarati) to Phan Thiết (part of historical Panduranga) is approximately 750 kilometres.[64]

BIBLIOGRAPHY

Aymonier, É. (1890). Légendes Historiques des Chames. *Excursions et Reconnaissances, XIV, 32.*

Aymonier, É. (1911). L'inscription čame de Po Saḥ. *Bulletin de la Commission Archéologique de l'Indochine*, 13–19.

Bửu, C., Đỗ, V. A., Pham, H. T., & Trương, B. L. (1962). *Hồng Đức Bản Đồ*. Tủ Sách Viện Khảo Cổ-Publications of the Institute of Historical Research - Publications de l'institut de Recherches Historiques - Số III.

Cao Hùng Trưng (Gao Xiongzheng) – Khuyết Danh. (17th century). *An Nam Chí Nguyên* (Hoa Bằng, Trans.; 2 ed.). Nhà Xuất Bản Đại Học Sư Phạm.

Chébaut–me Mougamadou, F. (2013). *Une géographie historique du Campa du Sud: l'exemple du pays de Panrang (MI XVIIIᵉ - début XXᵉ siècle)* École Pratique dé Hautes Études].

Đào, D. A. (2006). *Lịch sử Việt Nam – Từ nguồn gốc đến thế kỷ XIX*. Nhà Xuất Bản Văn Hóa Thông Tin. (1957)

Đào, D. A. (2005). *Đất nước Việt Nam qua các đời – Nghiên cứu địa lý học lịch sử Việt Nam*. Nhà Xuất Bản Văn Hóa Thông Tin.

Drohiêm, & Dohamide. (2018). *Dân Tộc Chàm Lược Sử* (2 ed.).

Dương, V. A. (2019). *Ô Châu Cận Lục* (Đ. V. Trần, Trans.). Nhà Xuất Bản Khoa Học Xã Hội – MaiHaBooks. (1555)

Dutton, G. E., Werner, J. S., & Whitmore, J. K. (2012). *Sources of Vietnamese tradition*. Columbia University Press. http://site.ebrary.com/id/10598855

Federal Research Division, L. o. C. (1994). *Laos, a country study* (3 ed.). https://tile.loc.gov/storage-services/master/frd/frdcstdy/la/laoscountrystudy00sava_0/laoscountrystudy00sava_0.pdf

Finot, L. (1903). V. Pānduranga. *Bulletin de l'Ecole française d'Extrême-Orient*, 630–648. https://www.persee.fr/doc/befeo_0336-1519_1903_num_3_1_1260

Golzio, K.-H. (2004). *Inscriptions of Campa based on the editions and translations of Abel Bergaigne, Etienne Aymonier, Louis Finot, Edouard Huber and other French scholars and of the work of R. C. Majumdar ; newly presented, with minor corrections of texts and translations, together with calculations of given dates*. http://www.shaker.de/de/content/catalogue/Element.asp?ID=&Element_ID=21301&Mode=Page

Hall, D. G. E. (1999). *A history of South-East Asia*. MacMillan.

Hồ, N. T. (2007). *Nam Ông Mộng Lục (combined with Việt Điện U Linh-Truyền Kỳ Mạn Lục)* (T. Nghĩa, Trans.). Nhà Xuất Bản Văn Học.

Hồ, T. T. (2019). *Có 500 năm như thế – Bản sắc Quảng Nam và Đàng Trong từ góc nhìn phân kỳ lịch sử* (6th ed.). Nhà Xuất Bản Đà Nẵng. http://books.google.com/books?id=KMTCxLyvLcoC

Hoàng, X. H. (2017). *Những bài khảo cứu của Giáo Sư Hoàng Xuân Hãn*. Nhà Xuất Bản Hồng Đức - Tạp Chí Xưa & Nay.

Le Breton, H. (1936). *Le Vieux An-Tinh: La Prehistoire, Les lieux et monuments historiques ou légendaires remarquables, Extrait du Bulletin des Amis du Vieux Hué, Avril-Décembre 1936*.

Lê, Q. Đ. (2007). *Đại Việt thông sử* (T. L. Ngô, Trans.). Nhà Xuất Bản Văn hóa - Thông tin. (1759)

Lê, T. D. (2018). *Niên Biểu Các Đời Vua Việt Nam*. Nhà Xuất Bản Hồng Đức.

Lê, T. K. (2018). *Lịch sử Việt Nam từ nguồn gốc đến giữa thế kỷ XX* (N. Nguyễn, Trans.; Vol. Nhã Nam, Nhà Xuất Bản Thế Giới). (1955, 1982)

Liên, N. S. (1998). *Đại Việt Sử Ký Toàn Thư*. Khoa Học Xã Hội (Social Science) (1998). (Chính Hòa version (1697).)

Lý, T. X. (2012). *Việt Điện U Linh* (Đ. R. Trịnh, Trans.). Nhà Xuất Bản Hồng Bàng. (1329)

Majumdar, R. C. (1927). *Ancient Indian colonies in the Far East. Vol. I, Champa / by R.C. Majumdar*. Punjab Sanskrit Book Depot.

Manich, M. L. (1967). *History of Laos (including the history of Lannathai, Chiengmai)*. Chalermnit, Bangkok. https://www.renincorp.org/bookshelf/history-of-laos_manich.pdf

Maspero, G. (1928). *Le royaume de Champa* (G. Vanoest, Ed.). Librairie Nationale d'Art et d'Histoire.

Nguyễn, H. S. (2001). *Nguyễn Trãi-Về Tác Giả và Tác Phẩm*. Nhà Xuất Bản Giáo Dục.

Nguyễn, L. B. (2003). *Nguyễn Trãi Đánh Giặc Cứu Nước*. NXB Quân đội nhân dân. https://www.quansuvn.net/index.php/topic,29967.20.html, https://pubhtml5.com/jfqx/yfxa/

Nguyen, L. Q. (1989). Traditional Vietnamese Law--The Le Code--and Modern United States Law: A Comparative Analysis. *Hastings International and Comparative Law Review*, *13*(1, Fall 1989), 141–177.

Nguyễn, N. N., & Nguyễn, T. N. (2006). *Quốc Triều Hình Luật - Luật Hình Triều Lê, Luật Hồng Đức*. Nhà Xuất Bản Thành Phố Hồ Chí Minh.

Nguyễn, T. (15th century). *Nguyễn Trãi Toàn Tập* (V. S. Học, Trans.; 2 ed.). Nhà Xuất Bản Khoa Học Xã Hội, 1976. https://dovanphuong.com/nguyen-trai-toan-tap-pdf.html

Nguyễn, T. (15th century). *Nguyễn Trãi Toàn Tập (Ức Trai Thi Tập) – Phúc Khê Nguyên Bản (1868)* (H. K. (1970), Trans.). Nhà Xuất Bản Văn Hóa Thông Tin (2001).

Nguyễn, T. (1431). *Lam Sơn Thực Lục* (Bảo Thần, Trans.; 3 (1956) ed.). Nhà Xuất Bản Tân Việt.

Nguyễn, T. (2010). *Beyond the Court Gate: Selected Poems of Nguyen Trai* (D. Nguyen & P. Hoover, Eds.). Counterpath Press.

Nguyễn, T. D. (2018). *Văn hóa Việt Nam thường thức*. Nhà Xuất Bản Hà Nội.

Nguyễn, T. P. C. (2019). *Thái Ấp – Điền Trang Thời Trần (Thế kỷ XIII-XIV)*. Nhà Xuất Bản Khoa Học Xã Hội – MaiHaBooks.

Nguyễn, V. G. (2019). Interpretations about Hoa Anh state. *Thu Dau Mot University Journal of Science*, *1*(1-2019), 66–77.

Nguyễn, V. T. (2012). *Mối bang giao giữa triều đình Huế với hai Phiên vương Thủy Xá, Hỏa Xá* Việt Nam Học - Kỷ Yếu Hội Thảo Quốc Tế Lần Thứ Tư,

Nhiều Tác Giả. (2014). *Họ Hồ và Hồ Quý Ly Trong Lịch Sử*. Nhà Xuất Bản Hồng Đức.

Peter and Sanda Simms. (1999). *The Kingdoms of Laos: six hundred years of history*.

Phạm, Đ. H., & Nguyễn, Á. (1806). *Tang Thương Ngẫu Lục* (T. K.-N. V. Triện, Trans.). Nhà Xuất Bản Hồng Bàng (2012).

Pham, T. (2021). *The Bronze Drums and The Earrings* (Vol. 1). 315Kio Publishing.

Pham, T. (2022). *One Thousand Years – The Stories of Giao Châu, the Kingdoms of Linyi, Funan and Zhenla*. (Vol. 2). 315Kio Publishing.

Pham, T. (2024). *Đại Việt and Champa: Panduranga, Kauthara, and Indrapura*. (Vol. 3B). 315Kio Publishing.

Pham, T. (2025). *Đại Việt and Champa: The Early Centuries – The Dynasties of Đinh, Tiền (Former) Lê, Lý, and Trần* (Vol. 3A). 315Kio Publishing.

Phan, Đ. T., & Trương, T. H. (2012). *Cải Cách Hồ Quý Ly*. Nhà Xuất Bản Tổng Hợp Thành Phố Hồ Chí Minh.

Phan, H. C. (2005). *Lịch Triều Hiến Chương Loại Chí - Tập 1* (V. S. H. Viện Khoa Học Xã Hội Việt Nam, Trans.). Nhà Xuất Bản Giáo dục.

Phan, H. C. (2014). *Lịch triều hiến chương loại chí – Tập 5 – Binh chế chí–Văn tịch chí–Bang giao chí* (Vol. XXXIX to XLIX). Nhà Xuất Bản Trẻ. (1819)

Phan, H. L. (2018). *Lịch sử và văn hóa Việt Nam tiếp cận bộ phận* (P. T. Phan, Ed. 4th ed.). NXB Đại Học Quốc Gia Hà Nội.

Phan, H. L., & Phan, Đ. D. (2019). *Khởi Nghĩa Lam Sơn (1418–1427)* (4 ed.). Nhà Xuất Bản Hồng Đức.

Phan, J. D. (2008). *The Ming Records: an Account of Annam (a partial translation)*. East Asian Literature, Department of Asian Studies, Cornell University.

Quốc Sử Quán Triều Nguyễn – Viện Khoa Học Xã Hội Việt Nam – Viện Sử Học. (2006). *Đại Nam Nhất Thống Chí* (T. Đ. Phạm, Trans.). Nhà Xuất Bản Thuận Hóa.

Quốc Sử Quán Triều Nguyễn, & Viện Sử Học. (1998). *Khâm Định Việt Sử Thông Giám Cương Mục* (Hoa Bằng, Trans.). Giáo dục.

Silā Vīravong (Mahā.). (1957). *History of Laos. Translated from the Laotian by the U.S. Joint Publications Research Service*. Paragon Book Reprint Corp. https://lao-online.com/all_files/books/B00720.pdf

Stuart-Fox, M. (1997). *A history of Laos*. Cambridge University Press.

Taylor, K. W. (1983). *The Birth of Vietnam*. Berkeley: University of California Press.

Taylor, K. W. (2014). *A History of the Vietnamese*. Cambridge University Press.

Tổng Cục Thống Kê – General Statistics Office. (2020). *Kết quả toàn bộ tổng điều tra dân số và nhà ở – Completed results of the 2019 Vietnam population and housing census*. Nhà Xuất Bản Thống Kê.

Tống, T. T. (2012). *A general outline on the history of archeology in Vietnam - Vài nét về lịch sử khảo cổ học Việt Nam*. Perspectives on the archaeology of Vietnam International Colloquium, Hanoi 29th February - 2nd March 2012 = Toàn cảnh khảo cổ học Việt Nam, Hanoi, Vietnam.

Trần, T. K. (1999). *Việt Nam Sử Lược*. Văn Hóa Thông Tin. (1921)

Trần, T. P. (2011). *Lĩnh Nam Chích Quái* (Q. Vũ, P. Kiều, G. K. Đinh, & N. S. Nguyễn, Trans.). Nhà Xuất Bản Trẻ, Hồng Bàng. (1492)

Trương, B. L. (1967). Patterns of Vietnamese Response to Foreign Intervention: 1858–1900. *Southeast Asia Studies, Monograph Series, Yale University, 11*, 55–62.

Vũ, Đ. Đ. (2011). *Proclamation of Victory (Bình Ngô Đại Cáo) - Translation and Annotations of a Fifteenth Century Vietnamese Document*. Publisher: Thế Giới Publishing ompany. https://www.amazon.com/Proclamation-Victory-B%C3%ACnh-Ng%C3%B4-%C4%90%E1%BA%A1i-ebook/dp/B006ZOEEAM

Vuving, A. L. (2001). The References of Vietnamese States and the Mechanisms of World Formation. *ASIEN (Journal of the German Association for Asian Studies), no. 79 (April 2001)*, 62–86.

Wade, G. (2005). *Ming Shi-lu by Reign*. National University of Singapore Press. http://epress.nus.edu.sg/msl/ming-shi-lu-source-study-southeast-asian-history

Wade, G. (2019). Campā in the Ming Reign Annals (Ming shi-lu). 14th–17th Centuries. In G. Arlo, H. Andrew, & W. Geoff (Eds.), *Champa: Territories and Networks of a Southeast Asian Kingdom* (Vol. 31, pp. 255–285). École française d'Extrême-Orient.

Whitmore, J. K. (2004). The Two Great Campaigns of the Hongduc Era (1470–97) in Dai Viet. *South East Asia Research*, *12*(1), 119-136. https://doi.org/10.5367/000000004773487965

Whitmore, J. K. (2013). *Ngo (Chinese) Communities and Montane–Littoral Conflict in Dai Viet, ca. 1400–1600* Maritime Frontiers in Asia: Indigenous Communities and State Control in South China and

Southeast Asia, 2000 bce–1800 ce, . Pennsylvania State University. https://www2.ihp.sinica.edu.tw/file/2170SgsZeWy.pdf

Whitmore, J. K. (2019). The Fall of Vijaya in 1471: Decline or Competition? Campā in the 15th Century. In G. Arlo, H. Andrew, & W. Geoff (Eds.), *Champa: Territories and Networks of a Southeast Asian Kingdom* (Vol. 31, pp. 179–191). École française d'Extrême-Orient.

Yao Takao. *Luật Quang Thuận đã từng tồn tại? - Nguồn gốc của Quốc Triều Hình Luật không phải là Luật Hồng Đức* Việt Nam Học - Kỷ Yếu Hội Thảo Quốc Tế Lần Thứ Tư,

PREFACE

1. Pham, T. (2021). *The Bronze Drums and The Earrings* (Vol. 1). 315Kio Publishing.

2. There are three different names in this period of independence: Đại Cồ Việt (Great Great Viet, 968 to 1054), Đại Việt (Great Viet, 1054-1400) and Đại Ngu (Great Ngu, where Ngu is the name of the founder's lineage, or it could mean Great Joy, Happy and Peaceful, 1400–1407). Between 1407 and 1427, the country was under the rule of the Ming dynasty from China, and its name was reverted to Giao Chỉ, its title under the Former Han dynasty 500 years earlier. Once the Ming was driven out, the name returned to Đại Việt (Great Viet, 1428-1804). I have adopted Đại Việt for this period as it was used for the longest period.

3. Pham, T. (2025). *Đại Việt and Champa: The Early Centuries – The Dynasties of Đinh, Tiền (Former) Lê, Lý, and Trần* (Vol. 3A). 315Kio Publishing. and Pham, T. (2024). *Đại Việt and Champa: Panduranga, Kauthara, and Indrapura.* (Vol. 3B). 315Kio Publishing.

4. While the Linyi rebellion started at the end of the 2nd century, the Jin dynasty (following the Later Han) did not move the border north of Ngang Pass until around the third century. Đào, D. A. (2006). *Lịch sử Việt Nam – Từ nguồn gốc đến thế kỷ XIX*. Nhà Xuất Bản Văn Hóa Thông Tin. (1957), p. 116, p. 123.

5. Taylor, K. W. (1983). *The Birth of Vietnam*. Berkeley: University of California Press. , p. 118. See also Đào, D. A. (2005). *Đất nước Việt Nam qua các đời – Nghiên cứu địa lý học lịch sử Việt Nam*. Nhà Xuất Bản Văn Hóa Thông Tin. , p. 106.

6. Referring to these kings by their names also helps readers relate to contemporary Vietnamese names. For example, *Lợi* or *Thành* are not uncommon names, but no Vietnamese is called *Thái Tổ* or *Thánh Tông*.

7. Hoàng Đế Citadel is located at W3GC+79V An Nhơn, Bình Định, Vietnam, coordinates 13°55'32.7"N 109°04'15.3"E.

8. Pham, T. (2025). *Đại Việt and Champa: The Early Centuries – The Dynasties of Đinh, Tiền (Former) Lê, Lý, and Trần* (Vol. 3A). 315Kio Publishing. , p. 191.

9. There are other translations of these titles; I have included them below for reference. Those by historian Keith Taylor are Đại Việt Sử Ký Toàn Thư (Complete Book of the Historical Records of Great Viet) and Khâm Định Việt Sử Thông Giám Cương Mục (Imperially Ordered Completely Researched General Survey of Viet History). See Taylor, K. W. (2014). *A History of the Vietnamese*. Cambridge University Press. , pp. 628-629. Those by historian John K Whitmore are Đại Việt Sử Ký Toàn Thư (Complete Chronicle of Dai Viet) and Khâm Định Việt Sử Thông Giám Cương Mục (The Imperially Ordered Mirror and Complementary on the History of the Viet). See Dutton, G. E., Werner, J. S., & Whitmore, J. K. (2012). *Sources of Vietnamese tradition*. Columbia University Press. http://site.ebrary.com/id/10598855 , pp. 588-596.

10. Cao Hùng Trưng (Gao Xiongzheng) – Khuyết Danh. (17th century). *An Nam Chí Nguyên* (Hoa Bằng, Trans.; 2 ed.). Nhà Xuất Bản Đại Học Sư Phạm.

11. Nguyễn, T. (1431). *Lam Sơn Thực Lục* (Bảo Thần, Trans.; 3 (1956) ed.). Nhà Xuất Bản Tân Việt. , pp. 20–30.

12. Quốc Sử Quán Triều Nguyễn, & Viện Sử Học. (1998). *Khâm Định Việt Sử Thông Giám Cương Mục* (Hoa Bằng, Trans.). Giáo dục.

13. Lê, Q. Đ. (2007). *Đại Việt thông sử* (T. L. Ngô, Trans.). Nhà Xuất Bản Văn hóa - Thông tin. (1759)

14. Nguyễn, T. (1431). *Lam Sơn Thực Lục* (Bảo Thần, Trans.; 3 (1956) ed.). Nhà Xuất Bản Tân Việt.

15. Nguyễn, T. (15th century). *Nguyễn Trãi Toàn Tập* (V. S. Học, Trans.; 2 ed.). Nhà Xuất Bản Khoa Học Xã Hội, 1976. https://dovanphuong.com/nguyen-trai-toan-tap-pdf.html , pp. 97–190.

16. Wade, G. (2005). *Ming Shi-lu by Reign*. National University of Singapore Press. http://epress.nus.edu.sg/msl/ming-shi-lu-source-study-southeast-asian-history

17. Liên, N. S. (1998). *Đại Việt Sử Ký Toàn Thư*. Khoa Học Xã Hội (Social Science) (1998). (Chính Hòa version (1697).)

CHAPTER I

1. SKTT, Vol. 2, p. 240, p. 264. See also Nguyễn, T. (15th century). *Nguyễn Trãi Toàn Tập (Ức Trai Thi Tập) – Phúc Khê Nguyên Bản (1868)* (H. K. (1970), Trans.). Nhà Xuất Bản Văn Hóa Thông Tin (2001). , p. 587.

CHAPTER 2

1. SKTT, Vol. 2, p. 100.

2. SKTT, Vol. 2, p. 148.

3. Lý, T. X. (2012). *Việt Điện U Linh* (Đ. R. Trịnh, Trans.). Nhà Xuất Bản Hồng Bàng. (1329)

4. SKTT, Vol. 2, p. 146. The play name was *Vương Mẫu hiến bàn đào* translated as The Queen Mother offers the peaches of longevity or The Queen Mother of the West presents the celestial peaches. *In Taoist lore, peaches aren't just seen as delicious fruits but are sacred symbols of immortality. Often called the "Peach of Immortality" (仙桃, xiāntáo), peaches are believed to grant eternal life to those who consume them, a motif that recurs across Taoist literature, art, and ritual. This symbolism can be traced to revered deities, especially the Queen Mother of the West, or Xiwangmu (西王母), who is linked to the divine peach. According to "The Classic of Mountains and Seas" (山海经, Shanhaijing), her garden on the Kunlun Mountains contains peach trees that bloom every 3,000 years. When harvested, these peaches are believed to grant immortality to those fortunate enough to consume them, symbolizing longevity and transcendence.*

   The Queen Mother of the West and the Peaches of Heaven. Xiwangmu, a prominent Taoist deity, is often depicted with a peach branch or holding a peach, symbolizing her role as the keeper of the fruit of immortality. Her peach garden is a frequent theme in Chinese art and literature, especially in works from the Tang and Song dynasties. According to legend, she hosts a grand banquet for the gods when the peaches ripen every 3,000 years, known as the "Feast of Peaches" (蟠桃會, Pántáo Huì), where gods partake in these fruits to gain. immortality. see https://www.the-taoism-for-modern-world.com/peaches-of-immortality/

5. SKTT, Vol. 2, p. 145.

6. SKTT, Vol. 2, p. 149.

7. SKTT, Vol. 2, p. 148.

8. SKTT, Vol. 2, p. 151.

9. SKTT, Vol. 2, p. 154.

10. SKTT, Vol. 2, p. 155.

11. SKTT, Vol. 2, p. 166.

12. SKTT, Vol. 2, p. 148.

13. Hồ, N. T. (2007). *Nam Ông Mộng Lục (combined with Việt Điện U Linh-Truyền Kỳ Mạn Lục)* (T. Nghĩa, Trans.). Nhà Xuất Bản Văn Học. , p. 63.

14. SKTT, Vol. 2, p. 159.

15. SKTT, Vol. 2, p. 164.

16. SKTT, Vol. 2, p. 196.

17. SKTT, Vol. 2, p. 187.

18. SKTT, Vol. 2, p. 196.

19. Trần Cảnh's coronation was on the 12th day of the 12th lunar month of 1225, which is 11 January 1226, so his reign began in 1226, not 1225 as commonly reported. Trần Cảnh's temple name is Trần Thái

Tông, not the usual Trần Thái Tổ that was bestowed on his father, Trần Thừa. Because of the different name, some historians refer to Trần Cảnh not as the first king of the Trần dynasty. Refer to SKTT, Vol. 2, p. 7, p. 9.

20. Trần Hạo died in 1369, and the next king was Dương Nhật Lễ — not a Trần — who was killed a year later and the throne returned to Trần Phủ, a member of the Trần clan.

21. Information taken from SKTT, Vol. 2, pp. 100–215.

22. Đại Việt suffered famine in 1302, 1308, 1309, 1311, 1321, 1333, 1344, 1345, 1354, 1363 and 1405. No famine was recorded between 1363 and 1405, which was probably due to the chaos caused by the Champa-Đại Việt conflict when documents were burned and the Trần court had to be evacuated.

23. SKTT, Vol. 2, p. 131, p. 132, p. 134.

24. https://eclipse.gsfc.nasa.gov/SEcat5/SE1301-1400.html

25. Edited from a photograph one taken by Proxodimec, CC BY-SA 4.0 <https://creativecommons.org/licenses/by-sa/4.0>, via Wikimedia Commons, https://upload.wikimedia.org/wikipedia/commons/4/4a/Vietnamese_opera.jpg, accessed 15 October 2024.

26. SKTT, Vol. 2, p. 141.

27. SKTT, Vol. 2, p. 86.

28. SKTT, Vol. 2, p. 313.

29. I could not locate these hamlets on contemporary maps. However, based on a 16th-century work which records some villages with similar names, these hamlets are likely in Thừa Thiên-Huế and Quảng Nam provinces. *Ô Châu Cận Lục* lists the villages of La Khê, La Miên in today's Hương Trà and Phú Vang of Thừa Thiên-Huế province and Đa Thử in today's Điện Bàn of Quảng Nam province. See Dương, V. A. (2019). *Ô Châu Cận Lục* (Đ. V. Trần, Trans.). Nhà Xuất Bản Khoa Học Xã Hội – MaiHaBooks. (1555), p. 68 and p. 70.

30. SKTT, Vol. 2, p. 91.

31. Phạm, T. (2024). *Đại Việt and Champa: Panduranga, Kauthara, and Indrapura*. (Vol. 3B). 315Kio Publishing. , p. 239, p. 282.

32. SKTT, Vol. 2, p. 91.

33. The temple is located at Trung tâm Văn hóa Huyền Trân, An Tây, Thành phố Huế, Thừa Thiên Huế, Vietnam, coordinates 16°25'08.8"N 107°36'30.1"E.

34. Photograph by the author, 21 February 2009.

35. Phạm, T. (2025). *Đại Việt and Champa: The Early Centuries – The Dynasties of Đinh, Tiền (Former) Lê, Lý, and Trần* (Vol. 3A). 315Kio Publishing.

36. The Hồ Sơn pagoda is at Liêm Minh, Vụ Bản District, Nam Định, Vietnam, coordinates 20°19'31.2"N 106°06'00.2"E.

37. The areas, in square kilometres, are: Quảng Trị province (4760.1), Thừa Thiên-Huế province (5065.3), the Red River Delta (15,070.70). See https://en.wikipedia.org/wiki/Provinces_of_Vietnam#cite_note-GSOV-3 and https://en.wikipedia.org/wiki/Red_River_Delta, accessed 16 September 2024.

38. Private communication with Prof. Hue-Tam Ho Tai, 7 September 2025.

39. Maspero, G. (1928). *Le royaume de Champa* (G. Vanoest, Ed.). Librairie Nationale d'Art et d'Histoire. , p. 188.

40. There are three places where C. 22 could have been found. These are at Cakling (Mỹ Nghiệp), between Hamu Craok (Vĩnh Thuận) and Bình Quý, and east of Lake Bầu Trúc. See Chébaut–me Mougamadou, F. (2013). *Une géographie historique du Campa du Sud: l'exemple du pays de Panrang (MI XVIIIe - début XXe siècle)* École Pratique dé Hautes Études]. , p. 169.

41. Golzio, K.-H. (2004). *Inscriptions of Campa based on the editions and translations of Abel Bergaigne, Etienne Aymonier, Louis Finot, Edouard Huber and other French scholars and of the work of R. C. Majumdar ; newly presented, with minor corrections of texts and translations, together with calculations of given dates*. http://www.shaker.de/de/content/catalogue/Element.asp?ID=&Element_ID=21301&Mode=Page , p. 197.

42. Aymonier, É. (1911). L'inscription čame de Po Saḥ. *Bulletin de la Commission Archéologique de l'Indochine*, 13–19. , p. 15.

43. Finot, L. (1903). V. Pānduranga. *Bulletin de l'Ecole française d'Extrême-Orient*, 630–648. https://www.persee.fr/doc/befeo_0336-1519_1903_num_3_1_1260 , p. 641. See also Golzio, K.-H. (2004). *Inscriptions of Campa based on the editions and translations of Abel Bergaigne, Etienne Aymonier, Louis Finot, Edouard Huber and other French scholars and of the work of R. C. Majumdar ; newly presented, with minor corrections of texts and translations, together with calculations of given dates.* http://www.shaker.de/de/content/catalogue/Element.asp?ID=&Element_ID=21301&Mode=Page , p. 197.

44. Pham, T. (2025). *Đại Việt and Champa: The Early Centuries – The Dynasties of Đinh, Tiền (Former) Lê, Lý, and Trần* (Vol. 3A). 315Kio Publishing. , p. 196.

45. Majumdar, R. C. (1927). *Ancient Indian colonies in the Far East. Vol. I, Champa / by R.C. Majumdar*. Punjab Sanskrit Book Depot. , Book I, The Political History of Champa, p. 126. Maspero, G. (1928). *Le royaume de Champa* (G. Vanoest, Ed.). Librairie Nationale d'Art et d'Histoire. , p. 198.

46. Trần Khắc Chung became a *Hành khiển*, also a *Tế tướng*, a role which is roughly equivalent to a Chief of Staff or a Prime Minister, the most powerful person after the king. See SKTT, Vol. 2, p. 101.

47. SKTT, Vol. 2, pp. 52–53.

48. SKTT, Vol. 2, p. 53.

49. SKTT, Vol. 2, p. 113.

50. SKTT, Vol. 2, p. 121.

51. SKTT, Vol. 2, p. 121.

52. SKTT, Vol. 2, p. 114.

53. SKTT, Vol. 2, p. 114.

54. SKTT, Vol. 2, p. 76.

55. SKTT, Vol. 2, p. 87.

56. SKTT, Vol. 2, p. 87.

57. Đại Việt and Champa fought twice in the 10th century (979, 982), six times in the 11th century (1020, 1043, 1044, 1069, 1074, 1075), six times in the 12th century (1103, 1104, 1132, 1152, 1167, 1177), twice

in the 13th century (1216, 1252), 20 times in the 14th century (1311, 1318, 1326, 1353, 1362, 1365, 1366, 1367, 1368, 1371, 1373, 1376, 1377, 1378, 1380, 1382, 1383, 1389, 1390, 1391), and nine times in the 15th century (1400, 1402, 1444, 1445, 1446, 1448, 1469, 1470, 1471). See SKTT, Vol. 1 and Vol. 2.

58. SKTT, Vol. 2, p. 96.

59. SKTT, Vol. 2, p. 98.

60. SKTT, Vol. 1, p. 274, Vol. 2, p. 112.

61. Maspero, G. (1928). *Le royaume de Champa* (G. Vanoest, Ed.). Librairie Nationale d'Art et d'Histoire., p. 197.

62. SKTT, Vol. 2, p. 103, p. 112.

63. SKTT, Vol. 2, p. 123.

64. CM, Vol. 1, p. 177.

65. Pham, T. (2022). *One Thousand Years – The Stories of Giao Châu, the Kingdoms of Linyi, Funan and Zhenla*. (Vol. 2). 315Kio Publishing. , pp. 186–189.

66. Federal Research Division, L. o. C. (1994). *Laos, a country study* (3 ed.). https://tile.loc.gov/storage-services/master/frd/frdcstdy/la/laoscountrystudy00sava_0/laoscountrystudy00sava_0.pdf , p. XV.

67. CM, Vol. 1, p. 683.

68. CM, Vol. 1, p. 343.

69. CM, Vol. 1, p. 947; SKTT, Vol. 2, p. 363.

70. Pham, T. (2022). *One Thousand Years – The Stories of Giao Châu, the Kingdoms of Linyi, Funan and Zhenla*. (Vol. 2). 315Kio Publishing. , pp. 227–231.

71. This has been identified with Suvarnabhumi, "Land of Gold" or Suvarnakudya, "Wall of Gold", Hall, D. G. E. (1999). *A history of South-East Asia*. MacMillan. , p. 27.

72. SKTT, Vol. 1, p. 318.

73. SKTT, Vol. 1, p. 274, p. 323; SKTT, Vol. 2, p. 115, p. 1337.

74. SKTT, Vol. 2, p. 123.

75. SKTT, Vol. 2, p. 123. Bia Ma Nhai is located at 3V48+94, Chi Khê, Con Cuông, Nghệ An, Vietnam, coordinates 19°03'22.0"N 104°51'55.1"E. It is on the south side of the Cả River and Highway QL7A, the main road from Vinh, Nghệ An to northern Laos.

76. Translated from Vietnamese in Trần, T. K. (1999). *Việt Nam Sử Lược*. Văn Hóa Thông Tin. (1921), p. 173. The original version in Chinese script is 皇越陳朝第六帝，章堯文哲太上皇帝受天眷命，奄有中夏，溥海內外罔不臣服，蔑爾哀牢，猶梗王化。歲在乙亥季秋，帝親帥六師巡于西鄙。占城國古子，真臘國，暹国及蠻酋道臣葵，禽，車，勒，新附杯盆蠻，酋道聲車蠻諸部各奉方物，爭先迎見。獨逆俸執迷畏罪，未即來朝。季冬帝駐蹕于宓州，巨屯之原。乃命諸將及蠻夷之兵入于其國。逆俸望風奔竄，遂降詔班師。嵓開祐七年，乙亥冬，閏十二月日勒石。Taken from https://vi.wikisource.org/wiki/Ma_Nhai_k%E1%BB%B7_c%C3%B4ng_

bi_v%C4%83n, accessed 6 October 2024. I am puzzled by the reference to 'Hoàng Việt' (皇越) and not 'Đại Việt' as expected. Note that Trần Mạnh was described as the sixth Trần king and not fifth since Trần Thừa was considered as the first king.

77. A footnote in SKTT explains the Tiết La river as a branch of the Lam (or Cả) river near Cửa Rào in Tương Dương district, coordinates 19°17'09.0"N 104°25'58.0"E. However, I would suggest that Đoàn Nhữ Hài was thinking of the Mekong River which would be the large river to Cambodia from northern Laos.

78. SKTT, Vol. 2, p. 123.

79. SKTT, Vol. 2, p. 127.

80. Wade, G. (2019). Campā in the Ming Reign Annals (Ming shi-lu). 14th–17th Centuries. In G. Arlo, H. Andrew, & W. Geoff (Eds.), *Champa: Territories and Networks of a Southeast Asian Kingdom* (Vol. 31, pp. 255–285). École française d'Extrême-Orient. , p. 281.

81. SKTT records several locations related to the various invasions of Champa up to this point. I have included them below to understand the extent of Đại Việt territory gains in the early 14th century. In the 1312 expedition, Đại Việt forces were divided into three columns at Lâm Bình. Lâm Bình was the name of Địa Lý (present-day Quảng Ninh and Lệ Thủy in Quảng Bình province). They reached Câu Chiêm which could be Chiêm Động, Đại Chiêm or present-day Quảng Nam province. On the way, they stopped at the sea gate Cần Hải, which a footnote in SKTT explains as *cửa Cờn* of Hoàng Mai in Nghệ An province. See SKTT, Vol. 2, p. 96, p. 98.

82. According to SKTT, the king of Champa in 1342 was Trà Hòa Bố Đề. SKTT first mentioned Chế Bồng Nga in 1376, and Ming shi records that the king of Champa, A-da-a-zhe, sent an envoy with a tribute in 1369, a year after the Ming dynasty was founded. Chế Bồng Nga died in 1390. These give us four fixed points in time: 1342, 1369, 1376, and 1390. If Chế Bồng Nga is A-da-a-zhe, then he must have been the ruler of Champa before 1369, but after 1342 and not in 1376. Working back from when he died in 1390, he could have been 30, 40, 50, or 60 years old at the time of death or was born in 1360, 1350, 1340, and 1330. We could rule out 1360 as a nine-year-old king would be too young and insufficiently thoughtful to send an envoy to the newly founded dynasty. We could also ignore 1330, as a 60-year-old man would be too old to command an army in the 14th century. These extremes can be ruled out. So, it is reasonable to assume that he was between 40 and 50 when he died; that means he was born between 1340 and 1350. Most information on Chế Bồng Nga suggests that his reign began in 1360 based on the Champa's raid of Hóa Châu in 1362. However, the Champa also raided Hóa Châu in 1353. If Chế Bồng Nga were involved in both raids, it would indicate that he was born closer to 1340 than 1350. On balance, it would seem that he was born sometime around 1340.

83. Wade, G. (2019). Campā in the Ming Reign Annals (Ming shi-lu). 14th–17th Centuries. In G. Arlo, H. Andrew, & W. Geoff (Eds.), *Champa: Territories and Networks of a Southeast Asian Kingdom* (Vol. 31, pp. 255–285). École française d'Extrême-Orient. , p. 268. *Rājādhirāja* appears on C. 22 (Po Sah, 1306) and C. 83 C (Mỹ Sơn B1, 1263).

84. Aymonier, É. (1890). Légendes Historiques des Chames. *Excursions et Reconnaissances, XIV, 32.* , p. 151, p. 165.

85. Drohiêm, & Dohamide. (2018). *Dân Tộc Chàm Lược Sử* (2 ed.). , p. 102, see also https://vi.wikipedia.org/wiki/Ch%E1%BA%BF_B%E1%BB%93ng_Nga, accessed 27 September 2024.

86. The districts south of Thu Bồn River of Thăng Bình, Tam Kỳ, Duy Xuyên and Quế Sơn in Quảng Nam province, see Vol. 2, p. 145.

87. Pham, T. (2025). *Đại Việt and Champa: The Early Centuries – The Dynasties of Đinh, Tiền (Former) Lê, Lý, and Trần* (Vol. 3A). 315Kio Publishing. , p. 59.

88. SKTT, Vol. 2, p. 154.

89. 1 dan = 10 dou = 67 litres, under the Song dynasty or 100 litres currently, 50,000*67/1000 = 3,350 cubic metres. A dan or shi, 石, is also known as a picul defined as 'as much as a man can carry on a shoulder-pole. So, to provide 50,000 dan of supplies, one would need around 50,000 men. A shi is equivalent to 175–195 pounds (79–88.5 kg) for milled rice, based on a milled rice density of 1.45 kg/l, this translates into 54.5–61 litres, 50,000*79=3950 metric tons.

90. SKTT, Vol. 2, p. 160.

91. The 23rd day of the first lunar month of 1377 is 3 March 1377.

92. SKTT, Vol. 2, p. 161.

93. Hong-wu: Year 10, Month 1, Day 28, 8 Mar 1377.

94. SKTT, Vol. 2, p. 164.

95. SKTT, Vol. 2, p. 166. Hiding the money and treasures close to the border with China seemed a little strange, given that Imperial China was Đại Việt's traditional enemy. Perhaps the Trần king may have planned for an escape to China should the Champa win the war and occupy Thăng Long for any length of time.

96. An Sinh Temple is at 4G8P+XRR, An Sinh, Đông Triều, Quảng Ninh 200000, Vietnam, coordinates 21.1175131606128, 106.53700506700359. The large complex is a temple for eight Trần kings: Trần Thái Tông, Trần Thánh Tông, Trần Nhân Tông, Trần Anh Tông, Trần Minh Tông, Trần Hiến Tông, Trần Nghệ Tông, and Giản Định Đế. The first three kings are described in Volume 3A. This volume includes the next five kings. Note that the information at the temple does not mention Trần Nhân Tông but includes Trần Dụ Tông.

97. SKTT, Vol. 2, p. 165.

98. SKTT, Vol. 2, p. 158.

99. SKTT, Vol. 2, p. 167 notes that the Ngu Giang River is the present-day Lạch Trường River, a branch of the Mã River.

100. His title was *Nguyên nhung hành Hải Tây đô thống chế*. SKTT, Vol. 2, p. 167.

101. SKTT, Vol. 2, p. 167.

102. I am unable to locate these locations. SKTT notes that Long Đại is today's Hàm Rồng, and Thần Đầu is in present-day Tam Điệp, Ninh Bình. These two places are some 50 kilometres from each other, which does not make sense because the two contingents of the Đại Việt army should be close together for mutual support.

103. SKTT, Vol. 2, p. 168.

104. SKTT, Vol. 2, p. 166.

105. SKTT, Vol. 2, p. 169.

106. SKTT, Vol. 2, p. 168. See also https://baotanglichsu.vn/vi/Articles/3098/15612/danh-tuong-tran-khat-chan-1370-1399-voi-chien-cong-djuoc-lich-su-ghi-nhan.html, accessed 22 September 2024.

107. SKTT mentions several locations related to the final battle of Chế Bồng Nga. These are the Lô River, where Trần Khát Chân and his men departed after bidding farewell to the senior king, Trần Phủ. SKTT

notes that the Lô River is the Red River, not the present-day Lô River that flows by Tuyên Quang. This explanation means that Trần Khát Chân left from Thăng Long. He then reached Hoàng Giang, where he first met the Cham army. Where is Hoàng Giang? There is a Hoàng Giang River close to the Cổ Loa Citadel that once connected the Red and the Cầu Rivers. However, since he decided to retreat and set up his defensive line at the Luộc River, which is south of Thăng Long, he must have travelled south on the Red River. Hoàng Giang is north of the capital, so this Hoàng Giang had to be a river near the Luộc River. Two rivers meet this assessment: the present-day Châu Giang River and the Nam Định River. Trần Khát Chân chose the Luộc River because, at that time, the senior king, and presumably the Đại Việt court, was at Bình Than near Chí Linh. Chế Bồng Nga could get to Bình Than via the Luộc River, so he had to block the entrance. Chế Bồng Nga came up from the south, most likely by the Đáy River. He could follow the Châu Giang or the Nam Định Rivers to the Red River. One is north, and one is south of the entrance to the Luộc River. Based on the previous and subsequent historical movements in the 11th and 15th centuries, I believe this Hoàng Giang is the present-day Châu Giang River.

108. SKTT, Vol. 2, p. 180.

109. SKTT, Vol. 2, p. 180.

110. SKTT, Vol. 2, p. 180.

111. https://en.wikipedia.org/wiki/Gunpowder_weapons_in_the_Ming_dynasty, accessed 24 September 2024.

112. Photograph by Gary Todd, 30 September 2008, Gary Todd from Xinzheng, China, CC0, via Wikimedia Commons, https://commons.wikimedia.org/wiki/File:Ming_Bronze_Gun_(9872947063).jpg, accessed 11 January 2025.

113. In recent times, a well-known Vietnamese singer of Cham ethnicity took on the profession name of Chế Linh so that everyone knows him as a Cham.

CHAPTER 3

1. SKTT, Vol. 2, p. 197.

2. SKTT, Vol. 2, p. 195.

3. Trần Nhật Duật died in 1330, Trần Khánh Dư died in 1339. SKTT, Vol. 2, p. 118, p. 126.

4. SKTT, Vol. 2, p. 188.

5. SKTT, Vol. 2, p. 189.

6. Đào, D. A. (2006). *Lịch sử Việt Nam – Từ nguồn gốc đến thế kỷ XIX*. Nhà Xuất Bản Văn Hóa Thông Tin. (1957), p. 246.

7. Ibid., p. 246.

8. https://en.wikipedia.org/wiki/History_of_Chinese_currency, accessed 23 October 2024.

9. SKTT, Vol. 2, p. 198, p. 301, p. 302.

10. Phan, Đ. T., & Trương, T. H. (2012). *Cải Cách Hồ Quý Ly*. Nhà Xuất Bản Tổng Hợp Thành Phố Hồ Chí Minh. , p. 193, p. 149.

11. Photographs by the author on 13 December 2019, the Hồ Citadel is located at 3JF4+PPH Vĩnh Lộc District, Thanh Hóa, Vietnam, coordinates 20°04'27.6"N 105°36'24.7"E. Figure 3-2 taken by vi:user:Silviculture, 30 June 2008, Public domain, via Wikimedia Commons, https://commons.wikimedia.org/wiki/File:Tay_Do_castle_North_gate.JPG.

12. https://vi.wikipedia.org/wiki/Th%C3%A0nh_nh%C3%A0_H%E1%BB%93#, accessed 22 October 2024.

13. *Đàn Nam Giao* is located at 2JWF+M29 Vĩnh Lộc District, Thanh Hóa, Vietnam, coordinates 20°02'48.0"N 105°37'21.4"E.

14. SKTT, Vol. 2, p. 197. Trần Khát Chân Temple is at 3J2F+2V7 Vĩnh Lộc District, Thanh Hóa, Vietnam, coordinates 20°03'00.1"N 105°37'28.9"E.

15. The information at the museum indicates that the outer wall connects the mountains (or hills) within the vicinity from Mount Hắc Khuyển (Vĩnh Long commune) in the north to Mount Đốn Sơn (Vĩnh Thành commune) in the south-east, Xuân Đài, Trác Phong, Tiến Sỹ (Vĩnh Ninh commune) in the south, along the Bưởi River to Mount An Tôn (Vĩnh Yên commune) and Mount Thổ Tượng (Vĩnh Quang commune) to the west, along the Nam Mã River. The outer wall covers a distance of over 20 kilometres as the crow flies. I am not convinced that the rampart is the outer wall since it is very long and would have taken a long time to construct. Besides, there should be no need for it since the Bưởi and Nam Mã Rivers already offer additional protection to the Hồ Citadel.

16. SKTT, Vol. 2, p. 185, p. 200, p. 201.

17. SKTT, Vol. 2, p. 193, p. 201.

18. SKTT, Vol. 2, p. 182.

19. SKTT, Vol. 2, p. 190.

20. SKTT, Vol. 2, p. 193.

21. SKTT, Vol. 2, p. 202.

22. SKTT, Vol. 2, p. 202.

23. SKTT, Vol. 2, 132.

24. The administrative units under the Hồ dynasty followed a hierarchy of *lộ* (a large province combining several smaller ones) such *lộ* Thuận Hóa (a combination of Thuận Châu and Hóa Châu) and *lộ* Thăng Hoa (a combination of Thăng, Hoa, Tư, Nghĩa. *Phủ* and *Châu* (province or prefecture) is a smaller than *lộ* and *huyện* is smaller again. Frontier or mountainous provinces are referred to as *trấn*. See Đào, D. A. (2005). *Đất nước Việt Nam qua các đời – Nghiên cứu địa lý học lịch sử Việt Nam*. Nhà Xuất Bản Văn Hóa Thông Tin. , pp. 126–166.

25. The total area of Quảng Nam (10,438.3 km2) plus Quảng Ngãi (5,152.7 km2) is 15,591 km2. Thanh Hóa is 11,136.3 km2. See https://en.wikipedia.org/wiki/Provinces_of_Vietnam#cite_note-GSOV-3 and https://en.wikipedia.org/wiki/Red_River_Delta, accessed 16 September 2024. I should point out that these are modern measurements that include all the mountainous regions. In the 14th century, the total area that Champa yielded most likely only included the river plains near the coast.

26. SKTT, Vol. 2, p. 202, p. 203.

27. SKTT, Vol. 2, p. 204.

28. Hồ, T. T. (2019). *Có 500 năm như thế – Bản sắc Quảng Nam và Đàng Trong từ góc nhìn phân kỳ lịch sử* (6th ed.). Nhà Xuất Bản Đà Nẵng. http://books.google.com/books?id=KMTCxLyvLcoC , p. 47.

29. Wade, G. (2019). Campā in the Ming Reign Annals (Ming shi-lu). 14th–17th Centuries. In G. Arlo, H. Andrew, & W. Geoff (Eds.), *Champa: Territories and Networks of a Southeast Asian Kingdom* (Vol. 31, pp. 255–285). École française d'Extrême-Orient. , p. 257.

30. SKTT, Vol. 2, p. 206.

31. SKTT, Vol. 2, p. 206.

32. https://en.wikipedia.org/wiki/Red_Turban_Rebellions, accessed 25 October 2024.

33. https://en.wikipedia.org/wiki/Hongwu_Emperor, accessed 25 October 2024.

34. SKTT, Vol. 2, p. 139.

35. SKTT, Vol. 2, p. 141.

36. Phan, J. D. (2008). *The Ming Records: an Account of Annam (a partial translation)*. East Asian Literature, Department of Asian Studies, Cornell University. , p. 2. See also https://chinesenotes.com/mingshi/mingshi321.html, History of Ming Dynasty, Volume 321 Biographies 209: Foreign States 2 - Annan Volume 321 Biographies 209: Foreign States 2 – Annan.

37. Ibid., p. 3. See also https://chinesenotes.com/mingshi/mingshi321.html, History of Ming Dynasty, Volume 321 Biographies 209: Foreign States 2 - Annan Volume 321 Biographies 209: Foreign States 2 – Annan.

38. SKTT, Vol. 2, p. 146.

39. SKTT, Vol. 2, p. 172.

40. SKTT, Vol. 2, p. 188.

41. SKTT, Vol. 2, p. 193.

42. Phan, J. D. (2008). *The Ming Records: an Account of Annam (a partial translation)*. East Asian Literature, Department of Asian Studies, Cornell University. , p. 4.

43. https://en.wikipedia.org/wiki/Yongle_Emperor, accessed 26 October 2024.

44. SKTT, Vol. 2, p. 201.

45. Phan, J. D. (2008). *The Ming Records: an Account of Annam (a partial translation)*. East Asian Literature, Department of Asian Studies, Cornell University. , p. 7. See also https://chinesenotes.com/mingshi/mingshi321.html, History of Ming Dynasty, Volume 321 Biographies 209: Foreign States 2 - Annan Volume 321 Biographies 209: Foreign States 2 – Annan.

46. SA MSL, Yong-le: Year 1, Month Intercalary 11, Day 15, 28 Dec 1403.

47. SA MSL, Yong-le: Year 1, Month Intercalary 11, Day 24, 6 Jan 1404.

48. https://zh.wikipedia.org/zh-hans/%E6%80%9D%E6%98%8E%E5%BA%9C, accessed 3 November 2024.

49. Ming shilu describes the event in more details with some variations. See SA MSL, Yong-le: Year 4, Month 3, Day 16, 4 April 1406.

50. SKTT, Vol. 2, p. 212.

51. https://vi.wikipedia.org/wiki/T%C3%B9ng_x%E1%BA%BBo, accessed 26 October 2024.

52. According to SKTT (pp. 211–212), two Ming generals led 100,000 men from Guangxi province, and on 25 April 1406, they attacked Đại Ngu forces at Lãnh Kinh. They took with them a Đại Ngu man named Thiêm Bình who claimed to be a Trần descendant, son of a Trần king. The fighting was intense and all four commanders of Đại Ngu, including Phạm Nguyên Khôi, the commander of the Champa expedition in 1403, were killed in action. Hồ Nguyên Trừng was surrounded as soon as he landed on the riverbank but was rescued an return to the boat safely. Fortunately, another Đại Ngu column from Vũ Cao arrived in time and caught the Ming troops from behind. That night, the Ming army decided to retreat but was halted at the Chi Lăng Pass. Instead of fighting their way through the pass, they offered Thiêm Bình to the Đại Ngu commander at the pass, Hồ Xạ, explaining that that they only came to help Thiêm Bình but discovered that no one in Đại Ngu supported him. Thiêm Bình had lied to Ming, and they were returning to report to the emperor and should be allowed to pass. Hồ Xạ agreed and took many Ming soldiers as prisoners but a few managed to escape, including the senior commander. Later, when Hồ Hán Thương handed out the awards for the victory, Hồ Xạ received a lesser award than others because of this mistake.

    The captured Ming soldiers were sent to Nghệ An to work in the paddy fields but the officers and other officials were retained in the capital to work as servants in aristocratic households. As for Thiêm Bình, he was sentenced to death by a brutal method called Lăng Trì (lingchi) or Tùng Xẻo (dismemberment) where the executioner used a knife to cut off pieces of flesh from his body over a long period, eventually leading to death.

    SKTT gives minimal detail about this invasion. The location of the areas where the Hồ court ordered the rice crops destroyed to deny the Ming army food, from north to south, are Lạng Châu (Lạng Sơn), Bắc Giang (Bắc Giang), Vũ Ninh (Vũ Ninh, Bắc Ninh), Gia Lâm (Gia Lâm), and Tam Đái (Yên Lạc, Vĩnh Phúc). See SKTT, Vol. 2, p. 212. Names in brackets are present-day locations. The first four locations are along CT01. Tam Đái is to the west. It appears that the Hồ court was expecting the Ming army to come from the north-west (from Yunnan) or from the north-east (from Guangxi). In the event, it appears that Ming invaded in one direction and retreated in the other. Based on this listing, the following route was most likely. The Ming army came down from Yunnan via today's Tuyên Quang and Thái Nguyên, north-west of Thăng Long. They fought Đại Ngu at Lãnh Kinh (present-day Đáp Cầu) by the Cầu River. Đại Ngu forces stationed in Bắc Giang then joined the fight from behind and routed the Ming forces. The Ming army then retreated to the border, following the direction of today's route CT01 to Lạng Sơn, where they were stopped and surrendered Thiêm Bình at Chi Lăng.

A line in SKTT indicates that Ming may have had another column from Guangxi in the direction of Lạng Sơn, but for some unknown reasons, they halted at the border. The battle appears to be over within a day or two. Unless Đại Ngu managed to kill a large number of Ming soldiers during the first battle, it would be difficult to believe that Ming would give up the remainder of their original 100,000 soldiers during the retreat as prisoners.

Trần Thiêm Bình appeared in SKTT as Nguyễn Khang, who rebelled when Chế Bồng Nga when the latter came up from the south in 1390. Following Chế Bồng Nga's death, he fled to join the Ming army and claimed to be a Trần descendant. SKTT, Vol. 2, p. 181. However, SKTT, Vol. 2, p. 212 explains Thiêm Bình was a servant of Nguyễn Khang.

53. CM, Vol. 1, p. 24.

54. SKTT, Vol. 2, p. 206.

55. SKTT, Vol. 2, p. 209.

56. Nguyễn, T. P. C. (2019). *Thái Ấp – Điền Trang Thời Trần (Thế kỷ XIII-XIV)*. Nhà Xuất Bản Khoa Học Xã Hội – MaiHaBooks. , p. 222.

57. SA MSL, Hong-wu: Year 2, Month 1, Day 20, 26 Feb 1369.

58. SA MSL, Hong-wu: Year 3, Month 1, Day 10, 6 Feb 1370.

59. SA MSL, Hong-wu: Year 27, Month 4, Day 11, 11 May 1394. The countries are Korea, Japan, Siam, Ryukyu, Champa, Cambodia, Annam, Java, Xi-yang, Suo-li, San-fo-qi, Bo-ni, Bai-hua, Lan-bang, Pahang, Dan-ba and Xu-wen-da-na.

60. SA MSL, Hong-wu: Year 24, Month 11, Day 7, 2 Dec 1391.

61. SA MSL, Hong-wu: Year 4, Month 7, Day 25, 5 Sep 1371.

62. SA MSL, Hong-wu: Year 6, Month 11, Day 12, 26 Nov 1373. Hong-wu: Year 12, Month 10, Day 1, 10 Nov 1379. Hong-wu: Year 12, Month 12, Day Jan/Feb 1380. Hong-wu: Year 13, Month 9, Day Sep/Oct 1380.

63. SA MSL, Yong-le: Year 1, Month 8, Day 8, 25 Aug 1403.

64. SA MSL, Yong-le: Year 1, Month 12, Day 28, 9 Feb 1404.

65. SA MSL, Year 2, Month 1, Day 15, 25 Feb 1404.

66. SA MSL, Yong-le: Year 2, Month 8, Day 1, 5 Sep 1404.

67. SKTT, Vol. 2, p. 201.

68. SKTT, Vol. 2, p. 207.

69. SKTT, Vol. 2, p. 210.

70. SKTT, Vol. 2, p. 209.

71. SA MSL, Yong-le: Year 4, Month 8, Day 1, 12 September 1406.

72. SA MSL, Yong-le: Year 4, Month 10, Day 10, 20 November 1406.

73. Wade, G. (2005). *Ming Shi-lu by Reign*. National University of Singapore Press. http://epress.nus.edu.sg/msl/ming-shi-lu-source-study-southeast-asian-history , Yong-le: Year 4, Month 12, Day 11, 19 January 1407.

74. Zhu Neng listed 20 major crimes, see Cao Hùng Trưng (Gao Xiongzheng) – Khuyết Danh. (17th century). *An Nam Chí Nguyên* (Hoa Bằng, Trans.; 2 ed.). Nhà Xuất Bản Đại Học Sư Phạm. , pp. 344–346. According to Ming shilu, Zhang Fu transmitted the list of the crimes from the emperor, see SA MSL, Yong-le: Year 4, Month 10, Day 9, 19 Nov 1406. The crimes included the killing of the 'legitimate' Trần kings, attacks on Champa's land and incursion into Ming's territory.

75. SKTT, Vol. 2, p. 214.

76. SKTT, Vol. 2, p. 215.

77. SKTT, Vol. 2, p. 215.

78. The roads are at 7946+3VC Ba Vì, Hanoi, Vietnam, coordinates 21°15'18.7"N 105°21'43.7"E. The old fort is at 79H7+8MW Ba Vì, Hanoi, Vietnam, coordinates 21°16'42.1"N 105°21'51.2"E.

79. SA MSL, Yong-le: Year 5, Month 6, Day 1, 5 July 1407.

80. Banens, M. (1999). Vietnam: A Reconstitution of its 20th Century Population History. hal- 00369251. https://hal.archives-ouvertes.fr/hal-00369251 , p. 38.

81. Presently, there is a Hoàng Giang River by the Cổ Loa Citadel, north of Hanoi, but this is not the same river as the one cited in Ming shilu and SKTT since it does not make sense for Đại Ngu to establish a defensive position there to stop the Ming army from getting to the coast. See CM, Vol. 1, p. 484. The Châu Giang River is a more likely candidate. See J29M+H4P Duy Tiên, Hà Nam, Vietnam, 20°37'08.2"N 106°01'58.2"E, as it connects the Đáy and the Red River. See also previous explnnation.

82. CM, Vol. 1, p. 730. Đào, D. A. (2006). *Lịch sử Việt Nam – Từ nguồn gốc đến thế kỷ XIX*. Nhà Xuất Bản Văn Hóa Thông Tin. (1957), p. 256.

83. SA MSL, Yong-le: Year 5, Month 3, Day 10, 17 April 1407.

84. SA MSL, Yong-le: Year 5, Month 4, Day 19, 26 May 1407.

85. SKTT, Vol. 2, p. 217.

86. SA MSL, Yong-le: Year 5, Month 3, Day 19, 4 May 1407.

87. Đào, D. A. (2006). *Lịch sử Việt Nam – Từ nguồn gốc đến thế kỷ XIX*. Nhà Xuất Bản Văn Hóa Thông Tin. (1957), p. 257. According to Phan, H. L., & Phan, Đ. D. (2019). *Khởi Nghĩa Lam Sơn (1418–1427)* (4 ed.). Nhà Xuất Bản Hồng Đức. , p. 155, Lỗi Giang is further upstream from Tây Đô along the Chu River toward Cẩm Thủy and Bá Thước.

88. The prisoners taken to Nanjing included Hồ Quý Ly, his sons Hồ Hán Thương, Hồ Nguyên Trừng, Triết, Uông; grandchildren Nhuế, Lô, and Phạm; a young grandchild Ngũ Lang; a younger brother Quý Tỳ; nephews Nguyên Cữu, Từ Tuynh, Thúc Hoa, Bá Tuấn, Đình Việp, Đình Hoàng; generals and senior officials Marquis Hồ Đỗ, Counsellor Nguyễn Ngạn Quang, Lê Cảnh Kỳ; generals Đoàn Bổng, Trần Thang Mông, Phạm Lục Tài.

89. SA MSL, Yong-le: Year 5, Month 6, Day 1, 5 July 1407.

90. His name was reverted to Li Cheng in Ming shilu's entries of 14 April 1426 and 18 January 1428. See SA MSL.

91. https://vi.wikipedia.org/wiki/H%E1%BB%93_Nguy%C3%AAn_Tr%E1%BB%ABng, accessed 20 November 2024.

92. SKTT, Vol. 2, p. 220.

93. SKTT, Vol. 2, p. 219.

CHAPTER 4

1. SA MSL, Yong-le: Year 5, Month 6, Day 1, 5 July 1407.

2. SA MSL, Yong-le: Year 13, Month 2, Day 15, 25 March 1415.

3. SA MSL, Yong-le: Year 5, Month 6, Day 21, 28 July 1407.

4. SA MSL, Yong-le: Year 5, Month 9, Day 23, 23 Oct 1407.

5. SA MSL, Yong-le: Year 5, Month 10, Day 7, 6 Nov 1407.

6. SA MSL, Yong-le: Year 9, Month 11, Day 13, 28 Nov 1411.

7. SA MSL, Yong-le: Year 5, Month 7, Day 26, 28 Aug 1407.

8. The commanderies are Tai-yuan (Thái Nguyên), Jia-xing (Gia Hưng), Guang-wei (Quảng Oai), Tian-guan (Tuyên Quang), Wang River (?), Lin-an (?) and Xin-ning (?).

9. SKTT, Vol. 2, p. 220.

10. SA MSL, Yong-le: Year 6, Month 6, Day 10, 3 July 1408.

11. SA MSL, Yong-le: Year 6, Month 6, Day 12, 5 July 1408.

12. 6.9 million (3,404,789 men and 3,538,089 women). See Banens, M. (1999). Vietnam: A Reconstitution of its 20th Century Population History. hal- 00369251. https://hal.archives-ouvertes.fr/hal-00369251, p. 38.

13. There is no information on the population of Đại Việt during this time. However, data from the Tang dynasty shows 299,377 heads and 78,099 households in 740 or 3.83 heads per household. In 742, these numbers are 153,144 and 50,963, respectively, or 3.0 heads per household. The figures in 742 include a large number of heads from Ái prefecture, which is contemporary Thanh Hóa province. See Pham, T. (2022). *One Thousand Years – The Stories of Giao Châu, the Kingdoms of Linyi, Funan and Zhenla*. (Vol. 2). 315Kio Publishing. , pp. 419-420. Between 942 and 946, these figures increased to 186,989 heads and 42,829 households, corresponding to 4.36 heads per household. In 1417, the numbers were 450,288 and 162,558 or 2.77 heads per household. Refer to Nguyễn, D. H. (2019). *Văn Minh Đại Việt*. Nhà Xuất Bản Hồng Đức. , p. 431. Suppose we interpolate the figures from 942 to 1417, assuming a straight-line growth ($y = 554.31x - 335174$); y=head, x=year; we arrive at a population figure of 219,139 in 1000; 274,571 in 1100; 385,433 in 1300; and 444,745 in 1417. Historian Li Tana uses the number of villages and estimates the population of North Vietnam in 1417 as 1,861,750, which is four times larger than the number of heads estimated. One explanation is that the number of heads only includes landowners for tax purposes, not landless peasants or servants. Thus, this number may not include children and older people. See Tana, L. (2002). *Nguyễn Cochinchina: Southern Vietnam in the seventeenth and eighteenth centuries* (Second ed.). Southeast Asia Program Publications. , p. 170. Using this multiplier of four, the population figures for Đại Việt are estimated at 876,559 in 1000, 1,098,284 in 1100, 1,320,010 in 1200 and 1,541,735 in 1300, and 1,778,981 in 1407.

    The annual population growth from an estimated five million in 1408 to 6.9 million in 1909 equates to 0.06%. By comparison, population growth in South and Southeast Asia between 1500 and 1900 rose from 120.7 million to 366 million, or an annual rate of 0.278%. See https://en.wikipedia.org/wiki/Estimates_of_historical_world_population. Applying this higher rate to Đại Việt, using the 1909 figure of 6.9 million, yields an estimated population of 1.7 million in 1408. At half that rate (0.14%), the figure would instead be about 3.4 million.

14. SA MSL, Yong-le: Year 5, Month 11, Day 1, 30 Nov 1407; Year 6, Month 1, Day 4, 31 Jan 1408; Year 6, Month 3, Day 22, 17 Apr 1407.

15. SA MSL, Yong-le: Year 5, Month 12, Day 10, 7 Jan 1408.

16. SA MSL, Yong-le: Year 6, Month 7, Day 19, 10 Aug 1408.

17. Đào, D. A. (2006). *Lịch sử Việt Nam – Từ nguồn gốc đến thế kỷ XIX*. Nhà Xuất Bản Văn Hóa Thông Tin. (1957), p. 260.

18. SKTT, Vol. 2, p. 222.

19. SA MSL, Yong-le: Year 6, Month 8, Day 10, 31 Aug 1408. SA MSL, Yong-le: Year 6, Month 8, Day 19, 8 Sept 1408.

20. SKTT, Vol. 2, p. 224.

21. SA MSL, Yong-le: Year 6, Month 12, Day 24, 9 Jan 1409.

22. SKTT, Vol. 2, p. 225.

23. SKTT, Vol. 2, p. 226.

24. SA MSL, Yong-le: Year 7, Month 1, Day 28, 12 Feb 1409.

25. SA MSL, Yong-le: Year 7, Month 5, Day 22, 5 July 1409.

26. Pham, T. (2025). *Đại Việt and Champa: The Early Centuries – The Dynasties of Đinh, Tiền (Former) Lê, Lý, and Trần* (Vol. 3A). 315Kio Publishing. , p. 205.

27. SKTT, Vol. 2, p. 223, p. 227.

28. SKTT, Vol. 2, p. 223, p. 227.

29. SA MSL, Yong-le: Year 7, Month 8, Day 21, 29 Sep 1409. Yong-le: Year 8, Month 1, Day 9, 12 Feb 1410. Yong-le: Year 8, Month 5, Day 11, 13 Jun 1410.

30. SKTT, Vol. 2, p. 227, p. 233.

31. SA MSL, Yong-le: Year 7, Month 8, Day 21, 29 Sep 1409.

32. SKTT, Vol. 2, p. 227. SA MSL, Yong-le: Year 7, Month 11, Day 10, 16 Dec 1409.

33. SA MSL, Yong-le: Year 8, Month 1, Day 9, 12 Feb 1410; Yong-le: Year 8, Month 5, Day 11, 13 June 1410; Yong-le: Year 8, Month 5, Day 12, 14 Jun 1410.

34. SA MSL, Yong-le: Year 8, Month 12, Day 26, 20 Jan 1411.

35. SA MSL, Yong-le: Year 9, Month 1, Day 18, 10 Feb 1411.

36. SA MSL, Yong-le: Year 9, Month 2, Day 25, 19 Mar 1411.

37. SA MSL, Yong-le: Year 9, Month 7, Day 17, 06 Aug 1411.

38. SA MSL, Yong-le: Year 9, Month 11, Day 13, 28 Nov 1411.

39. SKTT, Vol. 2, p. 233.

40. SA MSL, Yong-le: Year 10, Month 8, Day 1, 6 Sep 1412.

41. SA MSL, Yong-le: Year 10, Month 10, Day 26, 30 Nov 1412.

42. SKTT, Vol. 2, p. 235.

43. SA MSL, Yong-le: Year 12, Month 1, Day 17, 7 Feb 1414.

44. SA MSL, Yong-le: Year 12, Month 1, Day 19, 9 Feb 1414.

45. SA MSL, Yong-le: Year 11, Month 12, Day 7, 29 Dec 1413 records a major battle between Zhang Fu, Mu Sheng and Nguyễn Súy on 29 Dec 1413 at the Ai-zi (Ái Tử, modern Thạch Hãn) River in Quảng Trị province. The Ming army defeated Nguyễn Súy, but he escaped and was captured later in February further south.

46. SA MSL, Yong-le: Year 12, Month 8, Day 2, 16 August 1414; Yong-le: Year 13, Month 2, Day 15, 25 August 1414.

47. SKTT, Vol. 2, p. 232.

48. SKTT, Vol. 2, p. 233.

49. SKTT, Vol. 2, p. 233.

50. SKTT, Vol. 2, p. 235.

51. There are several Vietnamese translations of this poem from the Chinese scripts taken from https://vi.wikipedia.org/wiki/Thu%E1%BA%ADt_ho%C3%A0i_(%C4%90%E1%BA%B7ng_Dung) , accessed 22 December 2024.
感懷
世事悠悠奈老何
無窮天地入酣歌
時來屠釣成功易
運去英雄飲恨多
致主有懷扶地軸
洗兵無路挽天河
國讎未報頭先白
幾度龍泉戴月磨
Cảm hoài
Thế sự du du nại lão hà?
Vô cùng thiên địa nhập hàm ca.
Thời lai đồ điếu thành công dị,
Vận khứ anh hùng ẩm hận đa.
Trí chủ hữu hoài phù địa trục,
Tẩy binh vô lộ vãn thiên hà.
Quốc thù vị báo đầu tiên bạch,
Kỷ độ Long Tuyền đới nguyệt ma.
And from Trần, T. K. (1999). *Việt Nam Sử Lược*. Văn Hóa Thông Tin. (1921), p. 206.
Việc đời bối rối tuổi già vay,
Trời đất vô cùng một cuộc say.
Bần tiện gặp thời lên cũng dễ,

Anh hùng lỡ bước ngẫm càng cay.
Vai khiêng trái đất mong phò chúa,
Giáp gột sông trời khó vạch mây.
Thù trả chưa xong đầu đã bạc,
Gươm mài bóng nguyệt biết bao rày.

52. SA MSL, Yong-le: Year 9, Month 4, Day 24, 16 May 1411.

53. SA MSL, Yong-le: Year 14, Month 5, Day 15, 11 Jun 1416.

54. Five Classics (*Ngũ Kinh*): Book of Documents (*Kinh Thư*), Book of Odes (*Kinh Thi*), Book of Rites (*Kinh Lễ*), Book of Changes (*Kinh Dịch*), Spring and Autumn Annals (*Kinh Xuân Thu*). Four Books: The Great Learning (*Đại Học*), Analects (*Luận Ngữ*), Mencius (*Mạnh Tử*), The Doctrine of the Mean (*Trung Dung*).

55. CM, Vol. 1, pp. 765–767. Fortunately, a copy of *Việt Điện U Linh Tập* (Compilation of the Departed Spirits in the Realm of Viet) was found later and translated into contemporary Vietnamese.

56. SKTT, Vol. 2, p. 236.

57. SKTT, Vol. 2, p. 236.

58. SA MSL, Hong-xi: Year 1, Month 7, Day 12, 26 Jul 1425.

59. SA MSL, Hong-xi: Year 1, Month 7, Day 19, 2 Aug 1425.

60. SKTT, Vol. 2, pp. 236–237.

61. SA MSL, Yong-le: Year 12, Month 3, Day 27, 16 Apr 1414.

62. SA MSL, Yong-le: Year 13, Month 11, Day 28, 29 Dec 1415.

63. SA MSL, Yong-le: Year 14, Month 10, Day 14, 3 Nov 1416.

64. SA MSL, Yong-le: Year 15, Month 11, Day 4, 11 Dec 1417.

CHAPTER 5

1. SA MSL, Yong-le: Year 15, Month 2, Day 10, 26 Feb 1417.

2. SA MSL, Yong-le: Year 15, Month Intercalary 5, Day 11, 25 Jun 1417; Yong-le: Year 15, Month 6, Day 13, 26 Jul 1417. Also Phan, H. L., & Phan, Đ. D. (2019). *Khởi Nghĩa Lam Sơn (1418–1427)* (4 ed.). Nhà Xuất Bản Hồng Đức. , p. 81.

3. Ibid., p. 109.

4. Ibid., p. 128 dates the event of Lê Lợi's raising his banner to begin the uprising on 7 February 1418, the second day of Tết, the Vietnamese Lunar New Year.

5. Đào, D. A. (2006). *Lịch sử Việt Nam – Từ nguồn gốc đến thế kỷ XIX*. Nhà Xuất Bản Văn Hóa Thông Tin. (1957), p. 263.

6. Nguyễn, T. (1431). *Lam Sơn Thực Lục* (Bảo Thần, Trans.; 3 (1956) ed.). Nhà Xuất Bản Tân Việt. , p. 6. Phan, H. L., & Phan, Đ. D. (2019). *Khởi Nghĩa Lam Sơn (1418–1427)* (4 ed.). Nhà Xuất Bản Hồng Đức. , p. 157 indicates Khả Lam is Lam Sơn. Phụ Đạo is a chief of a semi-autonomous region like Cơ Mi or Ky Mi. It is a hereditary position. See Hoàng, X. H. (2017). *Những bài khảo cứu của Giáo Sư Hoàng Xuân Hãn*. Nhà Xuất Bản Hồng Đức - Tạp Chí Xưa & Nay. , p. 200. During the Tang Dynasty, the empire controlled the remote regions by allowing the local chiefs to rule with Tang-appointed titles such as chief, governor or prefect; these positions were passed on from father to son. These regions were called CO MI (Cơ Mi or Ky Mi). Literally, CO MI means a contraption of straps attached around the head of a horse and an ox respectively, to control them. See CM, Vol. 1, p. 199, p. 200.

7. According to the 2019 census, Ho Chi Minh City has 8,993,082 people; Hanoi has 8,053,663 people and Thanh Hóa has 3,640,128. See Tổng Cục Thống Kê – General Statistics Office. (2020). *Kết quả toàn bộ tổng điều tra dân số và nhà ở – Completed results of the 2019 Vietnam population and housing census*. Nhà Xuất Bản Thống Kê. , Table 1, pp. 9 –41. ANCN shows Thanh Hóa had slightly more people than Giao Châu prefecture during the Ming occupation.

8. Nga Lạc is likely to be a part of Ngọc Lặc and Thọ Xuân districts. See Đào, D. A. (2005). *Đất nước Việt Nam qua các đời – Nghiên cứu địa lý học lịch sử Việt Nam*. Nhà Xuất Bản Văn Hóa Thông Tin. , p. 156 and Đào, D. A. (2006). *Lịch sử Việt Nam – Từ nguồn gốc đến thế kỷ XIX*. Nhà Xuất Bản Văn Hóa Thông Tin. (1957), p. 272. Ngọc Lặc is located near Highway QL16, around 25 km north of the Historic Complex of Lam Kinh. Thọ Xuân, home to the Thọ Xuân airport, is approximately 12 kilometres to the south-east of the Historic Complex of Lam Kinh.

9. Photographs taken by the author on 19 December 2019.

10. SKTT, Vol. 2, p. 308.

11. The 22nd day of the eight lunar month of the year Quý Sửu (5 October 1433) and the 23rd day of the 10th lunar month of the same year (4 December 1433).

12. https://vi.wikipedia.org/wiki/Bia_V%C4%A9nh_L%C4%83ng, accessed 31 December 2024. Also Nguyễn, T. (15th century). *Nguyễn Trãi Toàn Tập (Ức Trai Thi Tập) – Phúc Khê Nguyên Bản (1868)* (H. K. (1970), Trans.). Nhà Xuất Bản Văn Hóa Thông Tin (2001). , pp. 373–375. The inscription is in Chinese characters. A version of which is as follows as taken from https://nnthannom.blogspot.com/2008/05/vn-bia-vnh-lng.html.
    10/5/08
    Văn Bia Vĩnh Lăng (Hán, 1433)
    Văn bia Vĩnh Lăng

維順天六年,歲次癸丑,閏八月,二十二日.太祖高皇帝賓天.本年十月,二十三日,葬于藍山之永陵.帝性黎,諱利.曾祖諱誨,清化府人也.常一日遊藍山,見衆鳥羣飛,翔繞於藍山之下,若衆人聚會之狀,曰:"此佳處也!".因徙家居焉.三年而產業成.子孫日繁,奴隸眾.建邦,開土,植基於此焉.自是世爲一方君長.皇祖諱汀克承其家以繼先志,有衆至千余人.皇祖妣阮氏,最有賢行,生二子,長曰從,次曰曠,帝之皇考也.愷悌慈祥,休休樂善,好養賓客,鄰境之民視同一家.是以人莫不感其恩而服其義也.皇妣鄭氏諱蒼,勤於婦道,閨門和睦,家日益昌.生三子,伯曰學,仲曰除,季則帝也.伯受祖父之傳不幸短命.帝承祖父之業惟勤.雖時遭大亂而志且益堅.晦跡山林,以稼穡爲業.由其憤強賊之陵暴,尤專心於韜畧之書,罄竭家資,厚待賓客.戊戌起集義兵,屯落水上.前後凡數十餘戰,皆殽伏,出奇,避銳,乘敝,以寡敵衆,以弱制強.丙午戰於窣洞,大捷,遂進圍東都.丁未,賊遣安遠侯柳昇領兵十萬,由廣西進,黔國公沐晟領兵五萬,由雲南進.支稜一戰,柳昇授首,斬賊衆數萬餘級,生擒賊將黃福,崔聚等三百餘人,軍下三萬餘口.所攫柳昇勅命,兵符送雲南軍.沐晟見之,擧衆宵潰,斬馘生拎,不可殫紀.時鎮守東關城成山侯王通等先與我軍講和未定,至是請盟於珥河之上. 各處鎮守成池俱開門出降.凡所擒獲賊人,及各成降卒,該十萬餘口,一皆放還. 水路送穀號船五百餘艘.陸路應付口粮,脚力.戒戢軍士,秋毫一無所犯.兩國自是通好,北南無事. 忙禮,哀牢,俱入本圖. 占城,闍婆,航海修貢.帝宵衣旰食,凡六載而國中大治.摯至是崩.順天六年,癸丑十月吉日,榮祿大夫,入內行譴,知三舘事,臣 阮薦奉 勅譔 翰林院待制,武文斐奉書.

13. ĐVTS, p. 35 lists his grandmother's name as Nguyễn Quách and his mother's name as Trịnh Ngọc Thương.

14. There is a modern Lạc Thủy district in Hòa Bình province near Phủ Lý but it would be too close to Đông Đô and the concentration of Ming's forces for Lê Lợi to setup his first camp there.

15. Official information shows Thanh Hóa had 364,622 Mường people in 2021. Nearly 279,398 of them live in Ngọc Lặc (94,676), Thạch Thành (76.106), Bá Thước (53,046) and Cẩm Thuỷ (55,570). See http://bienphongvietnam.gov.vn/dan-toc-muong-o-tinh-thanh-hoa.html, accessed 1 January 2025. These are the districts within 20 to 50 kilometres north of where Lê Lợi's family was believed to be in the 15th century.

16. https://baotanglichsu.vn/en/Articles/3181/8422/the-stele-vinh-lang-a-precious-historical-document.html, accessed 27 December 2024.

17. SKTT Vol. 2, p. 149.

18. SKTT Vol. 2, p. 171. SKTT records this incident in the 1385 entry. If Nguyễn Trãi were indeed born in 1380, as commonly believed, he would have been about five years old at the time, which would suggest that Nguyễn Phi Khanh was already married when he entered the Trần household as a tutor. It would seem unlikely that Trần Nguyên Đán would have invited a married man to tutor his daughter, so either SKTT records an event that happened five years prior or Nguyễn Trãi was born in 1385, not 1380.

19. Phan, H. C. (2005). *Lịch Triều Hiến Chương Loại Chí - Tập 1* (V. S. H. Viện Khoa Học Xã Hội Việt Nam, Trans.). Nhà Xuất Bản Giáo dục. , p. 274.

20. SKTT Vol. 2, p. 202.

21. SKTT Vol. 2, p. 218.

22. SA MSL, Yong-le: Year 5, Month 3, Day 27, 4 May 1407, *the Chief Minister of the Court of Judicial Review Ruan Fei-qing* [Đại Lý khanh Nguyễn Phi Khanh]… *all went to Fu and surrendered*.

23. Phan, H. C. (2005). *Lịch Triều Hiến Chương Loại Chí - Tập 1* (V. S. H. Viện Khoa Học Xã Hội Việt Nam, Trans.). Nhà Xuất Bản Giáo dục. , p. 274.

24. https://baohaiduong.vn/nguyen-phi-khanh-nguoi-het-long-vi-nuoc-vi-dan-337385.html, accessed 22 April 2025.

25. Phạm, Đ. H., & Nguyễn, Á. (1806). *Tang Thương Ngẫu Lục* (T. K.-N. V. Triện, Trans.). Nhà Xuất Bản Hồng Bàng (2012). , p. 116.

26. SKTT, Vol. 2, p. 170.

27. Nguyễn, L. B. (2003). *Nguyễn Trãi Đánh Giặc Cứu Nước*. NXB Quân đội nhân dân. https://www.quansuvn.net/index.php/topic,29967.20.html, https://pubhtml5.com/jfqx/yfxa/ , p. 30.

28. Nguyễn, T. (15th century). *Nguyễn Trãi Toàn Tập (Ức Trai Thi Tập) – Phúc Khê Nguyên Bản (1868)* (H. K. (1970), Trans.). Nhà Xuất Bản Văn Hóa Thông Tin (2001). , p. 587.

29. SKTT, Vol. 2, p. 306. The date was the 6th day of the 12th lunar month, 1431.

30. The version that I have referred to in this book was translated from a copy made by Hồ Sĩ Dương (1621–1681) under the reign of King Lê Hy Tông of the Restored Lê period during the Era of Vĩnh Trị (1676–1680) by Bảo Thần in 1944 and published in 1956. Lê Quý Đôn (1726–1784) mentions that the original version existed during his time and the 17th-century copy had several mistakes, see ĐVTS, p. 136. A more recent version of LSTL, reportedly based on the original, was published in 1976 and reprinted in 2006. This copy was translated into Vietnamese by Lê Văn-Uông and verified by Nguyễn Diên-Niên. Refer https://baotanglichsu.vn/vi/Articles/3091/13272/gap-go-nguoi-khao-chung-lam-son-thuc-luc.html and https://nghiencuulichsu.com/2015/04/25/loi-the-lung-nhai/, accessed 13 March 2025.

31. LSTL, p. 8.

32. ĐVTS, p. 191, p. 251, p. 255, p. 267, p. 269, p. 271. Also p. 6.

33. Hoàng, X. H. (2017). *Những bài khảo cứu của Giáo Sư Hoàng Xuân Hãn*. Nhà Xuất Bản Hồng Đức - Tạp Chí Xưa & Nay. , p. 200. See also Phan, H. L., & Phan, Đ. D. (2019). *Khởi Nghĩa Lam Sơn (1418–1427)* (4 ed.). Nhà Xuất Bản Hồng Đức. , pp. 116–117. The Kỷ Mão and Canh Dần dates of the second lunar month of the Bính Thân year is 15 and 26 March 1416, respectively.

34. The 18 men are Lê Lai, Lê Thận, Lê Văn Linh, Lê Văn An, Trịnh Khả, Trương Lôi, Lê Liễu, Bùi Quốc Hưng, Lê Nanh, Lê Kiệm, Võ Uy, Nguyễn Trãi, Đinh Liệt, Lưu Nhân Chú, Lê Bồi, Lê Lý, Đinh Lan, Trương-Chiến in one list. See Hoàng, X. H. (2017). *Những bài khảo cứu của Giáo Sư Hoàng Xuân Hãn*. Nhà Xuất Bản Hồng Đức - Tạp Chí Xưa & Nay. , p. 200. In another list, these are Lê Lai, Lê Thận, Lê Văn An, Lê Văn Linh, Trịnh Khả, Trương Lôi, Lê Liễu, Bùi Quốc Hưng, Lê Ninh, Lê Hiểm, Vũ Uy, Nguyễn Trãi, Đinh Liệt, Lê Nhân Chú, Lê Bồi, Lê Lý, Đinh Lan, Trương Chiến. See Phan, H. L., & Phan, Đ. D. (2019). *Khởi Nghĩa Lam Sơn (1418–1427)* (4 ed.). Nhà Xuất Bản Hồng Đức. , p. 117.

35. Phan, H. L., & Phan, Đ. D. (2019). *Khởi Nghĩa Lam Sơn (1418–1427)* (4 ed.). Nhà Xuất Bản Hồng Đức. , p. 119.

36. Lê Nhân Chú was from Thái Nguyên, Bùi Quốc-Hưng and Nguyễ Trãi were from Đông Quan. Lê Hiểm was a Mường. See ĐVTS, p. 251. Ibid., p. 123, p. 120.

37. Hoàng, X. H. (2017). *Những bài khảo cứu của Giáo Sư Hoàng Xuân Hãn*. Nhà Xuất Bản Hồng Đức - Tạp Chí Xưa & Nay. , pp. 200–219.

38. Ibid., p. 201.

39. SA MSL, Yong-le: Year 9, Month 3, Day 24, 16 Apr 1411.

40. LSTL, pp. 8–9.

41. SA MSL, Xuan-de: Year 4, Month 2, Day 11, 15 Mar 1429 and 1 May 1429. SKTT, Vol. 2, p. 297.

42. LSTL, p. 9.

43. LSTL, p. 9.

44. LSTL, p. 9. See also Hoàng, X. H. (2017). *Những bài khảo cứu của Giáo Sư Hoàng Xuân Hãn*. Nhà Xuất Bản Hồng Đức - Tạp Chí Xưa & Nay. , p. 180, p. 187.

45. ĐVTS, p. 192.

46. Phan, H. L., & Phan, Đ. D. (2019). *Khởi Nghĩa Lam Sơn (1418–1427)* (4 ed.). Nhà Xuất Bản Hồng Đức. , p. 132.

47. LSTL, p. 10.

48. Phan, H. L., & Phan, Đ. D. (2019). *Khởi Nghĩa Lam Sơn (1418–1427)* (4 ed.). Nhà Xuất Bản Hồng Đức. , p. 163. Phan suggests Khôi could be around Nho Quan in Ninh Bình province, but this is far from other battlefields along the Mã River mentioned earlier, where he operated. Since Lê Lợi retreated to Mount Chí Linh afterwards, Khôi is most likely be on the south side of the Mã River, possibly somewhere between Bá Thước and Quan Hóa districts.

49. LSTL, p. 11.

50. Nguyễn, T. (15th century). *Nguyễn Trãi Toàn Tập* (V. S. Học, Trans.; 2 ed.). Nhà Xuất Bản Khoa Học Xã Hội, 1976. https://dovanphuong.com/nguyen-trai-toan-tap-pdf.html , pp. 101–102.

51. Ibid., pp. 103.

52. LSTL, p. 11.

53. https://en.wikipedia.org/wiki/Yongle_Emperor, accessed 20 May 2025.

54. Phan, H. L., & Phan, Đ. D. (2019). *Khởi Nghĩa Lam Sơn (1418–1427)* (4 ed.). Nhà Xuất Bản Hồng Đức. , p. 178.

55. At that time, Nghệ An had four subprefectures: Trà Long (Trà Lung, Trà Lân)(Cha-long), Hoan (Huan, modern Vinh and surrounding area), Ngọc Ma (Yu-ma, west of Nghệ An, around today's Viengthong and Pha Khao in Laos), Nam Tĩnh (Nan-jing, present-day Hà Tĩnh). North of present-day Nghệ An was Diễn Châu (Yan-zhou) and Quỳ Châu (Kui-zhou). See SA MSL, 5 July 1407 and 13 May 1415.

56. ĐVTS, p. 48.

57. Phan, H. L., & Phan, Đ. D. (2019). *Khởi Nghĩa Lam Sơn (1418–1427)* (4 ed.). Nhà Xuất Bản Hồng Đức. , p. 180. On the current map, there is no direct road access from Tây Đô to Châu Nga. One has to go south on CT02 and then turn around to travel north on QL48 to get there. A more suitable place where the route south intersects the Hiếu River is around Thái Hòa (coordinates 19°18'57.6"N 105°24'59.2"E). This place would be a better candidate for Bồ-lạp. However, Phan also mentions two more places with vestiges related to the Lê Lợi's campaign of 1424. These are Tam Hợp, Quỳ Hợp (19°21'21.0"N 105°17'11.6"E) and Nghĩa Đàn (19°19'48.7"N 105°20'55.2"E), both are south of Châu Nga, along the Hiếu River and within the vicinity of Thái Hòa.

58. LSTL, p. 12.

59. Photograph by the author on 10 February 2025 from the bridge across the Hiếu River, 2XQF+GHH Anh Sơn District, Nghe An, Vietnam, coordinate 19°02'19.8"N 104°58'26.3"E.

60. Nguyễn, T. (15th century). *Nguyễn Trãi Toàn Tập* (V. S. Học, Trans.; 2 ed.). Nhà Xuất Bản Khoa Học Xã Hội, 1976. https://dovanphuong.com/nguyen-trai-toan-tap-pdf.html , pp. 103–104.

61. Tri Lễ Bridge is at W5X6+46V Anh Sơn District, Nghệ An, Vietnam, coordinates 18°56'52.3"N 105°09'38.0"E.

62. LSTL, p. 12.

63. Phan, H. L., & Phan, Đ. D. (2019). *Khởi Nghĩa Lam Sơn (1418–1427)* (4 ed.). Nhà Xuất Bản Hồng Đức. , p. 189.

64. The commanders were Lê Sát, Lê Văn, Lê Bí, Lê Lễ, Lê Nhân Chú, Lê Ngân, Lê Chiến, Lê Tông Kiều, Lê Khôi, Lê Bôi and Lê Văn An. See LSTL, p. 13.

65. SA-MSL, Yong-le: Year 13, Month 2, Day 20, 31 Mar 1415.

66. Quốc Sử Quán Triều Nguyễn – Viện Khoa Học Xã Hội Việt Nam – Viện Sử Học. (2006). *Đại Nam Nhất Thống Chí* (T. Đ. Phạm, Trans.). Nhà Xuất Bản Thuận Hóa. , Vol. 2, Book 5, Tỉnh Nghệ An, p. 168, p. 182.

67. Le Breton, H. (1936). *Le Vieux An-Tinh: La Prehistoire, Les lieux et monuments historiques ou légendaires remarquables, Extrait du Bulletin des Amis du Vieux Hué, Avril-Décembre 1936.* , Planche CLXIII, pp. 328–329.

68. According to ChatGPT, a typical army camp for 1,000 soldiers would require around 10 to 20 hectares, including sleeping quarters, food and mess areas, training and assembly areas, storage and armoury, horses and war elephants stables, medical and support facilities and defensive watchtowers.

69. Nguyễn, T. (15th century). *Nguyễn Trãi Toàn Tập* (V. S. Học, Trans.; 2 ed.). Nhà Xuất Bản Khoa Học Xã Hội, 1976. https://dovanphuong.com/nguyen-trai-toan-tap-pdf.html , pp. 104–106.

70. The commanders were Lê Lễ, Lê Sát, Lê Bị, Lê Triện, and Lê Nhân Trú. LSTL refers to them as Lê Lợi's grandchildren, which is possible but difficult to believe. Lê Lợi was 40 in 1425; if he had a son at 16 and his son had a son at 16, then Lê Lợi's grandson would be 18 in 1425. These men were likely to be older 18 to be commanders of his forces.

71. Present-day region around the Gianh River of Quảng Bình province.

72. 15 in 7 Jan 1408 and 2 in 5 July 1408, refer SA MSL.

73. The north-west column, led by Lê Triện, Lê Khả, Lê Bí with 2,000 men and advanced through Thiên-quan (modern Nho Quan, Ninh Bình), Quốc-oai, (Quảng Oai, Ba Vì, Sơn Tây), Gia-hưng (north of Hòa Bình, Sơn Tây, Phú Thọ), Lâm-thao (Yên Bái, Phú Thọ), Tam-đái (Phú Thọ, Vĩnh Phúc), Tuyên-quang. The central column, commanded by Lê Bị, Lê nhân Chú, also with 2,000 men, moved toward Thiên-quan, Thiên-trường (north-east Nam Định), Kiến-hưng (north of Thái Bình), Kiến-xương (south of Thái Bình). They went on to the north-east with over 3,000 men from Thanh-hóa, plus two war elephants, and marched toward Khoái-châu (Hưng Yên), Thượng-hồng (upper Red River), Hạ-hồng (lower Red River), Bắc-giang, and Lạng-sơn. See LSTL, p. 15.

74. The two commanders were Lê Lễ and Lê Xý. They were 'Quan Tư Không'.

75. Phan, H. L., & Phan, Đ. D. (2019). *Khởi Nghĩa Lam Sơn (1418–1427)* (4 ed.). Nhà Xuất Bản Hồng Đức. , p. 248.

76. Ibid., p. 249.

77. LSTL, p. 16.

78. Phan, H. L., & Phan, Đ. D. (2019). *Khởi Nghĩa Lam Sơn (1418–1427)* (4 ed.). Nhà Xuất Bản Hồng Đức. , pp. 283–293.

79. Quán Bến Temple is at VMG9+WWG, Anh Trỗi, Tốt Động, Chương Mỹ, Hà Nội, Vietnam, coordinates, 20°52'38.6"N 105°40'11.4"E. The Communal House of Tốt Động is nearby, at VMHF+5C Chương Mỹ, Hanoi, Vietnam, coordinates 20°52'40.8"N 105°40'24.6"E.

80. Mai Lĩnh Bridge is at WPPG+MWV Hà Đông, Hanoi, Vietnam, coordinates 20°56'12.2"N 105°43'38.3"E. Photograph taken by the author on 15 February 2025.

81. LSTL, p. 16.

82. SKTT, Vol. 2, p. 260.

83. https://vi.wikipedia.org/wiki/Qu%C3%A2n_trung_t%E1%BB%AB_m%E1%BB%87n-h_t%E1%BA%ADp#cite_note-ReferenceB-3, accessed 28 April 2025.

84. Nguyễn, T. (15th century). *Nguyễn Trãi Toàn Tập* (V. S. Học, Trans.; 2 ed.). Nhà Xuất Bản Khoa Học Xã Hội, 1976. https://dovanphuong.com/nguyen-trai-toan-tap-pdf.html , p. 107.

85. ĐVTS, pp. 274–277.

86. LSTL, p. 17.

87. Nguyễn, T. (15th century). *Nguyễn Trãi Toàn Tập* (V. S. Học, Trans.; 2 ed.). Nhà Xuất Bản Khoa Học Xã Hội, 1976. https://dovanphuong.com/nguyen-trai-toan-tap-pdf.html , pp. 111–112.

88. Ibid., pp. 118–119.

89. LSTL, p. 17.

90. SKTT, Vol. 2, p. 264, p. 265, 9. 267.

91. SKTT, Vol.2, p. 263.

92. Nguyễn, T. (15th century). *Nguyễn Trãi Toàn Tập* (V. S. Học, Trans.; 2 ed.). Nhà Xuất Bản Khoa Học Xã Hội, 1976. https://dovanphuong.com/nguyen-trai-toan-tap-pdf.html , p. 524.

93. SKTT, Vol.2, p. 282.

94. The Ancient Citadel of Xương Giang (Thành cổ Xương Giang) is located at 76R7+R7 Bac Giang, Vietnam, coordinates, 21°17'31.3"N 106°12'47.7"E. Photograph taken by the author on 16 February 2025.

95. Nguyễn, T. (15th century). *Nguyễn Trãi Toàn Tập* (V. S. Học, Trans.; 2 ed.). Nhà Xuất Bản Khoa Học Xã Hội, 1976. https://dovanphuong.com/nguyen-trai-toan-tap-pdf.html , p. 113.

96. LSTL, p. 17.

97. Nguyễn, T. (15th century). *Nguyễn Trãi Toàn Tập* (V. S. Học, Trans.; 2 ed.). Nhà Xuất Bản Khoa Học Xã Hội, 1976. https://dovanphuong.com/nguyen-trai-toan-tap-pdf.html , pp. 126–129.

98. LSTL, p. 17.

99. Nguyễn, T. (15th century). *Nguyễn Trãi Toàn Tập* (V. S. Học, Trans.; 2 ed.). Nhà Xuất Bản Khoa Học Xã Hội, 1976. https://dovanphuong.com/nguyen-trai-toan-tap-pdf.html , pp. 132–135.

100. Ibid., pp. 135–137.

101. In the letter, Lê Lợi mentions no less than 100,000 men in the prefectures in Giao Châu and 20,000 men in Diễn Châu, Tân Bình and Thuận Hóa.

102. Nguyễn, T. (15th century). *Nguyễn Trãi Toàn Tập* (V. S. Học, Trans.; 2 ed.). Nhà Xuất Bản Khoa Học Xã Hội, 1976. https://dovanphuong.com/nguyen-trai-toan-tap-pdf.html , pp. 137–140.

103. LSTL, p. 29.

104. The five commanders were Lê nhân Chú, Lê Sát, Lê Thụ, Lê Lãnh, and Lê Liệt. LSTL, p. 18.

105. Nguyễn, T. (15th century). *Nguyễn Trãi Toàn Tập* (V. S. Học, Trans.; 2 ed.). Nhà Xuất Bản Khoa Học Xã Hội, 1976. https://dovanphuong.com/nguyen-trai-toan-tap-pdf.html , p. 172, p. 174.

106. Ibid., pp. 144–145.

107. Phan, H. L., & Phan, Đ. D. (2019). *Khởi Nghĩa Lam Sơn (1418–1427)* (4 ed.). Nhà Xuất Bản Hồng Đức., Footnote 1, p. 353.

108. Mount Mã Yên is at HGWH+CJ3 Chi Lăng District, Lạng Sơn, Vietnam, coordinates 21°35'45.6"N 106°31'44.6"E. The stele is close to Highway QL1A, on the west side of the mountain. The stele marking the Chi Lăng Pass is at 21°37'12.0"N 106°32'31.4"E, Chi Lăng Museum (*Nhà Trưng bày Chiến thắng Chi Lăng*) is located at 21°36'47.7"N 106°32'23.8"E.

109. Photograph by the author, 19 December 2019.

110. According to SKTT, Vol. 2, p. 268, Liên Hoa Pass is by the Lô River flowing across the border between Hà Tuyên (Hà Giang) and Yunnan. However, Bửu, C., Đỗ, V. A., Pham, H. T., & Trương, B. L. (1962). *Hồng Đức Bản Đồ*. Tủ Sách Viện Khảo Cổ-Publications of the Institute of Historical Research - Publications de l'institut de Recherches Historiques - Số III. , p. 61, explains Liên Hoa is alongside the Thao River. (upstream of the Red River), just before the border of Lào Cai and Yunnan. I am inclined to support the latter, as the Red River is the usual route for Imperial Chinese armies to invade Vietnam.

111. Nguyễn, T. (15th century). *Nguyễn Trãi Toàn Tập* (V. S. Học, Trans.; 2 ed.). Nhà Xuất Bản Khoa Học Xã Hội, 1976. https://dovanphuong.com/nguyen-trai-toan-tap-pdf.html , p. 169.

112. SKTT, Vol. 2, p. 279.

113. Nguyễn, T. (15th century). *Nguyễn Trãi Toàn Tập* (V. S. Học, Trans.; 2 ed.). Nhà Xuất Bản Khoa Học Xã Hội, 1976. https://dovanphuong.com/nguyen-trai-toan-tap-pdf.html , pp. 173–185. Letter 19, p. 183. Footnote 2 in this letter explains that the offer of Nguyễn Trãi as a hostage is a mistake in copying the original text.

114. Nguyễn, T. (15th century). *Nguyễn Trãi Toàn Tập (Ức Trai Thi Tập) – Phúc Khê Nguyên Bản (1868)* (H. K. (1970), Trans.). Nhà Xuất Bản Văn Hóa Thông Tin (2001). , p. 587.

115. Nguyễn, T. (15th century). *Nguyễn Trãi Toàn Tập* (V. S. Học, Trans.; 2 ed.). Nhà Xuất Bản Khoa Học Xã Hội, 1976. https://dovanphuong.com/nguyen-trai-toan-tap-pdf.html , p. 181.

116. Ibid., p. 185. The full list of the participants in Vietnamese is *Tôi là đại đầu mục nước An-nam tên là Lê (Lợi) và bọn Trần Văn Hãn, Lê Nhân Chú, Lê Vấn, Trần Ngân, Trần Văn Xảo, Trần Bị, Trịnh Khả, Nguyễn Chích, Trần Lý, Phạm Bôi, Trần Văn An, Bế Khắc Thiệu, Ma Luân, cùng với:*

Quan tổng binh của Thiên triều là thái tử thái bảo Thành-sơn hầu tên là Vương Thông, và các quan tham tướng hữu đô đốc là Mã Anh, Thái giám là Sơn Thọ, Mã Kỳ, Vinh xương bá là Trần Trí, Yên bình bá là Lý An, đô đốc là Phương Chính, Chưởng đô ti sự Đô đốc Thiêm sự là Thuế Lự, đô đốc thiêm sự là Trần Hữu, giám sát ngự sử là Châu Kỳ Hậu, Cấp sự trung là Quách Vĩnh Thanh, bố chính là Đặc Kiêm, tả tham chính là Thanh Quảng Bình, hữu tham chính là Hồng Thừa Lương, hữu tham nghị là Lục Trinh, Án sát sứ là Dương Thời Tập, thiêm sự là Quách Hội.

117. LSTL, p. 19.

118. LSTL, p. 19.

119. Nguyễn, T. (15th century). *Nguyễn Trãi Toàn Tập* (V. S. Học, Trans.; 2 ed.). Nhà Xuất Bản Khoa Học Xã Hội, 1976. https://dovanphuong.com/nguyen-trai-toan-tap-pdf.html , pp. 187–188.

120. This translation comes from Trương, B. L. (1967). Patterns of Vietnamese Response to Foreign Intervention: 1858–1900. *Southeast Asia Studies, Monograph Series, Yale University, 11*, 55–62. , p. 55.

121. I counted these lines from LSTL, but different versions have different counts. For example, Vũ, Đ. Đ. (2011). *Proclamation of Victory (Bình Ngô Đại Cáo) - Translation and Annotations of a Fifteenth Century Vietnamese Document*. Publisher: Thế Giới Publishing Company. https://www.amazon.com/Proclamation-Victory-B%C3%ACnh-Ng%C3%B4-%C4%90%E1%BA%A1i-ebook/dp/B006ZOEEAM has 126 lines, and SKTT, Vol. 2, pp 282–284 has 151 lines, but my division of the paragraphs is roughly similar.

122. The Vietnamese lines read *Dù mạnh yếu có lúc không đều; Nhưng hào-kiệt chưa đời nào thiếu!*

123. LSTL, p. 23.

124. LSTL, p. 23.

125. The Vietnamese lines read *Khốn nỗi: tuấn-kiệt như sao buổi sớm! Nhân-tài như lá mùa thu!*

126. Liu Sheng died at Mã Yên on the 20th day of the 9th lunar month the year of Đinh Mùi (or 10 October 1427). LSTL, p. 28. See https://xskt.com.vn/lich-am-van-nien/nam/1427#toplich.

127. In LSTL, pp. 25–26, the text in Vietnamese is:

Chẳng những mưu-kế thực sâu-xa tột bực!

Mà cũng xưa nay chưa nghe thấy bao giờ!

…

Để gây-dựng nền thái-bình cho muôn đời!

Để gội-rửa nhục vô-cùng cho cả nước!

Cũng là nhờ Trời, Đất, Tổ-tông linh-thiêng, đã ngấm-ngầm phù-hộ mà được như thế này!

The original text in SKTT, Vol. 2, pp 282–284, is as follows:

非惟計謀之極其深遠盖亦古今之所未見聞.

Phi duy kế mưu chi cực, kì thâm viễn cái diệc cổ kim chi sở vị kiến văn.

于以開萬世太平之基于以雪千古無之恥是由天地之靈有以默將陰佑而致然也.

Vu dĩ khai vạn thế thái bình chi cơ, vu dĩ tuyết thiên cổ vô cùng chi sỉ! Thị do thiên địa tổ tông chi linh hữu dĩ mặc tướng âm hựu nhi trí nhiên dã.

Chẳng những mưu kế cực kỳ sâu xa,

Mà cũng xưa nay chưa từng nghe thấy.

….

Để mở nền thái bình muôn thuở,

Để rửa mối si nhục ngàn thu!

Âu cũng nhờ trời đất, tổ tông linh thiêng ngầm giúp mới được như vậy.

I have translated the Chinese script into English and there is no term for 'country' in this text.

128. The original text in SKTT, Vol. 2, pp 282–284, is as follows:

於戲一戎大定迄成無覺之功四海永清誕布維新之誥布告遐邇咸使聞知

Ô hô nhất nhung đại định, ngật thành vô giác chi công tứ hải vĩnh thanh, đản bố duy tân chi cáo, bố cáo hà nhĩ, hàm sử văn tri.

129. https://en.wikipedia.org/wiki/Hongwu_Emperor

130. SKTT, Vol. 2, p. 271, p. 282, p. 317,

131. https://leminhkhai.wordpress.com/2010/05/09/north-and-south-in-the-binh-ngo-d%e1%ba%a1i-cao/, accessed 19 April 2025.

132. Whitmore, J. K. (2013). *Ngo (Chinese) Communities and Montane–Littoral Conflict in Dai Viet, ca. 1400–1600* Maritime Frontiers in Asia: Indigenous Communities and State Control in South China and Southeast Asia, 2000 bce–1800 ce, . Pennsylvania State University. https://www2.ihp.sinica.edu.tw/file/2170SgsZeWy.pdf, p. 60, p. 66.

133. LSTL, p. 23.

Thử xét nước nhà: Đại Việt.

Vốn là xứ-sở văn-minh.

Cõi bờ của sông, núi đã chia.

Phong-tục của Bắc, Nam cũng khác.

Từ Triệu, Đinh, Lý, Trần, đã dựng thành một nước;

Cùng Hán, Đường, Tống, Nguyên, đều làm chúa một phương.

Refer to SKTT, Vol. 2, p. 283.

惟我大越之國實爲文獻之

Duy ngã Đại Việt chi quốc, thực vi văn hiến chi bang.

山川之封域既殊南北之風俗亦異

Sơn xuyên chi phong vực ký thù, nam bắc chi phong tục diệc dị.

自趙丁李陳之肇造我國與漢唐宋元而各帝一方雖強弱時有不同而豪傑世未嘗乏

Tự Triệu, Đinh, Lí, Trần chi triệu tạo, ngã quốc dữ Hán, Đường, Tống, Nguyên nhi các đế nhất phương, tuy cường nhược thời hữu bất đồng, nhi hào kiệt thế vị thường phạp.

Xét như nước Đại Việt ta,

Thực là 1 một nước văn hiến.

Cõi bờ sông núi đã riêng,

Phong tục Bắc Nam cũng khác.

Trải Triệu, Đinh, Lý, Trần nối đời dựng nước,

Cùng Hán, Đường, Tống, Nguyên đều chủ một phương,

134. Vuving, A. L. (2001). The References of Vietnamese States and the Mechanisms of World Formation. *ASIEN (Journal of the German Association for Asian Studies)*, no. 79 (April 2001), 62–86. , p. 67.

135. https://leminhkhai.wordpress.com/2011/04/05/the-problems-with-the-binh-ngo-d%e1%ba%a1i-cao-as-a-declaration-of-independence/, accessed 19 April 2025.

136. Nguyễn, T. (15th century). *Nguyễn Trãi Toàn Tập* (V. S. Học, Trans.; 2 ed.). Nhà Xuất Bản Khoa Học Xã Hội, 1976. https://dovanphuong.com/nguyen-trai-toan-tap-pdf.html , p. 112.

137. SA MSL, Yong-le: Year 5, Month 6, Day 1, 5 Jul 1407.

138. SA MSL, Xuan-de: Year 3, Month 2, Day 8, 22 Feb 1428.

139. SA MSL, Xuan-de: Year 3, Month 3, Day 15, 30 Mar 1428.

140. SA MSL, Xuan-de: Year 3, Month Intercalary 4, Day 27, 9 Jun 1428 and Xuan-de: Year 3, Month Intercalary 4, Day 29, 11 Jun 1428.

141. https://baike.baidu.com/item/%E7%8E%8B%E9%80%9A/8621712 accessed 8 April 2025.

142. SA MSL, Xuan-de: Year 3, Month 5, Day 30, 12 Jul 1428.

143. Nguyễn, T. (15th century). *Nguyễn Trãi Toàn Tập* (V. S. Học, Trans.; 2 ed.). Nhà Xuất Bản Khoa Học Xã Hội, 1976. https://dovanphuong.com/nguyen-trai-toan-tap-pdf.html , pp. 108.

144. SA MSL, Xuan-de: Year 3, Month 5, Day 20, 2 Jul 1428.

145. SA MSL, Xuan-de: Year 3, Month 5, Day 20, 12 Jul 1428.

146. Nguyễn, T. (15th century). *Nguyễn Trãi Toàn Tập* (V. S. Học, Trans.; 2 ed.). Nhà Xuất Bản Khoa Học Xã Hội, 1976. https://dovanphuong.com/nguyen-trai-toan-tap-pdf.html , p. 140.

147. SA MSL, Xuan-de: Year 3, Month 5, Day 16, 28 Jun 1428.

148. https://vi.wikipedia.org/wiki/M%E1%BB%99c_Th%E1%BA%A1nh, accessed 18 July 2025.

149. SKTT Vol. 2, p. 297. ĐVTS, pp. 274–277.

150. SA MSL, Xuan-de: Year 3, Month 3, Day 15, 30 Mar 1428.

151. SA MSL, Xuan-de: Year 3, Month 4, Day 1, 15 Apr 1428.

152. SA MSL, Xuan-de: Year 3, Month 5, Day 1, 13 Jun 1428.

153. SA MSL, Xuan-de: Year 4, Month 2, Day 11, 15 Mar 1429; Xuan-de: Year 4, Month 2, Day 22, 1 May 1429; Xuan-de: Year 5, Month 3, Day 11, 3 Apr 1430; Xuan-de: Year 5, Month 4, Day 15, 7 May 1430; Xuan-de: Year 6, Month 5, Day 3, 12 Jun 1431.

154. SA MSL, Xuan-de: Year 6, Month 6, Day 7, 15 Jul 1431.

155. SA MSL, Xuan-de: Year 9, Month 3, Day 9, 17 April 1434.

156. SKTT Vol. 2, p. 335.

157. https://en.wikipedia.org/wiki/Mu_Sheng, accessed 17 April 2025.

158. https://en.wikipedia.org/wiki/Zhang_Fu,

CHAPTER 6

1. SKTT, Vol. 2, pp. 260–261.

2. SKTT, Vol. 2, pp. 263–281.

3. SKTT, Vol. 2, pp. 269–270.

4. SKTT, Vol. 2, p. 298.

5. Photographs taken by Vũ Văn Khánh on 22 May 2025; 123 Lê Hồng Phong, P. Điện Biên, Thanh Hóa, Vietnam, coordinates 19°48'26.4"N 105°46'33.4"E.

6. https://vnexpress.net/tuong-dai-da-xanh-lon-nhat-thanh-hoa-duoc-tu-bo-3897826.html accessed 23 May 2025.

7. The list of 93 'meritorious officials (*công thần*)' are: First tier (3): Lê Vấn, Lê Sát, Lê Văn Xào. Second tier (1): Lê Ngân. Third tier (3): Lê Lý, Lê Văn Linh, Lê Quốc Hưng. Fourth tier (14): Lê Chích, Lê Văn An, Lê Liệt, Lê Thố, Lê Lễ, Lê Chiến, Lê Khôi, Lê Đính, Lê Chuyết, Lê Lỗi, Lê Nhữ Lãm, Lê Sao, Lê Kiệm, Lê Lật. Fifth tier (14): Lê Bị, Lê Bì, Lê Bĩ, Lê Náo, Lê Thụ, Lê Lôi, Lê Khả, Lê Bồi (Bôi), Lê Khả Lang, Lê Xí, Lê Khuyến, Lê Bí, Lê Quốc Trinh, Lê Bật. Sixth tier (26): Lê Lạn, Lê (Nguyễn) Trãi. Seventh tier (16): Lê Thiệt, Lê Chương. Eight tier (16): Lê Cuống, Lê Dao. Ninth tier (4): Lê Khắc Phục, Lê Hài. See SKTT, Vol. 2, p. 300. See also ĐVTS, p. 99 and CM, Vol. 1, pp. 853–856.

8. SKTT, Vol. 2, p. 292.

9. SKTT, Vol. 2, p. 293, p. 298.

10. ĐVTS, pp. 238–246.

11. CM, Vol. 1, p. 861. ĐVTS, p. 237.

12. According to ĐVTS (p. 234), Trần Nguyên Hãn resigned shortly after 1428 and returned to his home village where he built a large house and boats big enough to transport troops. Later, someone accused of him treason and Lê Lợi ordered him arrested. On their way back to the capital, the boat carrying him and his captors capsized and everyone on board drowned, except two servants who survived.

13. CM, Vol. 1, p. 852.

14. ĐVTS, p. 237.

15. ĐVTS, p. 201.

16. Nguyễn, T. (15th century). *Nguyễn Trãi Toàn Tập* (V. S. Học, Trans.; 2 ed.). Nhà Xuất Bản Khoa Học Xã Hội, 1976. https://dovanphuong.com/nguyen-trai-toan-tap-pdf.html, p. 262, p. 325.

17. SKTT, Vol. 2, p. 312. Lê, Q. Đ. (2007). *Đại Việt thông sử* (T. L. Ngô, Trans.). Nhà Xuất Bản Văn hóa - Thông tin. (1759), p. 254.

18. Four circuits: 1-Tây Đạo (West) includes Tam Giang, Hưng Hóa, Tuyên Quang and Gia Hưng; 2-Đông Đạo (East) includes Thượng Hồng, Hạ Hồng, Nam Sách Thượng, Nam Sách Hạ and An Bang; 3-Bắc Đạo (North) includes Bắc Giang, Thái Nguyên; 4-Nam Đạo (South) includes Khoái Châu, Lý Nhân, Tân Hưng, Kiến Xương and Thiên Trường. SKTT, Vol. 2, p. 261.

19. SKTT, Vol. 2, p. 340, p. 341.

20. SKTT, Vol. 2, p. 264, p. 272, p. 273.

21. SKTT, Vol. 2, p.273, p. 277.

22. CM, Vol. 1, p. 851.

23. Vietnamese historians count the year of birth as one, so their record shows Lê Quang Long as 11 years old in 1433, and Lê Lợi passed away at 49. They were born on 1423 and 1385, respectively.

24. SKTT, Vol. 2, p. 307.

25. SKTT, Vol. 2, pp. 307–308.

26. ĐVTS, p. 119.

27. Phan, H. L., & Phan, Đ. D. (2019). *Khởi Nghĩa Lam Sơn (1418–1427)* (4 ed.). Nhà Xuất Bản Hồng Đức. , p. 391. See also Lê, T. K. (2018). *Lịch sử Việt Nam từ nguồn gốc đến giữa thế kỷ XX* (N. Nguyễn, Trans.; Vol. Nhã Nam, Nhà Xuất Bản Thế Giới). (1955, 1982), pp. 249–254.

28. Đào, D. A. (2006). *Lịch sử Việt Nam – Từ nguồn gốc đến thế kỷ XIX*. Nhà Xuất Bản Văn Hóa Thông Tin. (1957), p. 285.

29. Taylor, K. W. (2014). *A History of the Vietnamese*. Cambridge University Press. , p. 180.

30. SKTT, Vol. 2, p. 240.

31. Phan, H. L., & Phan, Đ. D. (2019). *Khởi Nghĩa Lam Sơn (1418–1427)* (4 ed.). Nhà Xuất Bản Hồng Đức. , p. 123.

32. Nguyễn, T. (15th century). *Nguyễn Trãi Toàn Tập (Ức Trai Thi Tập) – Phúc Khê Nguyên Bản (1868)* (H. K. (1970), Trans.). Nhà Xuất Bản Văn Hóa Thông Tin (2001). , p. 587.

33. Phan, H. C. (2005). *Lịch Triều Hiến Chương Loại Chí - Tập 1* (V. S. H. Viện Khoa Học Xã Hội Việt Nam, Trans.). Nhà Xuất Bản Giáo dục. , p. 276.

34. Nguyễn, T. (15th century). *Nguyễn Trãi Toàn Tập (Ức Trai Thi Tập) – Phúc Khê Nguyên Bản (1868)* (H. K. (1970), Trans.). Nhà Xuất Bản Văn Hóa Thông Tin (2001). , p. 22, p. 25. 'Bắt ngôn công thành' (Do not speak of attacking the city), 'Nhi thiện ngôn công tâm' (But be skilled in attacking the heart/mind).

35. Phan, H. L., & Phan, Đ. D. (2019). *Khởi Nghĩa Lam Sơn (1418–1427)* (4 ed.). Nhà Xuất Bản Hồng Đức. , p. 115.

36. Taylor, K. W. (2014). *A History of the Vietnamese*. Cambridge University Press. , p. 186.

37. SKTT, Vol 2, p. 264.

38. ĐVTS, p. 66.

39. SKTT, Vol 2, p. 263.

40. SKTT, Vol 2, p. 293.

41. SKTT, Vol 2, p. 279.

42. Nguyễn, T. (15th century). *Nguyễn Trãi Toàn Tập (Ức Trai Thi Tập) – Phúc Khê Nguyên Bản (1868)* (H. K. (1970), Trans.). Nhà Xuất Bản Văn Hóa Thông Tin (2001). , p. 587.

43. Ibid., p. 450. Nguyễn, T. (15th century). *Nguyễn Trãi Toàn Tập* (V. S. Học, Trans.; 2 ed.). Nhà Xuất Bản Khoa Học Xã Hội, 1976. https://dovanphuong.com/nguyen-trai-toan-tap-pdf.html , p. 106.

44. Nguyễn, T. (15th century). *Nguyễn Trãi Toàn Tập (Ức Trai Thi Tập) – Phúc Khê Nguyên Bản (1868)* (H. K. (1970), Trans.). Nhà Xuất Bản Văn Hóa Thông Tin (2001). , p. 468. Nguyễn, T. (15th century). *Nguyễn Trãi Toàn Tập* (V. S. Học, Trans.; 2 ed.). Nhà Xuất Bản Khoa Học Xã Hội, 1976. https://dovanphuong.com/nguyen-trai-toan-tap-pdf.html , p. 111.

45. Nguyễn, T. (15th century). *Nguyễn Trãi Toàn Tập (Ức Trai Thi Tập) – Phúc Khê Nguyên Bản (1868)* (H. K. (1970), Trans.). Nhà Xuất Bản Văn Hóa Thông Tin (2001). , p. 522. Nguyễn, T. (15th century). *Nguyễn Trãi Toàn Tập* (V. S. Học, Trans.; 2 ed.). Nhà Xuất Bản Khoa Học Xã Hội, 1976. https://dovanphuong.com/nguyen-trai-toan-tap-pdf.html , p. 127.

46. SKTT, Vol. 2, p. 273.

47. Nguyễn, T. (15th century). *Nguyễn Trãi Toàn Tập* (V. S. Học, Trans.; 2 ed.). Nhà Xuất Bản Khoa Học Xã Hội, 1976. https://dovanphuong.com/nguyen-trai-toan-tap-pdf.html , p. 252.

48. Nguyễn, H. S. (2001). *Nguyễn Trãi-Về Tác Giả và Tác Phẩm*. Nhà Xuất Bản Giáo Dục. , p. 803.

49. Reproduced with permission by Do Nguyen, co-author of *Beyond the Court Gate: Selected Poems of Nguyen Trai*; see his email to Tan Pham dated 2 August 2025.

50. Nguyễn, T. (2010). *Beyond the Court Gate: Selected Poems of Nguyen Trai* (D. Nguyen & P. Hoover, Eds.). Counterpath Press. , p. 36. The original poem, translated into Vietnamese, reads: Nhờ người vẽ tranh Côn Sơn.

Nửa đời phải bỏ cái thú leo leo khe núi;

Sau loạn quê nhà chỉ phí chiêm bao mà tìm về.

Gió tùng trên bậc đá, không có ai thưởng thức;

Bóng hoa mai bên suối, đành phụ thú ngâm nga.

Thấy yên hà vắng vẻ, ruột ta muốn đứt;

Thấy vượn hạc tiêu điều tâm ý khó cầm.

Nhờ cậy tay vẽ giỏi trong thế gian,

Lấy ngòi bút vẽ ra cả tấm lòng của ta.

See Nguyễn, T. (15th century). *Nguyễn Trãi Toàn Tập* (V. S. Học, Trans.; 2 ed.). Nhà Xuất Bản Khoa Học Xã Hội, 1976. https://dovanphuong.com/nguyen-trai-toan-tap-pdf.html , p. 337.

51. https://vi.wikipedia.org/wiki/Tang_th%C6%B0%C6%A1ng_ng%E1%BA%ABu_l%E1%BB%A5c, accessed 24 September 2025.

52. Phạm, Đ. H., & Nguyễn, Á. (1806). *Tang Thương Ngẫu Lục* (T. K.-N. V. Triện, Trans.). Nhà Xuất Bản Hồng Bàng (2012). , pp. 116–128.

53. Lê Lợi will be king, Lê Trãi will be his servant (or subject) in Vietnamese is *Lê Lợi vi quân, Lê Trãi vi thần (Lê Lợi làm vua, Lê Trãi làm tôi)*.

54. CM, Vol. 1, p. 851.

55. ĐVTS, p. 179.

56. SKTT, Vol. 2, p. 347.

57. SKTT, Vol. 2, p. 340.

58. SKTT, Vol. 2, p. 341.

59. SKTT, Vol. 2, p. 360.

60. SKTT, Vol. 2, p. 341. *Lấy Nhập nội tư khấu Bắc đạo hành quân đô tổng quản Lê Ngân làm Nhập nội đại đô đốc Quy Hoá trấn phiêu kỵ thượng tướng quân đặc tiến khai phủ nghi đồng tam ty thượng trụ quốc, Quốc huyện thượng hầu.* Appoint Lê Ngân, currently serving as *Nhập nội Tư khấu* – Royal Judicial Commissioner; *Bắc Đạo Hành Quân Đô Tổng Quản* – Commander-in-Chief of the Northern Circuit; *Nhập nội Đại Đô Đốc* – Grand Admiral/Grand Marshal of the inner court; *Quy Hóa Trấn* – Quy Hóa Garrison; *Phiêu Kỵ Thượng Tướng Quân* – Cavalry General of the Highest Rank; *Đặc Tiến Khai Phủ Nghi Đồng Tam Ty* – Honorary Grand Councillor with Authority Equal to the Three Ducal Ministers; *Thượng Trụ Quốc* – Pillar of the State; *Quốc Huyện Thượng Hầu* – Marquis of the Highest Rank.

61. SKTT, Vol. 2, p. 346.

62. SKTT, Vol. 2, p. 340.

63. SKTT, Vol. 2, p. 319, p. 332.

64. SKTT, Vol. 2, p. 351.

65. SKTT, Vol. 2, p. 352. Tru Di Tam Tộc ("诛三族 (zhū sān zú)) refers to an ancient Chinese form of collective punishment known as 'execution of three generations'. There are several interpretations of who would be executed. In one interpretation, three generations include the criminal's father, mother, brothers, wife and children. In the other, the list consists of the criminal's father, children and grandchildren. In yet another, the list includes the father's side: parents, uncles, aunts, and their families; the mother's side: maternal grandparents and relatives; the wife's side: the spouse's family. In some interpretations, it could also refer to the criminal's immediate family (parents, siblings, children), their paternal and maternal relatives, and their wife's family. https://vi.wikipedia.org/wiki/Tru_di#cite_note-cct-21 accessed 29 May 2025.

66. SKTT, Vol. 2, p. 352.

67. I have assumed that Lê Nguyên Long, being 19 at the time, would be unlikely to be attracted to someone significantly older than himself.

68. SKTT, Vol. 2, p. 350, p. 370.

69. SKTT, Vol. 2, p. 352.

70. CM, Vol. 1, p. 920.

71. CM, Vol. 1, p. 929.

72. Phạm, Đ. H., & Nguyễn, Á. (1806). *Tang Thương Ngẫu Lục* (T. K.-N. V. Triện, Trans.). Nhà Xuất Bản Hồng Bàng (2012). , p. 127.

73. VRWQ+643, Nhị Khê, Thường Tín, Hà Nội, Vietnam, coordinates 20°53'44.1"N 105°50'16.1"E.

74. SKTT, Vol. 2, p. 355, p. 373, p. 377, p. 383,

75. SKTT, Vol. 2, p. 378.

76. ĐVTS, p. 261.

77. SKTT, Vol. 2, p. 362, p. 370.

78. SKTT, Vol. 2, p. 379.

79. SKTT, Vol. 2, p. 319, p. 327, p. 337, p. 379, p. 385.

80. SKTT, Vol. 2, p. 311.

81. SKTT, Vol. 2, p. 351.

82. https://en.wikipedia.org/wiki/Temple_of_Literature,_Hanoi, accessed 11 June 2025.

83. SKTT, Vol. 2, p. 367.

84. SKTT, Vol. 2, p. 347.

85. SKTT, Vol. 2, p. 371.

86. SKTT, Vol. 2, p. 355, p. 338.

87. SKTT, Vol. 2, p. 391.

88. ĐVTS, p. 194.

89. SKTT, Vol. 2, p. 397.

90. CM, Vol. 1, p. 1005.

91. http://www.chinaknowledge.de/History/Terms/wujue.html, accessed 12 June 2025.

92. CM, Vol. 1, pp. 1135–1136, pp. 1145–1147.

93. SKTT, Vol. 2, p. 189.

94. SKTT, Vol. 2, p. 319.

95. Nguyễn, T. D. (2018). *Văn hóa Việt Nam thường thức*. Nhà Xuất Bản Hà Nội. , pp. 208–209.

96. SKTT, Vol. 2, p. 365.

97. SKTT, Vol. 2, p. 465. SKTT, Vol. 3, p. 14. SKTT, Vol. 3, p. 72.

98. SKTT, Vol. 2, p. 189, p. 465.

99. The topics of the for the metropolitan examinations in 1475 were as follows, see SKTT Vol. 2, p. 465:

    Round I: choose and write on four topics out of eight topics from the Four Books (Tứ thư): Analects (Luận Ngữ), three topics; Mencius (Mạnh Tử), four topics; Doctrine of the Mean (Trung Dung), one topic. On the Five Classics (Ngũ king), each classic had three topics, except for the Spring and Autumn Annals (Xuân Thu), which had two topics.

    Round II: compose one poem (thơ) and one rhyme-prose (phú). The poem had to follow Tang-regulated verse, and the rhyme-prose had to follow the Lý Bạch (Li Bai) style.

    Round III: write one piece each in the following official document styles: Edict (chiếu), Decree (chế), and Memorial (biểu).

    Round IV: write a policy essay, where candidates answered questions on the similarities and differences in meaning of the classics and histories and the military strategies of generals.

100. SKTT, Vol. 2, p. 368, p. 466.

101. SKTT, Vol. 2, p. 396.

102. SKTT, Vol. 2, p. 390, p. 408.

103. CM, Vol. 1, p. 1019.

104. These are *Trung hư, Thường sơn xà, Mãn thiên tinh, Nhạn hang* (Flying goose), *Liên châu, Ngư đội* (Fish-scale), *Tam tài hành, Thất môn, Yến nguyệt* for the naval formations and *Trường cơ, Tường kích, Kỳ binh* for land combat tactics.

105. SKTT, pp. 407–408.

106. SKTT, Vol. 2, p. 473.

107. http://thanglong.chinhphu.vn/Home/Doan-mon--cua-thanh-luu-dau-got-rong/20107/5243.vgp, accessed 3 June 2025.

108. Photo by Alex 69200 vx, 16 April 2020, CC BY-SA 4.0 <https://creativecommons.org/licenses/by-sa/4.0>, via Wikimedia Commons, https://commons.wikimedia.org/wiki/File:Citadelle-thang-long-hanoi.jpg.

109. Photo by Gryffindor, 2008, CC BY-SA 3.0 <https://creativecommons.org/licenses/by-sa/3.0>, via Wikimedia Commons, https://commons.wikimedia.org/wiki/File:Hanoi_Citadel_0348.JPG.

110. SKTT, Vol. 2, p. 298.

111. SKTT, Vol. 2, p. 404, p. 407.

112. Tống, T. T. (2012). *A general outline on the history of archeology in Vietnam - Vài nét về lịch sử khảo cổ học Việt Nam*. Perspectives on the archaeology of Vietnam International Colloquium, Hanoi 29th February - 2nd March 2012 = Toàn cảnh khảo cổ học Việt Nam, Hanoi, Vietnam. , p. 315.

113. Phan , H. L. (2018). *Lịch sử và văn hóa Việt Nam tiếp cận bộ phận* (P. T. Phan, Ed. 4th ed.). NXB Đại Học Quốc Gia Hà Nội. , p. 776.

114. Co-ordinates (21°02'12.6"N 105°50'25.3"E).

115. Phan , H. L. (2018). *Lịch sử và văn hóa Việt Nam tiếp cận bộ phận* (P. T. Phan, Ed. 4th ed.). NXB Đại Học Quốc Gia Hà Nội. , p. 763.

116. Pham, T. (2022). *One Thousand Years – The Stories of Giao Châu, the Kingdoms of Linyi, Funan and Zhenla*. (Vol. 2). 315Kio Publishing. , pp. 239–242.

117. https://baotanglichsu.vn/vi/Articles/3101/72013/bi-an-nhung-kiet-tac-bao-vat-quoc-gia-thanh-bac-rong-them-djien-kinh-thien.html, https://special.nhandan.vn/ditichnendienkinhthien/index.html, accessed 4 June 2025.

118. Pham, T. (2025). *Đại Việt and Champa: The Early Centuries – The Dynasties of Đinh, Tiền (Former) Lê, Lý, and Trần* (Vol. 3A). 315Kio Publishing. , p. 126.

119. https://nld.com.vn/van-nghe/bao-vat-quoc-gia-them-rong-dien-kinh-thien-co-gi-dac-biet-20230903104513486.htm, accessed 4 June 2025.

120. SKTT, Vol. 1, p. 234.

121. SKTT, Vol. 1, p. 325.

122. SKTT, Vol. 1, p. 422.

123. SKTT, Vol. 1, p. 437.

124. SKTT, Vol. 1, p. 452. SKTT records that the effective date for the implementation of the new regulation was set for the 10th day of the first lunar month 'of that year'. As the entry itself is dated the 7th lunar month of 1471, I interpret 'that year' to mean 1472. It would seem unlikely for the chronicle to refer to an implementation date that had already passed by six months.

125. SKTT, Vol. 1, p. 507. The confirmed administrative units were 13 xứ thừa tuyên (circuits or provinces), 52 phủ (prefectures), 178 huyện (districts), 50 châu (subordinate territories), 20 hương (communes), 36 phường (urban wards), 6851 xã (villages), 322 thôn (hamlets), 637 trang (estates), 40 sách (military colonies), 40 động (highland regions), 30 nguồn (remote border zones), 30 trường (administrative outposts). See also Bửu, C., Đỗ, V. A., Phạm, H. T., & Trương, B. L. (1962). *Hồng Đức Bản Đồ*. Tủ Sách Viện Khảo Cổ-Publications of the Institute of Historical Research - Publications de l'institut de Recherches Historiques - Số III. , p. XIX.

126. CM, Vol. 1, p. 1024.

127. CM, Vol. 1, p. 1177, pp. 1073–1091

128. Bửu, C., Đỗ, V. A., Phạm, H. T., & Trương, B. L. (1962). *Hồng Đức Bản Đồ*. Tủ Sách Viện Khảo Cổ-Publications of the Institute of Historical Research - Publications de l'institut de Recherches Historiques - Số III. , p. XIV.

129. Ibid., p. 3.

130. Ibid., p. 5.

131. A full explanation of the grids is below, see ibid., p. 4.

    1. A - Nam giới Lung-lang giới [Lung-lang: có lẽ là một cách âm của những chữ Ran-Ran: tiểu vương quốc Panduranga của Chiêm Thành. Trong địa chỉ của Alexandre de Rhodes năm 1653, họ đã tìm thấy ghi: Province de Ran-Ran. Nhưng đây chỉ là một giả thuyết hơi bình]; E - Nam; H- Đông giáp đại-hải;

    2. A - Giáp Ai-lao; F - Thạch-bi [bia đá], Quảng-nam; G-Chiêm-thành.

    3. D - Nghệ an; E-Thuận-hóa, Hồng-linh sơn; F-Thiên-cẩm sơn; G - Tam độ sơn; H- Đại hải.

    4. B - Tây kinh; C Na-sơn - Thanh-hoa; D - An-hoạch Sơn; F- Tượng-sơn, Phô-minh tự.

    5. A - Thập châu C Hy-mã sơn, D-Sơn-nam- Trung đô; E - Nam-xương châu; F - Hải dương; G - An-tử sơn; H - An-ky-sinh đắc đạo xứ [An-kỳ sinh thành tiên tại đây], Hồng đàm.

    6. A - Ngải tích sơn sơn, Hưng-hóa; B - Tân-viên sơn; C - Phật tích sơn, Sơn-tây, Câu-lậu sơn; D - Tây hồ, Lý Ông Trọng miếu; E - Kinh bắc, Thiên đức giang, Kim-ngưu sơn, Tiên-du sơn, F - Lục đầu giang; G - An thù sơn, Quỳnh-lâm tự; H - An-bang, kim An-quảng [An-quảng: có lẽ địa danh này được đời dưới thời vua Lê Anh-tông (1556-1573) vì tên của vua là Duy-Bang], Vân-đồn sơn.

    7. A - Bạch thành, B - Tuyên quang; C - Hùng vương sơn -Bạch hạc giang; D - Lịch sơn; F - Phả lại tự - Xương giang; G – Mẫu sơn, Côn sơn; H - Quảng-đông, Việt địa Triệu Vũ đế đô [đất Việt kinh đô của Triệu-Vũ Đế] - Đại viên sơn.

    8. A - Vân-nam; B- Ngưu-dương động; C - Lũng sơn, Thái Nguyên; D - Phụ-dục Sơn, Bông sơn; E – Lạng-sơn, Khâu-bàn sơn; G - Ải quan, Quảng tây - Bách Việt địa; H - Nam cương, Đồng trụ giới, Bắc cương, Phân mao lãnh.

    9. A - Tây giáp Ai-lao giới; E - Bắc; H - Bắc giáp Quế-quản giới.

132. SKTT, Vol. 1, p. 376.

133. Yao Takao. *Luật Quang Thuận đã từng tồn tại? - Nguồn gốc của Quốc Triều Hình Luật không phải là Luật Hồng Đức* Việt Nam Học - Kỷ Yếu Hội Thảo Quốc Tế Lần Thứ Tư, p. 670.

134. Nguyen, L. Q. (1989). Traditional Vietnamese Law--The Le Code--and Modern United States Law: A Comparative Analysis. *Hastings International and Comparative Law Review, 13*(1, Fall 1989), 141–177. , p. 142.

135. Nguyễn, N. N., & Nguyễn, T. N. (2006). *Quốc Triều Hình Luật - Luật Hình Triều Lê, Luật Hồng Đức*. Nhà Xuất Bản Thành Phố Hồ Chí Minh. , p. 29.

136. Nguyen, L. Q. (1989). Traditional Vietnamese Law--The Le Code--and Modern United States Law: A Comparative Analysis. *Hastings International and Comparative Law Review, 13*(1, Fall 1989), 141–177. , p. 147.

137. SKTT, Vol. 1, p. 24.

138. SKTT, Vol. 1, p. 23.

139. SKTT, Vol. 1, p. 23.

140. Pham, T. (2021). *The Bronze Drums and The Earrings* (Vol. 1). 315Kio Publishing.

141. Pham, T. (2025). *Đại Việt and Champa: The Early Centuries – The Dynasties of Đinh, Tiền (Former) Lê, Lý, and Trần* (Vol. 3A). 315Kio Publishing.

142. SKTT, Vol. 1, p. 22.

143. https://vi.wikipedia.org/wiki/Ng%C3%B4_S%C4%A9_Li%C3%AAn, accessed 11 June 2025.

144. WMCX+PCJ, Ngọc Hoà, Chương Mỹ, Hà Nội, Vietnam, coordinates 20°55'18.7"N 105°41'54.6"E.

145. Hồ, T. T. (2019). *Có 500 năm như thế – Bản sắc Quảng Nam và Đàng Trong từ góc nhìn phân kỳ lịch sử* (6th ed.). Nhà Xuất Bản Đà Nẵng. http://books.google.com/books?id=KMTCxLyvLcoC , pp. 48–52.

146. SKTT, Vol. 2, 132.

147. SKTT, Vol. 2, p. 321.

148. SKTT, Vol. 2, 132.

149. SKTT, Vol. 2, p. 334.

150. SA MSL, Zheng-tong: Year 11, Month 6, Day 27, 20 Jul 1446.

151. SKTT, Vol. 2, p. 355.

152. SKTT, Vol. 2, p. 356.

153. Hoàng Đế Citadel is located at W3GC+79V An Nhơn, Bình Định, Vietnam, coordinates 13°55'32.7"N 109°04'15.3"E.

154. SA MSL, Jing-tai: Year 1, Month 3, Day 22, 3 May 1450.

155. SA MSL, Zheng-tong: Year 12, Month 6, Day 29, 10 Aug 1447.

156. SKTT, Vol. 2, p. 357.

157. SA MSL, Zheng-tong: Year 13, Month 5, Day 15, 15 Jun 1448.

158. SKTT, Vol. 2, p. 369.

159. SA MSL, Jing-tai: Year 3, Month 7, Day 1, 17 Jul 1452.

160. SKTT, Vol. 2, pp. 440–441.

161. SKTT, Vol. 2, p. 450.

162. SKTT, Vol. 2, pp. 441–445.

163. SKTT, Vol. 2, p. 445.

164. CM, Vol. 1, p. 1095.

165. SKTT, Vol. 2, p. 447.

166. SKTT, Vol. 2, p. 448.

167. Whitmore, J. K. (2004). The Two Great Campaigns of the Hongduc Era (1470–97) in Dai Viet. *South East Asia Research*, *12*(1), 119-136. https://doi.org/10.5367/000000004773487965

168. CM, Vol. 1, p. 1099.

169. SKTT, Vol. 2, p. 449.

170. SKTT, Vol. 2, p. 449.

171. https://www.cambridge.org/core/books/abs/cambridge-world-history-of-genocide/viet-nam-and-the-genocide-of-champa-14701509/6E8490A4C5670883A94DAD24BF5C899A

172. SKTT, Vol. 2, p. 450.

173. SKTT, Vol. 2, p. 450. According to CM, Bô Trì Trì held two-fifth of Champa, see CM, Vol. 1, p. 1100.

174. CM, Vol. 1, p. 1101.

175. Nguyễn, V. T. (2012). *Mối bang giao giữa triều đình Huế với hai Phiên vương Thủy Xá, Hỏa Xá* Việt Nam Học - Kỷ Yếu Hội Thảo Quốc Tế Lần Thứ Tư, , p. 756.

176. Nguyễn, V. G. (2019). Interpretations about Hoa Anh state. *Thu Dau Mot University Journal of Science*, *1*(1-2019), 66–77. , p. 67.

177. CM, Vol. 1, p. 1101.

178. Pham, T. (2024). *Đại Việt and Champa: Panduranga, Kauthara, and Indrapura*. (Vol. 3B). 315Kio Publishing.

179. SKTT, VOL. 2, p. 494.

180. SKTT, Vol. 2, p. 425.

181. Dương, V. A. (2019). *Ô Châu Cận Lục* (Đ. V. Trần, Trans.). Nhà Xuất Bản Khoa Học Xã Hội – MaiHaBooks. (1555), p. 75, p. 78.

182. Hồ, T. T. (2019). *Có 500 năm như thế – Bản sắc Quảng Nam và Đàng Trong từ góc nhìn phân kỳ lịch sử* (6th ed.). Nhà Xuất Bản Đà Nẵng. http://books.google.com/books?id=KMTCxLyvLcoC , 84–91.

183. SKTT, Vol. 3, p. 17.

184. Hồ, T. T. (2019). *Có 500 năm như thế – Bản sắc Quảng Nam và Đàng Trong từ góc nhìn phân kỳ lịch sử* (6th ed.). Nhà Xuất Bản Đà Nẵng. http://books.google.com/books?id=KMTCxLyvLcoC , p. 86. See https://baoquangnam.vn/an-trien-quang-nam-3070454.html. Accessed 21 June 2025.

185. Griffiths, A. (2019). Études du corpus des inscriptions du Campā, VI: Epigraphical Texts and Sculptural Steles Produced under the Vīrabhadravarmadevas of 15th-Century Campā. In G. Arlo, H. Andrew, & W. Geoff (Eds.), *Champa: Territories and Networks of a Southeast Asian Kingdom* (Vol. 31). École française d'Extrême-Orient. https://halshs.archives-ouvertes.fr/halshs-02292578

186. Pham, T. (2024). *Đại Việt and Champa: Panduranga, Kauthara, and Indrapura.* (Vol. 3B). 315Kio Publishing. , p. 122.

187. Châu Sa Citadel is located at 5R7V+QV5 Son Tinh District, Quang Ngai, Vietnam, coordinates 15°09'51.8"N 108°50'41.0"E.

188. Photograph taken by the author on 9 March 2024.

189. CM, Vol. 1, p. 947.

190. CM, Vol. 1, p. 947, p. 992.

191. SKTT, Vol. 1, p. 414, p. 417.

192. CM, Vol. 1, p. 1152.

193. SKTT, Vol. 2, pp. 473–477.

194. SKTT, Vol. 2, p. 479.

195. SKTT, Vol. 2, p. 477.

196. CM, Vol. 1, p. 1152; SKTT, Vol. 2, p. 419.

197. From Google Maps the following road distances are: for the first army: Hanoi-Điện Biên Phủ (434 km), Điện Biên Phủ-Luang Prabang (397 km); for the second army: Hanoi-Long Sap (221 km), Long Sap-Phonsavan (345 km); for the third army: Thanh Hoá-Bản Na Mèo (194 km), Bản Na Mèo-Phonsavan (325 km); for the fourth army: Vinh-Nậm Cắn (241 km), Nậm Cắn-Phonsavan (136 km); for the fifth army: Vinh-Nam Phao (91 km), Nam Phao-Phonsavan (325 km).

198. Stuart-Fox, M. (1997). *A history of Laos.* Cambridge University Press. , p. 42.

199. Peter and Sanda Simms. (1999). *The Kingdoms of Laos: six hundred years of history.* , p. 46.

200. Ibid., pp. 51–52.

201. The two Laotian generals were Mun-Luang and Phragna Khua-Thepa; the four lieutenants were Norasing, Norasnai, Noradeth and Norarath. The two defensive locations were Thong-Na-Mung-Khun and Na-Hai-Dieo. See Silā Vīravong (Mahā.). (1957). *History of Laos. Translated from the Laotian by the U.S. Joint Publications Research Service.* Paragon Book Reprint Corp. https://lao-online.com/all_files/books/B00720.pdf , p. 45. According to Manich, M. L. (1967). *History of Laos (including the history of Lannathai, Chiengmai).* Chalermnit, Bangkok. https://www.renincorp.org/bookshelf/history-of-laos_manich.pdf , p. 127, the two Laotian generals were Muen Luang and Phya Kwatepa; the four lieutenants were Norasing, Noranarai, Noradet and Norarat. The two defensive locations were Na Moungkon and Na Haidio. The two Vietnamese leading the invasion, Bua Kwangchun and Nerg-Ong, were killed.

202. Silā Vīravong (Mahā.). (1957). *History of Laos. Translated from the Laotian by the U.S. Joint Publications Research Service.* Paragon Book Reprint Corp. https://lao-online.com/all_files/books/B00720.pdf , pp. 45–46; Peter and Sanda Simms. (1999). *The Kingdoms of Laos: six hundred years of history.* , p. 52.

203. SKTT, Vol. 2, p. 482.

204. SA-MSL, Cheng-hua: Year 17, Month 6, Day 9, 5 Jul 1481.

205. SKTT, Vol. 2, p. 518, p. 520, p. 522.

206. SKTT, Vol. 2, p. 522.

207. SKTT, Vol. 3, p. 38.

208. SKTT, Vol. 3, p. 45.

209. SKTT, Vol. 3, p. 38.

210. SKTT, Vol. 3, p. 39.

211. SKTT, Vol. 3, p. 50.

212. SKTT, Vol. 3, p. 46.

213. SKTT, Vol. 3, p. 47.

214. Lê Dinh was the son of Kiên Vương Tân, SKTT, Vol. 2, p. 518.

215. SKTT, Vol. 3, p. 58, p. 73.

216. Trần, T. P. (2011). *Lĩnh Nam Chích Quái* (Q. Vũ, P. Kiều, G. K. Đinh, & N. S. Nguyễn, Trans.). Nhà Xuất Bản Trẻ, Hồng Bàng. (1492)

217. SKTT, Vol. 3, p. 52, p. 74.

218. SKTT, Vol. 3, p. 74.

219. SKTT, Vol. 3, p. 42, p. 65.

220. SKTT, Vol. 3, p. 62. ĐVTS, p. 281.

221. SKTT, Vol. 3, p. 75.

222. SKTT, Vol. 3, p. 77, p. 80.

223. ĐVTS, pp. 144–145.

224. ĐVTS, p. 163.

225. Information taken from ĐVTS.

226. Lê, T. D. (2018). *Niên Biểu Các Đời Vua Việt Nam*. Nhà Xuất Bản Hồng Đức. , p. 301.

227. https://ditichlamkinh.vn/vi/gioi-thieu-ve-khu-di-tich-lam-kinh-367faa79216f5876b616a2f-f6a7d4d5b.html, accessed 14 July 2025.

228. Photographs taken by the author on 19 December 2019.

229. Historic Lam Kinh is located at WCG4+JP9 Thọ Xuân District, Thanh Hoa, Vietnam, co-ordinates 19°55'35.5"N 105°24'24.7"E.

230. https://baotanglichsu.vn/vi/Articles/3096/4855/mo-vua-le-thai-to-o-djau.html, accessed 14 July 2025.

CHAPTER 7

1. ĐVTS, p. 124. Phan, H. C. (2014). *Lịch triều hiến chương loại chí – Tập 5 – Binh chế chí–Văn tịch chí–Bang giao chí* (Vol. XXXIX to XLIX). Nhà Xuất Bản Trẻ. (1819), p. 121.

2. Nhiều Tác Giả. (2014). *Họ Hồ và Hồ Quý Ly Trong Lịch Sử*. Nhà Xuất Bản Hồng Đức.

3. Whitmore, J. K. (2019). The Fall of Vijaya in 1471: Decline or Competition? Campā in the 15th Century. In G. Arlo, H. Andrew, & W. Geoff (Eds.), *Champa: Territories and Networks of a Southeast Asian Kingdom* (Vol. 31, pp. 179–191). École française d'Extrême-Orient. , p. 191. See also Pham, T. (2024). *Đại Việt and Champa: Panduranga, Kauthara, and Indrapura*. (Vol. 3B). 315Kio Publishing. , p. 177.

4. Whitmore, J. K. (2019). The Fall of Vijaya in 1471: Decline or Competition? Campā in the 15th Century. In G. Arlo, H. Andrew, & W. Geoff (Eds.), *Champa: Territories and Networks of a Southeast Asian Kingdom* (Vol. 31, pp. 179–191). École française d'Extrême-Orient. , p. 179, p. 180.

5. SKTT, Vol. 2, p. 327.

www.ingramcontent.com/pod-product-compliance
Lightning Source LLC
Chambersburg PA
CBHW051400070526
44584CB00023B/3237